BIG GIFTS

Big Gifts

How to Maximize Gifts From Individuals, With or Without a Capital Campaign

M. Jane Williams

FUND RAISING INSTITUTE
A Division of The Taft Group
Rockville, Maryland

Published by
Fund Raising Institute
A Division of the Taft Group
12300 Twinbrook Parkway, Suite 520
Rockville, MD 20852

Printed in the United States of America
96 95 94 93 92 91   6 5 4 3 2 1

Library of Congress Catalog Card Number: 90—085638
ISBN 0-930807-15-4

Fund Raising Institute publishes books on fund raising, philanthropy, and nonprofit management. To request sales information, or a copy of our catalog, please write us at the above address or call 1-800-877-TAFT.

Dedication

I would like to dedicate this book to the memory of William F. Balthaser, a longtime friend and colleague. Bill directed the Fund-Raising Institute, which is now part of the Taft Group, from 1976 until his death in December 1989. At FRI, Bill was dedicated to publishing books and newsletters to help the fund-raising professional.

All of the books that I worked on for FRI, including this one, were based on his ideas. Those who knew Bill will remember him for having an idea a minute, and he could always think of creative new ways to package those ideas. It was tough to write for Bill because his own style was so direct and effective. He taught me a great deal and did much to advance the field of development through his writings for FRI and his active role in the National Society of Fund-Raising Executives and the American Association of Fund-Raising Counsel Trust for Philanthropy.

Bill was trained as a journalist at Temple University and worked in radio news for NBC. His fund-raising activities began at Albert Einstein Medical Center in Philadelphia, where he served as director of information. He then became director of development and public relations at Haverford College before devoting himself full time to FRI.

Contents

Foreword

"To give away money is an easy matter and in any man's power. But to decide to whom to give it and how large and when and for what purpose and how, is neither in every man's power—nor an easy matter."

Aristotle

People have been giving away money since before Aristotle's time, but we can see from this quote that the process has always raised many questions for donors. To be successful at fund-raising, you must be able to provide the kinds of answers that will encourage people to think of your organization first when they are considering making a donation. And that's the purpose of this book: to show you how to cultivate the big donors who have the potential to make a significant difference in your fund-raising program.

In recent years, individuals have given over 80 percent of all philanthropic dollars in the United States, with corporations, foundations and other sources contributing the remaining 20 percent. The most significant resource that all nonprofit organizations have for private funding is the *major individual donor*. One person who makes a truly pacesetting gift can make more difference to an organization's future than hundreds of smaller donors.

Just what is a major gift? Depending on the size of the nonprofit group, a major gift could be anywhere from $5,000 to $50 million or more. Therefore, the real name of the game in fund-raising is the process of identifying, cultivating and soliciting major individual prospects.

This book provides a step-by-step guide to the process of interacting with major prospects,

both on an ongoing basis and during a capital campaign. In the first section of this book, we will look at what motivates a major donor, followed by a review of the basics of prospect identification, cultivation and solicitation. In the second section, you will learn how to organize a major gifts program, and in the third part, how to raise major gifts during a capital campaign. The aim is to show that major gifts fund-raising should be an ongoing part of every development program—even if you have only a handful of major prospects and even if you are not in a capital campaign.

We will also see how capital campaigns work and how vital they are to the process of raising major gifts. Campaigns can have a dramatic impact on individuals' gifts, raising them to new heights that will influence giving for years to come.

This book incorporates a revised version of *Capital Ideas,* a guide to capital campaigns. Like that book, this one includes many charts, brochures and reports that various organizations have used in the fund-raising process. For your convenience, there is a listing of these samples. You will note that many of them are found in the section on capital campaigns. A capital campaign usually requires more printed matter than an ongoing major gifts program because you have to create the campaign atmosphere and a sense of immediacy.

The importance of major gifts from individuals cannot be overstated. Gifts from individuals represent the one area of real growth in American philanthropy. Over the last 30 years, gifts from individuals have grown every year despite economic, political and tax turmoils. This book will show that it is worth expending considerable time and effort on the cultivation and solicitation of major individual prospects.

I will share here all that I've learned about interacting with major prospects during my more than 20 years in the development field. I hope that, after reading this material, you will agree that the most challenging and rewarding aspect of institutional fund-raising is the successful cultivation and solicitation of a major donor. The first time this process works for you will be the convincing factor—it will be exciting!

Whether you are a development staff member, a volunteer or a nonprofit administrator who is a reluctant fund-raiser, I hope this book will define the process in a way that will convince you that you, too, can raise a major gift—and that it's well worth the effort. After reading this book, you should feel better-equipped to tackle the big donors who can make a real difference to your organization's future or to mount a capital campaign that can move your gift totals to new heights.

—M. Jane Williams

Part I

THE BASICS OF ALL MAJOR GIFTS PROGRAMS

Chapter 1
An Introduction to Major Gifts

If we place all fund-raising activities on a spectrum, major gifts from individuals might be in the middle, with direct mail or the mass approach to prospects at one end and nurturing fund-raising, where you plan a lifetime of interaction with a single prospect, at the other end. An individual's "gift potential" determines where he or she is placed on the spectrum of fund-raising activities.

Direct-mail solicitations usually target all identifiable prospects for gifts that are anticipated to be smaller than "major." In some ways, direct-mail fund-raising can be seen as a speculative process involving many "asks" of many people on a recurrent basis. The aim of direct-mail appeals is to build a constituency. Once a donor gives regularly in response to direct-mail appeals, he or she might move along the spectrum and become a major prospect.

Major gifts fund-raising is a much more targeted process, seeking a specific amount for a specific project on a one-time basis. When we talk about raising major gifts from individuals, we are really talking about developing individualized gift plans for each major prospect. This is a very specialized and carefully orchestrated type of fund-raising. A separate game plan has to be developed for each prospect.

At the far end of the spectrum from direct mail is the epitome of major gifts fund-raising, which has been called nurturing fund-raising.

This occurs when you know a prospect has substantial potential and a lifelong interest in your cause. The aim is to continue regular interaction with the prospect over many years, seeking what Dave Dunlop, a longtime fund-raiser at Cornell University, calls the "ultimate" gift—his or her entire estate or close to it.

The focus of this book is on attracting gifts from individuals using techniques from the middle of the fund-raising spectrum (major gifts) through the far end (ultimate gifts). In these situations, half the time spent interacting with a prospect involves cultivating interest in the organization and the other half in deciding who should ask for the gift, when it should be sought and for what purpose. Cultivation of some kind is essential for all major gifts, and virtually no major gift comes without a direct personal solicitation. But all the cultivation in the world is misdirected if it does not culminate in an ask.

Many development programs create and maintain effective annual campaigns aimed at seeking regular support from a large number of prospects, but often those annual campaigns are seen as the entire fund-raising effort. No nonprofit organization can reach its fund-raising potential without targeting a limited number of prospects who have the potential to make major gifts. Without careful plans to cultivate and solicit major donors, organizations miss their best opportunity to raise significant gifts.

The main message of this book is that every nonprofit group can effectively raise major gifts, but it must organize itself to do so either through a capital campaign or through the establishment of an ongoing major gifts program. It is important to realize, however, that establishment of a major gifts program does not mean that you should stop asking for annual gifts. Major gifts should be raised on top of annual gifts, not instead of them.

Traditionally, campaigns have been viewed as the way to raise major gifts. But they are not the only way.

Capital campaigns are mounted to meet specific major needs. In the early days of campaigns, they usually aimed to raise funds for capital projects (bricks and mortar). Then they moved on to address endowment needs. Now campaigns often become comprehensive gift programs that include all gifts raised during the campaign period. They are a mechanism for substantially increasing total gift income for organizations and for reaching new plateaus of giving that are maintained after campaigns are completed. Until recently, organizations usually anticipated downturns in giving immediately following a campaign, but now fund-raising has become such a way of life that budget administrators expect gifts to remain at the new high levels even after a campaign is over.

Capital campaigns do provide an extra motivation to make major gifts, but the real challenge for all development programs is to increase giving every year whether during a campaign or not. That means major gifts from individuals must be sought on a continuing basis and not just during campaigns. There should be no beginning and no end to major gifts fund-raising. Once a donor is identified as having major gift potential, ongoing cultivation should never stop—not even after a donor's death if there are still family members who are interested in the organization.

A key point we will return to again and again in describing the cultivation of major gifts is *involvement*. Involving a prospect in an organization's activities is *the* most important factor in attracting a major gift.

For both donor and recipient, a big gift is more than money. To the donor, it represents influence, recognition and power. Major donors develop a real commitment to an organization's future. Their gifts become part of their lives, and the donors become part of the organization. For the organization, the first big gift represents only the beginning. That donor has the potential to make more than one gift, to find other donors for you and to become a board member with a real commitment to your cause. Major gifts should be a primary focus of all development programs.

Chapter 2
Major Donors

Who They Are

How do you spot a major prospect? The following list is compiled from the combined experience of many fund-raisers and nonprofit organizations. Although these are the most common attributes of major donors, we all know people who do not fit this mold. For example, women aren't on this list. But don't overlook them; they hold 50 percent of the wealth in this country.

In general these factors are good indicators that an individual has major gift potential:

■ Over 55
■ Male
■ Married
■ Conservative
■ Religious
■ Approaching retirement
■ History of giving
■ History of involvement
■ Holds mixed assets (a combination of stocks, bonds, real estate, venture holdings etc.)
■ Has a family foundation
■ Owns a business
■ Has inherited wealth

The most important of these characteristics is holding mixed assets. Major gifts usually are made from assets, unlike annual gifts, which usually come from income. Therefore a prospect must be able to sell or reorganize assets in order to make a major gift.

Changes in lifestyle and in the type of assets owned are excellent indicators of major gift potential. Consider the following situations when researching prospects:

■ A death in the family that leads to inherited wealth
■ Retirement—especially with a "golden parachute"
■ Marriage into wealth
■ Sale of a business or property
■ Success in a venture capital or real estate deal
■ No dependents or heirs
■ Financial windfall
■ Company takeover

To attract really significant gifts, you need to identify prospects who have the potential to give them. The number of affluent individuals is growing. The rich are getting richer. In 1963, the top one-half of 1 percent of the U.S. population held 25.4 percent of the nation's wealth. In 1983, the same percentage held 35.1 percent of U.S. wealth. There are now over 800,000 millionaire households in the United States, with many of them found in the Northeast and the South.

Although not all major donors must be millionaires, you should keep in mind the 20-to-1 rule. A donor should have 20 times the size of the gift in assets. That means a person would need total assets in the $20 million range to make a $1 million gift during his or her lifetime. Gifts made through estates can often be larger than this guideline suggests.

Although the wealthiest people have by far the highest rate of giving, a study by Eugene Steuerle for the American Enterprise Institute, reveals that "top wealth holders tend to give away only a tiny percentage of their wealth during their lifetimes." Steuerle compared income-tax returns with estate-tax returns and found that wealthy people gave 15 times as much through their estates as during the last year of their lives. He also concluded that for the very wealthy, charitable giving competes less with consumption than with the process of holding onto wealth itself.

Since we are often dealing with wealthy people when cultivating major gifts, we should remember that the accumulation or management of wealth is a primary interest for them. As fund-raisers, we must build natural ties with likely prospects who have significant financial resources and allow them to become involved in the organization so that significant gift-giving will follow.

When looking for major prospects, remember appearances can be deceiving. Truly wealthy persons often don't look it. They may drive a Volvo rather than a Ferrari. They may live modestly. Many wealthy people today took a long time to make their own fortunes, so they remember times when they had to live more frugally. Others who make money quickly, spend it just as fast and are cash poor. Still others, especially those with inherited wealth, follow long-established patterns of behavior and hold on to their assets tenaciously. Also remember that some inheritors of major wealth are actually far less wealthy than their ancestors. Many family fortunes are now spread among so many descendants that no one pool of wealth is nearly as significant as the original.

So if appearances don't always expose a prospect's potential, what else do you look for? Start by looking at who donates to your own annual giving program. Look for the prospect who consistently makes gifts that are higher than your average annual gift. Also look for donors who increase their gifts every time you ask them to, for donors who give more often than they are asked to and for donors who respond generously to challenge gifts.

Board members and other "insider" leadership should be looked to for major gifts. Individuals or families who receive services from an organization should also be researched for major gift potential. People who own businesses or significant real estate holdings and who have an interest in an organization usually have major gift potential.

In recent years, entrepreneurs have been identified as likely prospects. Entrepreneurs enjoy the process of making money, and if you can successfully involve them in your organization, they can enjoy making money for it too.

But entrepreneurs can also be difficult prospects because they often want to exercise significant control over the charities they support and over their gifts. The challenge is to identify entrepreneurs who have a natural interest in your mission and to channel their interests creatively so they will help your cause.

A national survey conducted by Yankelovich, Skelly and White Inc. called "The Charitable Behavior of Americans" draws these conclusions about those who give:

- People who are married or widowed give a higher percentage of their incomes than do single people.
- Retired persons are by far the most generous.
- The more educated the person, the higher the proportion of income to charity.
- Charitable giving increases with age, education, income and occupational status.

All these factors can have an effect on who becomes your major donors, but the key is *involvement*. People give where they feel a commitment. They give because they want to make a difference. Major gifts rarely come from individuals with no history of involvement. The real secret to success is to carefully identify and methodically cultivate a limited pool of major prospects to the point where they will ask, "What can I do for you?"

Why You Need Them

A major donor is significant because his or her gift is big enough to make a real difference.

Major gifts can get fund-raising efforts off to a great start, or they can complete a campaign in an exciting way.

In almost every development program, and certainly in every capital campaign, a few very large gifts make the difference. That's the significance of major gifts in a nutshell. Major gifts fund-raising, if done well, is the most successful and cost-effective way to seek private funds.

Some fund-raisers feel that the "big gifts" approach is *the* primary way to raise money. Charles E. Lawson, chairman of Brakeley, John Price Jones Inc., in Greenwich, Connecticut, says, "It's wise to start with the premise that you are looking for one donor who can give the entire amount you're seeking. Failing that, you next look for the total goal from two donors, and then on to three big gifts . . . . and so on."

Setting the stage by involving major prospects leads to a natural progression of increased interest, so that in the end most major donors have logical reasons to give. They want to identify themselves with the organization's mission and gain a "pride of association," according to Harold J. "Si" Seymour, the author of *Designs for Fund-Raising,* one of the first books on the subject.

Some large universities, Stanford and Princeton among them, see such significance in the largest gifts that they have organized "principal" gift programs. This is the nurturing fund-raising mentioned earlier. Principal gift directors at these schools do nothing but plan and orchestrate the step-by-step involvement of principal prospects—a very small number of prospects, who could each give $5 million or more. These schools have realized that it takes very careful planning to realize extraordinary gift potential from a very few substantial prospects. Even if

$5 million gifts are not out there for every nonprofit group, there is a level of extraordinary giving that is possible for every group. However, that type of giving will occur only if the prospect is very carefully cultivated in an appropriate way.

When talking about gifts at the very top levels, we begin to realize that such gifts usually come from those who have an extraordinary commitment to a cause or to an organization. Big gifts rarely come from strangers. They usually come from insiders—board members and other close friends who are really committed to an organization. Big gifts from insiders not only provide significant financial help for nonprofits, but also set the pace for giving from others. Major gifts from board members and community leaders can really set the stage for fund-raising success. These gifts also assure that major insider donors remain involved and committed to the organization.

But not all donors are insiders. Some truly major donors give because of emotional reactions to the cause. Jerold Panas, author of *Mega Gifts,* interviewed several major philanthropists and found that a few responded immediately to an ask just because the project sounded exciting. The major donor wants to share in the dreams of an organization and to feel a real joy in giving.

The significance of a major donor can be seen in looking at the profiles of successful development programs. Approximately 10 percent of the donors provide 90 percent of the funds. Major individual donors lead the way and in the end make goals reachable. Even if an organization has only one or two major prospects, the time spent increasing their involvement and interest is pivotal.

Chapter 3
The Truth Behind Giving

Why People Give

Figuring out what will motivate a donor to give is one of the most important aspects of major gifts fund-raising. The definition of motivation, as it relates to gift-giving, might be: those factors within a person combined with external forces that move him to make a donation.

We can apply classic theories of motivation to fund-raising. For example, consider Maslow's Hierarchy of Needs.

To apply this schematic to fund-raising, we must accept Maslow's theory that a person does not move up on the scale of needs until all the needs in a lower category are met. So an individual is not likely to become a major prospect until he or she has completely satisfied needs at

Figure 3.1. Maslow's Hierarchy of Needs

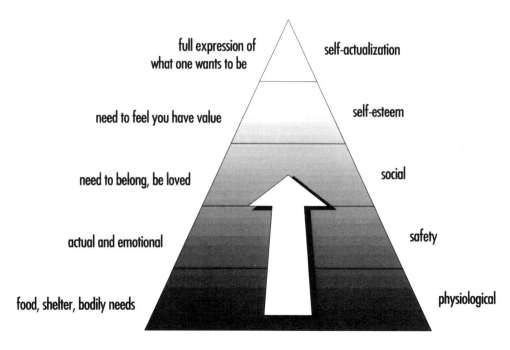

the safety and physiological levels. But once a person starts looking for connections and acceptance, relating to nonprofit organizations is a natural outlet.

Paul H. Schneiter in *The Art of Asking* points to seven motivations for gift-giving:

- Religious beliefs
- Guilt
- Recognition
- Self-preservation and fear
- Tax benefits
- Obligation
- Pressure

Other factors that can motivate philanthropy are:

- Acceptance
- Altruism
- Appreciation
- Enlightened self-interest
- Approval
- Being asked
- Belief in the cause
- Community interest
- Competition
- Gratitude
- Immortality
- Sympathy

Experienced fund-raisers agree that the primary motivator for a major gift is involvement. So the objective of all fund-raising techniques is to involve the major prospect in the mission of an organization. Commitment leads to money!

When approaching a new prospect or a recalcitrant donor, it is important to realize that you have to bring about an attitude change. You have to introduce new information that will change the prospect's view of your organization's mission.

One key motivator is the person who asks. People of influence who are connected with a nonprofit group can often be the best askers because prospects are impressed with being asked by them. Among wealthy people, there are many charitable trade-offs. Once a person asks for a gift, he or she can expect to be asked in return to support the prospect's charitable interests. The real challenge in such a setting is to be sure your organization is the *top* interest of at least several key supporters, so that these trade-offs do not eat away at your piece of the pie.

Are They Giving Just for Tax Reasons?

Most fund-raisers agree that the answer is "yes" but only in a secondary way. Commitment and interest in a particular cause are the key motivators. Then tax issues might come into play, affecting the size or timing of a gift. A donor's tax benefits are the same no matter which charity he or she supports, so selling tax benefits is not the best way to sell your own distinctive cause. Tax incentives often allow a donor to give more or to dictate when a gift is made, but they rarely spark the gift.

Some very wealthy people seem almost oblivious to tax issues. For example, when Disque D. Deane, a New York financier, gave $20 million to Duke University, he said, "I don't plan to seek a tax deduction for this gift and I don't believe it would be ethical to profit from a charitable deduction."

Another motivation for giving was revealed in a study of 200 wealthy Americans and their advisors made for the Council on Foundations and Yale University's Program on Nonprofit Organizations. "The key philanthropic motive expressed was a desire to maintain control over the money, a conviction that it was their money and they would decide where it goes, and not see it put in the Government's coffers as taxes." Some people would rather give money away than see it go to the government.

Major donors are also often motivated by their advisors—financial, legal, tax—to make gifts (or not to!). But advisors most often have an impact only if real commitment to a particular charity does not already exist. An advisor's suggestions are usually considered only in conjunction with a donor's own predispositions.

People do not give just because somebody *needs* their money. Major donors give because they see a chance to have an impact. Some major donors are seeking an improvement in their stature. Buying acceptability and wanting to be recognized as charitable and caring are real motivational issues to be considered.

We also must recognize that there will be a number of motivators for each gift. Some wealthy people respond emotionally, not logically, to an ask. Others feel a real obligation to give back some of their wealth. But most big givers are motivated by the chance to do something special.

For many major donors, the specific project they are being asked to fund is not nearly as important a motivator as overall commitment to the organization itself. However, part of the challenge is matching the interests of the prospect to the needs of the organization. It is only a board chairman or a similarly committed board member who will give to a project without being particularly attracted to it.

Here are some additional perspectives on why people give:

> "The act of philanthropy is a voluntary decision. It is a decision based upon two prime human motivations. The first motivation is caring; the second is sharing."
>
> *Arthur C. Frantzreb*
> *Fund-raising Consultant*

> "People give, ultimately, on a generous and sustained basis, not because they are conned into it, not because they have been convinced of the 'needs' of some worthy institution, not because of attachment to the abstract ideas of a nonprofit third sector. . . .
> "People give on an ongoing and substantial basis because they have come to share a vision of how to help people, how to build a better community, how to correct some social evil, how to right some human wrong. They give because they want to invest their money and themselves in some truly worthy purpose that transcends their own selfish desires and ambitions, because they want to volunteer themselves to help realize the vision."
>
> *Landrum R. Bolling*
> *Former Chairman*
> *Council on Foundations*

Ernest Dichter, psychologist and motivational researcher, says, "Giving is a proof of one's prowess, one's virility, one's capacity as a mighty hunter. . . . Giving buys power and makes us feel triumphant."

Dichter feels we should not play up needs by picturing problems but should stress the value of our causes to the community, thereby giving the donor the sense of "how wonderful he is because of his giving."

How They Give

Donors draw on their assets to make major gifts. They receive a proposal for support, determine their interest, and if they decide to give, they consider various gift mechanisms.

Wealthy donors and their advisors are more sophisticated about gift-giving today than ever before, but a surprising number still know little of the more complex gift techniques or of the tax advantages of giving.

More and more large gifts are coming in mixed formats; that is, some cash, some securities, some long-term or planned gift mechanisms. Planned gifts (such as bequests, trusts or life insurance, where the proceeds are realized at a later date) are playing an ever-increasing role. For example, during Princeton's capital campaign of the mid-1980s, 65 percent of the gifts from individuals came in the form of planned gifts. At the same time, Harvard reported that nine of the top 11 gifts to its campaign were planned gifts.

More than half of the wealthiest people in the United States belong to families that have formed private foundations, so their gifts may actually come through a foundation. If a foundation exists, the gift decision may be more complicated, involving other members of the family and foundation staff members.

Major gifts may be either outright or planned donations. Planned gifts involve contributing assets now or after death, often while retaining an income interest during one's life and the lives of beneficiaries.

Basically, the following are the types of major gifts individuals can make:

OUTRIGHT GIFTS

Cash.
- A check is the best gift of all because an organization can put it to use right away.

Securities.
- The donor delivers stock certificates directly to the organization and endorses the necessary stock powers.
- Or the donor sends *unendorsed* stock certificates by registered mail and mails the executed stock powers *under separate cover.*
- Or the donor deposits the securities with a bank or broker, and the intermediary advises the organization of the gift. This is the most convenient way to handle the transaction.

Real estate.
- This may be a simple outright gift or a planned gift (see below).

Gifts-in-kind.
- A donor may give valuable items or a partial interest in those items. Such items might include art, antiques, coin collections or jewelry. They might also include such things as computer equipment, employee time or printing services.

PLANNED GIFTS

Bequest.
- A donor leaves a nonprofit group a specific amount, a specific percentage of the full estate or the entire estate. A *residuary* bequest means that a donor leaves the organization the residue of the estate after other specific bequests are made. A *contingent* bequest means that the donor makes the gift dependent on certain events.

Real estate.
- *Gift with retained life income.* The donor uses the value of real estate to fund a unitrust (see below).
- *Live-at-home gift.* The donor transfers the ownership of his or her personal residence but retains the right to use the property for life.
- *Gift of partial interest.* The donor gives a percentage of interest, and the organization

receives a proportionate share of the proceeds when the property is sold.

Life insurance.
- A donor may name a nonprofit organization as one of the beneficiaries or the sole beneficiary of a life insurance policy. A donor may also transfer ownership of a policy to the organization. In the case of ownership transfer and/or sole beneficiary status, the policy's face value is removed from the donor's taxable estate. Also, future premiums paid on the policy by the donor can be treated as charitable gifts, and if the policy has a cash value, the donor can take an immediate tax deduction.

Charitable remainder trusts. The donor gives a specific amount that is placed in a trust managed by the recipient organization or by a financial institution. The donor gives up control of the funds but retains a *life income* interest in the funds. Once the donor and other beneficiaries die, the remainder of the funds comes to the organization. These trusts may take effect while a donor is still living (*inter vivos* charitable trust) or may be treated by the donor's will (testamentary charitable trust). The following are types of charitable remainder trusts:

- *Unitrust.* Federal law requires that a fixed percentage of the trust's assets be paid to the donor (or beneficiaries) as income each year. In the case of unitrusts, the percentage is based on the current market value of the assets, so the income can vary.
- *Annuity trust.* The annual income payment is set as a percent of the assets when the trust is established, and annual payments never change.
- *Pooled income trust.* Gifts from more than one donor are pooled by the trustee and invested. All of the net income must be passed to beneficiaries on the basis of the number of units owned.

Charitable gift annuity.
- This is an annuity contract between the recipient organization and the donor. The organization is obligated to pay the donor or other designated beneficiaries a fixed sum

annually for life. It differs from an annuity trust because the annuity contract creates a "debt" obligation to the donor, not a "trust" obligation. The assets given by the donor do not need to be held in a trust but are often placed in a separate fund.

■ A *deferred payment gift annuity* is a variation on this type of gift. Here annuity payments do not begin until a specified number of years after the gift is made, allowing a donor to take an immediate tax deduction, perhaps while in a high tax bracket. The income from the annuity payments is postponed until it is really needed, perhaps after retirement.

Charitable lead trust.

■ This is a *reversionary trust*. The donor gives the organization a specified amount that is placed in a trust for a specific period. During that time, the nonprofit group receives the income, and when the trust ends, the principal reverts to the donor. Usually, the donor is not taxed on the income that goes to the charity during the life of the trust.

Will They Keep on Giving?

The trends that concern fund-raisers most are economic and tax-related. Downturns in the economy can have an impact on how people feel about giving money away. If prospects feel their assets are growing and the economic picture is bright, they are much more likely to make substantial gifts.

The October 1987 stock market crash seemed to spell disaster for many fund-raising efforts. There certainly was an immediate cutback in giving (October through December 1987), but over the next 10 months, the stock market became less volatile, and overall giving for most nonprofits did not suffer dramatically. However, many newly affluent prospects, especially those with direct ties to investment banking or the securities industry, were at least temporarily knocked out of prospect pools. The long-term effect of this economic downturn and of others seems to be minimal on fund-raising. Except for dramatic downturns like the '87 crash, when the effect was felt immediately, most blips in the economy don't affect giving until almost a year later.

In recent recessions and economic downturns, two groups of individuals remained good prospects:

■ Those whose support had been in the middle-giving range
■ Those for whom a cause was one of their strongest philanthropic interests

Another impact of recessions that fund-raisers must plan to meet is the pressure to cut back their budgets. Once fund-raising activities are reduced, it is often hard to get the flow of gift income started again. So it is important to make your organization realize that fund-raising, especially for major gifts, is a cumulative effort and should be allowed to continue at least with top prospects during periods of economic stress.

Marts & Lundy Inc., a fund-raising consulting firm in Lyndhurst, New Jersey, has produced a study comparing giving with 30 years of economic history in the United States. The 30-year time line shows that despite economic blips, giving from 1957 to 1987 continued at a steady upward rate.

In addition to economic concerns, societal trends such as these will have an impact on major gifts fund-raising in the future:

■ Married couples are making more charitable decisions together, so if major prospects are married, husband and wife should be solicited together.
■ Women (wives, widows and prospects in their own right) make up the largest segment by number of our prospect pools, so we should tailor approaches to women's concerns. Although men's gifts tend to be bigger, women are on prospect lists in larger numbers, in part because they live longer.
■ A strong Jewish tradition of giving back is having a growing impact on gifts to many charitable causes beyond those with established Jewish ties.
■ The baby-boom generation will make up the largest proportion of our prospect pools. As baby-boomers reach middle age, nonprofits will have increased potential for sup-

port. However, this generation of donors has concerns and interests that are different from those of the traditional gift prospect. And many of them will be more sophisticated donors because they will be more knowledgeable about financial planning.

■ The racial and ethnic mix of American society is changing dramatically. Groups that have traditionally not been a part of the philanthropic picture will be growing. They will need to be motivated as givers.

■ The population (and therefore our prospects) is aging. Senior citizens will be growing in numbers and should be good prospects, especially for planned gifts.

Changes in government policies for funding society's needs, and potential (and seemingly continuous) tax-law changes will have an impact on the major donor. But since tax considerations have rarely been the primary motivation for large or small gifts, philanthropy will survive tax reform.

In the mid-1980s, changes in the tax laws made it less attractive for people to donate gifts of appreciated property, such as stocks, because they were now allowed to deduct only the original price, not the appreciated price. Though the number of these gifts has declined since then, they are still worth pursuing.

As fund-raisers, we must also learn how to capitalize on tax changes. For example, by lowering the highest income tax rates, some tax reforms actually increase discretionary income for the wealthy. The only thing certain about tax laws is that they will change, which will mean that charities will have to be creative in approaching their major prospects.

Public perceptions of how philanthropies manage their funds will also be increasingly important to donors. For example, dramatic cutbacks in gifts followed the revelations of scandals in some evangelical ministries. Non-profit causes will have to communicate more

effectively with major prospects and assure them that their gifts are being well-used. The media will be covering issues related to nonprofit management, so the public will be watching. Nonprofit organizations must learn how to mount effective media-relations programs.

Another trend that will have a significant impact on major gift-giving is the increased competition in the fund-raising marketplace. Many newer nonprofit organizations are now competing with established philanthropies. Also many nonprofits are becoming increasingly sophisticated in their solicitation techniques. So when you are approaching a major prospect, even within a small community, be aware that he or she has probably been asked to support other causes. But each organization has its own strengths, and if its case is of interest to a donor, there is a good chance for a gift.

Growing sophistication in prospect-research methods and prospect-tracking systems will also change major gift fund-raising. Much more will be known about prospects. Computers will give us the opportunity to carefully track all interactions with donors and to access data on them instantly.

Later we will talk about capital campaigns in detail, but for now you should know that campaigns are a major trend in themselves. They are now bigger, more frequent and more intense. Comprehensive campaigns seeking "mega-gifts" have raised campaign goals to new plateaus ($1 billion and more).

In summary, even though the future of economic developments and tax issues is uncertain, major gifts fund-raising will thrive and become increasingly important to all nonprofits. Even those organizations that relied for many years on securing large quantities of small gifts by direct mail are realizing the difference a small number of truly significant gifts can make and are entering the world of major gifts and capital campaigns.

Chapter 4

Before You Get Started

Four Prerequisites

Every nonprofit organization must have a clearly stated and well-recognized mission in place before funds can be raised. The following four prerequisites are essential to that mission. Although they are very basic and simple, they are often overlooked. These basics can also change over time, so a real effort should be made to keep them current because you want to have the most impact you can on your major individual prospects.

1. **Cause.** This is the concept around which your organization is built—the socially desirable result you hope to achieve. A donor must feel your cause is significant. Therefore your cause must have a direct impact on society and a sense of immediacy. For example, for a cancer research institute, the cause is finding cures and improving care for cancer patients.

2. **Case.** The case for support is a statement of how an organization is going to achieve that socially desirable result (the cause). A case must be valid for all of an organization's constituencies. There is only one case per institution, although specific explanations for specific programs can be developed as subsets of the case. The case shows why funds are needed and the specific funding priorities related to these needs. It gives prospects clear reasons why they should support your activities and shows what makes

your activities better or different from those of any other group. For example, the case for a cancer research institute would be an explanation of the specific research being done and the specific results being sought.

3. **Organizational identity.** Nonprofit organizations must be recognized for addressing the issues they are working on. Creating an organizational identity means linking in the public's mind the recognized case of the organization's programs to the cause being addressed. In other words, prospects must clearly recognize what you're doing and feel their support will be identified with meeting important societal needs. You also must be clearly identified as a nonprofit group, and the name of your organization should evoke a specific image in the minds of prospective donors. Ongoing news coverage and public relations activities create an organization's identity and position it for fund-raising.

You must be sure that your organizational identity is kept current. For example, the March of Dimes was originally identified with the fight against polio, but when that was won, the organization repositioned itself to battle birth defects.

4. **People.** The internal and external constituencies of an organization must all be drawn into the fund-raising process for it to be successful. While the word "constituencies" refers to all the

people you could possibly ask for donations, in terms of fund-raising statistics, it most often means the actual number of people solicited on an annual basis. These people include staff, administrative leadership, board members, volunteers, neighbors, community leaders, the public and most important—your major prospects.

The people involved are the real definers of whether a fund-raising program will work. You can't be successful at fund-raising unless people see it as part of their jobs, whether those jobs are paid or volunteer.

Long-range Planning for the Organization

In fund-raising, it's what you do ahead of time that determines whether you will be successful. To raise maximum gifts, you simply must do your homework. You cannot rush out and ask someone for a gift or start a capital campaign without carefully preparing a mission statement, maintaining a data base on your prospects and planning cultivation events. You must know your prospects and your organization's priorities, and what you are going to do to bring the two together.

Before any type of effective fund-raising can take place, two kinds of planning must be ongoing within an organization:

■ Long-range institutional planning
■ Fund-raising program planning

The second must be based on the first and really cannot be carried out effectively unless an organization's mission and current priorities are established. Development plans should be based on the results of long-range planning.

The CEO and board chairman of a nonprofit organization should institute long-range planning and monitor it carefully. Unfortunately, many development staff members find themselves in the uncomfortable position of forcing the planning process in order to get priorities for raising funds. The managers of nonprofit groups should themselves realize the need for a mission statement for fund-raising and create a plan without pressure from the fund-raiser.

The fund-raiser should definitely *not* be the only planner. He or she should play a part in the planning effort but should not be seen as charting the priorities alone. The planners should be representatives of all parts of the organization, including paid staff and volunteers. Broad-based planning is necessary to reach consensus on organizational direction.

Following an organized approach to long-range planning will give the fund-raiser the ammunition needed to attract funds. But few nonprofit organizations conduct effective planning. This creates a real problem for fund-raisers because a development plan should be based on an established mission and agreed-upon objectives.

The process of planning is often more important than the plan itself. The process provides an opportunity to involve representatives of all the organization's constituencies. Planning focuses thinking and clarifies issues that are sometimes long overlooked. And let's not forget the biggest advantage of having a plan: It makes an organization look good. Having a long-range plan shows that you have your act together.

To be successful, long-range planning must result in exciting new directions for an organization. But if drastic changes are planned, you can expect resistance.

How do you go about planning then? Long-range organizational planning means charting your organization's future by defining appropriate goals as well as ways to reach these objectives. The planning process can be divided into three phases:

■ A self-assessment of the organization both past and present: What have you done or not done?
■ Organizational goal-setting: Where do you want to be?
■ Strategic planning: How are you going to get there?

During the self-assessment phase, a planning committee, made up of representatives of all the organization's constituencies, should do a candid assessment of all recent activities. What has the organization been doing? What has worked and what has been overlooked? It is important to tell it like it is in this phase of planning. Admit failures and note successes. This self-study will begin to establish in everyone's mind what the organization should be doing.

Then the planning group moves on to a goal-setting stage. At this point, each area of recent activity (or what should have been recent activity!) is looked at in light of whether it should be continued or changed. Then three-to-five-year goals are set for each area.

Once these goals are set, the planning group moves on to the strategic-planning stage. Strategic plans are the plans that will enable an organization to implement its objectives. The strategic planning stage produces *the plan*.

The plan shows specific staff responsibilities, budget needs, facility and equipment needs, and the timetable for implementing each recommended objective.

Here is a more specific outline of the steps in the strategic planning process:

1. **Establishing planning premises.** Setting this baseline for planning is often overlooked. What are the parameters of the organization's purpose? What are the basic assumptions the organization is built upon?
2. **Situation analysis.** The most time-consuming but most important step. Where are you now? What's going on? Avoid editorializing or drawing conclusions. Be candid.
3. **Identifying obstacles and opportunities.** These evolve naturally from the situation analysis. What stands in the way of achieving certain objectives? What specific or timely advantages exist? Obstacles and special opportunities should be identified for each area of activity.
4. **Setting objectives.** What do you want to accomplish? Objectives should be measurable and generally are stated in numeric terms such as percentage of growth. Five to 10 overall objectives for the organization should be sought.
5. **Developing strategies.** Each objective should have at least one and may have several strategies. A strategy is a well-thought-out plan of action. These should be broad as opposed to specific actions.

6. **Creating a mission statement.** This involves combining specific plans into an overall organizational plan.
7. **Identifying critical factors for success.** What are the issues that will make or break your plans? These are vital to keep in mind as you go through the planning process. They can be formulated as the plan progresses. Five to 10 would be appropriate.

The time spent on long-range organizational planning can and should be considerable. What is the timetable for creating an organizational plan? This will vary depending on the readiness of the group to accept the planning process, but a good general estimate is eight to 15 months.

Let's look at the 15-month time frame this way:

■ Three months to develop the scope of the plan and to enlist participants
■ Six months for the core of the planning process, including discussions and work groups
■ Three months to pull the elements of the plan together
■ Three months for review and approval of the plan

There is a delicate balance in the time frame for planning. It gets boring and cumbersome if it takes too long, but it simply cannot be done too quickly. A reasonable period for this type of planning would be at least a year.

Planning for Fund-raising

Once organizational objectives are defined and agreed upon, the development staff can create a specific plan for raising the funds needed to pursue those objectives. This can be done in three steps:

■ Review the objectives and identify specific fund-raising goals to achieve them.
■ Determine the cultivation and solicitation activities needed to meet each goal. Are they currently part of the development program or must they be added?
■ Create a specific plan for each of the fund-

raising activities, including a timetable, schedule, staff and volunteer assignments, list of events and budget.

A fund-raising plan translates the overall organization plan into a step-by-step development plan. Within fund-raising plans, there should be both program and dollar goals.

A fund-raising plan will show volunteers and organization leaders exactly where they fit into the action. But the development staff itself actually benefits the most from creating detailed plans because they show exactly what has to be done and when it should be completed.

Fund-raising is an opportunistic business, and you can often be drawn off course by new but very worthwhile activities. Consulting your plan regularly will keep you on course even with many distractions.

In a large development program, plans are needed for each program area, and they should be brought together under general program guidelines. Month-by-month schedules for each program will show how various activities overlap. Seeing this overlap is important, especially when a single prospect might be involved in cultivation and solicitation activities emanating from several fund-raising programs within the same organization at the same time.

Here is what should be included in a fund-raising plan:

- **Statement of organizational purpose.** Don't create a new purpose just for fund-raising. Take the facts from your organization's long-range planning document. A statement of purpose describes the mission of the organization and tells what the fund-raising is supporting.
- **Goals of the program.** Include the dollar goals as well as a description of each area to be funded. Goals should be attainable. Base them on your record of fund-raising and on a careful assessment of your prospect pool. Don't set them high just to sound impressive. And they should relate well to your statement of organizational purpose.
- **Program components.** Describe the prospects to be targeted for cultivation and solicitation. Then define the fund-raising tech-

niques to be used with each constituency. Establish program goals for each area of activity, such as number of prospects to be contacted or percentage of participation to be sought.
- **Volunteer leadership.** Include a list of volunteer posts and brief descriptions of their responsibilities.
- **Staff and volunteer assignments.** State who will be responsible for each activity and how the staff and volunteers will interact. Ideally, you should assign a staff person to be responsible for each component of the effort. If you have a small staff or a one-person operation, you still must be sure to assign priorities and to divide available staff time accordingly.
- **Organization charts.** These help you and others see how the effort fits together. It is sometimes advisable to do *three* charts: one for the staff, one for volunteers and one showing how they interact. It is best to put your board and administration at the top of the pyramid, making it clear that they hold the ultimate responsibility for fund-raising. Then show how the lines of authority move down to the staff and volunteers.
- **Gift-policy statement.** Before you receive your first gift, you must be very clear on what types of gifts will be accepted, how they will be credited, who makes the decisions and how. Defining this ahead of time avoids difficulties later on.
- **Table of needed gifts.** This is an estimate of the number of gifts needed at various dollar levels if you are to make the goal. This estimate must be based on the results of your prospect research. And you must know that your constituency contains sufficient prospects within the gift ranges you outline. We will show how to develop a gift table later in reference to capital campaign planning.
- **Schedule.** You need a timetable for achieving your goals, including solicitations, special events, publicity.

Putting these elements together is a big job. But once it is done, you'll have a concise document that unites all the key components of the effort into a format that everyone involved can understand and agree on. The operating plan is your blueprint for action.

A long-range plan for an organization is produced on an infrequent basis, but fund-raising plans should be done every year. It is important to create and revise plans to meet dollar and program goals on an annual basis.

Chapter 5
Finding Major Donors

Where Are They?

The purpose of the research process is to estimate the maximum gift a prospect could make if properly motivated by the organization. Finding out facts about prospects helps you decide which activities will affect gift motivation. The ultimate aim is to find the *right person* to ask the *right prospect* for the *right amount* in the *right way* for the *right reason* at the *right time*.

Prospect information must be up-to-date to be helpful, so research must be ongoing and continuous. Changes in a prospect's financial holdings or family situation can obviously have a dramatic impact on his or her potential.

When preparing for a capital campaign, prospect research also helps identify volunteer leaders. People of standing in a community make effective spokesmen for a charitable cause.

Obviously you need to know a good deal about a prospect to appropriately plan such solicitation for a major gift. What are sources of this information?

- Reference books
- In-house records
- Reports from outside data services, such as an individual profile from Dun & Bradstreet
- Computer data banks that you can access yourself
- Newspapers
- Periodicals
- Interviews
- Surveys
- Personal contacts with prospects

Prospect identification and evaluation activities are much the same as marketing and sales techniques for identifying likely buyers. You start with a broad group of prospects and then zero in on the best individual targets.

Because you need approximately three prospects for every major gift you ultimately receive, you should identify three times the number of prospects you think you'll need. This is particularly important when working within a campaign framework.

How do you decide which prospects to research in depth? Start by looking at members of groups within the organization's constituency:

- Prior donors—
    individuals, businesses, foundations, associations, local clubs, corporations, unions etc.
- Users of your services and resources
- People who have shown an interest in the organization
- Vendors
- Past and present board members
- People with historical or family ties to the organization
- Employees
- Neighbors
- People or organizations with interest in similar causes

It is important to concentrate your research effort where it will be the most beneficial—at the top of the list in terms of potential. Zeroing in on the top targets and spending the most research time on them is a key to success.

What are some early indicators of significant potential?

- Address—pinpoint affluent locations
- Titles—business or volunteer leadership
- Business name and address—success of firm etc.
- Gift history—sizable gifts to your organization or to others
- Current level of involvement in your organization

- Marital status and family ties—who are the heirs, if any?
- Connections with people of wealth
- Recent sale of company or real estate
- Family business—successful history of growth could signify personal wealth
- Family foundation
- Real estate holdings
- Stock holdings—corporate proxy statements are a source of this data for executives and directors of public corporations

Figure 5.1. One way to find major donors is through a questionnaire. This alumni census was used by the University of Pennsylvania. Note the financial data requested.

■ Salary data—available on corporate executives in company proxy statements and 10K's, though you will have to request this information.

Research should begin on prospects already known to an organization and then move on to more removed targets. If your organization needs to identify prospects quickly, start by looking at people close to home who fit these categories:

■ Civic or corporate leaders
■ Persons of inherited wealth
■ Persons with a tradition of public service
■ Opinion leaders
■ The newly powerful and the newly rich

Computer data-matching techniques are helpful in obtaining names of new prospects. You can match the donors to your organization with a list of people in the general population, who have the same demographic or lifestyle charac-

---

SEASONAL ADDRESS INFORMATION

To assist us in keeping you informed of events at Penn, please supply address information for additional residence(s) where you spend a portion of your time on a regular basis.

Please forward my Penn mail to the following address from _____ to _____
                                                        mo/day   mo/day

Street Address _____

Apartment Number _____

City_____ State/Country _____ Zip Code _____

Phone (_____) _____
        Area Code

BIOGRAPHICAL INFORMATION

Date of Birth: ___ / ___ / ___   Sex: ☐ Male ☐ Female

Marital Status: _____ (Please select appropriate code from list below.)

Single   (S)   Separated (Z)   Married to an Alumnus(a) (A)   Widow/er   (W)

Married   (M)   Divorced   (D)   Widow(er) of Alumnus(a)   (B)

Spouse Name _____
             Pre title   First   Middle   Last   Post title

Please list any schools attended by spouse, degree received, and date of graduation:

School   U/G   G/P Degree   Date
                                                 ☐   ☐   _____   _____
                                                 ☐   ☐   _____   _____

Please use additional paper, if necessary.

How many children do you have? _____ How many of your children attended Penn? _____

Please list the names of your children, their birthdates, their schools and years of graduation or expected graduation.

Name   Birthdate   School   Yr of Grad
_____   _____   _____   _____
_____   _____   _____   _____
_____   _____   _____   _____
_____   _____   _____   _____

Please use additional paper, if necessary.

Please list the names and relationship of any living or deceased family members other than spouse or children who have attended Penn. Please include the schools they attend(ed) and the year they graduate(d).

Name   Relationship   School   Yr of Grad
_____   _____   _____   _____
_____   _____   _____   _____
_____   _____   _____   _____

Please use additional paper, if necessary.

Please list any other undergraduate and graduate or professional schools you have attended. Indicate the degree you received and the year of graduation, if applicable.

Schools Attended   U/G   G/P Degree   Date
                                                 ☐   ☐   _____   _____
                                                 ☐   ☐   _____   _____

Please use additional paper, if necessary.

2

teristics as your donors and who therefore might be prospects. For example, if you know the zip code of a major prospect, you might be able to find other potential prospects in that same area.

An in-depth analysis of your donors' motivations for giving will help you to further interest them and to identify new prospects with similar interests. This can be done through focus groups, interviews or surveys.

In focus groups, a well-briefed moderator guides a free-flowing discussion about your or-

ganization that can elicit very helpful—and sometimes surprising—information. Hearing the opinions of others sometimes stimulates people to say things that they wouldn't have thought of in a one-on-one interview. Those you invite to the focus groups should all be prospects themselves, and you should keep the groups small enough to encourage everyone to talk.

One-on-one interviews are probably *the* very best way to gain in-depth information on a prospect's interests as well as hints on gift potential. It is amazing how much some people

---

PENN ALUMNI ACTIVITIES

As a graduate, have you ever used Penn's Placement Service to assist you in obtaining employment? Yes ☐ No ☐
When did you most recently attend Homecoming or a Class Reunion? _____
Please put an "X" in the column marked "C" next to any activity in which you **participate currently**; put an "X" in the Column marked "F" next to any activity in which you **participated previously**.

Alumni Events and Activities	C F	Fundraising	C F	Other	C F
Alumni Tour	☐ ☐	Annual Giving Class Agent	☐ ☐	Admissions Interviewer/Recruiter	☐ ☐
Association of Alumnae Board	☐ ☐	Matching Gift Chairman	☐ ☐	Commonwealth Relations Council	☐ ☐
Black Alumni Society	☐ ☐	Regional Gifts Volunteer	☐ ☐	Continuing Education	☐ ☐
Class Officer	☐ ☐	Special/Capital Gifts Volunteer	☐ ☐		
Family Day	☐ ☐				
General Alumni Society Board	☐ ☐				
Organized Classes Board	☐ ☐				
Regional Alumni Club Officer	☐ ☐				
School Alumni Society Officer	☐ ☐				

Other: _____

In what areas of Penn are you most interested?

School of Arts and Sciences (includes C, CW, FAS, CGS, Grad Division)	(050) ☐	Annenberg Center (performing arts) (251) ☐	Academic Research:		
School of Engineering and Applied Science	(450) ☐	Athletics (001) ☐	Humanities	(135) ☐	
Wharton School	(150) ☐	Hospital of the University of Pennsylvania (501) ☐	Engineering	(459) ☐	
School of Nursing	(700) ☐	Institute of Contemporary Art (201) ☐	Health Sciences	(516) ☐	
School of Dental Medicine	(300) ☐	Library (600) ☐	Natural and Physical Sciences	(136) ☐	
Law School	(550) ☐	Morris Arboretum (800) ☐	Social and Behavioral Sciences	(137) ☐	
School of Medicine	(500) ☐	University Museum (650) ☐	Campus Beautification and Facilities	(918) ☐	
School of Veterinary Medicine	(750) ☐		Faculty Development/Professorships	(905) ☐	
School of Education	(350) ☐		Graduate and Professional Education	(902) ☐	
Graduate School of Fine Arts	(200) ☐		Student Financial Aid	(910) ☐	
School of Social Work	(400) ☐		Student Residences and Campus Life	(911) ☐	
Annenberg School of Communications	(250) ☐		Undergraduate Education	(903) ☐	
			University-Community Relations	(928) ☐	

Other: _____

☐ I have made provision in support of Penn in my estate plans, either through a trust or under my will.
☐ I would like to receive information about how to include Penn in my estate plans.
☐ I would like to receive information about how to make a gift through a trust which will provide me with a lifetime income.

My attitude toward the University of Pennsylvania is: (Circle one number):

0	1	2	3	4
Strongly Negative			Neutral	

3

will tell you about themselves if given the opportunity. But you must do initial evaluations to know which prospects you should spend this much time with.

Questionnaires, especially to known constituents, can also tell you a great deal about their potential and interests. To get a significant return, you will have to mail the questionnaire two or three times to non-respondents. Some colleges do regular alumni surveys to update their records and often ask for financial data that helps greatly in targeting prospects.

You may feel hesitant about asking for financial data, but experience has shown that asking those questions doesn't offend people to the point where they won't respond at all. If they don't want to tell you how much they earn, they'll just leave that answer blank. And if they do tell you, then you're just that much further along in your research. But it's important to incorporate the financial questions into the questionnaire in a nonthreatening way. Position them carefully so that they don't stick out. One word of warning: Check out the data you re-

---

PENN STUDENT ACTIVITIES

As a student, did you use Penn's Placement Service to assist you in obtaining employment?   Yes ☐ No ☐
Did you receive financial aid **from Penn** while you were a student?   Yes ☐ No ☐
What student activities did you participate in as a student at Penn? **If you attended one of Penn's undergraduate schools, see page 5.**

_____   _____

Please use additional paper, if necessary.

BUSINESS, PROFESSIONAL AND CIVIC INFORMATION

Please list any companies, philanthropic foundations, and professional or civic organizations with which you are affiliated. This includes parent or subsidiary companies of your primary business affiliation. Please include your title with this organization. Use additional paper if necessary.

Organization	Title

If you have an area(s) of specialization in your profession, please list.

_____   _____

Please include a copy of your vita, if possible.

My total family annual income is:

under $5,000	(A) ☐	$35,000 - $49,999	(E) ☐	$250,000 - $499,999	(J) ☐
$5,000 - $14,999	(B) ☐	$50,000 - $74,999	(F) ☐	$500,000 - $749,999	(K) ☐
$15,000 - $24,999	(C) ☐	$75,000 - $99,999	(G) ☐	$750,000 - $999,999	(L) ☐
$25,000 - $34,999	(D) ☐	$100,000 - $249,999	(H) ☐	$1,000,000 +	(M) ☐

My total net worth is:

Under $100,000	(A) ☐	$10,000,000 - $24,999,999	(H) ☐
$100,000 - $499,999	(C) ☐	$25,000,000 - $49,999,999	(J) ☐
$500,000 - $999,999	(E) ☐	$50,000,000 - $99,999,999	(L) ☐
$1,000,000 - $9,999,999	(G) ☐	More than $100,000,000	(M) ☐

4

2456

ceive. People have been known to say they make $5 million a year—as a joke.

Rating Them Once You've Found Them

In developing a prospect pool, an organization should begin by bringing together all of its internal resources to evaluate prospect potential. Then it should take those results to volunteer leaders and seek their advice on prospect ratings. The process of rating involves careful evaluation of gift potential for each prospect and then assignment of a gift range. These ratings are based on all the data your research produces, prior gift records and on the judgments of volunteers who know the prospects well.

Obviously a schedule of ratings must be established early on. A simple schedule of ratings for a major gifts program might look like this:

Rating	Gift Range
A	$5 million +
B	$1 million to 4.99 million
C	$500,000 to $999,999
D	$250,000 to $499,999
E	$100,000 to $249,999
F	$ 50,000 to $ 99,999
G	$ 25,000 to $ 49,999
H	$ 10,000 to $ 24,999
I	$ 5,000 to $ 9,999

When organizing a major gifts program, rating ranges should be selected in light of the history of giving to the organization. In other words, a prospect may have the ability to make a $1 million gift, but has he or she ever given more than $1,000 to your organization? Ratings should be realistic for the organization. Does anyone give $1 million gifts to your cause?

Ratings during a capital campaign might be pushed up beyond those ordinarily considered because the whole point of running a capital campaign is to get prospects to give more than they ever thought they could—stretch gifts. But these ratings still must relate to the ability to give.

Prospects should also be rated for both annual gifts and major gifts. Those who are close to an organization should be expected to make ongoing annual gifts even when they are solicited for a major gift to support a specific project.

The overall objective of rating prospects is to target the best prospects, so you can spend the appropriate amount of time cultivating them. Raising major gifts requires that you segment the prospect pool, emphasizing those who are worth the most effort. This is especially appropriate in light of the proven guideline that the bulk of private support for any cause comes from very few prospects. The aim of researching and rating prospects is to define the top 10 percent of the organization's constituency—the people who can make the real difference. But prospects at lower gift levels will also be determined through this process.

When assigning ratings, it is important to keep two factors in mind:

■ Ability to give
■ Inclination to give

The best way to begin, especially when asking for rating advice from volunteers, is to seek *ability* ratings only. In other words, ask volunteers to rate prospects based on their ability to give if properly motivated. In the early stages, you should eliminate factors that are suggested as limitations. When someone says, "John could give $1 million, but he doesn't like the president," rate John on ability only, hoping to have an impact on the negative factors through careful cultivation.

The rating process usually occurs on two levels. The first is a broad screening process where volunteers identify everyone with potential, and the second is a more detailed evaluation, especially of those at the higher levels. At the second level, you seek peer-level ratings from those who know prospects well. The rating process must be confidential and well-organized.

The first-level sessions are usually conducted as "silent" rating meetings. Volunteers can be given lists of up to 1,500 prospects to review in a two-hour session. Ask them to write in gift ratings for each prospect they know. The results of these sessions are then combined, and smaller lists are distributed to smaller volunteer groups, usually leaders in the development program, for further clarification. Here some discussion might take place, but confidentiality should be stressed.

At the second-level rating meetings, staff should take careful notes and stress that prospects are being rated for ability to give and not propensity to give.

Try to hold these meetings in a comfortable setting such as someone's home. It is helpful if a volunteer can host and chair these rating meetings, so it doesn't look as if the staff alone is probing for personal information.

After a period of socializing, the host can introduce the process by saying something like this: "We need to know who our best prospects are for large gifts, and the university can only find this out with our help."

To verify volunteer-generated ratings, you should look for three to five ratings at approximately the same level. This means a series of rating sessions on the same prospects will probably be necessary.

You must be specific about what you are seeking in rating sessions, but you should look primarily for three pieces of information:

■ Gift range by dollar amount
■ Areas of interest
■ Best solicitor

Especially at the second-level sessions, you should be able to get good ideas on how to go about the cultivation and solicitation of key prospects.

Volunteers will often ask for guidelines for establishing appropriate ratings. We have already noted that many personal factors will have an impact on the ultimate gift level, but you can suggest these overall guidelines:

■ 10 percent of annual income for an annual gift
■ 5 percent of net worth for a gift from assets

If you are seeking a major annual gift that will come from income, knowing the annual income is helpful and a gift range somewhere under 10 percent of that income is possible. If you are seeking a $1 million gift from assets, a prospect's net worth would need to be in the $20 million range according to these guidelines.

Remember, too, that these guidelines are usually suggested for stretch gifts to a capital campaign or major one-time gifts. When setting annual gift ratings, it is best to look at past gift history and suggest reasonable increases over prior gifts. The 10 percent of annual salary guideline can be considered for annual gifts, but a donor usually gives considerably less than that amount to all of his or her philanthropic interests in one year.

In summary, ratings are best determined by volunteer committees, working from data and guidelines supplied by the development staff. Their own personal knowledge of the prospect's attitudes, interests and abilities will be important factors in determining appropriate ratings.

E. Burr Gibson, board chairman of Marts & Lundy, fund-raising consultants, also suggests that ratings should be evaluated from time to time to see how accurate they are. He further notes that studies usually show the highest prospects are rated the most accurately. He suggests that if prospects are giving only 20 percent of their rated potential, ratings are too high. If the majority of prospects are giving at 70 to 80 percent of the rated figure, ratings are probably much too low.

Keeping Track of Everybody

Once prospects are identified, it becomes essential to have a record system to maintain information on them. Donor and prospect records are essential for any major gifts program or campaign.

Depending on the size of an organization and its budget, a prospect/donor record system may be anything from a manual gift-recording system in a card file to a completely computerized system. There are so many computerized options available that just about every organization should have access to one.

This is the basic data that you need on individual prospects:

■ Name
■ Salutation: Ms., Mr., Dr.
■ Address: home and business
■ Phone numbers: home and business
■ Business title

- Name of spouse
- Connections to your organization
- Community interests
- Corporate and foundation contacts
- Business connections
- Net worth, salary, stock and real estate holdings
- Charitable interests
- Gifts to your organization and to others (including outstanding pledges)
- Interests in your organization
- Existence of a family foundation
- Summary of significant contacts and correspondence with your organization

Other information that might be helpful:

- Nickname
- Date and place of birth
- Education—secondary and higher
- Spouse's affiliations (schools, clubs, charities)
- Names and birth dates of children
- Family ties to your organization
- Previous job titles
- Honors and achievements
- Club and organization memberships
- Political affiliation
- Religious background
- General interests
- Directorships
- Name of secretary
- Name of attorney or tax advisor
- Close friends

In addition to background information, detailed records on gifts to your organization are needed. Here are the details:

- Date of gift
- Amount
- Payments and pledge schedule
- Purpose of gift
- Solicitor
- Acknowledgments
- Total gift history showing amounts, dates and purposes of gifts
- High gift, purpose and date

Your record system might also include details on organizational events that the prospect is invited to and which ones he or she attends.

When setting up a record system, it is important to build in a plan for regular updates. A record system is helpful only if it is up-to-date. People move often, and their personal situations change. Therefore, it is essential to maintain records carefully and record new data on a regular basis.

Some organizations have one record system for prospect addresses (used for direct mail) and another for more detailed prospect information. If that is so, be sure both systems can be automatically updated as new address information is received.

It is essential to keep track of what's happening with major prospects once they are identified and cultivation has begun. The best way to do this is to set up a tracking system on a computer. Your tracking system is different from your prospect records in that it should include only the briefest gift and biographical data. The purpose of a tracking system is to know just where you are with each prospect. The most important data on a tracking system are:

- Prospect name
- Region (general address information)
- Capability rating
- Gift target and purpose
- Readiness
- Areas of interest
- Solicitor's name
- Name of staff person assigned to prospect
- Other people who have connections with prospect
- Date of last interaction with prospect
- Brief review of recent interaction
- Next steps
- Date of next action

A tracking system is a management tool that should be updated regularly so that current status with each prospect can be accessed quickly. Keeping biographical data at a minimum means updates are streamlined.

You do need the ability to sort prospects by the elements listed above, so that you can regularly report to volunteers and staff on progress with their prospects.

Chapter 6
Cultivation—Or Getting to Know You

Why You Must Make the Effort

In development terminology, the word "cultivation" means educating potential donors about an organization's mission and needs before they are asked for a gift. Some cultivation is needed for every gift. Usually the bigger the gift, the more preparatory steps have to be taken. In many ways, cultivation is the most vital part of the gift-seeking sequence, although gifts are rarely made without someone asking for them directly.

Cultivating a prospective donor's interest in your cause is a continuous information-sharing and bridge-building process that should go on before, during and after the solicitation.

The best cultivation takes place slowly over a period of time. Donors give more money to a cause if they can visualize it not as an organization but as people. Inviting major prospects to carefully planned events is the best way to create a face-to-face, personal relationship between the prospective donor and the people who carry out the services of your organization.

Cultivation begins when a prospect first hears about an institution. It reaches its peak when the prospect asks, "What can I do for you?" It should never end.

Cultivation should not really be aimed at getting only one gift. It should focus on establishing a habit of giving, with significant gifts coming at key points. Therefore your most important cultivation targets should be prior donors.

It is important to be honest about your cultivation activities. Don't leave prospects guessing about the purpose of invitations and about why they are targets. Your activities should not pretend to serve one end while really serving another. The truth sells best, so make sure everyone you're cultivating understands that your activities have well-calculated goals.

When planning cultivation events, think of being in the prospect's position yourself. Do only those things that you feel you would respond positively to.

Although you don't want to hit prospects over the head with the fact that you eventually need their financial support, let them know that your organization feels they are important to its future and that because of this, you want to keep them posted on what you're doing. Let prospects know you need their help.

The University of Pennsylvania organized a series of "Inside Pennsylvania" programs aimed at reintroducing major prospects to the university, including alumni, parents and friends. This is the program from one of these events, which included dinner at the president's house and a full day of on-campus briefings.

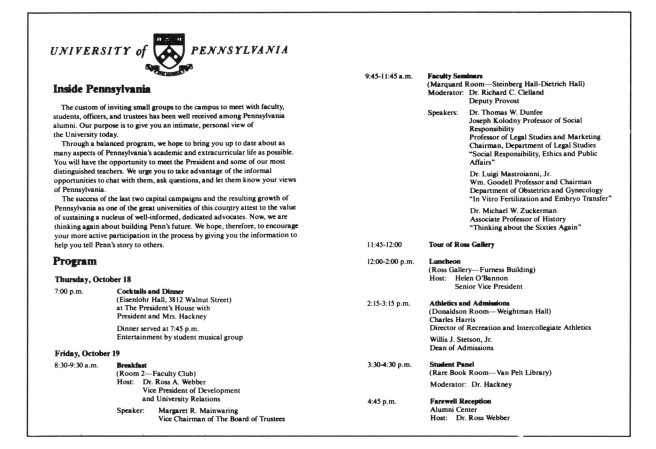

Figure 6.1. "Inside Pennsylvania" program

Making Your Moves

Cultivation occurs in three ways:

■ Mass impersonal events
■ Smaller directed events
■ One-on-one personal interaction

Even with major prospects, it is best to start cultivation in a more informal way by inviting them to events. However, with some major prospects, you might jump over that stage and go right into personal interaction. Very wealthy people often expect that kind of individualized treatment from the start.

G. T. Smith, a former college president and development officer, says there are five steps in what he calls "The Cultivation Cycle":

1. Identification
2. Information
3. Interest
4. Involvement
5. Investment

The last step, investment, is a gift. From there, you go right back to the second step, information. Smith sees the cultivation of potentially large donors as a systematic, continuous effort to develop the power structure of an institution. He feels that securing major gifts is the natural result of the cultivation process. The key to success with major gifts, he says, relates to thinking about a potential donor more as a "person" than as a "prospect." The aim is to involve wealthy people intimately and genuinely with your organization. Smith suggests these steps in cultivation:

■ Determine that the cultivation of major prospects is of primary importance. Get whatever approvals are necessary; the president's approval and endorsement are crucial.

■ Assign or hire one person—ideally the chief development officer—with full responsibility for prospect cultivation.

■ Establish clear-cut procedures for the cultivation process. To begin with, you should:

1. Make an initial list of all known potential donors and gather as much information as possible on each.

2. Assign estimates of gift potential, using four categories: $1 million and up, $100,000 to $1 million, $10,000 to $100,000, $1,000 to $10,000.

3. Within each category, rank potential donors in order, such as: 1-10, 11-30, 31-60 or 61-100.

4. Beginning with the top 10 in the highest category, estimate cultivation requirements. For example, the top 10 should probably have an average of 12 cultivation contacts per year, the next 20 should have 10, the next 30 should have eight, and the next 40 should have six. (This total of 800 contacts with the top 100 potential donors is about what one person can handle if he or she spends 80 percent of the time in major gifts cultivation.)

5. Plan specific cultivation initiatives for each potential donor as far in advance as possible.

Smith's cultivation theory has become known as the "moves" concept. Every development program should have a list of major prospects at whom a constant stream of initiatives or "moves" is aimed. These moves are planned by the development officer to advance a person's relationship with the organization. The theory is that the best way to cultivate the interest of these individuals is to have a series of regular but unexpected contacts with them.

In order to stimulate their interest in making significant gifts, individuals have to feel that an organization is part of their lives on a frequent basis. These moves can include anything from a personal visit, to a letter, to a newsletter, to participation in an organizational event, to a contact from another volunteer from the organization.

The characteristics of a prospect's involvement have to be real and not artificial. In other words, the moves or initiatives must seem natural to the prospective donor and not contrived. Therefore, the system of moves is really not a structured system that will work for every prospect but one that has to be orchestrated differently for almost every major donor. In many ways, this series of moves doesn't have as much to do with immediate gift-giving as with setting the stage for future financial return.

A development officer for an organization should be the orchestrator of a series of initiatives with a top list of major prospects. However, that development person does not have to be the prime mover in all these initiatives. The job of the development officer is to see that a number of people are in contact on a regular basis with major prospects.

In order to make the moves system work as it should, you need a tracking system to allow quick reference to the last contact with a prospect. As we mentioned before, a tracking system is best stored on a computer. It does not need to include all available data on donors because it is not a substitute for biographical record-keeping. A tracking system should provide a quick picture of where you stand with major donors.

Cultivation is often more important than solicitation. During the cultivation process, it is important to listen to prospects, find out what they think of the organization and what kind of involvement they are looking for.

The final result you want from the cultivation process is a true sense of *involvement,* even a feeling of ownership, which convinces the prospect to stretch to make a truly significant financial commitment.

An Example

To see how the moves concept might actually work, let's look at a hypothetical college alumnus:

PROSPECT: Joe Q. College

CLASS: 1950
PROFILE: Joe is a graduate of a small Midwestern college. He grew up in the state where the college is located but moved to Chicago 30 years ago. He is married with two adult children. Joe is the president of a real estate development firm, with business activities in the Midwest and on the East Coast. The firm has just been bought for $20 million. Joe has been a regular donor to the annual fund; his top gift is $5,000. He has never made a major gift nor has he ever been asked. He has not been on the campus in 25 years.
PLAN:

- *July.* Create a top prospect file for special consideration and include Joe.
- *September, December, April, June.* Send him regular "insider" newsletters on the college's progress four times a year.
- *October.* Invite him to a weekend on campus with 40 to 50 other alumni to become reacquainted with the institution.
- *March.* Invite him to a meeting with 10 to 50 other alumni in business in Chicago to hear a presentation by the dean.
- *May.* The president visits Joe's office to spell out the priorities of the college, seek Joe's input and tell him his support is vital to the college's future.
- *June.* President sends a letter outlining how Joe can be helpful. Might include an ask.
- *September.* Ask Joe to join college board of overseers.
- *September through February.* Continue regular contacts, increasing their level of importance.
- *April.* Ask Joe for a major gift.

This is a sketch of how a donor with significant potential might be effectively and slowly cultivated. Keep in mind that these steps don't just happen; they need to be planned.

Let's for a moment put this case in another light. Let's assume that the college is in the midst of a capital campaign when Joe is identified as a major prospect. Also consider the fact that Joe has already expressed his interest in the college by making regular gifts and that he may be receiving a quick influx of funds from the sale of his firm.

This second scenario might mean that Joe should be cultivated and asked *quickly* for a major gift. A campaign gives you the added impetus that can help shorten the cultivation process.

The best way to know what to do in this case, or with any other major prospect, is to get to know the prospect as well as possible and to read his or her situation. Learn how to pick up key issues. Plan interaction with the prospect in a way that will work. Knowing the prospect in detail is the key to success in mounting a cultivation effort.

Chapter 7
Asking The Big Question

Who Should Do the Asking?

Asking someone for money is all most people think fund-raising is. And it's the asking that most people dread. But if the stage has been set correctly, the ask can really be a very rewarding experience—both for the asker and the donor. It can be the first step in a truly meaningful relationship between the prospect and the organization.

Soliciting a major gift almost always requires a personal visit. Few donors can be convinced to part with large sums of money without being asked in a direct way by someone of influence who represents the organization. No solicitation technique works as effectively as the personal visit.

The asker should be of equal or superior status to the prospect. Prospects react best when they are asked by people of influence. Those people are:

- Prominent volunteer
- Chief administrative officer
- Key member of either the development staff or the administrative staff

Even though many development professionals argue that development staff can be just as effective in solicitations as anyone, a review of successful major gifts programs reveals that volunteer involvement in cultivation, and especially in solicitations, leads to the biggest gifts.

Volunteers need to realize that they will be respected for asking. A donor may figure that it is the job of the development staff and the CEO to ask for money. But volunteers can really make good impressions on donors because they are showing that they believe in the organization enough to donate not only their time but also their money.

Patricia L. Fleischer, director of development and marketing for the Washington Opera in the nation's capital, sees these points in favor of volunteer solicitors:

- Volunteers are likely to have a longer relationship with the organization than the development staff person. And the real relationship must be between the donor and the cause, not the donor and the staff.
- It is easier for a prospect to say "no" to a staff solicitor and easier to make a gift that is too small.
- You risk disenfranchising your volunteers when you assume their principal responsibilities.
- It saves staff time to have volunteers do the asking.

One very effective solution is team solicitation. Often the following combinations work very well:

- Volunteer (chairman of the board or key board member) and the CEO

- Volunteer (chairman of the board or key board member) and a development staff member
- CEO and a development staff member

When the team approach is used, it is important to be sure all participants are working on the same solicitation plan and have the same objectives in mind. Preparing a proposal for the prospect, which may or may not be left behind, is a good way to be sure both members of the team are on the same wavelength.

The key to defining the best solicitor is knowing as much as possible about the prospect and anticipating the approach that will work. Some major prospects will expect to be asked by the president and/or the chairman of the board. Others are more low-key and would expect the person they know best from the organization to ask for the gift. Reading this element of the solicitation process correctly is *the* key to success. People don't give to organizations or needs. People give to the person who asks, for the purpose they perceive as important.

How Should They Ask?

Play it by ear is probably the only accurate answer. We will review the established techniques for successful solicitations, but the most important element is the sensitivity and preparation of the asker. The solicitor must be attuned to the prospect and follow the prospect's lead, even if this lead strays a bit from the original plan. The asker must know enough about the needs of the organization to be flexible during the solicitation and to be able to move the conversation in a direction that is in the organization's best interest.

The ask itself is the culmination of a series of cultivation steps. Therefore the asker is simply extending an invitation for the prospect to do something for an organization that has already become attractive. Remember, it may take more than one personal visit to seal the deal.

The process of soliciting a major gift begins way before the personal meeting and should continue through follow-up visits and additional solicitations.

There are three stages in the solicitation process:

- Preparation for the face-to-face meeting
- The meeting
- Follow-up

The preparation includes, of course, the kind of cultivation activities necessary to warm up the prospect. Also involved are fact-finding about the prospect and training the asker. The more the asker knows about the prospect, the more effectively he or she can anticipate reactions and deal with them.

Solicitors should feel comfortable with their fund-raising assignments. They should take on only what they can handle in terms of the number and type of solicitations. They should choose the prospects they will ask. If a volunteer is being asked to solicit major prospects, being assigned no more than five prospects at one time—even during a campaign—is a good rule-of-thumb. Prospects should also be assigned based on who might be most successful in attracting the maximum gift.

In preparing for a solicitation visit, the first step for the asker is to convince himself or herself that the cause is worthy. This is best done by making a generous gift commitment. It is so much more effective if the solicitor can say, "Joe, I've already committed $100,000 to this project and I want you to join me."

Depending on how close the solicitor is to the prospect and how much is known about him, the first meeting may or may not be the right time to ask. Depending on how much the prospect knows about the organization or how ready he is to be asked, it may be best to use the first meeting only for cultivation and fact-finding.

There are important facts you might seek out during a first meeting. Keep in mind that "seek out" doesn't necessarily mean come right out and ask. If a solicitor can get a prospect started in meaningful conversation, it is amazing how much information will surface. Here are some questions to have in mind during that first visit:

- What are the prospect's main interests, both personal and philanthropic?

- What connections does he or she have with your organization or cause? Don't ask this if you should already know.
- What are the prospect's feelings toward the organization and its leadership?
- What recent events have had an effect on the prospect's ability to give?
- Are there other people who know the prospect well and could help in the solicitation?
- Who are the prospect's key advisors?
- How much impact will they have on a gift decision?
- Does the project you had in mind for the prospect make the most sense or are there others which are more appropriate?
- Is the prospect ready for an ask?

If you determine it is not the right time to ask, follow the meeting by sending the prospect further information, a remembrance of the organization or invitations to appropriate events. You might also ask for the prospect's direct participation in your programming, or seek his or her advice on specific issues. All of these steps should be aimed at preparing the prospect to be solicited.

Now let's look at other issues of importance during the first meeting, especially if the meeting will include a solicitation. It is best to call the prospect personally to set up the appointment and then confirm the date, time and purpose in a letter. You should suggest a meeting place where you feel the prospect will be most comfortable. Avoid meetings over meals or in public places so fewer distractions will occur. Ask for a one-on-one meeting. The only exceptions might be spouse and/or lawyer or financial advisor, if you really think the meeting will end in closure.

Once you get to the meeting, be aware of body language, both yours and the prospect's. As a solicitor, you should strive for eye contact and friendly gestures. Watch for squirminess or indirectness from the prospect. His or her body language will tell you a lot about whether it's an appropriate time to ask.

Here are some hints for your conversation with the prospect:

- Use questions to get started. Refer to items in the room or interests of the prospect.
- Listen well and patiently.
- Be sure the conversation returns frequently to the cause and its needs.
- Answer objections in a positive tone.
- Don't hurry the solicitation. The best response is to get the prospect to ask what is needed.
- Don't ask unless you feel the timing is right. Don't ask if the prospect seems out-of-sorts, rushed or preoccupied.
- Be sure you get an opportunity to ask for a specific amount.
- Stress people, programs and ideas, not costs or needs. Remember people give to help people, not to support causes or build facilities.
- Base your appeal on logic and facts.
- Talk about other people who are already major donors or prominent leaders of your organization.
- Sell your cause, not the tax advantages of giving.
- Know how to help the prospect make the gift. Be ready to talk about various gift mechanisms and mention advisors who might help.
- Mention available recognition for gifts such as naming a facility after a donor.
- Suggest that you will send a written proposal or be prepared to leave one with the prospect.
- Tell the prospect how his or her gift will motivate other donors.
- Be sure you actually ask for the gift at the highest level you can. Push for a figure at the high range of those suggested for the prospect.
- Be flexible and understanding.
- If a prospect says "no," ask under what conditions a positive response might be possible.
- Suggest appropriate follow-up to the meeting and be sure it happens.

By the end of a first visit with a prospect you should know the following:

- How does the prospect feel about the organization and its needs?
- What is of greatest interest?
- What size gift is likely? Did you ask too high, too low or not at all?
- What giving method is most likely?
- What should happen next?

Some other things to keep in mind during a solicitation meeting are:

- The prospect is under no obligation to give.
- The prospect is probably a busy person, so don't drag out the conversation.
- The prospect may react emotionally, rather than logically, to the ask and want to give immediately.
- Concede points if the prospect is argumentative. Never press your views over those of the prospect.
- Remember to mention the prestige and recognition afforded to major donors.
- Be prepared to help the donor decide on the size of the gift. Do so by noting the size of your gift and those of others, the average gift to date and the period of time over which the pledge can be paid.
- Don't stress your organization's needs but try to uncover the ways a gift can fill the prospect's personal needs. Determine which of the prospect's needs match the needs of your organization.

Many prospects respond to opportunities to make a difference. They want to see how their gift will challenge others and how it will help the organization capitalize on its assets. When you are asking for a gift, treat the prospect as if you were asking for an investment.

Remember this advice from John D. Rockefeller Jr., one of the earliest major philanthropists and fund-raisers:

"Never think you need to apologize for asking someone to give to a worthy object, any more than as though you were giving him an opportunity to participate in a high-grade investment."

How to Close

Whether it happens during the first meeting or after several follow-up meetings, the solicitor must push to close the gift, thereby bringing the solicitation to a conclusion.

Philip R. Walters, lawyer turned fund-raiser, says, "Closing is the process of helping prospects make decisions that are good for them." Walters notes that there is usually a certain tenseness in the air when a prospect is ready to decide on a gift. That is the time for the asker to begin the close. Walters suggests these six "go-ahead" signs:

- The pace of the conversation changes, either slowing down or speeding up.
- The prospect moves from being a listener to asking lots of questions.
- The prospect gives the first positive response: "I might be interested in . . . . "
- The prospect starts being agreeable.
- The prospect smiles.
- The prospect says, "Will you go over that one more time?"

Walters then suggests these five basic methods of closing:

- **Basic written close.** This method starts with the solicitor making notes on a gift form during the meeting and asking a key question at the pivotal time. "Mary, do you have a middle initial?" If she gives it, you continue asking questions to fill out the gift form and then ask her to approve it.
- **Secondary question close.** This technique uses an involvement question, one that makes prospects decide on something they would need to consider only *after* they agreed to make the gift. Such a question might be: "Jane, are you going to keep the gift you'll receive for supporting our organization, or do you plan to give it to a friend or relative as a present?"
- **Similar situation close.** Tell how other donors have worked through the issues affecting their gifts and are now satisfied investors.
- **Money-bracket close.** Instead of asking for a gift of a specific amount, give the prospect

three gift-range choices: one that is moderately higher than you expect, one that is twice as much and one that is exactly what you expect. Walters sees this as a "soft" close since you've avoided the issue of "gift or no gift."

■ **Balance-sheet close.** Here you make a list of the advantages and disadvantages of making the gift. You seek the prospect's help with the advantages but you offer no help with the disadvantages. Walters feels this is a good approach when the prospect says, "I'll have to think about it."

Whether you feel comfortable using methods like these or you take a more direct approach, it is essential to actually make the ask. Often the best way is to say, "Would you consider a gift in the X-dollar range?"

At this point, some solicitors are so relieved that the ask is over that they'll take any gift, even if the $10,000 prospect offers only $1,000. That's a natural reaction, especially if you are a bit hesitant about being a solicitor in the first place. But you should be careful not to accept the prospect's first offer right away if you think it is much too low. Consider whether you've learned some new things that you can capitalize on. For example, the prospect may have mentioned an area that he or she might be interested in, and you might want to go back to your office to do some more research on this. On the other hand, if this is the only time you'll be able to meet face-to-face with the prospect, you might want to take that low offer and then ask for a second gift at a later date. There is no right answer when you're dealing with the art of negotiation. It's all a game of nerve.

Remember that donors do not perceive themselves as *giving* to you or your organization. They see themselves as *sharing* with others, and in doing so, making what they feel is a positive impact on society.

In summary, the role of a solicitor is to *guide* and *gauge* the prospect's increasing interest, to *determine* the highest possible level of support the prospect can consider and finally to *ask* for that support.

The Follow-up

Always thank the prospect in writing for seeing you. Use this letter as an opportunity to share even more information about the cause.

If a gift was pledged at the level suggested, thank the prospect yourself and see that others (the president, the board chairman etc.) acknowledge the gift as well. Also repeat the recognition to be offered and tell the prospect about others he or she joins as major donors. If the prospect's name is not already on a mailing list to receive key information on the organization, be sure it is added. Also consider sending the person a memento of the organization such as a book, paperweight or another appropriate gift.

If no commitment was made because the prospect needed more information, be sure it is sent in an appropriate format, perhaps as a proposal. Then schedule a second meeting to discuss the proposal further. Suggest that another person be involved in the next meeting if that seems appropriate.

If the prospect raised objections you could not answer, be sure explanations are offered by the appropriate people. If the meeting simply did not go well, assess whether the prospect has enough interest in the organization to be pursued and by whom.

Don't give up if the answer was "no." Try again within six months. Most prospects will find it hard to say "no" too many times if they have an interest in the cause.

We have now completed the review of the basic techniques and concepts you must master to be successful in raising major gifts from individuals. In Part II, we will see how to use these ideas within a development program that has a structured major gifts effort and, in Part III, how to use them within a capital campaign.

Part II
THE ONGOING MAJOR GIFTS PROGRAM

Chapter 8

What's So Important About A Major Gifts Program?

"Major donors deserve and demand constant special treatment. If you deny them such treatment, you remove their primary incentives for giving. The feeling of being an insider, of having personal contact with organization leaders, provides powerful psychological satisfaction."
Dennis Myer
Epsilon Data Management

Where Major Gifts Fit Into Your Plans

The concept behind ongoing major gifts programs is that major prospects have the continuing potential to make one-time gifts or multi-year pledges that will meet significant needs of the organization. These major gift commitments are often made in addition to sizable annual gifts.

Cultivation of major prospects must be a careful and continuous process. Depending on the size of the organization, a major gifts program could be anything from the president carefully courting five prospects to a staff of development officers overseeing the cultivation and solicitation of hundreds of major prospects.

Larger nonprofit organizations should aim to have a well-structured major gifts program at the core of their development efforts. But even smaller groups should always have an identified pool of individuals, with the potential to make major gifts, and a staff member to work with them.

For a major gifts program to operate successfully, it should exist within an ongoing development program that already has an annual giving program and the capability of recognizing and dealing with planned gift prospects. There should also be an effort to encourage gifts from other sources, such as corporations and foundations.

To have a major gifts program, you need a pool of prospects as well as staff and/or volunteers to pursue them. Many organizations have strong annual giving efforts, but they never capitalize on that success by moving major prospects into a category for special consideration, the kind of consideration that can lead to truly significant gifts.

Larger nonprofit groups that do have major gifts programs often organize them by gift level. For example, the following gift categories might be established:

- Annual Gifts   Up to $10,000 a year
- Special Gifts $10,000 to $100,000
- Major Gifts $100,000 to $1 million
- Leadership Gifts $1 million to $5 million
- Principal Gifts $5 million +

These gift categories are then staffed separately, even though the functions carried out within each level are very similar.

While the gift-category approach has proved to be successful, this structure may be artificial. It is best to think about what types of fund-raising activities will be needed to raise gifts at each level, and then to group prospects accordingly and cultivate them as needed.

The number of prospects and the amount of staff time available will also determine program structure. For example, for gifts at lower levels ($25,000 to $100,000 or so), about half the time is spent cultivating the prospect and half preparing the asker for the ask. At higher gift levels, certainly at $1 million or more, each case must be dealt with individually and very carefully. In these top gift ranges, often 98 percent of the time is spent cultivating, but only 2 percent of the time may actually have to be devoted to the ask. By that time, the prospect is certainly expecting a solicitation and may even ask, "What can I do?"

Often development staff members and volunteers are most comfortable dealing with lower-level prospects, so the bottom of the prospect pool gets the most attention. That is fine if you do not have prospects with bigger gift sights, but remember, one very large gift can add up to many smaller gifts, so spend appropriate time on the biggest targets.

On the other hand, don't arbitrarily set up a program based on gift levels and assume that you spend the most time at the top. Think about what it will actually take to get gifts at different levels. It may take more time at the lower level because the prospect has never made a big gift before. In other words, the $25,000 donor may take more persuasion and cultivation than the one who gives $250,000.

The best way to define the structure of a major gifts program is to study your prospect pool carefully and plan cultivation activities in light of your organization's immediate fund-raising goals. Spend the most time analyzing the top prospects and what it will take to get gift commitments from them.

Because major gifts define the success of most fund-raising programs, cultivating and soliciting each prospect should be viewed as a mini-campaign in itself. To be successful with these mini-campaigns, fund-raising consultant John L. McCormick suggests the following steps:

■ A major gifts committee of volunteers must be recruited.
■ Research on prospects should be complete and ongoing, with background materials available for volunteers.
■ The staff and volunteers should agree on the basic strategy for each solicitation.
■ Training must be provided for volunteers.
■ A system for following up prospect calls must be designed.

McCormick also points out the importance of honoring the donor once a gift is made. Often this recognition is the first act of cultivation for the next gift.

In summary, the structure of a major gifts effort within an ongoing development program depends on several key variables:

■ What is the total makeup of the development program? Are there annual giving and planned giving programs as well as a major gifts program?
■ What is the composition of the major gifts prospect pool? How many prospects do you have? How many solicitors do you have? Are they staff or volunteer?
■ How close are the prospects to the organization? How much cultivation do they require?
■ Who can do the solicitations and how much time can they devote?
■ What are your budget constraints? Do you have the resources to allocate staff specifically to major gifts? Do you have computers to store data on prospects and your progress with them?

No individual prospect is the same as any other, but the ideal objective for interaction with every major prospect should be:

■ To attract an annual gift each year at the highest possible amount
■ To attract major gifts from time to time for specific needs
■ To encourage the inclusion of the organization in the donor's estate plan

This should be the plan for prospects who have an ongoing interest in any organization. The aim should rarely be to get one big gift at the expense of a lifetime of giving.

Annual giving, major gifts and planned giving programs should work together. In fact, planned gift techniques are often used to make a major gift larger. Every year a prospect should be solicited for an annual gift, and occasionally special plans should be made to seek a major gift commitment for specific needs. Then when an individual seems at the appropriate stage to think about long-term gifts, planned giving techniques should be introduced. There is a definite continuum in the gifts we are seeking: *Annual gifts* lead to *major gifts* lead to *planned gifts*.

However things are rarely this simple. For example, donors who are asked for major gifts during a capital campaign might want to cut back on their annual gifts. Or donors who put an organization in their wills might think a gift commitment of that type is all that is needed.

Also there is no longer really any clear definition between major gifts and planned gifts. Most large gift commitments include some type of planned gift. Large gifts are rarely outright gifts of cash, so planned giving often comes into play.

And then to confound the whole continuum argument, you will find some donors who won't give annually but who will respond nicely when asked to make a major commitment to a specific cause that is of special interest.

Even though these blips in the continuum do arise, it is best to consider a prospect in light of his or her potential to make gifts in all three of these categories. Because of the importance of pursuing major prospects for different kinds of gifts, let's briefly review the basics of annual giving and planned giving before we get into the mechanics of major gift fund-raising.

An Annual Giving Program

"Annual giving is the custom of making a yearly gift to an institution in which one has faith. It is a friendly, happy custom . . . a perennial reunion in spirit . . . a polling of hope and good wishes by those who wish the institution well."

From a University of Pennsylvania annual giving brochure

More pragmatically, annual giving is the lifeblood of most nonprofit organizations. Through annual giving programs, there is a chance to identify both potential major donors and volunteer leadership. Annual giving is literally the training ground for givers and getters. When it is done well, an annual giving program actually creates a partnership between donors and the organization.

Joe Bolster, director of annual giving at Princeton University, sees annual giving as "a school for philanthropy in which alumni learn basic rules about soliciting and being solicited."

Annual giving solicitations create an awareness of your organization's service to society and a desire among your constituents to support it. They get into the habit of giving on a yearly basis, and their gift sights are increased through devices such as challenge gifts or special gift clubs.

Annual giving is a broad recurring effort to seek funds for an organization's most pressing needs—usually to support ongoing operating expenses. Most organizations are especially interested in annual gifts because they are unrestricted and provide flexible funding in times of rising costs. Annual giving programs usually employ three basic solicitation methods:

- Direct mail
- Phonathons
- Personal solicitation

Annual giving promotes an organization's case for all types of fund-raising, but it alone usually cannot provide the total amount of private funding needed.

What role should annual giving play during a capital campaign? There are four basic options:

- Eliminate annual giving during the capital campaign, and include a sum to replace the missing annual gifts in the capital goal.
- Eliminate annual giving and do not include a replacement sum in the capital program.
- Continue annual giving as a separate program during the period of the capital program.
- Continue annual giving but incorporate it into campaign totals.

Which option is best? Most experienced fundraisers strongly suggest the third alternative. Although some small organizations may not be able to sustain the momentum, you usually end up getting more annual giving dollars during the capital drive, and after it, than before. This is partly because people are asked to increase their annual gifts during the campaign, but also because the general air of excitement surrounding a campaign makes gifts go up.

Marts & Lundy has found that "while annual giving may flatten out during the campaign period, there is usually a gain of 10 percent to 30 percent in the first full year after active capital solicitation, if the right techniques are employed."

It is important to time annual giving and major gifts solicitations so that you do not overburden volunteers or prospects. Actually, overworking the same volunteers rarely is a problem because they are usually different people. You can work up to becoming chairman of annual giving because you are a hard worker, but you are appointed chairman of a capital campaign because of your standing in the community and your own giving potential.

There are three ways to structure the interaction between annual giving and a capital campaign to the mutual benefit of both programs.

- Annual giving and the capital program can have separate goals, objectives and prospects—but be conducted simultaneously.
- The capital program can include increased annual giving support as a goal, thus merging the efforts.
- Solicitations can be staggered during the major fund drive, so that no one prospect is approached for both an annual and major gift in any one year.

If it is possible within your program, the best route to go is to keep annual giving functioning at all times and try to persuade a major donor to make an annual gift first and then consider major commitments above and beyond that amount.

A Planned Giving Program

Planned or deferred giving refers to several forms of philanthropy through which a donor makes a commitment to an organization now, but the benefits are not received until later. Planned giving really includes both current and deferred giving. Generally, however, planned giving programs seek future gifts from donors' accumulated assets rather than current gifts from their income.

Planned gifts are actually major gifts. The term "planned giving" refers to the gift vehicles used to make major donations that are not outright gifts. Today most people can give you more money through planned gifts than through outright gifts. A particular planned gift technique can sometimes cause a donor to make a gift that is much larger than he or she ever considered.

But keep in mind that people who make planned gifts are sometimes good prospects for large outright gifts later on. Often an individual's estate picture changes over time, and an outright major gift may become a possibility where it was not before.

Because of its complexity, planned giving has become the most staff-oriented of all fund-raising work. Building a knowledgeable planned giving staff is basic for future major gifts and capital campaigns. Planned gift solicitations develop close personal relationships between donors, volunteers and development staff members.

Involvement with an organization grows through a planned gift. Donors actually become investors in an organization, and their ties grow as they learn about its financial management. So planned gift programs cultivate potential major donors just as annual giving does.

In reality, all major gifts are planned gifts because they are made from assets and a donor has to *plan* which assets to use to fund a gift and how to transfer these assets. But in fundraising parlance, a planned giving program implies that an organization can and will receive gifts such as:

■ Bequests
■ Trusts (both revocable and irrevocable, meaning that the trust can be changed or it lasts forever)
■ Life-income gifts (the donor transfers property but retains a life-income interest)
■ Life insurance
■ Real estate

Having an organized planned giving program will allow you to be much more successful in soliciting major gifts both during a campaign and on a regular basis. In recent years, many major capital campaigns have seen a significant percentage of their largest gifts come in the form of planned gifts. But to do this, you must have knowledgeable staff or advisors who can solicit these intricate gifts, and you need to be able to provide donors with relevant tax and estate planning information.

One last point to consider, when looking at a major prospect, is that for most organizations, the priority is to seek outright gifts first (especially during a capital campaign) and then to pursue gifts that will be realized later on. It is important to remember how all gifts from individuals interact: We should look for the biggest annual gift and then major outright commitments before moving on to planned gift techniques to push the donor's sights even higher.

Chapter 9
Designing A Program

Just How Are You Going to Do This?

To be successful at raising major gifts on a regular basis, you need to design a program that takes into consideration the number and size of your funding objectives; the number of major gifts prospects in your constituency; the staff, volunteers and systems that are in place to support the program, and the stages you plan to go through in cultivating and soliciting the prospect.

The best way to plan your activities is to chart the steps to be completed, as the major gifts staff did at the University of Pennsylvania.

The first step was to identify the prospects. Penn used the combination of a census mailed to alumni, screening sessions held around the country and staff suggestions.

Then review committees, including staff and volunteer leaders, evaluated the pool and began to establish gift ratings for each prospect. Once gift ranges were established, the prospect's intercsts were paired with funding objectives, and cultivation strategies were formulated.

An important early step was assigning each prospect to a staff member for monitoring and to a solicitor for asking. Data on the prospect and the plans for cultivation and solicitation were entered into a tracking system.

Prospects were then invited to a series of cultivation events, moving from larger events down to specific targeted affairs with fewer participants. After a series of organized contacts with the prospect was completed, the decision was made as to whether this was the right time to ask or whether more cultivation was necessary.

Figure 9.1. Chart of the individual prospect cycle used by the University of Pennsylvania.

INDIVIDUAL PROSPECT CYCLE

PROSPECT IDENTIFICATION

census, screening, staff

PROSPECT EVALUATION
(Review Committee)

rating, interest, strategy

PROSPECT ASSIGNMENT

solicitor, development officer

TRACKING SYSTEM

major gifts liaison

CULTIVATION

visit, event, campus

READINESS DECISION

calling team, proposal

SOLICITATION

commitment or reassess and revisit

STEWARDSHIP

report, event

If this was the right time, plans were made as to who, when, where and how the solicitation would take place. Then if the prospect made a gift, stewardship and acknowledgment steps were in order. But if the prospect's answer was "no" or "not yet," plans for re-solicitation were made.

This outline provides a simplified view of the necessary steps that can help you determine how to design your major gifts program. Your design will depend on the elements you want to include. How many contacts and what type of contacts do you want to have with a major prospect each year? What will you use to make those contacts? Here are some ideas:

■ A newsletter to provide facts on your organization
■ Cultivation events to bring major prospects into your activities
■ A special mailing list of major prospects to receive "insider" news on a regular basis
■ Events hosted by board members
■ Events to bring your organization to your major prospects
■ Recognition events to honor donors

An assessment of who your major individual prospects are, where they live, how much cultivation they need and who needs to be involved in that process will suggest the design for your major gifts program.

Some other cultivation steps you should consider are:

■ Sending the prospect invitations to the organization's social events
■ Asking the prospect to serve as a volunteer
■ Inviting the prospect to orientation sessions
■ Sending the prospect regular publicity materials on the organization's activities
■ Asking the prospect for advice
■ Asking the prospect to join the board or an advisory committee

Once you design the steps to be followed by your major gifts program, you need to set goals. The goals should include dollar goals for amounts to be raised each year as well as goals for the number of new prospects to be uncovered each year and the number of contacts to be organized with individual prospects. In other words, a major gifts program is never standing still. You must always be actively pursuing gift commitments while, at the same time, adding new prospects to your pool and increasing meaningful contacts with identified prospects. The progress of your program should be measured not just on money raised, but on successful contacts with prospects that will lead to gifts at a later date.

To set a dollar goal for a major gifts program, start at the top of your prospect list and assess which gifts might be committed within the next year and at what gift levels. For a major gifts program that is operating without the framework of a campaign, dollar goals should increase by about 10 percent or so each year. Large one-time gifts may cause blips in your fundraising records, but you should have several big targets who are being pursued at all times to counteract the effect of large, sometimes unanticipated, gifts realized in previous years. Dollar goals for an ongoing major gifts program can be set only by reviewing your record of major gifts received and factoring in the gifts you expect to get during a given year. These anticipated gifts must be analyzed on a prospect-by-prospect basis.

Figuring Out a Budget

The budget for a major gifts program should include:

■ Staff salaries and benefits
■ Travel costs
■ Cultivation costs
  Events
  Mailings
■ Equipment and computer costs

Staff and cultivation expenses will be the largest expenditures, usually 80 to 90 percent of the total.

While a capital campaign needs a separate infusion of funds, the money for a major gifts program should be built right into the regular development budget. The size of a major gifts budget is directly related to the number of prospects and the size of the staff.

If you are just beginning a major gifts program, you might be able to start out by inviting major prospects to existing events. But you may soon find that you need new computer software for a tracking system or extra staff to monitor interactions with prospects. If you need to hold additional cultivation events, that will also require more money. And there may be extra costs involved in training volunteers, especially if you bring in outside counsel.

But the extra money spent on major gifts fund-raising is money well spent. The return on your investment is higher than it is for annual giving because the stakes are higher. It actually costs a lot more percentage-wise to do direct mail, and you must write or call the prospect several times to get a response. Even then, the donation is usually far less than what you receive through a major gifts program.

Once you make a budget, don't let it stay static. Your budget should increase annually because you should have more prospects every year and more activities will be necessary to cultivate them.

Managing the Cultivation and Solicitation Process

The key to success in raising major gifts is to *make* things happen with a prospect and not just let them happen. You need to carefully control the growing interaction between the organization and the prospect.

You should have a plan that defines the activities aimed at prospects, how long they will take and how much they will cost. Your plan should begin by dealing with the biggest prospects first. Spend the most time on prospects where the potential is the greatest.

Figure 9.2. The development staff at Lynchburg College used this work sheet to manage the solicitation process for major gifts.

```
WORK SHEET:  How to Manage the Solicitation
                    Process
NAME OF PROSPECT:
SOLICITORS NAMES:
    1.
    2.
    3.
MANAGER OF PROSPECT:
  Name:_____
GIFT SIZE AND TYPE:
    $_____
PERSONAL TIME SPENT LAST THIRTY DAYS
    1.  Office
    2.  Phone
    3.  Face-to-face with volunteer or with prospect
    4.  Call report
TIME PLANNED NEXT THIRTY DAYS AND TYPES OF MOVES
PLUS DATES AND TIMES


WHAT IS THE MOST IMPORTANT ACTION THAT NEEDS
TO BE DONE IN ORDER TO CLOSE THE MAJOR GIFT?


WHAT EVENTS SHOULD THIS PROSPECT BE INVITED TO
IN THE NEXT 6 MONTHS?
```

Even though it is important to manage the cultivation and solicitation process, you must also remember that raising major gifts is an opportunistic process. A new prospect with immediate potential may surface out of the blue, causing you to shift your current plans for prospect development. Take advantage of big opportunities as they arise, but don't forget to get back on schedule as soon as the new situation is dealt with.

Also remember to reevaluate your plan from time to time. Is it working? Are you reaching the right prospects? Should some prospects be dropped from the plan—or added? Are solicitations taking place? One of the biggest failings of major gifts programs is that too much time is spent on putting the systems in place and on orchestrating cultivation events but actual asks do not happen.

The amount of time required to cultivate and solicit major individual prospects will vary with each prospect. Therefore you really need a separate plan for each prospect. Although there are many variables, on average you should plan a six-to-18-month cultivation cycle, with a solicitation taking place right at the end of cultivation activities. Some prospects will cut the cultivation process short, but don't let that happen if the prospect wants to make a gift much below your target figure. Keep the cultivation plan moving on a regular basis, but be sure to take advantage of optimum situations for solicitations.

Chapter 10
Gift Management And Stewardship

Recording the Gifts

Once a gift comes in, you have to be prepared to manage it and to thank the donor. Important actions are needed:

- Record data on the gift, noting any special requests from the donor such as that the gift is to be anonymous.
- Set up appropriate gift accounts, an interest-bearing account for gifts to be invested and a spendable account for gifts that will be used right away.
- Transmit the gift for deposit.
- Prepare and distribute receipts.
- Prepare and send acknowledgment letters.
- Record and summarize data needed on the gift for organizational records.
- List the donor in gift reports.
- Publicize the gift.
- Send pledge payment reminders if necessary.
- Prepare a stewardship plan for the donor that aims at attracting more gifts in the future. ("Stewardship" is the term used to describe all the activities you do with a donor once a gift is made.)

Thanking the Donors

Saying thank you is usually thought of as the last step in the gift process. But it really should be considered the first step in cultivating the next gift from a major donor. You can never say thank you too often. Jerold Panas, author of *Mega Gifts*, thinks seven acknowledgments are not too many for a major gift.

Who should send acknowledgments to a major donor? Certainly the top administrative officer of an organization and the chairman of the board should send personal letters recognizing gifts at significant levels. If a volunteer has played a role in the solicitation, he or she should also send a written thank you to the donor. If the work of a particular staff person within the organization will benefit directly from the gift, he or she should thank the donor too.

The most important thing is to acknowledge gifts positively and quickly. You want the donor to know that the top people within your organization are aware of the gift and that his or her generosity will serve as a motivator for other prospects. You also want the donor to know that you will use the money wisely.

Here are some basic guidelines for saying thank you:

- **Promptness**. A receipt and an acknowledgment letter should go out as soon as possible after the gift is received.
- **Legality**. Mention on the receipt the portion of the gift that is tax-deductible.
- **Flexibility**. Be able to respond in different ways to different types of gifts, with truly pacesetting gifts receiving very special attention.

Figure 10.1. This gift-acknowledgment plan was developed at Cedars of Lebanon Health Care Center in Miami, Florida, for gifts at all levels. It is a good example of the details that must be considered in the acknowledgment process.

1) Donor Gift Acknowledgment
A) Gift Size
—Under $25, send an acknowledgment card.
—$25 to $100, send a personal letter from the director of development.
—$100 or more, send a personal letter from executive director.
—$1000 or more, send a letter from chairman of board in addition to a letter from executive director.
—Show appropriate carbons to physicians when indicated.
—Send new donor envelope with acknowledgment card.

B) If gift is a memorial, acknowledge to next-of-kin.
—Send card if one donor.
—Send letter if two or more donors.
—Make a special folder with name of deceased into which all correspondence to next-of-kin is placed.
—Start an adding machine tape and keep a running total of gifts.
—When tributes total $1000, contact the family regarding the establishment of a named fund.

C) If gift is made in honor of someone, acknowledge to the honoree.

2) Accounting Procedures
A) Make one photocopy of donor correspondence.
B) Make one photocopy of check (or stock) and one copy of acknowledgment.
C) Fill out cash sheet in duplicate, noting donor, fund name and number.
D) Give check, one copy of cash sheet, and copy of donor correspondence to cashier. (Cashier signs both copies of cash sheet.)
E) Record gift amount on profile sheet in donor file folder. (If it is a new donor, make up file folder.)
F) File copy of check, original donor correspondence and copy of acknowledgment in donor folder.
G) File cash sheet in fund-file folder. Record donor's name and gift amount on fund sheet.

3) Type of Gift
A) Cash — write amount in on donor acknowledgment. (Never photocopy cash.)
B) Check — photocopy and attach to donor acknowledgment.
C) Stock — proceed as follows:
—Gift date is determined by postmark if stock is mailed to the Hospital. If stock is brought to the Hospital personally, then the date on which it is received is the gift date.
—Mean value is the figure given to the donor. Call the Hospital's broker for the mean value of the stock on the gift date.
—Take stock certificate, after a photocopy has been made, to Hospital's comptroller; do this on the same day as it is received.
—Write a letter to the donor confirming the gift date and amount.

4) Monthly Gift Summary
—Prepare monthly summary of gifts received by fund categories.

5) Quarterly QUEST Listing
A) Each quarter, supply a listing of all new donors to the public information office for inclusion in the Hospital's publication, QUEST. Obtain needed information from fund-file sheets.
B) The listing is alphabetic, by fund.
C) A copy of QUEST is kept in the development office for reference.

6) Quarterly Fund Balance
A) Each quarter, check with the accounting office to determine any accrued interest on fund investments. Add to balance on fund sheet.
B) Requests for expenditure of special funds must be approved by the development office as well as other administrative team members:
—To ensure purchase is in keeping with any restrictions specified by the donor;
—To ensure that sufficient funds are available; and,
—To maintain an accurate fund balance (expenditures are entered on fund sheets).

- **Personalization**. The more personal the thank you, the better.
- **Multiplicity**. For major gifts, more than one thank you is always in order.
- **Focus**. Emphasize the gift's impact. Show what it will accomplish.
- **Appropriateness**. The thank you should be appropriate to the organization as well as to the nature and level of the gift.
- **Organization**. The gift-acknowledgment procedure should be documented in writing, showing exactly who does what, when and how.

In summary, the right thank you comes quickly, is appropriate to the organization and the donor, and leaves the donor in a favorable frame of mind toward making another gift.

Sending an acknowledgment is just the first step in the stewardship process. A staff person should be assigned to this activity, or it will not be done well. To be effective, a stewardship plan has to be structured and well-managed, or opportunities for effective stewardship will slide by unnoticed.

One way to avoid this is to schedule donors for stewardship activities on a monthly basis. Just prior to the anniversary of a donor's gift is a good time to be in touch because the contact may trigger another gift.

Reporting back to the donor on the use of the gift is also an important part of the stewardship plan. Show how the gift specifically benefited the organization. Public reports on the progress of projects, which were made possible by major gifts, can invite further support from current donors and stimulate new prospects.

Harvard University has made extensive use of written stewardship reports to major donors. These are guidelines that have been used by the stewardship staff there:

- Use the most impressive signature you can obtain; "the stature of the person signing the stewardship report shows the importance your institution attaches to a donor and a fund." Make the source of the report believable by including some details from the signer's personal or professional life.

- Prepare the signer for a response—especially a telephone response—from the donor.
- Raise the consciousness of others in your organization, so that they will help with the stewardship job, perhaps by providing information. Make them know the donor is a "flesh-and-blood person who is contributing personal resources."
- Look for hidden information—good things to report on—in your financial printouts, departmental reports and other internal documents.
- Use the full name of the donor early in the report.
- Show that you know why the gift was made.
- The report should look personally prepared: blue-ink signature, real postage stamp.
- Make the report human, lively and interesting; "don't edit out the sidelights and small touches."
- Let the donor know in advance—before any public announcement—of something new and significant that is associated with the gift: an important research finding, new personnel, a prestigious award etc.
- Even if the donor doesn't respond, keep reporting. It will build the donor's confidence in your cause.

It is important to honor donors, by providing special recognition to them and special services as appropriate. Here are some of the ways to honor a donor:

- Publishing or putting on prominent display an honor roll listing the donors' names. This might be an honor roll listing only gifts at certain levels or gifts for a specific project.
- Place a plaque with the name of the donor in a prominent location commemorating a specific gift.
- Prepare and place news stories about the donor in the local or national press.
- Hold a recognition event, either specifically for one donor or for a group of donors of significant gifts.
- Invite the donor to a special event attended by organizational and community leaders that the donor might want to "rub shoulders with."

- Provide direct services to the donor such as tickets for events, parking etc.
- Pay special tribute to the donor at scheduled events such as commencement, a convocation or a board meeting.
- Prepare an individualized recognition item for the donor to keep at home or in the office.

How Cornell Does It

Another way to recognize a donor very effectively is to bring special significance to major lifetime giving. Cornell University was founded by a major gift of $500,000 made by Ezra Cornell in 1865. Cornell has built on that philanthropic tradition by creating a five-point program to recognize donors whose total lifetime giving to Cornell reaches $500,000.

Donors of $500,000 or more are sent personal letters by the university president acknowledging their generosity, describing how they will be honored and asking if they will allow the university to recognize them through a program that includes the following elements:

- **Wall**. The primary honor is the inscription of the donors' names on stone panels set in a low wall. A university booklet predicts: "Here, generation after generation of students will pause for a moment to reflect on the debt they owe to those who have gone before." An inscription at the entrance to the wall reads: "Those whose names are recorded on this wall have given generously to build and strengthen Cornell."
- **Visitors' guide**. A drawing of the wall, with each section identified by a letter, appears in the visitors' guide folder. Then, the name of each benefactor is listed alphabetically, showing the letter of the section in which his or her name appears. Mr. Cornell's name, for example, appears in section "A."
- **Book**. Titled *The Builders of Cornell: A Record of Cornell University's Foremost Benefactors*, the hardcover book contains 190 pages and leads off with a short biography of Ezra Cornell, "a self-

made man, honest and perseverant." Other names include: Astor, Gannett, Grumman, Olin, Pew, Rockefeller, Sloan and Westinghouse. A one-page biographical sketch of 250 to 300 words describes each benefactor.

These texts are reviewed and approved by the donors if they are living, or by family members if the donor is deceased. As needed, new biographies are bound into the book, which eventually will be reprinted in a new edition. One leather-bound copy of the book is the centerpiece of a permanent exhibit in Cornell's library. This book rests in an open position, and each day a page is turned, exposing two fresh biographies to view.

- **Statue**. A 10-foot high statue of Ezra Cornell, unveiled in 1919, still stands on the campus. For its donor recognition project, the university commissioned 12-inch bronze replicas of that statue. Each benefactor receives a replica, along with a booklet that describes the statue's history. "The gift of the statue is intended as a tangible expression of appreciation," the university explains, "and, perhaps more importantly, the statue itself serves as a daily reminder of the benefactor's involvement in the University's history."
- **Ceremony**. When possible, the benefactor is invited to the campus where, in a private ceremony, the book and the statue are presented by the president or another university representative. If the donor can't make the trip, sometimes the ceremony is held in his or her home.

Some of the sophistication and success of this project comes from what the university *does not* do. For example, it avoids creating the appearance that the wall is a memorial to the dead. New names are mixed with old; there is no clear chronological or hierarchical order; space is left in each section for addition of new names. No public name is assigned to the project. The university explains: "The trustees and administrators did not want this honor to be thought of as a 'super-giving club.'" And there is no "grand celebration" to which all honorees are invited. The focus is on "the individual generosity, wisdom and vision of each benefactor."

The success of this program is attested to by the fact that $156 million in *new* gifts and pledges came from the honorees in the project's first four years. Much of the new gift income certainly came because of the donors' involvement with the university, but probably some of it also came because of the recognition program.

In summary, your donor-recognition program should be well-organized and be seen as a vital ingredient of your major gifts effort. No single step is more essential to future gifts than reporting accurately and regularly to donors of major gifts.

Chapter 11

Personnel: Insiders and Volunteers

Who Are They and What Are They Doing?

For a major gifts program to reach its potential, some staff time must be specifically devoted to the cultivation and solicitation of major prospects. Large gifts don't just happen. They must be orchestrated by experienced staff who know the constituency and the basics of gift-giving.

Volunteers are also very important to a major gifts program. The ideal solicitation is done by a volunteer with careful backup from staff members. Administrative leaders also have an important role to play in the major gifts program.

The number of prospects will have a definite impact on how your program is organized. Comparing the number of prospects to the number of staff, administrative leaders and volunteers is an important first step.

Here are some guidelines for gauging the number of staff and volunteers needed:

- One development staff person can adequately handle only about 100 prospects at a time. Handling usually means tracking and being responsible for the progress of the organization's interaction with a prospect and making sure that the process is continuous and is leading to a solicitation. The staff person may or may not be the solicitor. Some large organizations have stretched staff assignments to 200 prospects and more, but the quality of staff follow-up suffers as the pool expands.

- Volunteers do best if the number of prospects assigned to them is limited to three to 10, with five being the ideal. If volunteers are actually soliciting gifts, keeping the number as low as possible at any one time is best. If a volunteer has more prospects than he or she can handle, progress with every prospect will be slow.

- High-level prospects usually require interaction with the president and/or the board chairman, so the availability of their time will dictate the organization of a major gifts program. Their time needs to be available on an organized basis (several days a month should be spent on prospect contacts) and also on an as-needed basis. Since fund-raising is an opportunistic business, the organization's leaders should make time to interact with major prospects as opportunities arise. The way to guarantee that your leaders spend time on major prospects is to have days on their calendars set aside so that you can fill them.

The most important function of a major gifts staff person is to keep things moving with a prospect. The cultivation process should be continuous and carefully staged. Staff members must have detailed knowledge of prospects to be successful.

What are the characteristics of effective staff members? Good "people skills" are essential. They should be able to talk to a prospect about his or her personal and/or business interests. If you can carry on conversations with prospects about things that interest them, you will be much more successful in the cultivation process than if you just talk about your organization and its needs.

Major gifts staff members should be well-read and well-educated. Listening and absorbing pertinent facts are essential traits. You cannot have an effective conversation with a prospect unless you know what you're talking about and what the prospect is talking about.

It is also important to know about trends in philanthropy and of other fund-raising campaigns within the immediate community. Of course, detailed knowledge of the organization and its needs is vital to encouraging support. But major gifts staff members should avoid references to organizational issues or jargon that may not be familiar to the prospect. And finally, the staff person should have strong language skills and knowledge of proper grammar.

In summary, if a major gifts staff person will have contact with your best prospects, he or she must make a good impression and be responsive to the prospect's requests.

But there are many other people besides development staff who are involved in the process of cultivating and soliciting major gifts. And they often have different responses to the work they are called on to do. One of the most difficult and most important roles for a development officer is to rally recalcitrant participants into the process of seeking major gifts. Attracting large gifts requires interaction with the organization's leadership, so your leaders must be prepared and willing to participate. Development staff cannot do the job alone.

Some people are naturals for fund-raising. They are outgoing, responsive, committed to the cause and willing to spend some time on the fund-raising process. But, too often, that is not the case with key administrators and volunteers, and a development officer has to engage in the delicate task of creating an effective asker and cultivator.

The first step is to convince your leadership that you as a development officer cannot effectively seek major gifts alone. If you are forced to, the gifts will be significantly lower than if the organization's CEO or a board member is involved.

The reason most "non-fund-raisers" are hesitant about the process of asking is that they fear being told "no." Eventually that happens to everyone, but you have to select a situation for each participant where you feel relatively certain success is at hand. Put your key leaders in a situation where the prospect is likely to say "yes." Then move them on to more difficult targets.

This may seem like a simplistic plan, but it is important to get off on the right foot with the leaders you must rely on. Of course, training in the process of asking and cultivating is also vital. Let's look at the various people who should be involved in seeking major gifts and how you need to prepare them.

The president or chief operating officer of an organization must define the objectives to be funded through major gifts and be the chief spokesman for the fund-raising effort. The president should create the vision for an organization that serves as the basis of fund-raising activities. He or she should also be a chief asker for major gifts.

The president's main role is bringing a vision for the organization to its various constituencies. He or she creates, refines and sells this vision to prospects.

During major campaigns, whether they are targeted capital campaigns or special initiatives for major gifts, the president may have to spend significant time on cultivating and soliciting major gifts. For example, at some major universities during a campaign, the president has taken a leave of absence from administrative duties, so that he can spend one-third to one-half of his time on fund-raising. That may sound like a lot, but the more time the chief administrator spends on major gift activities, the more large gifts will be raised.

The president is also the leader of a team of volunteers and development staff who make fund-raising happen. He or she manages the participants, sells the case and interprets the organization to its constituencies. The case for fund-raising should be the president's case and not one that is determined by others without his or her participation. The president must also provide the necessary budget for raising major gifts.

With some major individual prospects, the president may be the first and only contact. Some wealthy people expect an approach from an organization to come only through the president—even the initial approach.

Sometimes, but hopefully not too often, the president may have to decline a gift. This may be because the gift is not high enough or because the purpose of the gift does not fit into the organization's current priorities. For example, a donor may want to construct a building that you don't need or want. Accepting a gift an organization cannot use effectively can be more serious than declining it.

The president or chief administrative officer is therefore:

■ the titular head of the fund-raising effort
■ the chief asker for major gifts
■ the definer of funding priorities
■ the chief spokesman for the organization
■ the provider of the fund-raising budget

Other key administrators can also play a role in fund-raising. Deans, vice presidents, department chairmen and others who can be good representatives of the cause should be involved. They too must be trained and supported in the process.

A Special Word About Board Members

The next most important group of participants in a major gifts program is the board. In seeking major support, the leadership of the governing board is a critical factor. Board members should themselves be visible donors and be committed to giving time to encourage others to give. If board members do not play an active role in a major gifts program, it is very difficult to be successful in mounting such an effort.

Board members should bring the following traits to the organization:

■ Time   ■ Work
■ Talent   ■ Wealth
■ Treasure   ■ Wisdom

In addition to the three T's and the three W's, board membership is often categorized by the three G's:

■ Give
■ Get
■ Get off

Board members are the organization's chief volunteers. Being a board member gives one a stake in the responsibility for the organization's future. A governing board should "accept ownership" of the organization's fund-raising programs, especially at the highest gift levels. The active involvement of the board (or at least of a number of board members) in fund-raising is essential. They have connections you cannot create. No organization can hope to have all its board members be excellent fund-raisers, but at least a few, even a handful, must accept that role. You will probably find some of them are actually challenged and motivated by a fund-raising role.

Board members, just like all volunteers, are only as effective as the staff backup they receive. Active boards are created by inspired executive leadership and detailed staff support.

Leadership gifts from board members are essential. They must stretch and make larger than usual gifts to motivate other prospects. Not every board member can give the biggest gift, but each one should make a gift that is significant, according to his means.

Various guidelines exist for board giving. In some capital campaigns, the nucleus fund (an initial fund-raising effort prior to the public announcement of the campaign) might total 30 to 50 percent of the goal. And often 80 to 100 percent of those nucleus fund gifts come from board members. Some fund-raisers feel a board must give the first 20 percent of the goal and be responsible for raising another 20 percent.

In addition to giving, board members set the style and establish the guidelines for fund-raising. Board members should assess the fund-raising programs of an organization and be sure the necessary elements are in place. They should also reach out to key people in the community and make the organization's needs known.

Michael Radock, an experienced professional fund-raiser, suggests in a publication for the Association of Governing Boards of Universities and Colleges, that trustees use the following checklist to assess whether they are reaching their fund-raising potential for their organization:

■ Have I contributed substantially according to my means? On an annual basis? To capital campaigns? Restricted or unrestricted gifts?
■ Have I tried to influence members of my family, professional associates, corporation or foundation officials to provide support?
■ Will I be prepared to enlist fund-raising leadership from my fellow trustees and friends?
■ Am I willing to accompany the president or another volunteer on a solicitation visit?
■ Can I list my institution's 10 most urgent needs?
■ Am I ready to insist that the president be deeply involved in fund-raising and be ready to join him or her in strategy and priority-setting meetings?
■ Will I be willing to enlist outside counsel when appropriate to review development programs, provide advice or conduct campaigns?
■ Do I support the budget and staff needed to provide a good campaign? Will I support the president and administration when certain policies are needed to ensure a smooth operation of fund-raising programs?
■ Will I use my influence to establish priorities for the institution?
■ Will I be prepared to authorize or assist in the conduct of feasibility and planning studies?

James K. Looney, a fund-raising consultant with Donald A. Campbell & Company Inc. in Chicago, suggests that for board members to be effective fund-raisers they must be closely involved in the process—as policymakers, as planners, as leaders, as solicitors and as donors.

He suggests these guidelines for board involvement:

■ The board will perform effectively in fund-raising only to the extent that it performs effectively in other board functions. This means the board must be well-managed.
■ The staff must view the board as its partner in, and resource for, achievement of organizational objectives. It shouldn't be seen as an adversary or "legal necessity."
■ The selection of board members should be based on the objectives of the institution. The nominating committee must determine how prospective new members can contribute to these objectives, and that committee should also evaluate the way present board members are contributing to the objectives.
■ This evaluation will produce stronger board members who have a sense of identification and ownership. It will also eliminate marginal performers.
■ Board members who have a strong sense of ownership and a feeling of helping the organization achieve its objectives will also: volunteer to raise dollars, interpret the organization's story effectively to the public and give significant gifts themselves.
■ A sense of ownership comes when board members are deeply involved in assessing the organization and its environment, developing long-range plans, establishing policy to achieve objectives and monitoring the outcome of that policy.

To sum up, let's look at two quotes from board members on how boards interact with the development process:

"The professional development officer can prepare lists of prospects, but only the trustee can identify those prospects with which he or she has a special relationship. The development officer can plan a luncheon, a dinner, a tour, or whatever sort of cultivation and fund-raising event may be appropriate, but only the trustee can get prospects to attend. The development officer can prepare proposals and leads for personal solicitation, but only the trustee can effectively solicit the pledge or the gift. . . . The role of the development person is key to success in these endeavors because the kind of trustee who has the most contacts and is best at cultivation and solicitation is usually a terribly busy and committed person who needs superior staff work if he or she is to be effective."

John W. Eckman,
Life Trustee of
The University of Pennsylvania

"Nothing has greater cumulative impact in fund-raising outreach than the continuing, persistent, personal witness of the trustee. People are persuaded by those people whom they respect and who talk warmly and supportively of the causes they espouse. Your board should be well-populated by such people. And they need a good platform from which to operate. . . . Why leave them as an amorphous dark cloud which hovers over the crest of the institution and from which lightning bolts occasionally descend? The board should be brought into public view in its role in governance, and its presence should be established in the minds of your constituencies. Many of the things that boards do are even interesting and newsworthy. Promote a public appreciation of the importance and strength of your board and of the hard-working volunteers who serve on it. Such a growing recognition serves as a validating backdrop against which the individual trustee can pursue his or her cultivation and promotion tasks far more effectively."

John W. Pocock
Former Chairman of the
Board of Trustees of
The College of Wooster

Besides the board, other volunteers are also needed to round out the team of people charged with raising major gifts. For example, you might enlist an advisory board or major gifts subcommittee, which would include people with major gifts potential who are willing to ask others for donations. You might have subcommittees working specifically on scholarships or on raising gifts for a specific project.

Volunteers could also be enlisted based on the gift levels you're seeking. For example, if one group is the $10,000 to $100,000 range, you could ask for help identifying, cultivating and soliciting potential donors within that group.

We're not talking about licking envelopes here. These volunteers will have one-on-one contact with prospects. They will be helping to customize the cultivation strategy for individual prospects. They should be viewed as key liaison people.

Enlisting and Training Volunteers

For board members as well as other important volunteers, the enlistment process is a vital step. People have to know right up front exactly what is expected of them in order to be successful, especially at fund-raising.

We often hear administration officers and professional fund-raisers lament that their boards do not have wealthy members and that their board members simply will not ask for money. The problem in those cases is almost always that board members were not recruited on the right basis and they have not been oriented properly to understand their roles. If you expect a board member to do major gift fund-raising and to make significant gifts, you have to say so right up front. Don't tell new board members that fund-raising will not be required and then introduce it later on.

What traits should you look for in a good volunteer, especially a board member?

- Commitment to the organization
- Desire to become involved
- Desire for a new challenge
- Commitment to the general welfare of society
- Time to devote to the organization
- Established stature that will enhance the organization
- Financial ability to give

Volunteers should be enlisted by someone they know or by the top leadership of the organization. If you are asking an influential person to help, he or she should be impressed by who does the asking. If a personal contact begins the enlistment process, it should be followed up by an official letter from the appropriate person within the organization.

After enlistment, you must motivate board members and other key volunteers for fund-raising by involving them in planning the fund-raising program. Inform them early on of your objectives and educate them constantly about the organization.

When board members and other key volunteers are first enlisted, they should attend orientation sessions on the organization, including site visits to its major programs. Let board members get to know the staff and learn first-hand about organizational priorities. By seeing these programs in action, trustees will buy into supporting them.

The initial orientation of board members should include sessions on development, where you explain your fund-raising efforts, with a special emphasis on the role board members are expected to play in raising major gifts. Tell them you will provide training, especially if you are going to ask them to solicit gifts. Be straightforward about the fund-raising process from the very beginning.

Trustees and other important volunteers should be involved in major gift fund-raising on an organized basis, not in an ad hoc way. You should set up committees and enlist leadership based on the functions to be carried out.

Recruit volunteers in a sequential fashion starting at the top. Enlist a development committee of the board and perhaps a major gifts subcommittee. Create job descriptions for the committee chairmen and for members. This will make it clear exactly what is expected. Once board committees are enlisted, you might add representatives of other constituent groups, community leaders and major donors. If it is not appropriate to add outsiders to board committees, enlist separate committees and create a fund-raising steering committee with representatives from each constituency including the board.

When asking volunteers, including board members, to cultivate and solicit major prospects, it is best to limit their assignments and to choose their prospects very carefully. If people are given too much to do, they won't do any of it. Allow volunteers to pick prospects they know and to choose assignments where their influence will be the most meaningful. Volunteers should take on prospects only after they have made substantial gift commitments. They should also take on prospects in the same gift range as their own.

An effective way to train volunteers for solicitations is the role-model approach. Simulate an ask and involve the volunteer in acting out responses. Or stage a successful solicitation using volunteers and staff as participants. This can be fun and constructive because it gets volunteers to think about the actual solicitation process. Some nonprofit groups have prepared videotapes of model solicitations for their volunteers.

Another way to prepare volunteers for a personal solicitation is to suggest they review a work sheet prior to each meeting. Questions for review can include:

- How is the organization servicing the prospect?
- Do you know everything you can about the prospect?
- What objections can you anticipate? What concerns will the prospect raise about the organization?
- Be ready to demonstrate your own commitment, by mentioning your gift and by being enthusiastic.
- Don't overstay your welcome.
- Pay attention to what the prospect says.
- Watch prospect's body language.
- Be prepared to cite pacesetting gifts already received.
- Be direct, confident and simplify the request.
- Aim to develop a pleasant rapport with the prospect.
- Make the ask before you leave if no barriers have arisen.

Effective busy volunteers, especially board members, prefer structure for their activities. Tell them what you want them to do and when. Show how their activities will affect the entire major gifts program.

Volunteer interaction is essential to raising major gifts at the highest levels. But you must work to keep them on schedule. Here are some ideas for doing that prepared by the consulting firm of Barnes & Roche Inc. of Rosemont, Pennsylvania:

■ Involve volunteers in planning the activities in which they will later participate. This will heighten their understanding and commitment.

■ Don't recruit volunteers when there is really nothing for them to do. Don't form committees unless there are specific needs for them.

■ Busy volunteers are far less likely to stray from the timetable if they feel that their energies are being used in a productive way.

■ Schedule regular meetings for key volunteers—meetings at which each person reports on his or her progress. "This creates a subtle and effective peer pressure."

■ Provide volunteers with a monthly or quarterly schedule of their activities.

■ Don't expect volunteers to respect the timetable if your staff does not. "The development officer should be certain that the staff meets every deadline under its control."

Training of major gifts volunteers has to be done in an organized way, but remember that all major prospects are different. Therefore volunteers should not be trained to solicit by rote. They must learn to be attuned to different situations and always be looking for the opportunity to obtain a bigger gift.

Not all volunteers will be good major gifts solicitors. Look for the best among your leaders and pair them with your best prospects.

Chapter 12
Two Successful Ongoing Major Gifts Programs

In order to show how ongoing major gifts programs actually operate, here are illustrated profiles of programs at two very different organizations—Bryn Mawr College and the Metropolitan Opera.

Bryn Mawr College

The plan of action for a major gifts program at Bryn Mawr College came directly from the success of a capital campaign at the suburban Philadelphia institution. The college's ability to raise major gifts from individuals during the campaign led to the establishment of an ongoing major gifts program.

Bryn Mawr took advantage of the existing fund-raising structure and volunteers from the capital campaign to build in a major gifts program. That way, the college raised a significant amount of money without a significant increase in the fund-raising budget.

The Centennial Campaign had gone over its goal of $41 million, for a total of $46.5 million in outright gifts and pledges, and just over $50 million, counting new deferred gift contracts and government research grants. Bryn Mawr's major gifts activities made enormous progress during the planning and execution the Centennial Campaign. In fact, Donna L. Wiley, current director of resources at Bryn Mawr, credits the campaign with strengthening the development program's entire approach to major gifts.

For the first time, the college appointed two staff members, in addition to the director of the Resources Office, who were charged with working with major prospects. The office produced a pyramid of gifts that were needed to reach the goal, and a computerized tracking system was set up to match prospective donors with targeted gifts at various levels.

As is so often the case at the close of major campaigns, the Resources Office faced a number of staff changes. The director of the office began a year of sabbatical leave; the two staff members most directly concerned with major prospects left the office, and two out of three staff positions for the annual fund changed over. The volunteer major gifts committee that had been assembled was disbanding, as were all of the campaign volunteer structures.

The question was obvious and the need immediate: how to capture the wealth of information gained about prospective donors during the course of the campaign and create a structure for continued cultivation work in the inter-campaign period to come.

The development staff immediately assembled a group that included all of the outgoing staff members, as well as the retiring chairman of major gifts, and undertook a painstaking review of the over 400 major prospects (rated at $10,000 or more), who had been identified during the campaign. In each case, the volunteer who seemed likely to have the most current

7/1/88

NAME	STATE	CLASS	CODE	STAFF ASSIGNED	VOLUNTEER ASSIGNED	RATING	REVIEW DATE	COMMENTS
	CT	1932		NYM			1/89	
	TX	1933	C	MLN	RKN		9/88	
	MD	1942		NYM			1/89	
	CT	'31 R'91		KPA			9/88	
	DC	'30 R'91		KPA			9/88	
	CA	1957	C	DLW	RKN		9/88	
	CT	'61 R'90	C	DLW	MPMcP		9/88	
	CT	1969	C	DLW			9/88	
	PA	1919		KPA			9/88	
	PA	1925		KPA			8/88	
	NM	'55 R'89	C	MLN			7/88	
	NY	'54 R'89		DLW			9/89	
	IL	1933	S	DLW	MPMcP		8/88	
	NY	'51 R'91	Z	KPA			9/88	
	MA	1941	S	DLW	BAT		3/89	
	NY	'31 R'91	C	DLW	PMcP		7/88	
	PA	'59 R'90	C	DLW	BGA		10/88	
	PA	P		AQA	R.Cooper		9/88	

A = Future Review	S = Solicit	D = Deferred Gift	P = Parent	
C = Cultivate	Z = In Progress	R = 89, 90, 91	F = Friend	

Figure 12.1. This page from the Bryn Mawr tracking system shows how prospects were followed.

information on that prospect was also identified.

Letters explaining the situation were mailed to these volunteers, recommending cultivation and solicitation activities for the prospects during the next two years or removal from the major prospect list. Based on the volunteers' rankings of the list, a new refined list was made up of just over 200 individuals, who would form the basis of a post-campaign tracking system for major prospects.

That new tracking system became the basis of the major gifts program. Each prospect was assigned to a staff member, and regular review dates were set up. The primary goal was to develop a travel schedule and series of cultivation events that would allow at least one member of the staff, many of whom were new to the Resources Office, to meet each prospective donor over a period of two years. At the same time, a list of about 40 of the most important prospective donors was developed. That list was reviewed repeatedly in a monthly meeting of the senior resources staff with the president of the college. A volunteer major gifts committee was reconstituted, and a chairman was appointed, who was a trustee of the college and whose energy and commitment to working on Bryn Mawr's behalf were exemplary.

Since Bryn Mawr's Centennial Campaign, the Resources Office has been fully engaged in an active program of major prospect cultivation across the country. This has involved the president of the college, three to four resources staff members and a volunteer major gifts committee. With the exception of the chairman, the activities of that committee have centered on arranging gatherings of Bryn Mawr alumnae, rather than on actual solicitations.

The following figures give some idea of the scope of this activity. In the 1985-86 fiscal year, 475 individuals attended various major gifts events. Sixty people were visited individually during that year. In 1986-87, the chairman of major gifts visited 149 people, individually or in small groups. The president of the college, usually accompanied by the director of resources, saw about 100 people, not including those at larger-scale campus events, and 17 cultivation events were held across the country. In 1987-88, 179 people were visited individually, and 20 events were held on and off campus.

Although there is, of course, some overlap among these various contacts, the Resources Office has orchestrated outreach to a significant portion of the alumnae body (which numbers 11,000 undergraduate alumnae and about 4,500 alumni of the graduate schools). At the same time, the tracking system was expanded by 60 percent, to a list of 320 prospective donors.

What impact did all of this activity have on major gifts to the college? First of all, in 1986-87, the college received more gifts from individual donors (cash received plus new deferred gift

Figure 12.2. Although Bryn Mawr created no special fund-raising materials for its major gifts program, this donor report, which we have excerpted, gives a comprehensive view of the development program that reflects the major gifts effort.

GIFTS TO BRYN MAWR COLLEGE 1987–88

Outright Gifts		
Alumnae/i and Alumnae/i Foundations		$2,950,170
Parents		90,626
Friends		241,383
Corporations		321,715
Foundations		1,827,256
Bequests		
Alumnae/i	1,578,274	
Friends	1,066,784	
Parents	5,879,078	
		8,524,136
		$13,955,286 *
Deferred Gifts		1,051,008
Total		$15,006,294

* Includes all cash gifts received by Bryn Mawr College between
June 1, 1987 and May 31, 1988.

DEAR FRIENDS,

As I look back over a very productive year, I am impressed by how much we have accomplished with the help and understanding support of our friends—the alumnae, alumni, parents, friends of the College, corporations, and foundations that we salute in this report. It is a pleasure to thank you all for your interest in Bryn Mawr.

This has been the first year of our five-year effort to achieve sustainable financial equilibrium for the College. Our planning last year is showing some results, as we have been able to budget more adequately for campus and building maintenance, and to make much needed improvements in faculty and staff salaries. A college of Bryn Mawr's extraordinary breadth, diversity, and small size is difficult to manage in these times, but I believe that the measures that we have taken will enable us to meet the challenges before us.

Our efforts to improve faculty salaries received a tremendous boost this year through the addition of four new endowed professorships: the Eleanor A. Bliss Chair in Biology, the Eugenia Chase Guild Chair in the Humanities, the Mary Hale Chase Chair in the Social Sciences and Social Work, and the Rachel C. Hale Chair in the Sciences and Mathematics. We also look forward to appointing a scholar to a new Assistant Professorship in British History, established in memory of Helen Taft Manning '15 by generous gifts from her family, friends, and the many students and colleagues whose lives she touched.

We are gratified that the College continues to attract an extraordinary group of students. Their energy and ideas invigorate us each year. The hard work of our alumnae volunteers in admissions deserves our praise and thanks. Financial aid remains one of our major priorities, and we can report not only several special gifts this year to the College's endowment for undergraduate and graduate student aid, but the continued success of our Alumnae Regional Scholarship Program.

This year's Mary Flexner Lecturer, the historian Natalie Zemon Davis of Princeton University, shared with us fascinating insights into the history of the gift in sixteenth-century France. She spoke not only of the history of giving, but of the special relationship that existed between donor and beneficiary. It was a lesson we understood very well. It is always a pleasure to acknowledge our debt to each of you for your generosity to Bryn Mawr. We hope that you will make your claim on the College in exchange, whether by returning for Reunion, Alumnae College, or a tour of the campus, or by attending one of the district conferences and alumnae gatherings across the country. I look forward to thanking you in person in the near future here or abroad.

With gratitude and warm regards,

MARY PATTERSON McPHERSON PhD '69
President

1987–88 Volunteers

Dear Friends,

I t is a great pleasure for me to thank all of you who serve Bryn Mawr as volunteers. Your dedication to our efforts to recruit potential students, to secure funds for all areas of the College's operations, and to support a myriad of activities by and for the alumnae across the country and around the world, is very much appreciated. Your involvement and loyalty serve as a collective vote of confidence in Bryn Mawr and a testament to the significance that the College has had for all of us.

This volume celebrates in particular those who have supported Bryn Mawr this past year with gifts of time and of dollars. Please accept, on behalf of all of the Bryn Mawr Trustees, our deep gratitude and warmest regards.

Sincerely yours,

Hanna Holborn Gray

Hanna Holborn Gray '50
Chairman, Board of Trustees

TRUSTEE DEVELOPMENT
COMMITTEE
Jacqueline Koldin Levine '46, Chair
Barbara Goldman Aaron '53
Annie Leigh Hobson Broughton '30 MA '36
William S. Cashel, Jr.
Anthony T. Enders
Hanna Holborn Gray '50
Johanna Alderfer Harris '51
Ruth Kaiser Nelson '58
Marie Salant Neuberger '30
R. Anderson Pew
Martha Stokes Price '47
Rosalyn Ravitch Schwartz '44
Sally Shoemaker Robinson '53
Barbara Auchincloss Thacher '40
Barbara Janney Trimble '60
Deborah Jackson Weiss '68

ALUMNAE RESOURCES COUNCIL (ARC)
Sally Shoemaker Robinson '53, Chairman
Ruth R. Atkiss '36
Annie Leigh Hobson Broughton '30 MA '36
Sheila Cunningham '72
Constance Collier Gould PhD '75
Mary Beth Krebs '75
Ruth Kaiser Nelson '58

ANNUAL FUND COMMITTEE
Mary Beth Krebs '75, Chairman
Judith Anne Calhoun '82 MA '85
Ashley Dorien Dartnell '80
Epsey Cooke Farrell '57
Jane Karr Fortin '73 MA '75
Margaret Parlin Hutchinson '61
Nancy Porter Morrill '60
Elinor Bissell Offill '39
Kathryn Geib Plympton '49
Elinor Beidler Siklossy '64
Beth Brumbaugh Steffian '61

REUNION GIVING CO-CHAIRMEN
Ruth R. Atkiss '36
Sheila Cunningham '72

MAJOR GIFTS COMMITTEE
Ruth Kaiser Nelson '58, Chairman
Patricia Castles Acheson '46
Barbara Bettman Allen '49
Sally Ankeny Anson '52
Lois Miller Collier '50
Ruth N. Cooper '44
Barbara Kates-Garnick '72
Melissa Emery Lanier '55
Marie Salant Neuberger '30
Patricia McKnew Nielsen '43
Joanne d'Elia Payson '75
Martha Stokes Price '47
Patricia Cain Schramm '59 PhD '71

GIFTS IN KIND CHAIRMAN
Constance Collier Gould PhD '75

DESIGNATED GIFTS

Many individuals, foundations, and corporations choose to support Bryn Mawr with gifts and grants intended to meet specific needs. These restricted gifts can advance the College's programs in a number of innovative ways. This year, a gift is supporting a capital renovation project in the sciences; a grant allowed science students to conduct research in the science laboratories over the summer; gifts helped to meet our challenge grants from the Hewlett Foundation and the National Endowment for the Humanities; and the support of the Alumnae Regional Scholarship Program brought talented and promising young women to study at Bryn Mawr.

Gifts for the endowment are particularly valuable, as they lay the groundwork for Bryn Mawr's long-term fiscal viability. In 1987–88, alumnae, friends, and family members, as well as two private foundations, gave gifts that were used to establish 25 new endowed funds. Their names and purposes are described below. In addition, gifts were added to 145 of the College's more than 1,000 endowed funds.

NEW ENDOWED FUNDS

Elizabeth Baer Fund
Established by the bequest of Elizabeth Baer '31 for the general purposes of the College.

Eleanor A. Bliss Chair in Biology
Established by the bequest of Eleanor A. Bliss '21, Professor Emeritus of Biology, Dean Emeritus of the Graduate School of Arts and Sciences, and a member of the Board of Directors from 1944 to 1952, to support a Professorship in the Department of Biology.

Elisabeth Tyson Broekhuysen Fund
Established by the bequest of Elisabeth Tyson Broekhuysen '27 for the general purposes of the College.

The Frank W. and Elinor West Cary Fund
Established by the bequests of Elinor West Cary '21 and her husband Frank W. Cary for the general purposes of the College.

Collier English Fund
Established by Reginald and Lois Miller Collier '50 to provide library support for the Department of English.

Collier Psychology Fund
Established by Reginald and Lois Miller Collier '50 to provide library support for the Department of Psychology.

Amelia Sanborn Crist '19 and Elizabeth Crist Nicholson '50 Fund
Established by Elizabeth Crist Nicholson '50 in memory of her mother, Amelia Sanborn Crist '19, to provide support for advanced research and study in the fields of Classics and Classical and Near Eastern Archaeology.

Emily Grace Fund
Provided by Phyllis Goodhart Gordan '35 in memory of Emily Grace '33 MA '34 for the general purposes of the College.

Emma and Fritz Guggenbuhl Fund in Mathematics
Established by the bequest of Laura Guggenbuhl Ph.D. '27, in memory of her parents, Fritz Guggenbuhl and Emma Marie Wildhaber Guggenbuhl, to provide scholarship support for graduate students in the Department of Mathematics.

Maude F. Hallowell Fund
Established by the bequest of Maude Frame Hallowell, who was a graduate student at Bryn Mawr in 1934, to support the Department of Anthropology.

Dorothy Grant Hammond Library Fund
Established by the family of the late Dorothy Grant Hammond '38 to provide unrestricted support for the Canaday Library in her name.

Margaret B. Hays Fund
Established by the bequest of Margaret B. Hays, who was a graduate student at Bryn Mawr from 1927 to 1929, to support the general purposes of the Department of Physics.

Marguerite Krantz Iwersen Fund
Established by the bequest of Marguerite Krantz Iwersen '19 for the general purposes of the College.

Ruthalia Keim Fund for the Graduate School of Arts and Sciences
Established by the bequest of Ruthalia Keim, who was a graduate student at Bryn Mawr in 1932, to support the Graduate School of Arts and Sciences.

Louise Kerr Book Fund
Established by the bequest of Louise Chamberlin Kerr '46 to support library acquisitions.

Helen Taft Manning Scholarship Fund
Provided by the Reginald and Julia B. Fleet Foundation in memory of Helen Taft Manning '15, Professor Emeritus of History and Dean Emeritus of the Undergraduate College, for unrestricted undergraduate scholarship support.

Matilda McCracken Peck Book Fund
Provided by the bequest of Matilda McCracken Peck '33 for library materials with preference given to purchases related to architecture and/or horticulture.

Edna K. Paine Fund
Established by the bequest of Edna Kraus Paine '15 for the general purposes of the College.

Margaret J. Reed Fund
Established by the bequest of Margaret Jane Reed '16 for the general purposes of the College.

James Logan Rhoads Fund
Established by the bequest of Esther Rhoads Houghton '23 MA '29 in memory of her brother, James Logan Rhoads, to provide support for special needs of the faculty.

Frederic C. Sharpless Fund
Established by the bequest of Frederic C. Sharpless, former member of the Haverford College Board of Managers, for the general purposes of the College.

The C.V. Starr Scholarship Fund
Provided by the C.V. Starr Foundation of New York for scholarship support, with preference given to undergraduate students.

Marian Frances Statler Fund
Established by the bequest of Ellsworth Morgan Statler, twin brother of Marian Frances Statler, who attended Bryn Mawr in the 1920's, to provide support for undergraduate scholarships.

Elizabeth K. Tyson Fund
Provided by the bequest of William C. Broekhuysen in memory of his wife, Elisabeth Tyson Broekhuysen '27, to support the purchase of books, periodicals, equipment, or special lectures in the Departments of History of Art and Classical and Near Eastern Archaeology.

BEQUESTS, DEFERRED GIFTS, AND GIFTS IN KIND

Bequests

The generosity of alumnae, parents, and friends who remembered Bryn Mawr in their wills yielded extraordinary results in 1987–88. Legacies from 56 individual donors came to a total of $8,524,136, more than double the highest level of bequests ever before received by the College. Many were unrestricted bequests, some of which have been used to help meet the College's challenge grants and to build the general endowment. A trust established by Rachel C. Hale, mother of Mary Hale Chase '25 and grandmother of Eugenia Chase Guild '52, allowed the establishment of three fully-funded professorships and the naming of the Eugenia Chase Guild Computing Center. Other generous bequests established library funds, scholarship funds, and funds for the support of specific academic departments.

DONORS

Seymour Adelman
Eleanor A. Bliss '21
Donita Ferguson Borden '31
Barbara Schiettelin Bosanquet '27
Alice Gibson Brock
Elisabeth Tyson Brockhuysen '26
William C. Brockhuysen
Eleanor Newell Burry '21
Mary Almack Carpenter PhD '24
Elinor West '21 and Frank W. Cary
Louise Catterall '21
Mary Hale Chase '25
Lucy Evans Chew '18
Fanny T. Cochran '02
Cristina Coney D'Arms '25
Louis Darmstadt
Margaret Simpson David '35 MA '43
Adelaide M. Davidson MA '36
Avis Wickins Evans MA '29
Mary S. Gardiner '18 PhD '27
Charles M. Goethe
Celia Newman Grau g '08
Laura Guggenbuhl PhD '27
Rachel C. Hale
Maude F. Hallowell g '34
Elizabeth Luciemay Hannah '32
Margaret Blanche Hays g '29

Esther Rhoads Houghton '23
Marguerite Krantz Iwersen '19
Arnold D. Kates
Ruthalia Keim g '32
Louise Chamberlin Kerr '46
Elisabeth Washburn King '16 MA '37
Marguerite Lehr PhD '25
Helen Tatt Manning '15
Edna Kraus Paine '15
Matilda McCracken Peck '33
Frances Van Keuren Pestalozzi '35
Marie Pinney '15
Margaret Yost Reed '15
Nancy Mitchell Riepe '28
Elizabeth M. Rowley '04
Lena B. Salisbury g '14
Mary Wingfield Scott '18
Elizabeth Williams Sikes '20
Elizabeth K. Stark '16 MA '18
Ellsworth Morgan Statler
Martha Taylor Stedman '31
Anne Hampton Todd '02
Sara Clark Turner '30
Jean Loeb Whitehill '26
Dorothy Miller Wright '31
Edith A. Wright PhD '35
Gertrude M. Wright
Edith F. Wyatt 1896
Lillian Wyckoff '22

Deferred Gifts

Last year, Bryn Mawr received a total of $1,051,008 in deferred gifts from 25 alumnae who chose to invest in the College by making a gift that would yield life income to them or to a beneficiary of their choice. Their gifts included three separately-invested trusts and several life insurance policies in the name of the College, as well as gift annuities and new and additional gifts to the College's two pooled funds.

DONORS

Cathleen A. Asch '74
Page Hart Boteler '48
Andrea Lorraine Bridgeman '77
Eleanor Fabyan Burlingham '36
Amie Smith Chabrier '43
Julia Grant Dietz '38
Clarissa Compton Dryden '32 MA '35
Isabelle Seltzer Fleck '37
Mary Moon Hemingway '39
Jeanne Dulebohn Kress '43
Diana Daniel Lucas '44
Ellen Woodbury Ober '61
Alice Little Payne '24

Margaret Haskell Pierce '34
Delia Marshall Pitkin '39
Marie A. Richards '35
Marion Bridgman Slusser '36
Florence Green Turner '26
Marilyn Hanback Van Keppel '57
Elizabeth Gray Vining '23
Cristobel Locke von Hemert '47
Vera Ames Widder PhD '38
Rita P. Winston '78
Ellery Yale Wood '52
Ledlie Laughlin Woolsey '40

The Bryn Mawr College Pooled Funds (one invested for income, the other for growth) have attracted an increasing number of donors in recent years.

Year Ending	6/30/84	6/30/85	6/30/86	6/30/87	6/30/88
Size of Funds	$1,588,716	$1,682,131	$1,830,574	$2,912,551	$3,213,118
No. of Donors	79	83	88	98	102

Gifts in Kind

A Matisse etching and a sterling tea service from 1890 were among the treasures alumnae and friends gave to the College in 1987–88. The proceeds from the sale of these gifts of tangible property helped Bryn Mawr to meet its operating expenses.

DONORS

Seymour Adelman Estate
Anne Lord Andrews '31
Darthela Clark '20 Estate
Clarissa Compton Dryden '32 MA '35
Diana D. Lucas '44
Ella Berkeley Pettee '33

Elisabeth W. Russell
Lianne C. Scherr MSS '65
Elizabeth Kindleberger Stone '33
Flora Tallman
Joan Wilson
Virginia Atmore Wilson '28

WAYS OF GIVING TO BRYN MAWR

There are many different ways to make a gift to Bryn Mawr College, some of which may be particularly advantageous to you as an individual donor and to the College. Your own attorney or financial adviser should be consulted as to the best plan of action for you.

OUTRIGHT GIFTS

Gifts of Cash
A gift of cash is available immediately for the use of the College, and provides important tax benefits for those donors who itemize deductions.
Your check should be made payable to Bryn Mawr College.

Gifts of Securities
Gifts of appreciated securities may be deducted at full market value on the date of transfer to the College, and, except in the case of donors who are subject to the Alternative Minimum Tax, will not be subject to tax on the appreciated value of the securities.
To make a gift of securities, please contact Margaret M. Healy, Treasurer of the College, at 215-526-5160.

Gifts of Real Estate and Other Tangible Property
A gift of real estate or other capital assets (stock in closely-held companies, oil or mineral rights, works of art, jewelry, books, and so forth) can be sold for the immediate benefit of the College. Although the responsibility for appraisal rests with the donor, that expense is tax-deductible for donors who itemize.
It is also possible to make a gift of real estate to Bryn Mawr and to retain the right to live on the property during one's lifetime.

DEFERRED GIFTS

Pooled Income Funds
Bryn Mawr offers two pooled income funds: an Income Fund, which is expected to yield 7.4% income in 1988-89, and a Growth Fund with 4.4% yield, invested for long-term growth of principal. Both offer life income, as well as current tax deductions based on the age of the beneficiary.

Gift Annuities
A gift annuity offers donors a fixed rate of life income, a portion of which is exempt from federal income tax, as well as a tax deduction at the time of investment. A donor of age 65 years or older may establish a gift annuity with a gift of $10,000 or more.
A deferred gift annuity, in which the donor defers income until a specified age (say, 65 or 70) offers a particularly high tax deduction at the time of investment and may offer an attractive retirement alternative for those no longer able to take full advantage of Individual Retirement Accounts.

Life Insurance
A gift of life insurance, which names Bryn Mawr owner and beneficiary of a policy on the life of the donor, is a good way to make a significant gift to the College which might otherwise not be possible. Donors may deduct the cost of premium payments. It is also possible to give Bryn Mawr an existing policy and to claim a tax deduction for the cash surrender value.

Charitable Remainder Trusts
Charitable remainder trusts, which can be established with a gift of $50,000 or more, are individually invested and managed by a trustee of the donor's choice. A unitrust yields a specified percentage of the assets, revalued annually; an annuity trust pays a fixed dollar amount each year. Both types of trusts provide attractive tax deductions and life income for the donor or other designated beneficiary.

Charitable Lead Trusts
A charitable lead trust pays a percentage of income to Bryn Mawr for a predetermined number of years, after which time the assets pass to a recipient of the donor's choice. In some cases, lead trusts may be used to shelter assets, to reduce income and/or estate taxes, or to relieve heirs of capital gains tax.

BEQUESTS

An individual may include the College in her will, either by naming a specific bequest or by naming Bryn Mawr as the residual beneficiary. Bequests to Bryn Mawr have been essential in providing for the College's future.

MATCHING GIFTS

Many corporations will match gifts made by employees, family members, and directors to charitable institutions. Some corporations will provide matches for deferred gifts as well as outright gifts. If you would like information about your own company's matching gift program, please contact your personnel office or the Resources Office at Bryn Mawr.

If you are considering a gift to Bryn Mawr, and would like information about ways of giving, please call or write: Donna L. Wiley, Director of Resources, Bryn Mawr College, Bryn Mawr, PA 19010, 215-526-5121.

Early College rings featured a different design for each class, often incorporating the class animal or bird.

UNDERGRADUATE COLLEGE

1896-1914

ANNUAL FUND
$920

Goodhart
Cleos Rockwell Fenn '14
Lantern
Mary Wilmarth Brown '12
Other Annual Fund Gifts
Katharine Huntington
Annin '14
Janet Baird '14
† Mildred Baird '14
Lillien Cox Harman '14

OTHER DESIGNATIONS
Fanny T. Cochran '02
Estate
Helen Strong Hoyt 1897
Trust
Gertrude Ziesing
Kemper '13
Elizabeth M. Rowley '04
Estate
Anna Stearns '11
Anne Hampton Todd '02
Estate
Edith F. Wyatt 1896 Estate

TOTAL $46,622

1915

ANNUAL FUND
18% $150

Dorothea May Moore
Isabel Fothergill Smith

OTHER DESIGNATIONS
Helen Taft Manning Estate
Dorothea May Moore
Edna Kraus Paine Estate
Marie Pinney Estate
Margaret Yost Reed Estate
Isabel Fothergill Smith
Margaret Free Stone

TOTAL 27% $43,961

1916

ANNUAL FUND
7% $150

Georgette Moses Gell

OTHER DESIGNATIONS
Elisabeth Washburn King
Estate
Elizabeth K. Stark Estate

TOTAL 7% $199,381

1917

ANNUAL FUND
20% $250

Alice Beardwood
Esther Johnson
Janet Grace McPhedran
Florence Iddings Ryan

OTHER DESIGNATIONS
Alice Beardwood

TOTAL 20% $275

1918

ANNUAL FUND
31% $2,205

Pembroke Arch
Helen Catherine Schwarz
Other Annual Fund Gifts
Ella Lindley Burton
Elizabeth Downs Evans
Harriet Hobbs Haines
Katharine Dufourcq Kelley

OTHER DESIGNATIONS
Lucy Evans Chew Estate
Mary S. Gardiner Estate
Mary Wingfield Scott
Estate

TOTAL 31% $43,442

1919

ANNUAL FUND
42% $5,680

Thomas
Beatrice Sorchan Binger
Pembroke Arch
Elizabeth Dabney Baker
Other Annual Fund Gifts
Elizabeth Hurlock
Beckman
† Eleanor Marquand
Delanoy
Meribah C. Delaplaine
Annette Stiles Greeley
Nanine Ray Iddings
Mary Thurman Martin
Anita Ehlers Mortensen
Katharine Tyler Wessells

OTHER DESIGNATIONS
Elizabeth Dabney Baker
Meribah C. Delaplaine
Marguerite Krantz Iwersen
Estate
† Helen Elizabeth Spalding
Katharine Tyler Wessells

TOTAL 46% $17,524

1920

ANNUAL FUND
59% $2,079

Pembroke Arch
Millicent Carey McIntosh
Lantern
Phoebe Helmer Hawkins
Other Annual Fund Gifts
Julia Cochran Blunt
Martha Prewitt
Breckinridge
† Darthela Clark
Mary Hardy
Monica Healea
Margaret Ballou Hitchcock
Helen Humphrey Jackson
Martha Jane Lindsey
Katharine Roberts Ludden
Teresa James Morris
Edith Stevens

OTHER DESIGNATIONS
Monica Healea
Margaret Ballou Hitchcock
Katharine Roberts Ludden
Millicent Carey McIntosh
Elizabeth Williams Sikes
Estate
Marian King Tichvinsky

TOTAL 64% $2,414

1921

ANNUAL FUND
57% $4,205

Pembroke Arch
† Julia Peyton Phillips
Goodhart
Jean Flexner Lewinson
Helen Hill Miller
Nancy Porter Straus
Lantern
Cecile Bolton Finley
Elizabeth Hole Mills
Alice A.S. Whittier
Other Annual Fund Gifts
Edith Farnsworth Brann
Margaret Morton Creese
Margaret Crile Devine
Ellen Lyons Donovan
Marian Eadie Farrow
Grace Lubin Finesinger
Bettina Warburg Grimson
Margaretta Archbald Kroll
Minor Banks Lewis
Rebecca Snowden
Marshall
Margo Murtha
Mary Anngenette Noble
Winifred Worcester
Stevenson
Beatrice Spinelli Stover
Laura Ward Sweany
Helen Hutchins Weist
Emily Kimbrough Wrench

OTHER DESIGNATIONS
Clarinda Garrison Binger
Eleanor A. Bliss Estate

1922

ANNUAL FUND
51% $1,725

Goodhart
Vinton Liddell Pickens
Lantern
Elizabeth Wilson Pharo

Garden party following commencement, 1906.

DONOR GROUPS

Taylor Tower	$5,000 and over
Thomas	$2,500 to $4,999
Pembroke Arch	$1,000 to $2,499
Goodhart	$500 to $999
Lantern	$250 to $499
Senior Row (classes of 1983-87)	$100 to $249

Donor group membership is based solely on an individual's contributions to the Annual Fund, Graduate Fund, and/or Parents Fund. Matching gifts are not included.

Eleanor Newell Burry
Estate
Elinor W. & Frank W. Cary
Estates
Louise Catterall Estate
Ellien Lyons Donovan
Rebecca Snowden
Marshall
Passya Ostroff Reefer
Alice A.S. Whittier
Emily Kimbrough Wrench

FRIENDS OF THE CLASS
Haffner Foundation

TOTAL 62% $218,208

Other Annual Fund Gifts
Marie Willcox Abbott
Jeanette Palache Barker
Isabel Coleman Cutler
Barbara Clarke Fuller
Virginia Randolph Grace
Katherine Stiles Harrington
Byrd C. Hazelton
Anne Gabel Hildenbrand
Mary Ecroyd Hinkle
Elizabeth Hobdy Hobart
Mabel Anna Meng
Jane Yeatman Savage
Margaret Bailey Speer
Malvina Glasner Wessel

OTHER DESIGNATIONS
Isabel Coleman Cutler
Katherine Stiles
Harrington
Elizabeth Hobdy Hobart
Lillian Wyckoff Estate

TOTAL 51% $105,364

Fundraising Volunteers are highlighted in italics.
† Deceased

Every effort has been made to ensure the completeness and accuracy of the donor lists. Please call the Resources Office collect at 215-526-7377 if you have questions or concerns.

contracts) than in any other year in Bryn Mawr's history. In fact, individual donors gave 19.7 percent more than they had in 1983-84, the highest year of the Centennial Campaign. Although the impending threat of the Tax Reform Act of 1986 made that year a banner one for most development offices, the resources staff is firmly convinced that the heavy schedule of major prospect cultivation and solicitation visits encouraged many people to think of Bryn Mawr when planning their charitable giving that year. A more significant indicator may be the fact that there were outright gifts of $10,000 or more from 43 individuals, for a total of over $1.6 million, all of which were solicited in that same year. For a college of Bryn Mawr's size, that is an unusually high level of support to be gained in a non-campaign period.

As the college began to plan its next major fund-raising campaign, contact with the most significant prospects had been maintained, and that fact put the college in good position to launch another comprehensive campaign.

The Metropolitan Opera

The Metropolitan Opera in New York City has one of the most successful fund-raising programs of any cultural organization in the country. After completing a $100 million capital campaign in the mid-1980s, a program was organized to attract potential donors of $25,000 and more. By 1989, $8 to $10 million of the $30 million raised annually by the opera came in the form of major gifts.

According to Vincent J. Spinelli, director of development for the Metropolitan Opera during the late 1980s, the major gifts program was

Figure 12.3. A brochure listing the privileges of membership in the Metropolitan Opera Patron Program

Some of the privileges you will enjoy as an active participant in the Metropolitan Opera Patron Program:

Contributing Patron — $1,500 a year

Personalized ticket service by mail or phone for opera and ballet performances at the Metropolitan Opera through Patron Ticket Service

Priority in requests for Metropolitan Opera and Dance at the Met subscription series, changes or seat improvements

Listing in the Metropolitan Opera performance program

Invitation to special Season Preview

Invitations to Patron dress rehearsals

Invitations to special events with Metropolitan Opera artists

Admission to Patron Room during intermissions

Use of private Patron coat-checking facility

One-year subscription to *Opera News* magazine

Lecture series on new productions

Gift of annual *Broadcast Guide*

Special Patron's backstage tour

Supporting Patron — $2,000 a year

Includes all of the above, *plus:*

Listing of your name in the annual Souvenir Book

Increased ticket priority

Sponsor Patron — $3,500 a year

Includes all of the above, *plus:*

Invitation to a special seminar and a reception with Metropolitan Opera artists and senior management

Complimentary copy of the annual Historic Broadcast Recording

Increased ticket priority

Additional dress rehearsal passes

Benefactor Patron — $6,000 a year

Includes all of the above, *plus:*

Invitation to an annual event on the Metropolitan Opera Stage with Met artists

Preferred reservations at the Grand Tier Restaurant

Increased ticket priority

Invitations to selected working rehearsals

President's Circle — $10,000 a year

Includes all of the above, *plus:*

Highest priority in all Patron privileges and benefits

Exclusive use of the Second Century Circle Ticket Service

Invitation to annual briefing on artistic and institutional planning with the Metropolitan Opera's President and senior management

Special listing in the opera performance program and annual Souvenir Book

Invitations to private social activities with Board members, Metropolitan Opera management and artists

How to participate in the tradition of Metropolitan Opera patronage

To make a tax deductible gift to the Metropolitan Opera, please send your check made payable to the Metropolitan Opera Association to:

Mrs. Thomas S. Brush
Chairman, Patron Program
Metropolitan Opera
Lincoln Center
New York, New York 10023

You might also wish to consider the Metropolitan Opera's Planned Giving Program which offers an array of financial strategies and custom-tailored gift arrangements including bequests and gifts of stock, bonds, life insurance or real estate.

Should you have any questions or require additional information about the Patron Program or planned giving opportunities at the Metropolitan Opera, please call the Director of the Patron Program at (212) 870-4589.

All privileges are on an annual basis and are renewable on the anniversary of the gift.

Figure 12.4. This brochure lists the privileges of Golden Horseshoe membership. Members are also listed in all of the opera's programs.

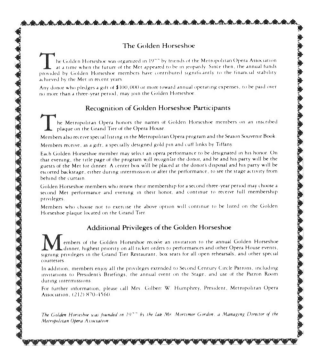

■ Leadership for the Second Century$250,000 +
■ Second Century Guarantors $100,000 +
■ Second Century Benefactors $ 50,000 +
■ Second Century Sponsors $ 25,000 +

In addition, the Golden Horseshoe group was organized in the late 1970s and has grown significantly. It is interesting to note that the major gifts to the opera through the Golden Horseshoe primarily provide funds to meet annual operating costs, although in some cases these gifts can be applied to specific projects such as sponsoring the production of an opera.

The staff involved in the major gifts program for the Metropolitan Opera is relatively small. The assistant general manager of the opera has a good deal of contact with major prospects and is supported in this activity by the director of development and an associate director of development, who is the director of major gifts.

Because the opera's programming provides many opportunities for cultivation activities, the development staff concentrates on using performances to draw prospects into the opera's orbit. Staff members and key volunteers invite prospects to dinner, followed by the chance to see a performance from a box seat. Prospects also get the opportunity to go backstage during and after performances.

The chairman of the opera's board also serves as chairman of the major gifts committee. He takes prospects to the opera as often as two to three times a week. Giving prospects the opportunity to meet performers is, needless to say, a great cultivation tool.

The opera also organizes a series of cultivation events at the opera house during the day. Luncheons are followed by working rehearsals. Prospects go behind the scenes and visit the opera's shops.

The chairman of the opera's board and the president of the Metropolitan Opera Association are often the solicitors for major gifts, but there is also a significant amount of solicitation by staff members. The staff concentrates on building close relationships with key prospects, so it often becomes a natural process for the staff to ask for gifts. The staff usually asks for gifts in the $1,000 to $100,000 range, and volunteer leaders ask for the larger gifts.

built on an existing patrons program. Major prospects were initially identified from the opera's patrons who were making gifts of $1,000 or more annually. Over the years, some of these patrons have moved up the ladder of gift categories to $25,000. There is even a $100,000 gift group, the Golden Horseshoe.

The gift categories that are part of the Patron's Program for the Opera are:

■ President's Circle $10,000 +
■ Benefactor Patron $ 6,000 +
■ Sponsor Patron $ 3,500 +
■ Supporting Patron $ 2,000 +
■ Contributing Patron $ 1,500 +

There is a second group of categories for major donors of $25,000 or more called the Second Century Circle. The gifts in these categories, which usually support special projects, are:

Figure 12.5. The opera describes ways that planned gifts can be made and how they can benefit donor. This brochure also tells how to become a member of the Encore Society.

Generation after generation, thanks to the loyal and generous support of our national family, the Metropolitan Opera has brought the best of grand opera to its great stage and, by radio and television, into millions of homes throughout the country.

We are pleased to announce a new program, The Metropolitan Opera Encore Society, established for the growing number of men and women who are ensuring that this tradition of support continues into the Met's Second Century by providing for the Metropolitan Opera through their Wills or other aspects of their estate plans.

By contributing to the Metropolitan Opera in one or more of the ways that would allow you to join The Encore Society, you may:

- receive substantial income tax and estate tax deductions
- avoid capital gains tax
- increase your income (by contributing through one of our charitable trust plans), and
- increase the amount ultimately transferred to your heirs or to other purposes of interest to you.

The Metropolitan Opera Encore Society

Associates of The Encore Society will have the opportunity to learn about an array of financial strategies and custom-tailored gift arrangements that can help both the donor and the Metropolitan Opera. Moreover, to express our appreciation for your special commitment to the future of the Metropolitan Opera, we will recognize your participation in The Encore Society by listing your name in the Metropolitan Opera performance program (with your permission, of course).

You may become an Associate of the Encore Society simply by completing and returning the enclosed reply card to let us know that you have remembered the Metropolitan Opera in your estate plans. This commitment may be fulfilled through your Will, a charitable trust, a life insurance policy, or a gift of real estate. What a wonderful way to share your love of opera with future Metropolitan Opera audiences!

Contributing through one or more of the following arrangements will entitle you to become an Associate of The Encore Society:

A Gift Through Your Will
Your bequest may take a number of forms, including a specific dollar amount or a percentage of what remains of your estate after your obligations to others are fulfilled. You may also name the Metropolitan Opera as a contingent beneficiary, in case none of your other beneficiaries survives you. Your estate will receive an estate tax charitable deduction for your bequest to the Met.

A Gift From Which You Receive Income
Under our "life income" charitable trust plans, you transfer cash or other assets to a trustee, who then invests the amount transferred and pays you (or another) income for life or a period of years. These charitable trust arrangements provide income tax and estate tax advantages and allow you to keep and often increase the income that you receive from the assets you donate. You may fund such a trust with as little as $2,500.

A Gift of Life Insurance
As an individual grows older, the need for life insurance protection usually lessens. For example, if your

(continued on the back panel)

children are now grown and support themselves, or if the mortgage on your home has been paid, you may no longer need all of the insurance that you own. Perhaps an insurance policy that has served its original purpose may now be contributed to the Metropolitan Opera. You may also want to consider purchasing a new insurance policy to contribute to the Met. In either case, you would receive income tax and estate tax benefits.

A Gift of Real Estate
Real estate can be contributed outright or through a "life income" charitable trust plan. You may even contribute your residence and retain the right to reside there for life, thereby making a significant gift to the Metropolitan Opera without diminishing your standard of living. Moreover, there is no capital gains tax due on a charitable gift of appreciated real estate.

To join The Encore Society or to request additional information, please complete and return the enclosed reply card or call Mr. Harold Gunn, Director of Planned Giving, at (212) 870-4592. We welcome your inquiries and the opportunity to work with you and your advisors in planning your gift to the Metropolitan Opera.

A copy of the last annual report filed by the Metropolitan Opera Association, Inc. with the New York Secretary of State may be obtained upon request addressed to: Metropolitan Opera Association, Inc., Lincoln Center, New York, New York 10023 or State of New York, Department of State, 162 Washington Avenue, Albany, New York.

Photo © Beth Bergman

The volunteer solicitation process is headed by a major gift committee of the board, which has six members. They have before them at all times a running list of assignments, but they concentrate on a small number of prospects at once. The staff develops the gift strategies that are carried out by the major gifts committee. A tracking system, which monitors progress with major prospects, is updated every two weeks.

The recognition of donors is a very important part of the opera's fund-raising program. Donors to the opera want their names associated with its programming. The names of donors in all Patron and Second Century categories are listed in every opera program as well as explanations of these categories. Donors are also recognized in the book that describes the operas and performers for the current season.

The opera places great emphasis on personalized acknowledgments. Every major donor receives at least three thank you letters, one each from the chairman of the board, the president and the general manager. Volunteers also do personalized thank yous to donors of $2,000 and up.

Many events are also held to thank donors. At least 14 cocktail parties are held each year as well as various dinners at the homes of board members. One weekend each year, 100 to 150 out-of-town prospects and donors are invited to New York for cultivation activities.

The Metropolitan Opera also gives a lot back to its donors. The higher the gift, the higher the priority given for ticket requests. The opera spends a great deal of time and money cultivating and entertaining past donors. Staff and key volunteers work to develop a personal rapport with these prospects. For example, when the Met is putting on a new production, the director of development reserves several boxes and invites donors to attend. This special attention is very well-received and is excellent cultivation for the next gift.

One more step that the Metropolitan Opera has taken to carry the major gifts concept into the planned gift arena is to establish the Encore Society.

The Metropolitan Opera has combined an effective mix of cultivation events and solicitation techniques to create a successful ongoing major gifts program. The secret to its success is the same point we have emphasized—*involvement.*

Both of these major gifts programs give insight into the steps involved in the ongoing cultivation and solicitation of major prospects. We now move on to a detailed review of capital campaigns and how they can have a significant impact on raising major gifts from individuals.

Figure 12.6. A pledge card for the Encore Society.

Mr. Harold Gunn
Director of Planned Giving
(212) 870-4592

Metropolitan Opera Association, Inc.
Lincoln Center, New York, New York 10023

☐ Yes, I would like to be recognized as an Associate of The Encore Society. I have remembered the Metropolitan Opera in my estate planning:

    ☐ through my Will.   ☐ by this other means: _____ .

☐ I/We wish to be listed in the performance program as: _____ .

☐ I understand that I need not reveal the size of my gift in order to join The Encore Society. However, in order to help the Met with its long term planning, I want you to know, in confidence, that the approximate size of my gift will be $ _____ .

☐ I may be interested in joining The Encore Society. Please send me more information about how to make a gift:

    ☐ through my Will.   ☐ of life insurance.

    ☐ from which I would receive income.   ☐ of real estate.

Name _____   Address _____

City _____   State _____   Zip _____

Part III
THE CAPITAL
CAMPAIGN

Chapter 13
Some Background Information

The Past, the Present and the Future

Capital: "The wealth, whether in money or property, owned or employed in business by an individual, firm or corporation."

Campaign: "Any systematic course of aggressive activities for some special purpose."

These dictionary definitions of "capital" and "campaign" describe the essence of capital fund-raising programs. But the use of the word "capital" may now be somewhat outdated because "capital" implies facilities, and campaigns now seek to raise major gifts of all kinds, not just for "capital" needs.

David Gearhart, who directed Penn State's $352 million campaign, feels that campaigns should be called "major gifts" campaigns because all needs are wrapped together in an effort to get big gifts. However, the public still knows the term "capital campaign" as the intensified, targeted effort to raise funds.

Capital campaigns are made up of a specified group of activities, aimed at producing a specified amount of new funding within a specified period of time. Raising major gifts from individuals plays a key role in capital campaign success. In this section, we will examine how campaigns are organized and how major gift potential from individuals can be expanded during a campaign.

Classically, the capital campaign was a big fund-raising effort to finance significant institutional needs such as buildings or equipment. More recently, endowments have been the goal of many campaigns. The effort usually involves prospect research, long-range planning, production of campaign literature, volunteer organization, complex logistics, careful scheduling and effective publicity—all conducted within a specific time period and on a prescribed budget.

Traditionally, capital campaigns have aimed to reach large dollar goals within a definite period of time. They have included all the trappings of a "campaign"—deadlines, publicity, events, hordes of volunteers and much hoopla. In fact, George J. Cooke, Jr., who was involved in educational fund-raising for many years, described the capital campaign as "total war." He saw it as "a mobilization of your people and your resources, for disruption of every accustomed routine and way of life, for the reassignment of people to new and unwanted tasks—all on a crash basis."

One constant remains in campaigning: Campaigns are not to be entered into without considerable thought and planning. A great deal of intensified effort goes into a capital campaign, and much of that work is completed before a campaign is even launched.

Over the years, three classic principles of capital campaigning have emerged:

■ The Rule of Thirds stated that most of your gift money would come from a small number of donors. Si Seymour estimated that "a third of the money has to come from the top ten gifts, the next third from the next 100 gifts and the last third from everybody else." Actually, recent statistics show that the top 10 prospects, in many campaigns, produce approximately 50 percent of the gifts, with 40 percent coming from the next 100 gifts and the last 10 percent from everyone else.

■ Larger prospective donors should either be part of the campaign leadership or solicited by volunteers who are on an equal or higher plane socially or economically.

■ Gifts should be solicited from the top down, so that the larger gifts will help raise the sights of those expected to give smaller gifts, inspiring the smaller donors by the example of the people they respect the most.

A capital campaign usually seeks to accomplish new objectives that go beyond regular annual fund-raising efforts. Recent large comprehensive campaigns have included all funds raised over a certain period of time. These campaigns push for larger goals, but it is important not to lose sight of needs goals in the process. Campaigns should not seek just to raise a big dollar goal. They should also seek to meet specific funding needs for the organization.

The designs of campaigns are constantly changing, but it is helpful to look briefly at the history of campaigns for perspective and for the essential features that remain.

"The most important single factor in the amazing increase in giving during the 20th century was the creation of a new technique for inducing people to give—the financial campaign." So observed veteran fund-raiser Arnaud C. Marts in his 1953 book, *Philanthropy's Role in Civilization*. Marts credits a pair of YMCA secretaries, Lyman L. Pierce and Charles S. Ward, for initiating the campaign idea in the 1890s. By 1913, they had evolved the modern whirlwind-campaign concept to the point where they were able to raise $4 million for new buildings for the New York City YMCA and YWCA. That same year, the University of Pitts-

burgh became the first institution of higher learning to use such a campaign effectively. Soon the idea had spread to hospitals, and welfare and religious organizations.

The first capital campaigns of major size came in the late teens and 1920s. These were followed by a period of inactivity that lasted from the Depression through the end of World War II. But after 1945, it all picked up again. And the campaigns began getting longer, and their goals started getting larger. During the 1960s, goals of $5 million to $10 million were common. By the late 1980s, goals of over $1 billion were set.

In addition to the larger goals, you also see more frequent campaigns. Organizations used to have one capital campaign every 10 or 20 years. Now they follow one another much more closely, with starting a new campaign every six years as a common option. Or else campaigns are merged into a continuing capital program with periodic spurts. And while it used to be that one community could handle only one fund-raising campaign at a time, now it's not unusual to see several institutions in the same community seeking capital funds at the same time.

The goals are changing as well. Capital campaigns have been launched to underwrite such things as equipment, salaries, expanded endowment and, most recently, even daily operating expenses. The purpose of the funds being raised is just as important as the total dollar goal.

Capital fund-raising programs are lengthening. The minutes of a 1938 meeting of the American Association of Fund-Raising Counsel noted that "fund-raising campaigns are tending to be lengthened from the traditional four-to-five-week period to six weeks." Today churches, and occasionally hospitals, still run such brief capital-fund drives, but many institutions are announcing programs up to 10 years in length. But these long campaigns rarely have the focus and motivational aspects of the shorter efforts.

The focus of capital solicitations is shifting. In the beginning, everyone was a prospect—the whole constituency. Then concentration shifted to the small percentage of donors who could make the biggest gifts. So in the late 1950s and early 1960s, fund-raisers started paying more attention to the lucrative top 10 to 20 percent, sometimes not even soliciting the rest of the constituency at all. But this, too, had drawbacks. A mounting body of statistics indicated that the top prospects for the next campaign might be hiding in the lower ranks of prospects for the present campaign. So, since the 1960s, we have seen a mixture of approaches. During the 1980s, renewed emphasis was placed on the major prospects at the top, rather than on the full constituency.

In the late 1980s, capital campaign goals began to top $1 billion. And these comprehensive campaigns included in their goals all funds raised from private sources during the campaign period. That is an important shift. Campaigns originally counted only funds raised for the specific objectives of the campaign. Now all funds raised for anything during the period of the campaign are often counted. Campaigns are used by many organizations to raise their entire fund-raising programs to new heights. It is often expected that those new highs will be maintained after a campaign is over—and in many cases they are.

The future of capital campaigns will be affected by a number of trends both societal and financial:

■ They will take place within an environment of increased competition for private dollars.
■ They will take place concurrently with many other campaigns, both regional and national.
■ There will be more frequent, more numerous, bigger and longer capital campaigns.
■ There will be more emphasis in campaigns on "sustenance dollars." Supporters will have to be shifted away from making gifts for imposing new buildings toward gifts for endowment and even operating needs.
■ Organizations will rely more heavily on detailed prospect research and computerized methods for tracking prospect development.
■ More planned gifts will be received with payouts at a later date. Even gifts of cash will be spread out over longer payment periods, perhaps delaying the actual receipt of the gift for as long as 10 to 20 years. The disadvantage to this is that a $10 million gift made over 10 years is worth less to an

organization than $10 million right now.
■ The campaign length and payment period will differ. For example, a five-year campaign may allow seven-to-10-year payment periods for gifts. These long payment periods will also have an impact on when the next campaign can be started.
■ Campaigns will employ more sophisticated marketing techniques.
■ The end of campaigns will not lessen goals. Organizations will have to raise more in the year following the completion of a campaign than they did during the last year of the campaign. This is partly because success in campaigns builds expectations of continued gifts at those levels. It is also because these increases are then built into budgets.
■ Large comprehensive campaigns for large organizations will be followed by a series of mini-campaigns for specific needs.
■ Campaigns will meet overall dollar goals but may not fully fund specific needs.
■ The volunteer will continue to be the best campaign solicitor, but staff will play a growing role, especially in organizations with a well-known mission and history of fund- raising success.
■ Campaigns will tend to include annual giving in totals to allow bigger goals to be sought.
■ Increasing unrestricted giving will be a partial goal of more capital campaigns.
■ Well-trained professional staff will be needed to be competitive in capital campaigning.

There's More to Be Gained Than Money

The process of organizing a capital campaign has a substantial impact on the entire organization. The sudden infusion of new funds is just one issue. Beyond the cash it produces, the research and organization necessary for a successful campaign can produce a legacy of other benefits. Here are the most important issues to consider beyond the money raised:

■ The publicity motivates volunteers.
■ The campaign creates wide acceptance for needs.

- It achieves broad visibility for the organization and focuses attention on its purposes.
- A campaign discovers and develops new leaders for the organization.
- It unites all constituents in a common activity and strengthens the morale of the staff and volunteers.
- It identifies new prospects for ongoing annual support programs and provides a better data base on prospects.
- A campaign raises the sights of donors for future fund-raising programs.

The campaign style of capital fund-raising has its own special benefits. It creates a finite framework for the involvement of large numbers of workers in an organization's activities. They get information. They sense an atmosphere of urgency and great need. A campaign forces your organization to set priorities and crystallize them into fund-raising needs that can be described convincingly. The deadlines of a campaign move people to action. And another important consideration: Capital fund-raising can be the least expensive type of fund-raising and the most productive you'll ever do. That's because it raises a substantial amount of money in a set period and it is oriented toward major gifts.

A campaign serves as a cohesive agent that brings together an organization. The effort involves everyone. It educates everyone about fund-raising and provides a solicitation and cultivation rationale that makes asking easier. Sometimes a campaign creates fund-raising converts by allowing volunteers or administrators to have instant success, thereby convincing them that fund- raising isn't so bad after all.

The prospect of having a campaign also forces institutional planning. You cannot have a capital campaign unless you identify funding objectives.

A campaign provides new self-knowledge to an organization and provides a perfect opportunity for reexamination of its purposes. A campaign also forces a reevaluation of the development staff and provides an opportunity to strengthen staff and volunteer resources. A campaign may provide budget to add staff and upgrade the development program, not just for the campaign but permanently. Organizations should plan to emerge from a capital campaign with a more effective development program that will serve the cause's future needs. Campaigns are no longer one-shot deals.

A capital campaign creates the bandwagon effect. Everyone wants to be part of the action. The structure and dynamics of a campaign should permanently enhance the development effort. Campaigns are exhilarating and exhausting!

Chapter 14
Are You Really Ready to Launch a Campaign?

Take a Look at Your Organization First

In a nutshell, what you need to be successful in a capital campaign are:

- A long-range plan
- Clearly defined institutional objectives
- Cultivated major prospects
- Program and dollar goals
- Influential volunteers
- Trained staff
- Committed administrative leadership

The error most frequently made in capital fund-raising is deciding to have a campaign before you're ready. It is essential to be ready—and to have most of the work done—before a campaign is announced.

A capital campaign is not *the* answer to all fund-raising problems. Don't start a capital campaign just because you need money. A campaign does not create a full-blown development effort; it should be built on one that is well-established.

Organizations that are successful with capital campaigns already have well-run development programs and a successful track record for attracting major gifts.

When assessing the overall readiness of your organization, consider these questions:

- Does your organization really know itself and its aims?
- Is there a history of philanthropic support for the organization?
- Is your organization seen as a positive and necessary asset to its community or constituency?
- Is there agreement among board members and staff that the cause is worthwhile? Will they give time and funds to the effort?
- Is your case for support valid and salable?
- Do you have the leadership to make the campaign work?
- Do you have an active prospect cultivation program?
- Can you identify at least 50 to 100 prospects in a substantial gift range and a loyal giving constituency below that level?
- Can you obtain one gift that is at least one-tenth of the total campaign goal?
- Do you know who the campaign chairman should be? Will he or she accept this role?

We will look now at the five most critical elements in determining campaign readiness.

You must have an *identified constituency*. When assessing the readiness of your constituency to support a capital campaign, start with your board.

- Is your board active in giving and getting?
- Do you have at least eight major prospects on your board?
- Can your board give 25 to 30 percent of the campaign goal?
- Is 100 percent of your board making annual gifts?
- Are there board members who will lead the campaign?

Once you ask these hard questions about your board, look carefully at your other constituencies. To be successful in a campaign, you must have approximately three times the number of prospects at various gift levels for every one gift you expect to receive. In other words, it usually takes three asks to realize one gift.

When you look at your rated prospect lists, also consider how close these prospects are to the organization and how ready they are to be asked. Prospects do not have real, immediate potential unless they have been cultivated and are informed about the organization. One technique to chart the potential of your constituency is to select various gift target amounts and list how many current prospects you have in those gift ranges. Here are samples of charts that compare the gifts needed with the gifts received. One was used by Princeton and the other by Harvard.

You must have a *history of fund-raising success*. Capital campaigns should be built upon an active fund-raising program. As we have already noted, you cannot hope to raise major gifts in a campaign timetable without an identified cultivated constituency that is already giving.

To assess the success of your organization's fund-raising, you must look at two factors: What is the actual history of gifts raised and what development programs are in place to raise those funds.

When looking at your fund-raising records, see if you can document regular growth in annual support, at least in the 8 to 10 percent range, each year. Also look to see if you have five to 10 significant major gifts each year (and not from the same donors each time). Review the average gift range over a period of years, and check if it is continuing to rise. Determine if you have a backlog of unpaid pledges. Are

Figure 14.1. Princeton (top) and Harvard tables of gifts needed and gifts received.

	Needed		Received	
Size of Gift	Approximate No. Donors	Approximate Amount	Number Donors	Amount
$1 million & over	10	$15,000,000	9	$16,165,396
$100,000 & over	100	18,000,000	107	24,543,879
$10,000 & over	500	10,000,000	499	10,723,475
$1,000 & over	3,000	7,000,000	3,208	6,887,380
Under $1,000	17,000	3,000,000	14,102	2,391,237
Totals	20,610	$53,000,000	17,925	$60,711,367

Princeton

	Needed		Received	
Size of Gift	Approximate No. Donors	Approximate Amount	Number Donors	Amount
$10,000,000 & up	1	$10,000,000	None	None
$5,000,000 - 9,999,999	2	12,000,000	None	None
$1,000,000 - 4,999,999	7	10,000,000	15	$30,127,169
$100,000 - 999,999	110	29,000,000	115	27,144,352
$50,000 - 99,999	100	5,000,000	45	2,867,106
$10,000 - 49,999	500	9,000,000	537	9,704,376
$5,000 - 9,999	400	3,000,000	519	3,119,944
$1,000 - 4,999	1,500	2,000,000	3,408	5,743,472
Less than $1,000	20,000	2,500,000	23,124	3,814,105
Group-gift donors	—	—	3,933	255,036
Totals	22,620	$82,500,000	31,696	$82,775,554

Harvard

these pledges unpaid because donors have lost interest in the organization or because you do not have a regular pledge reminder system? In reviewing your fund-raising history, try to think of all the factors that show the strength of your efforts as well as the loopholes. Be serious in assessing the problems. It is better to chart specific plans to improve specific programs than to mount a capital campaign to solve systemic problems.

The other factor to study is the design and makeup of the current fund-raising effort. Do you have successful ongoing annual giving and planned giving programs? Do you have a research staff as well as people experienced in soliciting major gifts? Do you have a stewardship program aimed at keeping past donors informed about the use of their gifts and the organization in general?

In summary, what you have already raised,

and how you are raising it, will help determine the likelihood of campaign success.

You must also have a good *public relations program*. A major purpose of the public relations program of any nonprofit organization is to foster fund-raising. For some organizations, it is the only purpose. In the long run, a public relations effort should be judged, to a great degree, by how much money you raise.

What are the fund-raising purposes of public relations?

■ To help identify and build your constituency
■ To create greater and improved understanding of your services
■ To create a climate of acceptance for your cause
■ To show people why your cause is needed
■ To support fund-raising itself, by creating an awareness of your various fund-raising programs and the good represented by their goals

Public relations is a series of actions designed to build interest, affect attitudes, create goodwill and eventually to alter human behavior to your advantage. One of its most important goals is to influence opinion leaders. An organization must put its case before those who can most help its cause. At the same time, some type of ongoing press coverage is also necessary to create a basic level of awareness among the general public of your organization and its work.

The priorities of the public relations office should reflect those of the organization. The public relations program should be totally coordinated with the organization's fund-raising programs. In some organizations, the public relations and development offices are separate. But from a fund-raising viewpoint, the most effective system seems to be one where both functions are combined under the person in charge of fund-raising. For a campaign to be successful, an established and active public relations program must exist. campaigns themselves are, in large part, public relations vehicles, so you need a good base of ongoing activities.

You must have *long-range institutional planning*. We reviewed earlier the long-range planning process, but nowhere in fund-raising is it

more vital than in a capital campaign. Long-range institutional planning must become a more integral part of development programs, especially as organizations prepare for campaigns. Fund-raising is inextricably linked with institutional planning. An institution must know where it is going before it can raise funds necessary to get there—particularly major gifts through a capital campaign. First you create a comprehensive institutional plan that charts, in specific terms, the future direction of your institution. Then you create a fund-raising program designed to finance the institution's voyage to these future goals.

Robert N. Anthony, professor of management control at Harvard and an authority on planning, describes institutional planning as "the process of deciding on objectives of the organization, on changes in these objectives, on the resources used to attain these objectives, and on the policies that are to govern the acquisition, use and disposition of these resources."

The long-range planning process is never completed. A plan must be kept up to date, so that it can respond as priorities change and the organization grows. And the matching fund-raising program must do likewise.

Barry Mastrine, president of Davon Management Company, puts it this way: "No single condition has as great a potential for destroying the morale and collective energy of an organization as the lack of a plan of action, or the existence of a plan that was developed in a vacuum and focuses on obviously unobtainable results."

Good planning also comes with a means for monitoring achievements, for defining staff responsibilities and for measuring how well they're being carried out.

You must have *organizational commitment*. A development officer cannot force a capital campaign on an organization. The organization and its top leadership must want it—not just the money, but also the campaign—and they must be willing to work on such an effort. A capital campaign should ideally be a total institutional effort: initiated by the administrative head, prepared by staff, reviewed by key leadership from all constituencies, approved by the administration and board, and implemented by the entire organization.

Many organizations unfortunately decide to launch a major effort to raise private support through what Bill Balthaser, a fund-raising expert, called "the coefficient of desperation." Organizational leaders begin to feel financial pressures closing in, and it is only then that they will commit themselves to fund-raising. It should be a development staff's primary aim to avoid this crisis approach to fund-raising.

How do you get organizational commitment? The first step is to integrate the institution's long-range goals into a fund-raising program that is feasible. Assess your staff and build their skills to the point where institutional leaders will feel comfortable about entrusting a major gifts effort to them. A sense of trust is of key importance. But this feeling must go both ways. The administration must believe in your development skills, and you must believe that your superiors are committed, capable and ready to help.

What the Experts Say

Over the years, the Fund-Raising Institute has asked fund-raising experts to comment on campaign readiness. To conclude our section on this topic, here are the views of several experienced fund-raisers:

Paul A. Netzel

Paul A. Netzel of Los Angeles has been a leader in fund-raising for YMCAs. He has identified seven success factors that can help you predict the outcome of a capital campaign.

1. **Your gift prospects and potential leadership**. Netzel asks you to identify nine groups within your constituency or area: 1) five people or corporations, each capable of making a gift equal to 15 to 20 percent of your campaign goal; 2) eight to 10 people or corporations, each with the capacity of giving 10 percent of the goal; 3) the five wealthiest individuals currently contributing to your organization; 4) the five wealthiest members of your constituency; 5) your 10 largest current contributors; 6) the 10 largest contributors to your last capi-

tal campaign; 7) the five most influential people in your service area; 8) the 10 wealthiest individuals or families in your service area, and 9) from the preceding lists, the five people or groups that are most committed to your organization. **Assessment**. Has your group involved at least six people representing a minimum of four of these lists in the key planning stages of your campaign? If not, then corrective action is needed.

2. **Your board of managers**. Do you have from six to eight people on your board representing at least four of the categories just listed? Do your board members have a collective capacity to contribute, over a three-year period, 20 to 25 percent of your goal? Do you currently solicit board gifts in a formal way? Do 100 percent of your board members contribute now? Do your entire board and staff know exactly what your organization needs in the way of facilities and why? Can they articulate the need? **Assessment**. If you answer "no" to any of these questions, you need corrective action.

3. **Your program**. Netzel asks: "Is there an established pattern of growth in each key program area?" **Assessment**. "If not, why? What corrective action is being or will be taken?" Will your capital campaign goals make any appreciable difference in this? Why? "Is there an ongoing annual process for evaluating the quality of each key program area? Is there a formalized process for making improvements in program quality each year?" **Assessment**. If either answer is "no," you need corrective action.

4. **Your current support**. Has annual support grown by 8 to 10 percent per year over each of the past three years? Has the number of volunteer solicitors recruited each year remained at least stable over the past three years? Does at least 50 percent of your current support come from the largest donors? How successful have your annual support programs been over the past three years? ("Ideally," says Netzel, "there should be two consecutive current-support campaigns reaching 100 percent of goal prior

to a capital campaign.") Are your contributors thanked immediately for their annual gifts? Are they told what your organization is doing with their funds? Is your number of uncollectable pledges 5 percent or smaller? **Assessment.** If the answer to any of these is negative, you probably need corrective action during the next annual giving drive.

5. **Your reputation.** Is there evidence that your organization is under sound management and provides a unique and needed service to its community? How are you viewed by various segments of your community? **Assessment.** Netzel suggests having executive committee members conduct a series of interviews to get strictly subjective answers to these questions.

6. **Your communications.** 1) Does your group have a plan for communicating regularly with the public? With your program participants (such as students of a school, patients of a hospital)? With contributors? 2) Do you have a program of communication and involvement for major gifts prospects? 3) Do you have a good working relationship with the local press? 4) Is your chief executive officer a member of at least two community groups? Actively? Are they the right groups? **Assessment.** If any of the answers is "no," corrective action is needed. What improvements can be made to your communication programs with the public, program participants, donors and major contributors?

7. **Your competition.** Are there plans for another major capital campaign in your area when your group may be holding its campaign? **Assessment.** If so, try to figure out the impact it will have on your campaign— competition for media coverage, campaigners, donors etc.

Jerold Panas

Jerold Panas, a Chicago-based fund-raiser, suggests 10 groups of questions to guide your thinking in determining your readiness for a major fund-raising effort.

■ Is there wholehearted agreement among the board and staff concerning the worthwhileness of the cause?

■ Are the board and staff committed enough to the success of the project to make personal sacrifices for the campaign—both in time and money?

■ Is your institution well-regarded in the community? Are your services considered important and relevant?

■ Is there a valid and urgent need for funds? Can the case for supporting your group be dramatized easily and effectively for emotional appeal?

■ Is top-level leadership available and interested?

■ The largest gift—the initial one, if possible—should be for one-tenth to one-sixth of the campaign goal. Will this be possible? Can half the goal be secured from 10 to 15 donors? Can 65 to 70 percent be secured from about 100 donors?

■ Can enough enthusiastic volunteers be enlisted and trained to work on the project?

■ Is the timing and planning of the campaign sound?

■ If it is a building project, are operating funds for the structure available after it is completed?

■ Have you discussed your plans with professional fund-raising counsel?

American City Bureau

American City Bureau, a fund-raising consulting firm in Hoffman Estates, Illinois, uses these 12 guidelines to help clients see if they're ready for capital fund-raising.

Good reason. Don't waste energy on a campaign that cannot provide a sense of urgency.

Leadership. Unless the right person is willing to serve as chairman, one who can command support (and give it), the campaign is better postponed.

Reputation. Is your organization well-regarded in the community? Donors give emotionally—for a job well-done.

Feasibility. Can your constituency raise the money needed? A shrewd evaluation is important.

Understanding. Does your constituency really understand the need?

Organization. Is your group well-managed enough to stand the strain of a campaign?

Competition. Make sure your organization performs unique and needed work.

Planning. Do you know exactly what you need the funds for? Indecision shakes a donor's confidence.

Next campaign. When will it be? Its force will be blunted if you have to return to the same donors for funds too soon.

Plans to hold support. A donor's interest should be rewarded and kept alive in a variety of ways; plans to do so should be part of your campaign strategy.

Machinery. Do you have the procedures needed to follow up on campaign pledges? Between promise and payment, you can expect to lose about 3 to 5 percent, but the loss may be much greater if pledges are allowed to slide.

Expertise. Do you have the experience needed to run the campaign?

Perry Laukhuff

Perry Laukhuff, a fund-raising consultant, created this checklist for his clients:

- Don't head into a campaign with a sense of compulsion or adventure.
- Don't use a capital campaign as a crutch to rescue poor annual support programs.
- Be sure you can demonstrate the efficiency and prudence of your financial management. "Good husbandry is valued these days, at least by those called on to give."
- Be sure your board is well cued in. *The board should be a propeller and not an anchor.*
- Have a good supply of specific prospect names.
- Be sure your records are in good order. You will need accurate background information.
- Remember your performance in annual giving is a real barometer of things to come.
- Pull your team together. Heal serious dissension among trustees, administration and others beforehand.
- Keep the fine edge on the blade of your eagerness. "But be sure you don't swing it with a swish through empty air."

Chapter 15
How to Prepare for a Campaign

Internal Audit

"Pre-campaign procedures are paramount. It is what you do ahead of time and how it is done that usually decides whether you win or lose."

Harold J. (Si) Seymour

Si Seymour, the first guru of fund-raising, stressed preparedness in all his discussions of capital campaigns. And experience has shown that he was 100 percent correct. It is what you do before the campaign is launched that is most important.

We will now look at three approaches to determining campaign potential: an internal audit, a market survey and a feasibility study. Some organizations will want to conduct all three; others may opt to merge elements of the internal audit and market survey into the feasibility study.

To get an objective point of view, the best approach is to use an outside consulting firm. If that is impossible because of budget, your own staff can do the work, as long as adequate staff is available. You don't want to spread this out over four years because, by the time you're done, your research will be out of date. Some organizations have been able to save money by doing part of the work themselves. For example, if you have a big staff and need to conduct 100 interviews, your staff could do half of them while an outside consultant does the rest.

Besides budget, there is one more factor to keep in mind: People will tell things to an outsider that they won't tell to a staff member. You'll get different information if a consultant does the interviewing. Besides, you don't want everyone to say that everything is running smoothly just out of fear that their criticisms will get back to the president. A guarantee of confidentiality is essential, and when that exists, important facts will surface.

The best place to start in preparing for a capital campaign is to do an internal audit of your current development program. You should review:

- Staff capabilities and size
- Budget
- Existing development program structures such as annual giving, planned giving and major gifts programs
- Existing space and equipment
- Existing materials and publications that explain the organization's purpose, including the case for support
- Existing constituencies and the quality of available data on prospects
- Gift management system
- Gift recognition program
- Cultivation program
- Volunteer base
- Recent fund-raising progress
- Your organization's financial health

- Board strength
- Involvement of key administrators and board members in fund-raising
- Consensus on future organizational direction
- Proposal preparation capabilities
- Willingness of staff and leadership to commit time, energy and funds to a campaign

As part of an internal development audit, you should also consider carefully any specific problems or situations that may impede capital campaign success. For example, has there been a scandal in your administration? Has a member of the board been forced to resign? Is your board in general very weak? Is your president or board chairman not willing to do fund-raising? Have you had real budget problems such as a negative cash flow? Are you facing the potential closing of one of your units? Try to think of anything that might create a negative image.

Assessing internal fund-raising capabilities is just as important as studying constituency strength and other external variables. Remember that one of the benefits of a capital campaign should be the permanent strengthening of a development program. If an organization is not prepared internally to capitalize on the benefits of a campaign, it will lose much of the rationale for conducting one.

An internal audit is a comprehensive review of the total development effort, including an assessment of program strength and success in reaching out to prospects. While a program audit can be done by experienced internal staff, it is best conducted by an outside fund-raising professional, or at least under the guidance of an experienced observer. A consultant can conduct a series of interviews and make on-the-scene observations of how the development program works. These observations should include a review of gift records and all internal development infrastructure. The results of these interviews and on-site visits are combined with a critical review of existing written materials on the organization. The end result is a formal report on the health of the fund-raising program.

The results of an internal audit will suggest steps that should be taken to strengthen existing development programs prior to a campaign, and the issues to be dealt with during campaign planning. This review process also lets key administrators know how the fund-raising process works. As a result, they should become more involved and comfortable with development, an essential prerequisite for a campaign.

Market Survey

A market survey is a review of *external* factors that will have a direct impact on the success of a capital campaign or an ongoing development program. In order to conduct a market survey, an organization must first clearly define its mission and its funding objectives, so that they can be presented to interviewees for review.

To many people, a market survey and a feasibility study are the same. But to give you the total range of possible pre-campaign activities, let's make a subtle but useful distinction. First of all, a market survey may be conducted at any time and doesn't have to be tied to a campaign. A market survey focuses on attitudes and perceptions, while a feasibility study ties those feelings directly to one's inclination to give. A feasibility study also includes elements of the internal audit, thereby assessing both external and internal issues. So a market survey can be somewhat more global, but less specific, than a feasibility study.

Through a series of interviews with major prospects and community leaders, a market survey attempts to assess the organization's image, its perceived functions and needs, and the climate for raising funds to meet these needs. The market survey has two primary purposes: to determine how the organization is perceived and how close prospects feel to it.

One issue a market survey must address is the competitive environment for campaigns in the community. Are several others going on that might appeal to the same prospects? If so, is the case for yours strong enough to differentiate it from the others?

Experience has shown that public-opinion surveying is a tricky business, best done by outside professionals. You should expect those professionals to follow a procedure similar to this outline:

■ Carefully determine the list of people to be surveyed, making sure a broad spectrum of interest and wealth is reviewed.

■ Try to let one person handle the entire survey process, especially the interviews. This will make the responses more consistent.

■ Design the survey to measure more than just gift potential for your organization. It should uncover the level of support given by community leaders to other organizations, their depth of commitment to charitable interests and the history of their personal involvement in such interests—especially those similar to yours.

■ Try to determine the image your institution has in the community. Are those being interviewed interested in your programs? Do they approve of your purposes? Will they contribute or influence others to do so?

■ Assess attitudes toward the current development program, the organization's leadership and the quality of service.

A market survey should take four to eight weeks, if an interviewer can see approximately 20 to 30 people a week. For some organizations, a sample of 40 to 50 may be large enough to assess interest, and therefore the time frame might be shorter. Remember to allow time not only for the interviews, but also for planning the survey and its objectives, and for a written report to be prepared.

The cost of such a survey depends on how many people are interviewed. Ask for estimates and for names of other clients for whom the consultant has done similar studies. The cost will be determined by the time that will be required and the per diem charge of the consultant. When inquiring about the per diem charges, be sure to ask if there is a different rate for different staff people, depending on their level of experience.

Feasibility Study

It is common practice, and highly advisable, to have a fund-raising consulting firm conduct a feasibility study prior to a campaign. This study is the most crucial pre-campaign step because it reveals whether your constituents will support your projected fund-raising plans. Some fund-raising consultants merge the market survey with the feasibility study, but for some organizations, it may be better to first assess community feeling through a market study, before getting involved in a more detailed feasibility study.

Basically the feasibility study involves a careful review of institutional records and needs, plus a series of interviews with key people: potential donors, board members and staff. The report summarizes the facts, analyzing the potential of the funding program, estimating a realistic goal, reviewing the sources of support and suggesting a plan of action.

A professionally conducted feasibility study is an expensive but important item. A feasibility study is detailed and comprehensive, so it will cost more on average than a market survey.

Consultant Jerold Panas feels that the feasibility study is the most effective way possible to evaluate the outcome of your campaign program in advance. A feasibility study identifies the amount of money that can be raised. It establishes both strong and weak points in the salability of your project and your case. It defines a plan for the complete development effort and puts that plan within a certain time frame. And he feels that total giving can be projected within a range of plus or minus 10 percent.

How is a feasibility study actually conducted? First, a capsule case statement for the campaign should be prepared. It is then sent out with a letter from a key leader, CEO or campaign chairman, asking participants to agree to be interviewed and giving the purpose of the study. Then calls are made to set up appointments. A detailed questionnaire should be designed and followed carefully by the interviewers. It is best to limit the number of interviewers to two or three people, so there is a similar context for responses. Once the interviews are completed, a feasibility study report is prepared.

The feasibility study should identify potential campaign leadership. Normally, as a result of the study, you are able to indicate the person who should be the general chairman of the program and, in most cases, you are able to indicate everyone else who will occupy key leadership roles in the major divisions of the program. Very often, you are also able to identify the nucleus of your campaign steering committee.

The study measures your program's appeal—whether people feel the program is necessary and how responsive they will be to the project. A feasibility study also indicates how responsive organization leaders are to the program—whether they are genuinely interested and sufficiently enthusiastic to work for the effort.

If any negative factors exist, the study should indicate how these can be corrected. Positive factors will also be described, and there should be a plan showing how these may be enhanced and developed to their full potential.

The study defines the proper timing and strategy for your campaign. In most cases, the firm that conducts your survey will develop a master plan and schedule, based on its report and recommendations.

When you're all done, the study should have answered these questions for you:

■ Is your organization pursuing its stated mission?
■ What are your major needs?
■ Can they be documented?
■ Do potential donors know these needs exist?
■ Who are your key prospects?
■ Do they have the potential for meeting your needs?
■ Do the potential donors have a good feeling about your institution and its leaders?
■ Is there active support from the governing board of your institution?
■ How will the record of your previous fund-raising affect the campaign?
■ Is the right kind of fund-raising leadership available?
■ What kind of capital fund-raising program should be considered?
■ What is a realistic goal? Does it justify a campaign? What is the time frame, not only of the campaign, but also of the preliminary steps?
■ Are there any problems that must be overcome before starting the fund-raising effort?

What should the final report on a feasibility study tell you? James J. Biggins, CEO of American City Bureau, describes the ideal contents of a study's final report this way:

■ The *opening* section should tell you: the purpose, why the study was commissioned; the study's plan (how it was conducted, the schedule, the questions asked), and the procedures used.
■ Then should come a section on the *findings*: how people reacted to a description of the program for which you plan to raise funds; whether volunteer leadership is available and interested; whether your constituency has the needed money and can provide a volunteer fund-raising organization; your fund-raising potential, the realistic goal; your cause's public image (whether it should and could be improved); the local fund-raising climate (the economy, competing campaigns), and the ideal timing for the campaign.
■ Next come *conclusions* on: how to strengthen your case for fund-raising "to make it more viable," leadership, public image, community financial support, problem areas, favorable factors (your cause's "pluses" in the eyes of the community) and an appraisal of your potential for conducting the campaign in your hoped-for time schedule.
■ Finally come the *recommendations* on: adoption of the report by your board, retaining fund-raising counsel, preparation and organization of the campaign, publicity, the period during which solicitations will be made and the schedule of campaign events.

Screening Sessions

Before you launch a campaign, there are several other ways to gauge public opinion of your organization and its fund-raising potential.

Screening sessions are pre-campaign activities aimed primarily at identifying new major prospects, but they can also serve as an opportunity to introduce potential prospects to campaign objectives.

Key volunteers, who are close to an organization, are invited to screening sessions to review existing constituent lists and to identify prospects who have major gift potential. You can either ask the screeners just to note prospects with potential or ask them to suggest possible gift levels. The basis for these judgments can be 10 percent of annual income or 5 percent of net worth, depending on the size of the gift being considered. Usually a prospect will give less than 10 percent of annual income to your organization because 10 percent might represent the total of all annual gifts made by that donor. If a prospect is being considered for a truly major gift from assets, that amount might represent 5 percent of total wealth.

These rating sessions usually take the format of "silent screenings," with each participant recording his or her suggestions on separate lists. Then these lists have to be compared by the development staff. What you are really looking for are recurrent suggestions of similar gift levels for the same prospect, rather than relying on one person's opinion.

As an introduction to screening meetings, it is effective to treat the screeners as insiders and give them the inside scoop on campaign plans. Since screening should take place very early in the campaign planning process, it is possible that details of the campaign might still be evolving.

But remember, those invited to your screening sessions should themselves be prospects, so you should use the opportunity to cultivate them. An organizational leader might be invited to the screening session to give an update on current activities and on campaign planning.

During the late 1980s, the University of Pennsylvania conducted an extensive screening program aimed at identifying prospects for a major campaign. Screening sessions were held around the country over a two-year period. These are the materials used.

Figure 15.1. Invitation to University of Pennsylvania screening session

Dear James,

    I would be delighted if you would join me and other San Francisco area Penn alumni on Thursday June 23, 1988 to participate in a special San Francisco alumni meeting. We will plan to meet at Arthur Andersen & Co., Spear Street Tower-Suite 3500, One Market Plaza, in San Francisco from 5:30 to 7:30 p.m. for cocktails.

    University representatives will be present at the meeting to offer a preview of Penn's plans for a major capital campaign. This will be a campaign of unprecedented size and scope, the second largest in history, and is designed to carry Penn well into the 21st century. After their presentation, they will be asking you to review a customized list of alumni and friends as part of the Penn Screening Program, a national alumni effort to identify potential donors for the future. If you have any special list preferences (i.e. class, fraternity/sorority, residential area, etc.), please indicate them on the reply form.

    In a very real sense, during our meeting you will be providing immeasurable assistance to the University in its preparation for the campaign. No solicitations will be made. I can assure you that all screening information will be handled in a confidential and professional manner.

    Please return the enclosed reply form by June 6th so that customized lists can be prepared for your perusal.

    I appreciate your consideration. Thanks for all that you are doing for Penn. I look forward to seeing you on June 23th.

                    With best regards,

                    James D. Kirsner W'65, WG'66

Enclosures

Figure 15.2. The information collected on this University of Pennsylvania reply form allowed tailored lists to be prepared for each screener.

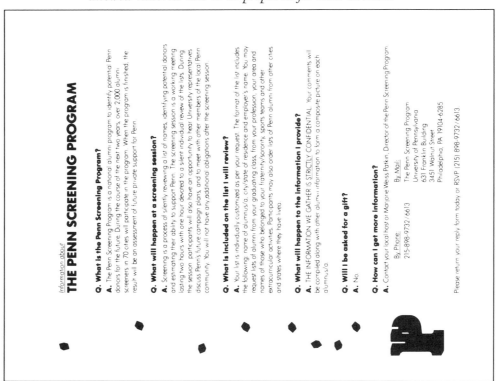

Figure 15.3. Information sheet that explained what would happen at the Penn screening session

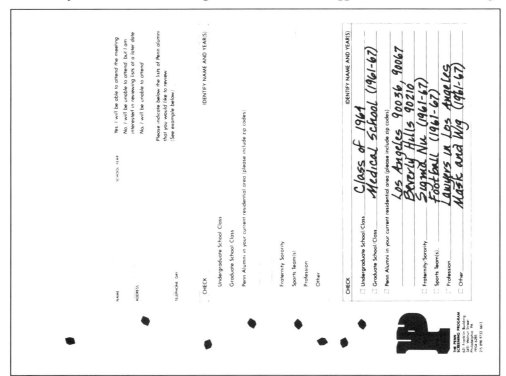

Figure 15.4. A Penn prospect report shows ratings by four people. (Their names would go under the column marked Current Opinions by Screeners.) Because the ratings vary so widely, the numbers couldn't just be averaged. Staff input was required, and a final rating of $25,000 was established.

```
                         Prospect Inquiry              05/30/89 10:35am
------------------------------------------------------------------------
Prospect Soc. Sec. #:

Prospect:
                              LOS ANGELES, CA 90049

Current Opinions By Screeners:            Opinion Comments
   1.                                     5K


   2.                                     25K


   3.                                     25K


   4.                                     100K


Final Gift Potential Rating: ** No Final Rating **
------------------------------------------------------------------------
   Next  Previous  View  Edit  Opinion-edit  Help  Return
View all the Prospects for a given search criteria.
   ALT-F10  HELP 3 VT-100   3 FDX 3  9600 E71 3 LOG CLOSED 3 PRT OFF 3 CR   3 CR
```

Focus Groups

Focus group meetings can be organized to get broader reactions to campaign plans and organizational mission. They are often used to supplement feasibility study interviews. Focus groups allow a larger segment of the constituency to react to the organization's needs.

A focus group meeting is best hosted by a volunteer leader. The main speaker or discussion leader should be a key administration member (even the CEO), or a trained focus group moderator might be hired. Materials on the campaign plan are usually circulated to invitees in advance, and then they are asked to respond to the plans through a structured discussion.

The leader should carefully target issues for discussion, and volunteers may be asked in advance to spark the discussion by raising certain points.

Remember that those invited to focus group sessions should also be prospects. So once again, focus group meetings allow an opportunity for further prospect cultivation.

Focus group meetings usually come at a point much further into campaign planning than screening sessions, which might even occur before specific campaign planning starts. Focus groups are held after the case for support exists, so that broad reaction can be sought before brochures and other campaign literature are actually printed.

Be prepared for some very frank opinions to be expressed in the focus group setting. A group discussion sometimes offers more stimulation to participants than a one-on-one interview.

It is usually a good idea to keep focus groups small (10 to 15 participants) to encourage everyone to speak up. It also helps to limit each session to individuals who have a similar link to the organization, such as local alumni or ex-patients.

A series of focus group sessions will elicit varied and valuable comments. They should be reported in an organized way, so that campaign planners can benefit from the process. A report on focus groups should list the range of reactions on each topic.

One thing to remember is that if you seek this kind of broad input into campaign planning, you must be prepared to take the advice offered. Don't give the impression that everything has already been decided. If you seek input, use the best advice you get to actually improve your campaign plan.

Sizing up Foundations and Corporations

Although we are focusing on major individual donors in this book, that does not mean that you should ignore other sources of donations during your capital campaign. Foundations and corporations have a very important role to play, and you need to do some research on them before beginning your campaign.

Foundation research is different from research on individuals. Most foundations will give to some philanthropic cause. The trick is to determine whether a foundation's interests correspond to your institution's needs. After you spot foundations with the right interests, you design an individual plan for approaching and soliciting each one. Here are some of the facts you should be looking for on foundations:

■ The correct name of the foundation
■ Precise street address and phone number
■ The officers or directors of the foundation and their professional connections
■ Brief historical sketch—when founded, by whom and for what purposes
■ Current assets
■ Amount of recent grants—by year and by individual recipient
■ Decision-making process—who, when?

■ Pattern of giving—to what kinds of institutions and for what programs, citing specific examples
■ Who is your best contact—the person you might send a proposal to or visit?
■ Connections with your institution
■ History of your institution's contacts with the foundation

Research on corporations is much the same as for foundations, although there are differences in emphasis and reference materials. Also remember that the key to determining whether corporations will give is what's in it for them. Increasingly, corporations are looking for a direct quid pro quo to guide their giving. They look for the public relations impact and maybe even to get an executive on your board.

Here are the key facts to know about corporations:

■ Corporate assets
■ Type of business
■ List of corporate officers and directors
■ List of corporate foundation officers, if a corporate foundation exists
■ Sales volume
■ Previous giving record
■ Decision-making process—who, when?
■ Gifts to other institutions (This is harder to learn if there is no corporate foundation.)
■ Connections with your institution—list of alumni-employees, if you're an educational institution, or patient-employees, if you're a hospital
■ History of your dealings with the corporation
■ Local subsidiaries and officers

Chapter 16

A Dozen Campaign Formats

You must analyze where your organization stands in terms of its current fund-raising in order to determine the type of campaign to conduct. Has your group ever had a campaign before? What programs (annual, major or planned giving) do you have? What are your most pressing needs? How extensive is your prospect pool?

Don't feel obligated to do the latest thing. Decide what type of campaign will work best for your organization as it is currently structured.

Here is the menu of capital fund-raising formats to choose from. Perhaps a combination of formats will work best for you.

The One-Time Campaign

This is the traditional approach to capital fund-raising. It involves an intensive campaign, with a definite goal, within a definite time span, for special needs. "The intensive campaign is here to stay because no other method has been found which equals it in raising dollars," says David S. Ketchum, former president of Ketchum Inc., a fund-raising counseling firm headquartered in Pittsburgh. Here's how he supports his statement:

■ The intensive campaign—properly integrated with the long-range development program—works.

■ The intensive capital campaign raises more money in less time than any other form of fund-raising because it provides built-in targets and deadlines to which volunteers and donors respond.

■ The intensive campaign is the least expensive method of raising money.

■ Campaigns have long demonstrated their value in developing volunteer leadership, in identifying those who should be considered for election as trustees, in broadening the base for an institution's gift support and in attracting favorable attention to its long-overlooked merits.

The Comprehensive Campaign

A format that has gained popularity during the 1980s is the comprehensive campaign. All funds raised during a specific campaign period (usually three to five years) are included in the totals. This means counting all annual giving, endowment and funds for capital needs. The main reason to run a comprehensive campaign is to give everyone a chance to participate, but this type of campaign also allows the organization to attract more attention because of a higher goal.

The Continuing Campaign

This type of capital fund-raising never stops; it just changes direction from time to time. Campaigning becomes an integral part of the ongoing funding programs of the institution. Some organizations have announced 10-year or longer campaigns, which include all funds raised. The biggest questions with this type of effort are how to maintain the momentum and whether establishing a very long-term goal really helps raise money for the things you need. Most long-term campaigns simply do not have the immediacy or the impact of a shorter one-time effort.

The Project-Oriented Campaign

Raising capital funds for a specific project is another form of the traditional one-time campaign. A project-oriented campaign sometimes funds a top priority by commemorating an important individual or a key date in an institution's development. This is an especially effective method when an institution's total needs are not particularly well-documented or easy to publicize.

The Endowment Campaign

Many institutions have endowment funds that are intended to provide a permanent source of annual operating income. When the fund was established, there was probably no intention to spend this endowment—just its income. But with increasing financial pressures, many institutions have dipped into their endowments to make ends meet. This trend and other factors have caused many institutions to launch capital drives for new endowment money. These include losses in the value of endowment funds brought on by stock market declines, the inability of endowment income to keep up with rising costs and a decline in capital gains income. Not long ago, most fund-raising experts would have said that you couldn't have a capital campaign for endowment. But today, for some organizations, endowment money has proven to be as readily available as that for buildings.

In this type of campaign, you must offer donors a variety of named options to commemorate their gifts: named endowment funds, scholarships, professorships, lectureships, library funds, orchestra chairs, even maintenance funds.

The Every-Member Canvass

As you would guess from its name, in this type of drive, every member of a constituency becomes a prospect and is solicited for a gift. This technique has worked well in church fund-raising efforts. But its validity in major institutional fund-raising programs has been questioned. Some fund-raisers feel that the needs of some institutions are so large that the average contributor just cannot have an impact on them. On the other hand, many fund-raisers feel that this type of program develops new donors and raises the potential of future fund-raising programs. The bandwagon effect, they say, is still an important one. But remember, the capital effort aimed at an entire constituency costs more than the limited campaign, requires a more elaborate volunteer organization and usually needs a larger professional development staff.

The Limited Campaign

Because of the generally accepted theory that most of the money raised in a capital campaign comes from a relatively small number of donors, many institutions and fund-raising consultants favor going after these prospects alone. You pinpoint your key prospects through research, and concentrate all your efforts on getting a big gift from each. This type of campaign is, by its nature, a quiet effort, but general publicity may follow the completion of the program or some phases of it.

The Regional Campaign

A regional campaign assumes that your constituency is national in scope or at least divided up in some geographic way. You concentrate on each geographic area separately—one at a time—and staff the program locally in each region if needed. This usually involves moving staff people and even key leadership from place to place as the campaign progresses. Each regional drive is intensive and short—a tiny one-time campaign in itself.

The Blanket (Regional) Campaign

If you have a national constituency, but if the capital program is conducted in all areas at the same time, this is considered the blanket approach to a regional campaign. It usually requires a large and well-trained staff. Such a campaign can become unwieldy. A blanket campaign can be advantageous, though, if the regions involved are reasonably close together geographically.

The Federated Campaign

This approach typically involves combined campaigns run jointly by several institutions, usually offering similar services to the community. Community support for federated fund-raising efforts is often strong. In one federated campaign involving five hospitals, for example, the combined results represented more than all that the hospitals had raised collectively over the previous 20 years. Cost savings can be achieved through the federated approach because the professional fund-raising staff will be smaller than that needed for several separate campaigns. Use of common literature and other campaign material purchased in large quantity could represent an important saving, and there often are significant savings in time and human energy—both of which are expensive. The support of community leaders is essential, of course, to any federated campaign.

The Challenge Grant Campaign

Occasionally an organization gets an opportunity to use a large challenge grant as the basis for a campaign. A donor or group of donors offers a sum of money to be given only if the organization can match the funds. Often members of the board make the challenge.

The time factor of a challenge campaign usually forces instant action. If the challenge is worthwhile, you might consider trying, even if time does not allow for as much planning as you would like. A challenge grant can create great momentum for a campaign.

The Mini-Campaign

This term refers to the opposite of the comprehensive campaign. A large university decides to have a series of mini-campaigns for separate schools or projects. There is no overall organizational message. Separate constituencies are approached to fund the separate needs of several projects. Often if a large comprehensive campaign does not reach its needs goals, a series of mini-campaigns, directed at specific projects, may follow.

Chapter 17
Who's Going to Raise the Money?

In-house Staff

To conduct a capital campaign, you need people—a skilled and effective in-house staff of planners, organizers, motivators and solicitors. At the very minimum, you need a campaign director; researchers; writers; solicitors for individuals, corporations and foundations, and someone knowledgeable about planned gifts. These could all be the same individual, but this would indicate a very small campaign effort. Most likely, the number of staff members will be greater than you first estimated.

You must have this inside staff lined up before the capital campaign starts. It is dangerous to wait until you see how things progress or until an emergency situation arises. Assess your current staff. Get rid of the deadwood. Use your new campaign plans to energize the existing staff and to hire more people.

Your major decision is this: Do you have the in-house expertise and clout to run a capital campaign, or do you need additional staff members? This decision should be made early, so you can proceed from a position of strength. There is no formula. Your needs will simply be based on what you plan to do.

The two basic prerequisites for capital campaign staff members are technical fund-raising skills plus the ability to deal effectively with people. Because a capital campaign is a series of related activities, which must happen on schedule, staff members should be team people and detail-oriented. They should be self-starting, too, because the staff keeps the volunteers moving and keeps top leadership involved—not vice versa. Ideally your campaign staff should combine those who know the institution well with those who know development well—without being weighted too much in either direction.

While your campaign staff members will concentrate on their own work, they must also be knowledgeable about the other development programs under way at your institution. And the people running those other programs must know what is happening with the capital campaign. This all speaks to regularly scheduled staff meetings. Lines of authority must be clear. Your staff must know how much program money is available, and who controls the various parts of the budget. Long before the first cocktail is raised at the kickoff meeting, you must have a smoothly working team. Otherwise you will have problems.

In-house staff for a campaign should have the following traits:

- Positive outlook
- Energy
- Ability to work with a variety of personalities
- Motivational
- Good communication skills

- A complete understanding of the environment of the organization
- Willingness to play a behind-the-scenes role and to be directly involved in solicitations
- Commitment to the organization's goals
- Confidence

During a campaign, you need staff members who can carry out different kinds of activities. A campaign director or manager should have a broad view of the campaign. A campaign office manager keeps the flow of details moving. Field representatives might be actual solicitors, who need to be backed up by researchers. You need a team of inside and outside staff who will work together to meet campaign goals.

The President or CEO

We have already emphasized the role of the president of a nonprofit organization in raising major gifts. That role becomes even more pivotal during a capital campaign. Some college presidents have been known to spend one-third to one-half of their time on fund-raising during a campaign. The president or CEO must be the chief spokesman for the campaign and be involved in critical solicitations.

The president is probably the key asker during the nucleus fund stage (the first part of the campaign when those closest to the organization are asked for substantial contributions.) It is also important that the president is heavily involved in cultivation events. The president must buy into the total campaign process because the campaign is literally the president's campaign. He or she is the embodiment of the campaign's goals and its chief salesman.

If you find that your president cannot shoulder this role, other alternatives must be put into place. The chairman of the board may have to carry the leadership role or another strong internal administrator can be tapped. But without campaign leadership from the president, you are left in a weakened position.

Volunteers

For a capital campaign, the type of volunteer you want is somewhat different than the types you'll meet in other fund-raising programs. Capital campaigns need men and women with clout. They should be prominent individuals with the capacity to make pacesetting gifts. They should have positions in the community that allow them to ask other key prospects— their peers—for sizable gifts. This type of campaign leadership is usually found among people who are already very close to your organization. Always remember that your prospective campaign leaders are also potential donors. Here are some important points to consider when selecting the leaders for your program:

- Does the individual believe in and understand the purpose and objectives of your institution—and of the campaign?
- Is the prospective volunteer leader respected by colleagues? Does he or she have the stature to attract important friends?
- Is this individual convincing? Is he or she a follower or a leader?
- Will this person contribute to the campaign and at what level?
- Will he or she ask others to contribute?
- Does the person have the time and energy needed?
- Is the volunteer a good and appropriate spokesman for your cause?

The following guide for the selection of campaign committee leaders may help you plan your own volunteer structure. It describes a specific type of effort—a community-wide campaign. But it is broad enough to give a pretty good idea of the type of volunteer staffing needed by any capital effort.

The general chairman. This should be an outstanding leader, who represents the organization well. The individual must be willing to use influence without restriction. He or she must be willing to devote the necessary time to the campaign, even if, as sometimes happens, this means devoting more time to the campaign than to his or her business. The leader must command respect without demanding it. The chairman must be the type of person to whom others will respond enthusiastically. He or she should be able to make a substantial personal gift.

The special-gifts chairman. This person must also have strong influence and be able to enlist an especially effective group of people, who are able to give substantially themselves and to influence others to give equally large gifts. He or she should be unusually dedicated to the campaign cause and be willing to devote the necessary time and energy. This person must have a sense of dedication sufficient to motivate the entire campaign division because most of the campaign's success will come in special gifts.

The chairman of the board. Already installed in office, he or she must not hesitate to insist that each board member make a pacesetting gift. The fact that a person is a board member means some sort of generous gift is expected.

Corporate and business division chairmen. It might be useful to have one person who can approach major corporations in your area and another who will be the small-business chairman. These volunteers should be successful in their own businesses. They must be well-known and compatible with others of equal caliber in the business community. They must be tenacious enough to hold their campaign workers to the task until it's finished, even if conditions change in mid-campaign. It is important for them to be people who can strongly influence their own company's gifts, so that they automatically represent pacesetting donations.

Major and/or planned gifts chairman. Someone who is close to the organization and who has made a pacesetting gift might help the board chairman and the CEO to motivate other individuals to give large gifts. If this chairman is someone with specific knowledge of gift mechanisms (such as a lawyer or estate planner), that would be a plus.

Organizations chairman. This individual must be popular and well-known by the leaders and members of many clubs and organizations. He or she must have the influence to enlist these leaders in the campaign, and with them, many of their club members. But throughout the campaign, no one club or organization should be favored.

Foundations chairman. Here you need someone with an intimate knowledge of the local philanthropic foundations, as well as their motivations, trustees and philosophies. He or she must be able to help select the best approach to each foundation.

Professional-staff chairman. Depending on your organization, the professional staff might be made up of doctors, nurses, administrators or faculty. The chairman must be a successful, respected staff member, who is willing to make clear to this group its responsibilities to the institution and to the campaign. He or she must be willing to set the pace personally and then to persevere in reaching the goal.

Regional or area chairman. He or she must be respected and popular. This chairman needs a vast knowledge of the area to be solicited, including its weaknesses or peculiarities. He or she must be a good detail person, with a strong sense of follow-through to see that the job assigned to large numbers of campaign workers—the door-to-door and telephone people—gets done.

Publicity chairman. This person should be a knowledgeable professional, strongly attached to the institution and its cause. He or she should be able to work within a plan of action and a budget. The chairman must be able to enlist specialized personnel and follow through on the publicity plan throughout the campaign.

Many organizations do not have the volunteer resources or the need to enlist a campaign committee as complete as the one just described. However every capital campaign needs a steering committee or executive committee, consist-

Figure 17.1. These forms were used by the Paoli Memorial Hospital and Bowdoin College to show committee enlistments.

```
PAOLI MEMORIAL HOSPITAL
EXPANSION FUND
Lancaster Pike
Paoli, Pennsylvania 19301
Phone: 644-8734



            ENLISTMENT REPORT FROM
            GENERAL GIFTS DIVISION

Your Name _____ Section No. _____

I have enlisted the following to serve as Team Members of the
General Gifts Division.  I have reviewed with each person the
"Duties of a Team Member" and the Schedule.

        1.  Name _____

            Address _____

                    _____

            Phone:  _____


        2.  Name _____

            Address _____

                    _____

            Phone:  _____


        3.  Name _____

            Address _____

                    _____

            Phone:  _____


Special Note:   Please make th
                yourself, senc
                and one to the
```

Bowdoin College 175th Anniversary Campaign Program

ENLISTMENT REPORT

The following persons have been enlisted to serve as _____

in the _____
(Division, Area, Section, Team)

(Area Chairmen, Section Chairmen, Captains, Committeemen, Team Members, etc.)

PLEASE PRINT OR TYPE

NAME	ADDRESSES (Please indicate zip codes)	TELEPHONES
1. _____	Bus: _____ (NAME OF COMPANY) _____ (ADDRESS) Res: _____	_____ _____
2. _____	Bus: _____ (NAME OF COMPANY) _____ (ADDRESS) Res: _____	_____ _____
3. _____	Bus: _____ (NAME OF COMPANY) _____ (ADDRESS) Res: _____	_____ _____
4. _____	Bus: _____ (NAME OF COMPANY) _____ (ADDRESS) Res: _____	_____ _____
5. _____	Bus: _____ (NAME OF COMPANY) _____ (ADDRESS) Res: _____	_____ _____

Do not delay sending the first two copies of this report to the Campaign Office. Two or three names may be filed at one time and additional forms used for further enlistments.

(Please Check)

☐ This completes my list

☐ More to come

Number of persons still to be enlisted ☐

Date _____

Your Name _____ (PLEASE PRINT)

Business Address _____

Business Telephone _____

Home Address: _____

Home Telephone: _____

(Please check address preference for mailing)

CAMPAIGN OFFICE #1

ing of top volunteer leaders, who will make major decisions about the conduct of the effort. If your organization has a national constituency, you might want to have a national campaign committee led by a smaller local executive group. Make sure that prominent people and top prospects are represented on the steering committee. Members of your board should serve on that committee. In fact, a campaign steering committee should be named by the board and possibly even be a subcommittee of

the board. This is the policymaking committee of the campaign, and it has ultimate responsibility for the campaign's success.

The number of volunteers needed for a capital campaign will vary with the size of the organization and the geographical spread of fund-raising activity. A general guideline is the 1-to-5 rule. Each key volunteer should be given five prospects. Five is enough at one time. If large gifts are involved, the volunteer will have to make numerous contacts with each potential donor.

Figure 17.2. The Saint Joseph Medical Center Foundation in Burbank, California, used this donor call report.

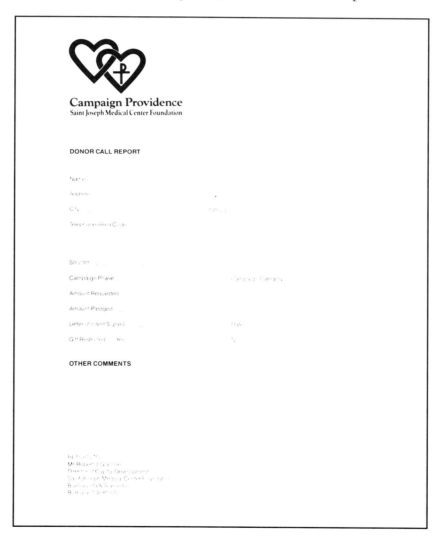

Limiting assignments especially at the top gift levels is more effective than spreading volunteers too thin.

As in most fund-raising work, forms are extremely helpful in the process of interacting with volunteers.

Once you have enlisted volunteers, you need to match them with an appropriate list of prospects. Peers should be asked to solicit peers, based on social standing, professional standing and gift potential. Start with your board because some of your top prospects and your best volunteers should come from that group. Each board member should be assigned to line up major gifts early in the effort—probably even prior to the official start of the campaign. Board gifts are often used to provide an early boost to a major fund-raising effort. When campaigns are announced, it is common to report that a sizable portion of the goal has already been committed in advance gifts—usually from board members and other close friends.

Once your board is solicited, take the list of your other volunteers and prospects, and begin making assignments. Suggest assignments based on what you know about your prospects, but let volunteers choose the prospects they want to solicit. By the time you get to the point of making prospect assignments, your research should have provided enough data for you to make suggestions that turn out to be pretty acceptable to the volunteers. Once again, forms are a help in the assignment process; you must keep track of which solicitor has which prospect.

Chapter 18

The Role of a Consultant

What a Consultant Does

The role of a professional fund-raising consultant during a capital campaign will largely be determined by the size of the campaign and the general development experience of the in-house staff.

Experience is an excellent teacher of the fund-raising art, so utilizing the expertise of outside counsel can be of tremendous help to the in-house staff that is light on campaign experience. Consultants can also help experienced staff plan a campaign effectively, based on their knowledge of what has worked for campaigns at other organizations. Outside counsel can help you analyze your needs, plan your course of action and keep you on track. And often, your leadership will take advice from a consultant that they simply would not take from you—or that you wouldn't dare give!

A typical fund-raising counseling firm offers the following services:

Consultation. Usually this is done by a senior member of the firm on a per diem basis to guide the administrators of an institution as they plan a capital fund-raising program and to help keep the campaign going at maximum efficiency.

Resident campaign or program direction. A senior staff member of the firm can be assigned to a client on a full-time basis for an agreed-upon period. This staff member discusses the client organization regularly with a senior member of the firm, who usually visits the institution on a scheduled basis.

Provision of staff. Such staff could include a campaign director, supervising consultant, publicity director—the whole package, if needed. This staff can be recruited or assigned by the consulting firm, with the approval of the organization's leaders.

A consultant can be your insurance policy during a campaign, by helping to define reachable goals and suggesting appropriate steps to attain them.

John J. Schwartz, former president of the American Association of Fund-Raising Counsel, defines the following *wills* and *will nots* of professional fund-raising counsel. The *wills* come first.

- They *will* identify the strengths and the weaknesses of the institution, and present a program to convert the latter into the former if possible.
- They *will* set up the conditions for action.
- They *will* backstop and strengthen the institutional staff.
- They *will* predict costs and maintain budget controls.
- They *will* provide an overall plan, the goals, the priorities and the deadlines.

- They *will* stimulate and organize top leaders to make them effective and to take advantage of the most priceless commodity any institution has—volunteer time.
- When problems arise, they *will* provide manifold and collective experience toward the solutions. . . .
- They *will* be the first to tell you if you cannot do what you are trying to do.
- And perhaps as important as any of the preceding, they *will* help an institution avoid the letup that happens so often when you have a few successes but still aren't there yet. They have to be professional needlers.

Now, here are the *will nots*.

- They *will not* normally be active in the solicitation of contributions.
- They *will not* attempt to sell the institution's case, unless it really is a salable one.
- They *will not* relieve top people of responsibilities in the fund-raising effort. As a matter of fact, they will increase both the responsibilities and the activities of the key people.
- They *will not* take over, hire or fire staff, but they will do their best to maximize the efficiency of those on the scene.
- They obviously *will not* give you any magic formula; no one can get blood from a turnip.

How to Pick the Right One

An important step in selecting professional counsel is to consult present or former clients of the firms you are considering. You should ask for an evaluation of the firm's services, an indication of how realistic their cost estimates turned out to be and whether the client would engage that particular firm again. As important as it is, goal attainment can never be the sole measure of a consultant's success. There are other measures, such as: improvement of the organization's program, increased involvement of influential leadership, an improved public image of the institution and an improvement of the extent to which administrators and board members work well together. A good consultant

should help them all—and reach the goal. Some important questions to ask the firm:

- What is the hands-on fund-raising experience of the key executives? In other words, what did they do in the field of fund-raising before they became consultants?
- Has the firm consulted with institutions or agencies similar to yours? What is their track record with those groups?
- How will the firm bill you for services? The American Association of Fund-Raising Counsel suggests you work on a fixed-fee basis, meaning on a per diem or fixed monthly fee. The reason for a fixed fee is so that you can be certain of the objectivity of the consultant in setting fund-raising goals. If a commission-based fee is suggested, question it strongly. There have been situations where a commission structure has pushed an organization toward too big a goal. Also question carefully if the initial fees are low and then will be raised once success is achieved. You want to be sure you get consistent—not sporadic—support from counsel.
- Will you have to pay out-of-pocket expenses? If so, how will they be billed—in advance or when they're incurred?
- Will the firm provide general plans for your effort, including cost estimates and a schedule of events?
- Will it conduct a feasibility study?
- Where are the firm's permanent offices? If they are far away, how often will the staff visit you? What costs are involved in these visits? How much does the firm know about your community? Has it done business here before?

Robert E. Nelson, an Elmhurst, Illinois, consultant, adds these cautions:

- Be sure the commitment to working with a consultant is based on a conviction, on the part of the executive head of your institution, that he or she actually wants counsel. It should also be based on board action—full discussion and hearty approval of the hiring of counsel by your board of trustees.

- Do not employ a consultant organization without retaining absolute control over which consulting personnel do your work.
- Seek a consultant who has had staff experience running a program for an institution similar to yours, sharing an awareness of your methodology and your operating problems. Check such references as thoroughly as if you were conducting a presidential search.
- Do not employ fund-raising counsel under the delusion that doing so will exempt the institutional administration from responsibility for the program.
- Do not expect counsel to bring in a divining rod to locate large new resources that you have never known about or tapped before. Once in a great while, a consultant may have the luck to do so, but this is rare.
- Be wary of a consultant who limits his or her concerns only to fund-raising techniques. Most fund-raising problems relate closely to areas of institutional governance and management, and to understanding and interpreting your organization's service.
- Do not buy a package of techniques that have worked somewhere else. Invest your counseling dollars in the experience and outlook that you believe will best serve your institutional situation. Achieving the correct match of consultant and institution means everything; the variations in costs are relatively incidental.
- Include in your agreement with counsel the understanding that the relationship can be concluded readily without prejudice, if either party comes to believe that the relationship is unproductive.
- Recognize that the relationship of institution to consultant is fundamentally one of mutual faith and respect. Recognize that it will succeed to the extent that it rests upon a foundation of mutual candor and honesty.

And if you want an extremely tough list of questions to ask when considering a consultant, the YMCA of Metropolitan Los Angeles has advised its branches to ask these!

- During the past three years, what percent of the goals were achieved in all the campaigns you directed?
- What services do you provide prior to the campaign?
- Can we accept or reject the on-site campaign director prior to the campaign? What's the process for changing a director and how quickly can it be done?
- What's your fee? When is it due? Is it refundable?
- What total expenses can we expect before, during and after the campaign?
- Do we get a complete campaign general plan for approval prior to the campaign?
- How do you work with us: in the early planning stage, in the nucleus fund stage, in the clean-up stage?
- Name all the services you provide.
- Name three organizations for which you directed campaigns in the past five years where the goal was achieved; name three where the goal was not achieved.
- Who is responsible for producing all campaign materials? Is any portion of the cost of these included in your fee? Do you provide any reporting materials?
- What's your attitude on studies—internal audit, feasibility and/or marketing? What are the costs?
- What do you expect of our volunteer and staff leadership?
- What kind of office space, equipment and staffing do you require, and for how long?
- If the goal is not achieved, is your full fee payable?
- Give a brief resume of each of your top six campaign directors—their backgrounds and the results of their last three campaigns.
- If you think our goals are too high, what steps will you take to help us resolve the issue?
- Give us a typical budget breakdown, including dollar amounts and percentages for campaigns of our size.
- Does your firm provide public relations services before and during the campaign?

■ What happens if we postpone or cancel the campaign?

■ If we want extra consultation services, what is the per diem charge?

■ Will you make a detailed report of the results of the campaign to our board? In writing?

How do you locate names of fund-raising consultants for consideration? The American Association of Fund-Raising Counsel Inc., 25 West 43rd Street, Suite 1519, New York, New York 10036, can provide a list of member firms. But many good consultants do not belong to AAFRC. Another source for a directory of consultants is the National Society of Fund-Raising Executives, 7720 Wisconsin Avenue, Suite 215, Bethesda, Maryland 20814. The Council for Advancement and Support of Education lists affiliated counsultants in its directory. CASE is located at 11 Dupont Circle, Suite 400, Washington, D.C. 20036.

The best way to seek out firms to interview is to check with organizations similar to yours and find out which ones they have used. Find out from other nonprofits in your area who the best local consultants are. Sometimes it is an advantage to choose a firm that knows your community well. Don't hire any fund-raising consultants until you find that they have satisfied clients.

The American Association of Fund-Raising Counsel requires that fees for fund-raising consulting services not be like a commission, based on a percentage of the sums raised. Fees are based primarily on the number of hours the firm's personnel apply to the client's program. Sometimes monthly retainer fees are required.

This is a set amount paid by the client every month for an agreed upon level of service such as one or two days a month of service.

Fees should be specified in advance and agreed upon by both parties. The agreement between an institution and a professional fund-raising firm should specify both fixed fee and budgeted expenses, and it should be in writing. It is best to agree that either party can give notice to end the relationship within a set period, such as 30 days.

Another word of advice on fund-raising consultants: Their role should not be to raise money but to help your organization raise it. Counsel supplements in-house abilities. In order to take full advantage of professional counsel, you must have in-house staff to act upon the advice. Consultants should bring a broad range of experience to your cause. Their advice should be unbiased and help put your organization's fund-raising plans in perspective. Hire a consultant you're comfortable with and one your leadership will respect.

When hiring consultants for a capital campaign, be sure to bring them in early. Then your staff can work with them in a partnership, and you can take full advantage of their expertise. You must trust and feel comfortable with your consultant because the real aim is to listen to the advice you pay for.

Fund-raising firms should also help you assess the success of a capital campaign. The American Association of Fund-Raising Counsel has designed, with the help of long-time consultant Maurice G. Gurin, a final campaign report for their member firms. This form is an excellent model for you to use when assessing your results.

Figure 18.1. American Association of Fund-Raising Counsel final campaign report.

AMERICAN ASSOCIATION OF FUND-RAISING COUNSEL, INC.

FINAL CAMPAIGN REPORT

This report form is designed for two major purposes: 1) to provide firms with a record of each completed campaign (firms may want to modify some sections of the form to reflect their particular interests or the specific characteristics of campaigns for different types of organizations and institutions); and 2) to improve the quality of the data available for AAFRC surveys. Future studies by the Research Committee will focus on the information presented in these reports.

Firm _____ Form completed by _____

Type of Organization: Educational _____ Health _____ Cultural _____ Other (specify) _____

CAMPAIGN SUMMARY

1. Name of client _____
2. Address _____
3. Geographical area served: City _____   County _____   State _____
    Regional _____   National _____
4. Total number prospect base _____
5. Campaign goal: $_____
6. Pledge payment period (months) _____
7. Service provided (months):   Resident _____   Counseling _____
8. Was pre-campaign counseling provided?   Yes _____   No _____   Duration (months) _____
    If so, by: Firm _____   Other (specify) _____
9. Was a pre-campaign study conducted?   Yes _____   No _____   Duration (months) _____
    If so, by: Firm _____   Other (specify) _____
10. Other services provided _____
    _____

11. Services began: _____ / _____   Services ended: _____ / _____
                        mo.   yr.   mo.   yr.
12. Previous campaign: Completion date _____   Goal $ _____
                                                    Pledged $ _____
    Was counsel used?   Yes _____   No _____
    Name of firm used _____

FINANCIAL REPORT

13. Institution's annual budget for last year of campaign: $ _____
14. Annual support* raised in last year of campaign: $ _____
15. Total pledges made during firm's service: $ _____
    Total pledges received in campaign: $ _____
    Is campaign complete?   Yes _____   No _____
    Receipts vs. goal: Excess $ _____   or Deficit $ _____
    (To be completed when full information is available)
16. Allocation of goal: Endowment _____%   Physical facilities _____%
                           Annual support _____%   Other (specify) _____%
17. Institutional campaign budget: $ _____
18. Firm's fee and expenses as a percentage of campaign goal: _____%
19. Firm's fee and expenses as a percentage of amount subscribed: _____%
20. Total cost as a percentage of campaign goal: _____%
21. Total cost as a percentage of amount subscribed: _____%
22. Effect of campaign on annual support during campaign period:
    Increase _____%   Decrease _____%
23. Total amount of bequests: $ _____
24. Total amount of planned gifts: $ _____
25. Number of volunteer workers _____

*As defined by client

26.   RANGE OF PLEDGES RECEIVED

Size of Pledges	**Number of Pledges**	**Total Amount**
$10 million & over	_____	$ _____
1 million to 9,999,999	_____	_____
500,000 to 999,999	_____	_____
250,000 to 499,999	_____	_____
100,000 to 249,999	_____	_____
50,000 to 99,999	_____	_____
25,000 to 49,999	_____	_____
10,000 to 24,999	_____	_____
5,000 to 9,999	_____	_____
1,000 to 4,999	_____	_____
Up to 1,000	_____	_____
Total	_____	_____

27.   TEN LARGEST PLEDGES

Amount	**Percentage of Goal**	**Type of Donor**	**Type of Pledge***
1) $_____	_____	_____	_____
2) _____	_____	_____	_____
3) _____	_____	_____	_____
4) _____	_____	_____	_____
5) _____	_____	_____	_____
6) _____	_____	_____	_____
7) _____	_____	_____	_____
8) _____	_____	_____	_____
9) _____	_____	_____	_____
10) _____	_____	_____	_____
Percentage of goal, cumulative top ten	_____		

Cash, securities, planned, personal property, in-kind, etc.

28.   TOTAL GIFTS AND PLEDGES

Donor	**Amount**	**Percentage of Goal**
Individuals	$_____	_____
Trustees	_____	_____
Alumnae/alumni	_____	_____
Members/clients/students	_____	_____
Parents	_____	_____
Employees	_____	_____
Other (specify)	_____	_____
Corporate	_____	_____
Corporations	_____	_____
Corporate foundations	_____	_____
Small business	_____	_____
Other (specify) _____	_____	_____
Foundations	_____	_____
Church/denominational support	_____	_____
Government	_____	_____
Other (specify) _____	_____	_____
_____	_____	_____
_____	_____	_____
Total	$_____	_____

American Association of Fund-Raising Counsel, Inc.
25 West 43rd Street, New York, NY 10036
212/354-5799

11/87

Chapter 19

Setting Your Goal

How Much Can You Really Raise?

Before you begin a campaign, your organization must have its act together. You must know the amount of gift income that is needed and then set some feasible goals.

The goal for a capital campaign must be a "stretch" goal that is within reach. This means that the goal should challenge donors to make their biggest gifts ever but should also be realistic.

A feasibility study is the very best way to determine reachable goals. A question in the study should actually ask how much each person interviewed will give. Proposed participation by the board and other lead givers must be carefully analyzed to determine the top gifts and what percentage they will be of the total goal.

The total number of prospects and their potential must also be considered when setting the goal. Remember the 3-to-1 rule: It usually takes three prospects to get one gift. Board and leadership gifts should be more certain than this, but gifts at lower levels probably won't be.

You should also compare your proposed campaign goal and timetable with similar efforts at similar institutions. (This is usually done with the help of outside counsel.) You can compare where you're starting from with the experience of other groups to help predict your success. Analytical models have been used, especially for some of the biggest campaigns, to compare similar organizations and predict the range of potential success. At most, these models should

be seen as outside tests to compare with your actual feasibility study results. Their predictive value is not as critical as a feasibility study's results, but modeling can help further define the range for a goal.

Building a Gift Table

Once you set the goal, you must estimate the types of gifts needed to fund your campaign. You must translate the dollar amounts into a table of gifts needed to complete the campaign.

Winthrop B. Wilson, a hospital fund-raiser, suggests this process for creating a gift table: The prime use of the gift table is *motivational*. It helps promote a mind-set among prospects and workers that motivates larger pledges. Its secondary use is as a tool for *analysis and planning*, including an analysis of your campaign's feasibility. You measure how well projections, which are based on the giving potential of your prospects, stack up against an ideal table. The rub comes in drawing up that ideal. The ideal table is a geometric progression of sorts, based on tried-and-true fund-raising precepts. Here is Wilson's explanation, using a $2 million goal.

The starting point is that age-old fund-raising truism: "10 percent of the money will come from a single gift."

1 gift at $200,000   for a total of $200,000

The next step is simple. Double the number of givers and halve the amount of the gift at that level.

2 gifts at $100,000   for a total of $200,000

Again, following the same rule, doubling the number of projected donors and halving the gift size, you get this:

4 gifts at $ 50,000   for a total of $200,000
and
8 gifts at $ 25,000   for a total of $400,000

Now, this is a good place to pause for reflection. From here on, *adjustments* to the math will be necessary. But let's summarize what the math has provided so far.

1 gift at $200,000	for a total of $200,000
2 gifts at $100,000	for a total of $200,000
4 gifts at $ 50,000	for a total of $200,000
8 gifts at $ 25,000	for a total of $200,000
15 gifts	for a total of $800,000

If we continued on with the same projection system, we would build the following table.

16 gifts at $12,500	for a total of $200,000
32 gifts at $ 6,250	for a total of $200,000
64 gifts at $ 3,125	for a total of $200,000
128 gifts at $ 1,562.50	for a total of $200,000
256 gifts at $ 781.25	for a total of $200,000
512 gifts at $ 390.625	for a total of $200,000

It's a nicely balanced mathematical sequence. Unfortunately, it has a good deal *wrong* with it as a fund-raising tool.

Exactly what is wrong? For one thing, some of the numbers, such as $781.25, don't even *look* like gifts. Further, our fund-raising experience tells us the drop from $25,000 to $12,500 is too great. Many gifts should come in at levels *between* these two figures. The answer to the problem is to change the formula after the top four levels. Therefore:

10 gifts at $20,000	for a total of $200,000
15 gifts at $15,000	for a total of $225,000

And continuing:

20 gifts at $10,000	for a total of $200,000
25 gifts at $ 7,500	for a total of $187,000
30 gifts at $ 5,000	for a total of $150,000

And finally:

many gifts under $ 5,000	for a total of $237,500

Below, we see the completed table.

1 gift at $200,000	for $ 200,000
2 gifts at $100,000	for $ 200,000
4 gifts at $ 50,000	for $ 200,000
8 gifts at $ 25,000	for $ 200,000
10 gifts at $ 20,000	for $200,000
15 gifts at $ 15,000	for $ 225,000
20 gifts at $ 10,000	for $ 200,000
25 gifts at $ 7,500	for $ 187,500
30 gifts at $ 5,000	for $150,000
numerous gifts under $ 5,000	for $ 237,500
1500-2000 gifts	$2,000,000

This is a reasonably good ideal table, but you might still want to tinker a bit. For example, you might want to show a shift toward gifts in the upper ranges. This could be managed by putting another level into the scale near the top such as:

3 gifts at $ 75,000	for a total of $225,000

While this is a very detailed and helpful process to follow, another simple way to begin a gift table is to start with the top gift you know you can raise, and then work down the table to see how many gifts are required at lower levels. Keep in mind the number of prospects you have and that most of the money must come from the biggest gifts.

There are all kinds of ideals, and the one ultimately tailored for a given situation should be a *comfortable fit*. For instance, there is little to be gained by showing more gifts in the upper ranges than you know you can ever expect to get (unless, of course, the purpose of the table is to demonstrate that a drive for a particular goal is not feasible).

In developing a gift table, remember some of the points mentioned earlier. The top 10 gifts should yield approximately 50 percent of the total, with one gift yielding 10 percent. The next 100 gifts should yield approximately 40 percent of the goal, and all the rest of the gifts should yield 10 percent.

Another helpful guideline is that in most significant capital campaigns, with goals of $25 million or more, approximately 50 percent of the gifts will need to come in contributions of $1 million or more, and 70 percent of the total will come in gifts of $100,000 and up.

Figure 19.1. Here is a gift table used by Carleton College for a $19.5 million campaign.

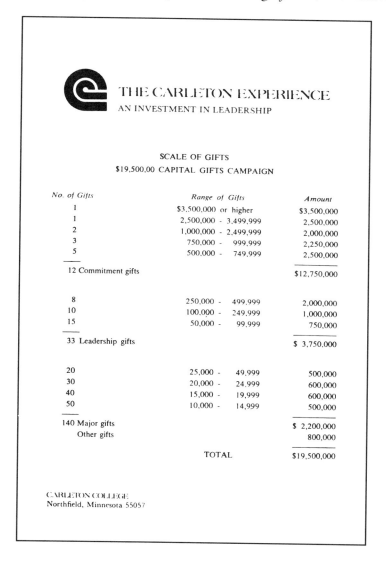

Chapter 20
How to Prepare a Campaign Case Statement

Once the needs and goals have been established, you must create a fund-raising program to meet those goals. If your institutional planning process has been successful, your organization knows where it wants to go, how it is going to get there, and what resources it will need.

As the development officer, it is your duty to take these plans and recast them into a convincing literary form, so attractive and lucidly written that your constituents will feel that they must be part of the effort. This case statement usually ends up as a brochure, and it is usually the keystone of a group of publications produced to support a capital campaign.

A case statement defines the programs of an organization, summarizes the basic philosophy underlying these programs, describes how these programs relate to society's changing needs, outlines the current fund-raising campaign and explains specific program goals. It may also help strengthen an institution's commitment to its plans by giving those plans graphic tangibility and a widespread reading.

Above all, though, a case statement is a selling document. Its purpose is to sell shares in an organization's future to the people within its constituency. The word "people" should be emphasized. The case statement will not be read

by governments or committees, nor will it be analyzed by computers. It will be read by people who will be moved by its logic and by the desirability of what it proposes. They then will direct their resources to the effort. They will volunteer their time; they will pledge their money; they will plan the organization's future into their estates; they will influence other sectors of society to share their interest in your plans.

The case statement also keeps everyone in an organization—staff and volunteers alike—pointed at the same goals and speaking the same language. A case statement need not be a long or elaborate document, although sometimes it is. However, it should be appropriate to the institution and to the plans it describes, both in the way it is written and in the way it is reproduced.

Who writes the case statement? Clearly someone with good writing skills and the ability to understand the institution's case for support. Fund-raising consultant Herbert N. Heston points out that it should be written by one person, never a committee. Heston thinks that the development director should do the first draft. Other consultants suggest that the text be written by someone closely involved with the institution, but not by a member of the fund-raising staff. The development office, they say, might be seen as creating its own kind of statement, fine for raising funds, but not reflecting the real concerns and plans of others within the organization. The case statement is an institutional, not departmental, document.

At any rate, all the leaders of an organization should review the draft of the case statement. Professional fund-raising counsel can help evaluate the potential philanthropic appeal of the text and produce the graphics. But the first draft of a case statement, most agree, is best done by one person—a person who is involved with the organization on a day-to-day basis.

How do you go about writing a case statement? Proceed as if addressing "the most resistant or recalcitrant donor imaginable," advises Heston. The case statement should be written and designed so the reader cannot resist opening it and reading it through. It should be brief and factual, with its logic and arguments aimed at the donor. It should tell prospective donors what their gifts will do for the things they hold most dear. It should do this in words donors will understand. And it should do so in a way that is also completely acceptable to an organization's insiders.

Several formulas have been proposed for writing case statements. The John Grenzebach consulting firm in Chicago suggests this approach:

■ State the needs and the rationale for those needs.

■ Answer all important questions and establish the arguments for your case.

■ Explain the proposed plan for raising the funds necessary for the project.

■ Show how gifts can be made and review the tax deductibility of contributions. (Sometimes the details of this information are separated from the case and printed as an independent but coordinated "how-to-give" booklet.)

■ Identify the people who are behind the project.

■ List those who will give the project leadership and direction.

In his *Designs for Fund-Raising*, Si Seymour puts it this way: "The case for support should aim high, provide perspective, arouse a sense of history and continuity, convey a feeling of importance, relevance and urgency, and have whatever stuff it needs to warm the heart and stir the mind." Here is Seymour's formula for constructing a case statement:

■ Expose the problem right away in the first paragraph.

■ Relate the case to an area of current general interest. Cite a parallel example that will lead the reader to go on.

■ Include approval by top authorities, testimony by consultants etc.

■ Note that the plan is clear and simple, the leadership team first-class.

■ Make clear that association with this project will bring long-lasting satisfaction to the reader.

How do you know if your case statement is well-written? Duncan M. Laidlaw, senior vice president for development at St. Leonard's Center in Dayton, Ohio, suggests this checklist:

■ **Interest**. Does the case sustain the reader's interest through to the end?

■ **Logic**. Are the main points sound? Do the ideas follow each other smoothly and logically?

■ **Clarity. Is it easy to read?**

■ **Brevity**. Is it short enough to read and digest at one sitting?

■ **Objectivity**. Are your benefits substantial and distinctive enough to set the appeal apart from others?

■ **Tone**. Does it sustain a positive, upbeat tone? Does it emphasize words like "opportunity," "potential," "success" and "benefits"?

■ **Perspective**. Does it address itself to donors and their interests, or is it a monologue in which an isolated cause talks to itself?

■ **Ideology**. Do the points in the case mesh with the values of the intended readers?

■ **Effectiveness**. Is the central argument the most effective that can be used?

■ **Motivation**. Does it lead naturally to the conclusion that the need for action is immediate?

■ **Concreteness**. Is the case supported by concrete facts?

■ **Accuracy**. Can you back up every fact and conclusion? Does it portray your cause and its work without misrepresentation?

The case statement is the most important document of a campaign. It needs to be compelling with a central theme. And above all it must be readable and believable.

To accompany a written case statement, you might consider a video presentation of the case.

For some organizations, it is hard to capture the real essence of their services in words. But showing the organization in action can help set the stage for an effective solicitation. A video case should not aim at detail but at effect and feeling.

Here are some case statements for your review.

Figure 20.1. These excerpts are from a case statement for Penn State's $200 million campaign, which actually raised $352 million. It used a 9-by-12-inch four-color format and stressed the fact that this was Penn State's first major gifts campaign.

A turning point for Penn State: The first major gifts campaign

Launching The Campaign for Penn State marks a significant turning point in the University's history. The Campaign will provide new and exciting possibilities for our faculty and our students. We will begin to see many of the most challenging and exhilarating of those possibilities take shape through the five-year life of the Campaign, which is committed to raising $200 million from private sources.

It may come as a surprise to some that Penn State, a **public** university, is seeking support from **private** sources. The need to do so becomes readily apparent when we realize that in 1985-86 only 23 percent of the University's operating budget was supported by the state. This percentage has declined about one percentage point per year since 1975-76, when the state supported about one-third of Penn State's budget.

Despite that trend, which accompanied a period of economic strain for Pennsylvania, Penn State continues to grow in achievement and promise. It is the quintessential university, a place of paradox, where one is constantly confronted by the unexpected and by fresh perceptions that show Penn State in an entirely new light. Its traditions are continually renewed by the need to meet society's changing needs. Consider that:

— Penn State is rooted in a strong agricultural heritage, yet, at the same time, is a leading pioneer in space technology.

— Penn State is renowned for its prowess in sport, but also is internationally acclaimed for the research achievements of its faculty. Among many such accomplishments are the field ion microscope (which allowed scientists to "see" the atom for the first time), the synthesis of progesterone, computerized weather forecasting, and the first long-term heart pacemaker – as well as the artificial Penn State Heart.

— Penn State serves its students at twenty-two locations in urban and rural Pennsylvania. Yet, regardless of the setting, it equips its graduates with the tools necessary for exceptional success in the fierce competition of the major professions, industry, and finance.

— And, along with a strong commitment to collegiality and an emphasis on merit within the University community, Penn State is recognized by its peers as a leader in the Association of American Universities – an influential group of the most important universities in the United States and Canada.

Penn State's Campaign goal of $200 million is far from arbitrary. It is the carefully calculated means to an all-important end. Every dollar has been allocated to fill a particular and pressing need.

The Campaign is designed to make the University richer, not ultimately in dollars, but in essential resources that only dollars can provide. These include advanced research facilities; innovative academic programs; scholarships to attract the brightest and neediest students; and newly endowed chairs of learning to afford prominent scholars and teachers the freedom to carry their work forward.

Giving to the Campaign is by no means a one-sided gesture. Support to Penn State is returned to the community in many ways: through outstanding research and its practical applications; through the education of highly qualified graduates who have made their mark in many fields; and through its programs of service. Investing in Penn State is as sound and productive an investment as you will find and one that will yield long-term benefits in which we can all take pride.

Yet, important as it is, our financial goal of $200 million is only a stepping stone to the broader goal of making a great university greater. We must achieve the financial goal to realize our visions, to fulfill our almost limitless potential, and to satisfy our obligation to society. These are the true goals of The Campaign for Penn State. Penn State graduate or friend of the University, we are asking you, urging you, to help us achieve them.

Bryce Jordan

Bryce Jordan
President, Penn State

A sense of balance: The arts at Penn State

Barbara R. and James R. Palmer see Penn State as embodying a precious vision of excellence—an inspiring vision that merited the support of an equally inspiring gift. The Palmers recently gave Penn State a multimillion dollar donation, to be divided three ways: for the University's Museum of Art; to endow a chair in communications or engineering; and to endow Pennsylvania Centre Stage.

Slep Student/Faculty Center, Altoona Campus

What do the highly successful Broadway play **Agnes of God** and the latest research into the mechanisms of enzyme reactions have in common? Their association with Penn State. Together they represent the special balance fostered at Penn State between art and science.

For years, Penn State has been quietly building a powerful reputation in many disciplines, until today it is an undisputed leader in engineering, medicine, and many branches of science.

The University also has a long tradition in creative writing—demonstrated in such memorable works as the stage play **Agnes of God,** the works of Penn State alumni Julius Epstein and John Pielmeier, respectively. And in the 1985 American Academy Institute of Arts and Letters Award in Literature received by Paul West, professor of English and comparative literature in the College of the Liberal Arts.

In the field of literary criticism, Penn State is the place to study Hemingway with Philip Young, the leading authority on the novelist, or to explore the ideas and writing of George Bernard Shaw with the eminent Shaw scholar, Stanley Weintraub.

The University's fourteen-year-old Museum of Art—the only major visual arts facility between Pittsburgh and Philadelphia—has a rapidly growing core collection in the history of Western art; mounts fifteen exhibitions a year ranging in subject from German expressionism to the drawings of Benjamin

West; and maintains an active program of community involvement in the Centre Region.

Penn State's commitment to the arts is reflected, too, in the impressive Holtkamp pipe organ in the Music Building recital hall; in significant research in medieval ivory carving; and in the vigorous and exciting program for Pennsylvania Centre Stage, the nation's newest professional regional theater.

What do the arts contribute to Penn State's overriding goal of excellence? An ageless, yet at the same time highly contemporary, sense of perspective. No matter what our long-term goals, this enlightening, perspective must be constantly invigorated and renewed.

The Campaign for Penn State seeks funds to expand the possibilities in what is already an exciting and flourishing environment for the arts.

Funds are needed to establish an annual residency for professional writers, whose presence and involvement in the life of the University will provide fresh impetus to young writers and will enrich the community at large.

The Campaign will also fund the construction of a new wing for the museum, endowments for new collections, and expansion of existing collections.

"Penn State represents, to us, a balanced emphasis on art and science. Just one example: Penn State has the highest enrollment of engineering students of any university, yet it's also ranked first in art education. Penn State's combination of diversity, quality, and accessibility makes it an extraordinary institution."

Barbara R. Palmer
James R. Palmer

An active partnership with industry

For Benjamin Franklin it was possible to achieve a major scientific breakthrough using nothing more elaborate than a kite, a door key, and a length of string.

Today, the needs of research are more complex. With physicists in search of the elusive "quark" and "charm," and biologists exploring the behavior of infinitesimal bacteria, significant research now calls for major investment in equipment and facilities.

Throughout the world, only a few universities have made a commitment to research on the scale of Penn State's. And many of our most ambitious research programs are made possible by industry sponsorship. In fact, in 1984, according to the most recent National Science Foundation figures, Penn State ranked fourth among all U.S. universities in industry-sponsored research funding.

The four-year-old Cooperative Program in Recombinant DNA Technology provides a channel for the exchange of information between Penn State faculty members and biotechnology-related industry.

Within Pennsylvania, the Technical Assistance Program known as PENNTAP has provided free expert advice for more than two decades to small businesses and industries across the state. And the Advanced Technology Center of Northern and Central Pennsylvania helps create and save jobs by sharing research, development, and training expertise with small companies, as part of the state's Ben Franklin Partnership Program.

And Penn State's contribution to industry isn't limited to technological development. More Penn State alumni work at IBM, General Electric, and Armstrong, for example, than graduates of any other university. The University is second only to Harvard in the number of specialized programs designed for senior corporate executives. And, not long ago, a group of Fortune 500 executives ranked our business executive education programs the best in the country.

The success of Penn State's relationship with U.S. business and industry is reflected in the gifts it receives. Corporate giving accounted for 41 percent of the $37.6 million received in nongovernment donations in 1985-86. And in the past year, this sum increased by 18 percent —a sizable vote of confidence.

To meet its $200 million goal in five years, The Campaign for Penn State must attract major corporate funding for a wide variety of major projects. And the sooner the funds are committed, the more we will benefit. Because nothing encourages potential donors like the generosity of other donors.

But what Penn State takes, it repays with interest. The thriving relationship between Penn State and industry is both innovative and productive—and constantly developing.

Jean E. Brenchley is an internationally recognized microbiologist. She serves as director of the Biotechnology Institute at Penn State, heads the Department of Molecular and Cell Biology, and is president of the American Society for Microbiology. She's a longtime advocate of stronger links between academic research and industrial applications. She is seen here on the site of the new Biotechnology Institute building, currently under construction at University Park.

University Hospital, Milton S. Hershey Medical Center

"If our industries are to compete in the coming decades, they must have partners, especially in the rapidly developing and exciting area of biotechnology. Japan has its MITI. Top universities are the logical choice for America. The multidisciplinary achievements at Penn State make it ideal for university-industry partnerships. Research here has helped industry develop countless new products and production methods. The Biotechnology Institute is the most recent example of how our research efforts interface with the needs of the private sector. The construction of new headquarters for the Institute, development of a modern pilot plant, special workshops and short courses, and application-oriented research all make the Penn State institute unique and place it at the forefront in biotechnology."

Jean E. Brenchley

How much to give? Our success depends on you

We cannot overemphasize the importance of The Campaign for Penn State to the University. And its success is assured, provided every friend of the University gives in proportion to his or her means.

We have designed the Campaign to provide every Penn State alumnus, alumna, and friend with the chance to make a significant gift, whatever the amount they are able to contribute.

At the same time, we are also calling on a few major donors to take the lead.

Although this is Penn State's first major gifts campaign, experience of hundreds of comparable university campaigns across the country shows that a relatively small number of donors are always responsible for a large proportion of the final total. In fact, as few as 10 to 15 percent of the contributors generally account for as much as 85 to 90 percent of the total sum raised.

Edward R. Hintz, '59, is past president of the Penn State Development Council and president of Hintz & Holman, Inc., a New York investment management firm. He currently serves as vice chairman of The Campaign for Penn State.

(from left) **Frable Building, Main Building, Science Building,** McKeesport Campus

Campaign Goal: $200,000,000

	Number of Gifts	Gift Level	Total $ Required
Leadership Gifts	1	$ 10,000,000 +	$ 10,000,000
	3	$ 5,000,000 +	$ 15,000,000
	40	$ 1,000,000 +	$ 40,000,000
	40	$ 500,000 +	$ 20,000,000
	60	$ 250,000 +	$ 15,000,000
Major Gifts	250	$ 100,000 +	$ 25,000,000
	400	$ 50,000 +	$ 20,000,000
	2,000	$ 10,000 +	$ 20,000,000
Annual Support Gifts	Many	Up to $10,000	$35,000,000 to 50,000,000

"Successful investors look for companies that are led by strong, imaginative senior executives. Penn State is guided by new, energetic, and dedicated leaders. They are committed to building on its traditional and solid values. This first Campaign will provide the resources to enhance Penn State's reputation and that of its alumni.

"I hope all of its loyal alumni and friends share my belief that anyone whose life has been enriched by his or her association with the University has an obligation and an opportunity to assist in this effort. Penn State has done so much for us. When it comes to repaying just a small part of this debt, we must respond generously."

Edward R. Hintz

Six ways to give—and make an impact

The preceding pages contain some insights, not only about how Penn State sees its future, but about the different perspectives of some of those who have already made generous gifts.

Their interests and outlooks, their relationships to Penn State, all are very different. Yet they have one thing in common. For all of them, Penn State embodies some cherished personal vision—a vision they have judged important enough to encourage.

If Penn State represents something of importance in your...either for what it has given you, or for what you believe it can give...ture generations, we urge you to support that judgment, with a...ribution. A contribution as generous as you can possibly make...nd, if at all possible, one you are prepared to commit to now.

The following suggestions for contributions are just that—suggestions. The Campaign for Penn State offers a number of different ways to link the name of an individual, a family, or a company permanently with the University and its aspirations. We will be happy to discuss others in detail. But we hope that these examples will at least start you thinking about how you best can help Penn State.

1. University Named Chairs — Minimum endowment: **$1 million**

The highest honor that can be bestowed on a faculty member, the endowed chair provides an eminent scholar with a salary, as well as additional sums to fund graduate assistant salaries, secretarial help, course development, and traveling expenses. An endowed chair is key in attracting and retaining the acknowledged leaders in their fields—the stars of the academic world.

2. University Named Professorships — Minimum endowment: **$250,000**

An endowed professorship allows the University to attract—and to keep—top-flight faculty, by supplementing departmental support. Funds are used to provide salary supplements, graduate assistant stipends, secretarial help, and travel expenses. As with named chairs, this kind of support can influence the caliber of faculty we are able to recruit, as well as the quality of teaching and instruction a department is able to provide.

3. University Endowed Fellowships — Minimum contribution: **$100,000**

Faculty fellowships allow the University to provide extra funds to outstanding faculty members. These funds help those who receive them to further their work in teaching, research, and public service. Endowment income goes toward paying graduate assistants, secretarial support, and travel expenses.

4. Graduate Fellowships — Minimum contribution: **$50,000**

To further its mission as a great research and teaching institution, Penn State must recruit the brightest graduate students and reward them in keeping with their respective needs, responsibilities, and stages of academic development.

5. Undergraduate Scholarships

The Penn State scholarship program has a dual purpose: to attract the most promising students to the University and to make a University education available to every qualified student, regardless of the individual's background or financial position. Endowed scholarship funds provide the necessary support.

There are three ways to institute a named scholarship:

A. A gift of $25,000

A gift of $25,000 or more will be used to fund an **Academic Excellence Scholarship.** As a specially targeted area of scholarship funding within the Campaign, this premier scholarship is offered to students who are invited to participate in the Penn State University Scholars Program.

B. A gift of $15,000

A gift of $15,000 or more is used to establish a separate endowment fund scholarship. The donor is free to establish selection requirements for those receiving the scholarship, provided the established terms fall within the law and do not unreasonably restrict the scholarship.

C. A gift of $10,000

A gift of at least $10,000 can be used to establish a named scholarship in one of four already existing University endowed scholarship programs. These cover the areas of greatest need for scholarship support. Separate guidelines have been established for each of these programs:

i. Alumni Memorial Scholarship — These scholarships are awarded on merit, to recruit students of the highest caliber.

ii. Penn State National Merit Scholars Scholarship — Selection for these scholarships is based on procedures administered by the National Merit Scholarship Corporation.

iii. Penn State National Achievement Scholars Scholarship — These scholarships are awarded to black students selected under the National Achievement Scholars Program of the National Merit Scholarship Corporation.

iv. Renaissance Scholarship — These are awarded to the "brightest of the neediest" students.

6. Buildings, Roads, and Plazas

Where buildings are constructed using private funds, such as the Greenberg Indoor Sports Complex and the Ag Arena, whole buildings or parts of buildings may be named for donors. Roads and plazas can also be named. Each instance is individually reviewed, in accordance with established University policy. Proposed names must be approved by the President and the Board of Trustees.

Again these are only examples of ways in which a generous contribution can be a lasting reminder of the donor, or someone the donor wishes to honor or commemorate. The Campaign committee will be happy to discuss ideas for other kinds of named gifts.

THE CAMPAIGN FOR PENN STATE

How to make your gift:
Outright gifts and deferred gifts

The academic world is just as intensely competitive as the world of business; we are by no means immune to market forces and economic constraints. Neither our size nor our achievements can protect us. If Penn State is not only to survive, but to prosper in its established academic goals, we must reward and support scholars of outstanding distinction; attract the most promising students; and see they have what they need to realize their potential and meet new challenges as they arise.

We hope that the preceding pages have given you a broader and more vivid impression of the true worth of the University. Now we turn to you for your support.

The Campaign for Penn State aims to secure both immediate, outright gifts, and pledges of contributions to be completed over a number of years. So, if you are wondering how you can best help the University, we suggest you consider the following alternatives.

Outright gifts are the simplest to make, provide the greatest tax benefit to the donor, and enable the University to take advantage of immediate opportunities.

Under present tax laws, gifts of cash are deductible for the full amount of the gift, unless they exceed 50 percent of the donor's adjusted gross income. In this case, the donor may not deduct the full amount in a single year. The excess can be carried forward for up to five more years.

Gifts of appreciated securities and real estate owned by the donor for at least six months may be deducted for the full fair market value at the time of the gift. This deduction can be claimed provided it does not exceed 30 percent of adjusted gross income, with a five-year carryover for any excess. No capital gains tax is levied on the appreciation.

Certain gifts of property are subject to valuation and substantiation requirements, and current law imposes penalties for overvaluing such gifts. If you are considering a gift of real or personal property, we recommend that you consult the Office of University Development and your legal advisers.

In general, deferred gifts are those—legally committed to the University during the donor's lifetime—in which the donor retains some personal interest, such as the right to use the property or to receive income from the gift. Deferred gifts cannot be put to use by the University until some time later, usually after the death of the named beneficiaries.

The University encourages these gifts, since they provide an endowment for the future. And donors often find that they are in a position to make a larger gift by careful selection of the most appropriate form of contribution. For example, by reserving the right to receive income on a gift, it is possible to protect an estate and provide for family members. A charitable deduction is allowed for a part of the value of the assets transferred.

Older alumni and friends may prefer the deferred gift or they may choose to combine a deferred gift with an outright gift in making their Campaign commitment. The most suitable kind of gift depends on the contributor's circumstances, but whatever your circumstances, the staff of Penn State's Planned Giving Office can provide you, as well as your legal and financial advisers, with the help you need to make your decision.

Woodland Building, Ogontz Campus

Hayfield House, Wilkes-Barre Campus

Classroom Building, Schuylkill Campus

Science Hall, Mont Alto Campus

Figure 20.2. Penn State also prepared a separate smaller piece that described the rationale for the campaign. This is a summary of the case statement, which answers key questions about the campaign.

1.
What Is
The Campaign for
Penn State?

The Campaign for Penn State is a five-year effort to raise $200 million from private sources. Campaign funds will be used to strengthen Penn State for continued academic leadership on a national scale.

2.
In What Ways Will
Campaign Money Be Used?

The $200 million goal is targeted for six critical areas of need:

— $57.5 million to create endowed faculty positions — chairs, professorships, and fellowships — to retain and attract the best teacher-scholars;

— $32.7 million to endow scholarship funds for undergraduates and fellowship funds for graduate students;

— $12.9 million to enhance existing academic programs and to support new initiatives in instruction, research, and public service;

— $9.3 million to augment the collections — special and disciplinary — of the University libraries;

— $52.6 million to construct new academic facilities throughout the Penn State system, and to purchase research/instructional equipment; and,

— $35-$50 million in annual support enhancement to strengthen a variety of academic areas, according to donor specifications.

3. Who Is Running the Campaign?

The Campaign is being mounted by an executive committee of thirty-two national business and civic leaders, most of them Penn State graduates. The Campaign chairman is William A. Schreyer, chairman and CEO of Merrill Lynch and Company, Inc. The three Campaign vice chairmen are Edward Hintz, president of Hintz and Holman, Inc.; Frank Smeal, limited partner in Goldman, Sachs Company; and Joe Paterno, Penn State head football coach. The Campaign treasurer is Robert Eberly, Sr., chairman of the board of Gallatin National Bank.

In addition, a national campaign committee, consisting of about 100 volunteers from across the country, is being formed. Staff support for the Campaign is being provided by the Division of Development and University Relations, under the leadership of Vice President G. David Gearhart.

4. When Does the Campaign Begin?

The Campaign is well under way. Campaign gifts have been counted since July 1, 1984. When the Campaign was announced publicly on September 13, 1986, $85 million — or 43 percent of the $200 million goal — had been raised.

5. Is This Penn State's First Major Gifts Campaign?

Yes, for all intents and purposes. An Emergency Building Fund Campaign was conducted from 1921 to 1924, and limited fund-raising campaigns for buildings have been held at various Commonwealth Campuses. The current Campaign, however, is by far the most comprehensive major gifts effort ever undertaken by the University. And the purpose is primarily to create endowments for academic programs, rather than to expand the physical plant.

6. Are the Commonwealth Campuses, King of Prussia Graduate Center, Behrend College, Capital College, and The Hershey Medical Center Involved in The Campaign for Penn State?

Yes. The Campaign for Penn State is a comprehensive, systemwide effort. All of the Commonwealth Campuses have set specific goals for endowment and enhancement funds for academic enrichment and/or building projects. A total of $3.25 million will be raised for endowment or enhancement at seven campuses (Allentown, Beaver, Delaware, Fayette, McKeesport, Mont Alto, Ogontz) and the King of Prussia Graduate Center. A total of $13.95 million will be raised from community-based campaigns for major building projects at ten campuses (Altoona, Berks, DuBois, Hazleton, New Kensington, Schuylkill, Shenango Valley, Wilkes-Barre, Worthington Scranton, and York). *The total goal for the Commonwealth Campuses and King of Prussia Graduate Center is $17.2 million.*

In addition, *Behrend College* in Erie has identified $12.25 million of needs to be funded. Penn State's *Capital College* in Harrisburg plans to raise $1.35 million for specific needs. And the University's *Milton S. Hershey Medical Center* has a $20.15 million Campaign goal.

7. Why Is a Public University Such as Penn State Seeking Private Gift Support?

Although Penn State is the Commonwealth's land-grant university, it is not state-owned, but *state-related.* As such, Penn State receives only about 23 percent of its total *operating budget from the state.* The fourteen state-owned universities, by contrast, receive about 50 percent of their revenue from the state.

The proportion of state support for Penn State's operating budget has been declining for years. In 1975-76, the state appropriation composed 33.1 percent of Penn State's total operating budget; in 1985-86, the state appropriation accounted for 23.3 percent of the total operating budget, a decline of about 1 percent per year.

Thus, in order to provide the Commonwealth and the nation with instruction, research, and service programs of the highest quality, Penn State must seek its operating revenue from a variety of sources, including private gifts.

8. If Penn State Attracts Substantial Sums of Private Support Through The Campaign for Penn State, Is it Likely the Legislature Will Decrease Penn State's Appropriation Accordingly?

No. Based on the record of other states where public institutions have conducted successful campaigns for private funds, there is no reason to expect reduced legislative support. To the contrary, voluntary gift support can present compelling evidence to legislators of the quality and value of a university.

And in Pennsylvania, the Governor's Commission on the Financing of Higher Education (1985, chaired by Robert E. Kirby) has recommended that:

Private support should be considered to be supplemental to state support and no public institution raising private funds should receive less state support because of its success in doing so.

9. Why Are So Many Public Universities Launching Capital Campaigns?

Because of declining levels of support from state governments, in addition to the continuing uncertainties of state and federal support for higher education. Moreover, state support, for the most part, covers basic operating expenses. It does not provide the discretionary money to support improvements and enhancements to academic programs in the way that private funds do. It should be emphasized, as well, that the leading American universities are extraordinarily competitive with one another. They compete fiercely for talented faculty, students, and facilities in an era of limited governmental resources. Today, in fact, it's rare to find a major public university that is not in the midst of a major gifts campaign, or at least planning one.

10.
What Are the Most Compelling Arguments for Philanthropic Support of Public Colleges and Universities?

The most compelling reasons for private support of public universities lie in their intrinsic value to our nation. Public higher education extends an opportunity to millions of students — especially minority students — who otherwise could not afford college. Moreover, public college and university students — who compose about 80 percent of all college students — deserve an education that is better than adequate.

Public universities also offer a range of instructional programs unavailable elsewhere. Nearly nine out of every ten American engineers are graduates of public universities, and virtually all instruction in agriculture is offered at these same institutions. In addition, public universities receive about half of all funds allocated to research in all American universities. Because of their critical contributions to a knowledge-driven society, public universities must not be allowed to languish. That would not be in the national interest.

11.
How Will the Campaign Enhance Penn State's Competitive Posture?

By giving the University the means to compete more vigorously for the very best faculty and students in a national market. Many of Penn State's top faculty are being actively recruited with attractive compensation packages from other institutions. In 1984-85, Penn State had to scramble fifteen times to retain eminent faculty members who were being lured with offers from other leading institutions.

For instance, a professor in Penn State's College of Science received this offer from a prestigious university: $100,000 annual salary; a $300,000 grant for new equipment; 5,000 square feet of lab space; and secretarial support.

And just as endowed faculty positions help to attract and retain superb faculty members, endowed scholarship and fellowship funds do likewise for talented students. Consider the impact of the $5.6 million bequest Penn State received in 1984-85 from the estate of Homer Frick Braddock '06. The Braddock bequest was designated for the creation of endowed scholarship and fellowship funds in the College of Science.

In the fall of 1985 alone, the College of Science awarded Braddock Scholarships to twenty talented undergraduates — most of whom turned down attractive offers from Ivy League institutions to attend Penn State. At the graduate level, the college used the Braddock endowment to attract three National Science Foundation (NSF) Graduate Fellowship winners, five NSF honorable mention winners, and four outstanding graduate students who were outside the NSF competition. In one year, the Braddock bequest has had a dramatic effect on enhancing quality in the College of Science.

12.
More Precisely, How Does The Campaign for Penn State Fit in with Penn State's Goal for the Future?

Penn State's overarching goal is to achieve recognition as one of the nation's very best public research universities — in a league with the University of California at Berkeley and at Los Angeles, the University of Texas at Austin, and the Universities of Minnesota, Washington, Illinois, Wisconsin, Indiana, North Carolina, and Virginia.

Penn State has a three-part strategy to achieve that status: to generate increased funding from the public sector, through increased state appropriations; to generate increased funding from the private sector, through The Campaign for Penn State; and to apply those funds in the most effective manner — in areas where they will do the most good — as determined by the University's strategic planning process.

13.
What Kind of Progress Has Penn State Been Making in Private Gift Support in Recent Years?

Dramatic progress. In the last ten years, Penn State's private gift support has increased sixfold. In 1975-76, the University attracted $5.77 million from donors; in 1985-86, the University raised $37.6 million from private sources.

14.
In What Ways Can a Gift Be Made to The Campaign for Penn State?

A Campaign gift may be given in one or more of the following ways:

— A pledge with payments spanning three to five years
— A onetime cash payment
— Appreciated, marketable stocks or securities
— Closely held securities
— Real estate (mortgaged or unencumbered)
— Gifts-in-kind (works of art, equipment, crop shares, livestock, warehouse receipts, etc.)
— Life income plans such as charitable remainder unitrusts, charitable remainder annuity trusts, pooled income funds, and gift annuities
— Charitable remainder lead trusts
— Remainder interests in residence or farm
— Corporate matching gifts

For further information, contact:

THE CAMPAIGN FOR PENN STATE
116 Old Main
The Pennsylvania State University
University Park, PA 16802
(814) 863-4826

Figure 20.3. Not all case statements must be as elaborate as Penn State's. Here are some excerpts from a case for the Pine Canyon Ranch for Boys in Salt Lake City, Utah. The case explains the history of the organization, its plans and its needs.

To Help With Your Contribution

CASH
Checks payable to Pine Canyon Ranch for Boys should be mailed to the address listed above.

SECURITIES
Registered securities should be sent unassigned to the address listed above. Stock powers or Bond powers, endorsed with signatures guaranteed by bank or broker, should be forwarded under separate cover. You may deliver the securities to your broker requesting him to contact the Development Office.

REAL ESTATE
Send a deed naming Pine Canyon Ranch for Boys Inc. as the owner of the property by registered mail to the Development Office.

TANGIBLE PROPERTY
Call or write the Development Office to arrange for pickup of items of tangible property.

CHARITABLE REMAINDER TRUSTS
The Development Office can make arrangements for the establishment of a tax-saving charitable remainder trust. There is no obligation for this service.

INSURANCE POLICIES, COLLECTIONS, AND OTHER ASSETS
Please name Pine Canyon Ranch for Boys, Inc.

BEQUESTS BY WILL
Bequest should specify "Pine Canyon Ranch for Boys, Inc. a non-profit Utah charitable corporation." We will be pleased to provide additional information to your legal or financial counsel upon request.

18

Tax Information

Pine Canyon Ranch for Boys, Inc., became a non-profit corporation in the State of Utah, April 15, 1969. On August 5, 1969, Internal Revenue Service granted the following exemptions: a charitable and educational organization; contributions made to the organization are deductible by the donors; bequests, legacies, devises, transfers or gifts are deductible for Federal estate and gift tax purposes. A favorable response to Form 4653, determining Pine Canyon Ranch for Boys not to be a private foundation, was granted November 9, 1970; this classification has not been challenged. Our Federal Identification number is 87-0280502.

Chapter 21
Getting it all Done on Time and Within Budget

Campaign Master Plan

We reviewed the details of the planning process earlier when talking about major gifts programs. The same elements of planning play a big role in capital campaigns. An important early step in campaign planning is to translate the organization's long-range plan into a master plan for the campaign. This master plan is for distribution to everyone involved with the organization and the campaign. It should include:

■ Overall campaign objectives
■ Campaign policies
■ Campaign organizational chart
■ Table of needed gifts
■ Campaign job descriptions—staff, volunteers, consultants and administration
■ Budget and rationale for increased expenditures
■ Campaign schedule
■ Basic strategy outline for the campaign
■ Proposed printed materials
■ Cultivation plans
■ Prospect pool analysis

Figure 21.1. This is the master plan prepared for the Wayne Hospital Building Fund Campaign in Ohio.

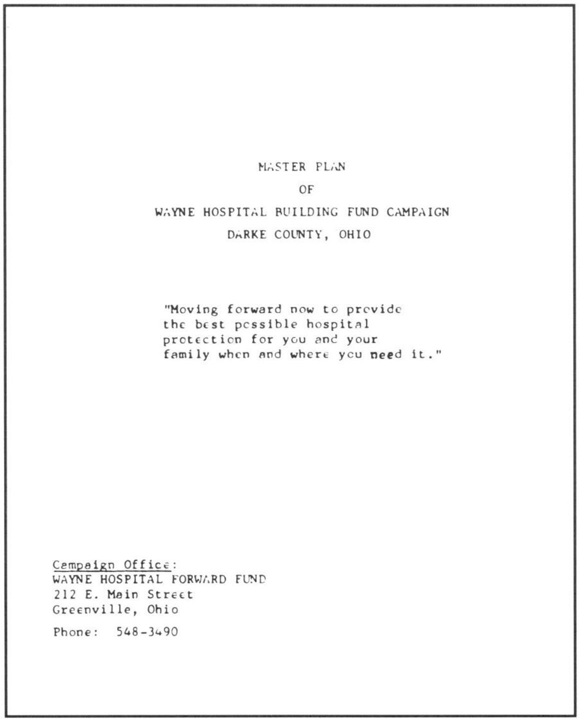

```
                    MASTER PLAN
                        OF
        WAYNE HOSPITAL BUILDING FUND CAMPAIGN
                DARKE COUNTY, OHIO


            "Moving forward now to provide
            the best possible hospital
            protection for you and your
            family when and where you need it."




    Campaign Office:
    WAYNE HOSPITAL FORWARD FUND
    212 E. Main Street
    Greenville, Ohio
    Phone:  548-3490
```

PURPOSE

To obtain a minimum of $1,000,000 in a public subscription campaign for the $2,300,000 modernization and expansion program of Wayne Hospital to meet the Hospital's needs so it may provide the best health care possible for its patients.

NEW WING

Medical Records	Administrator's Office
Drug Room	Office, Director of Pharmacy
Central Kitchen	Dietitian's Office
Employee Dining Room	X-Ray Storage
Central Linen Supply	Conference and Class Room
Employee Locker Rooms	Mechanical Power Plant
25-Bed Medical-Surgical Nursing Unit	

MODERNIZATION

8-Bed Special Care Unit including 5-Bed Intensive Care and Postoperative Recovery, and a 3-Bed Coronary Care Unit. Special equipment will include Cardiac Monitoring Equipment, Closed TV Circuit, and direct telephone communications system with Cardiology Clinic in Dayton.

New areas for Out-Patient Department, X-Ray, Eye Examination and Treatment Room; Physical Therapy and Inhalation Therapy, Visitor's Lounge, Private Room for seriously ill patients.

NEW EQUIPMENT

New surgical instruments, portable x-ray, x-ray accessories, electronic calculator, oxygen analyzer, microscope, Coulter Counter, dietary equipment, office equipment and furnishings, McBee data processing equipment.

PLAN OF OPERATION

The following outlines the campaign organization and sets forth the guide lines as related to policy in the conduct of the campaign.

PREPARED BY:

Daniel J. Polito, Campaign Director

CAMPAIGN CABINET

The Campaign Cabinet shall have the responsibility
for establishing the policies to be followed. This
group shall be composed of the Campaign General
Chairman, the Chairman of the Executive Committee
of the Hospital, the Chairman of each Soliciting
Phase and the Chairman of the Service Divisions.
The Administrator of the hospital shall serve as a
member of the Cabinet.

The responsibility for the conduct of the Campaign
shall be vested in the Cabinet with full authority
to act in all matters effecting the Campaign in
accordance with general policies established by the
Executive Committee.

The basic purpose of this group is to hear reports
of progress or problems of all committees and assist
the campaign director in policy decisions.

The Campaign Cabinet should meet regularly once a
week. Friday meetings, perhaps lasting less than
an hour, are recommended. The main consideration
is that the committee can review what has happened
during the week and can anticipate needs for the
next week.

GENERAL POLICY STATEMENT

1.   Pledge Period

      a. This will be a pledge campaign; payments
          thereunder to be made over a period of
          three years.

      b. Payments on pledges may be made at the
          option of the donor; annually, semi-
          annually, quarterly or monthly, or under
          such arrangements as he may specify within
          the period indicated.

2.   The Campaign Cabinet will be authorized to accept
      "Letters of Intent" from corporations, individuals
      and certain non-profit associations to permit com-
      mitments beyond their current fiscal year.

3.   The Campaign Cabinet may, in special circumstances
      involving major gifts, extend the period of pro-
      jected payment as the situation may warrant.

4.   Where circumstances require, the Campaign Cabinet
      may permit donors to qualify their pledges to the
      effect that in the case of death or other desig-
      nated reasons, such portions of the pledge due at
      the time of death or other designated reason shall
      be declared void and not become a liability against
      the estate of the deceased.

5.   The Campaign Cabinet shall be authorized to accept
      gifts from any source provided, however, that
      there is no condition attached thereto inconsis-
      tent with the purpose of the campaign or in viola-
      tion of any legal or ethical principles or policies
      of the hospital.

GENERAL POLICY STATEMENT (con't)

6.   The Campaign Cabinet shall be authorized to accept gifts of real and/or personal property, including securities. All securities will be immediately transferred to the Campaign Treasurer who shall issue an acknowledgement to the donor indicating the fair market value of such securities as of the date of transfer.

7.   A policy must be determined relative to the sale of securities. A committee may be appointed to determine whether such securities should be converted immediately or held for future conversion. Campaign credit will be based on the fair market value of such securities as of the date of transfer.

8.   The Campaign Cabinet shall be authorized to establish and accept memorial gifts under such terms and conditions as it may determine.

9.   A Finance and Audit Committee shall be appointed to assist in the receipt and audit of all monies and pledges received during the progress of the campaign, and shall be responsible for the safekeeping of such funds.

10.   A Campaign Treasurer shall be designated to be responsible for the receipt of all monies, securities, personal and/or real property, and all pledges received during the period of the campaign. He shall issue receipts to the Campaign Office for all monies, securities, pledges and records turned over to him; and he shall deposit all funds in accordance with the instructions established by the Hospital Executive Committee.

PROCEDURES

The Trustees and Executive Committee of Wayne Hospital have the responsibility for the raising of the necessary funds for the expansion program through the duly appointed General Campaign Chairman

The Campaign Cabinet will administer the fund-raising efforts, with full authority to act under such policies as may be determined:

1.   To launch an education and publicity program through all media to create a wider understanding of the total expansion program.

2.   For the preparation of prospect lists, the study and analysis of potential areas and sources of support, and the assignment of the prospect card to the individual best able to contact and obtain a subscription.

3.   To enlist volunteers to serve on committees and to make personal solicitation of corporations, firms, individuals, clubs and organizations, foundations, estates and trusts for subscriptions to this program.

4.   To effectively prepare the prospect prior to solicitation by use of brochures, other printed matter, newspaper and radio publicity, speakers at meetings, etc.

5.   To provide training and indoctrination of volunteer workers to insure that each solicitor is thoroughly familiar with the program, is prepared to answer questions and is instructed in the proper technique of approaching the prospect to secure maximum support.

6.   To arrange announcement and Kick-Off dinners to create enthusiasm and to weld the volunteer organizations into a loyal, cohesive, determined and dedicated force working for better hospital care.

7.   To establish a series of report meetings to check the progress of the solicitation by the several divisions.

8.   To effect an organization of mop-up operations to insure that all prospects are covered, and the establishment of administrative and collection procedures to follow the campaign.

SPECIFIC AREAS OF POTENTIAL SUPPORT

OFFICIAL FAMILY   This area is composed of the Trustees,
                   Executive Committee, Medical Staff,
                   Auxiliary, and full time and part time
                   employees of Wayne Hospital.

CORPORATIONS   Major industrial and corporate busi-
                   nesses in the hospital service area
                   should be approached to subscribe to
                   the Forward Fund on the basis of cor-
                   porate good citizenship invoked in
                   their interest in providing total,
                   modern hospital care for their execu-
                   tives, employees and their dependents.

INDIVIDUALS   In every community there are men and
                   women of substantial means who can be
                   interested in supporting a worthwhile
                   cause even though they may never re-
                   ceive any direct benefit from it. They
                   will act as a matter of community
                   responsibility.

                   Consideration must be given to contact-
                   ing not only those individuals active
                   in business and industry, but also those
                   who are not so identified and whose
                   potential giving ability warrants their
                   cultivation and solicitation.

SPECIFIC AREAS OF POTENTIAL SUPPORT (con't)

FOUNDATIONS   Foundations, Trusts and Estates whose
                   fields of interest are Ohio and Darke
                   County philanthropic institutions
                   including hospitals, should also be
                   approached for they are excellent
                   sources of support.

COMMERCIAL AND
SERVICE BUSINESSES Retail and service concerns throughout
                   the hospital service area should be
                   solicited for support from the firm
                   owner and/or executives and employees.

CLUBS AND ORGANIZATIONS There are many community, service
                   and civic clubs, labor union organiza-
                   tions, fraternal and veteran organiza-
                   tions and other groups that can be
                   interested in supporting this campaign.
                   Such support will be sought as treasury
                   gifts, and not as a basis of soliciting
                   or assessing their members.

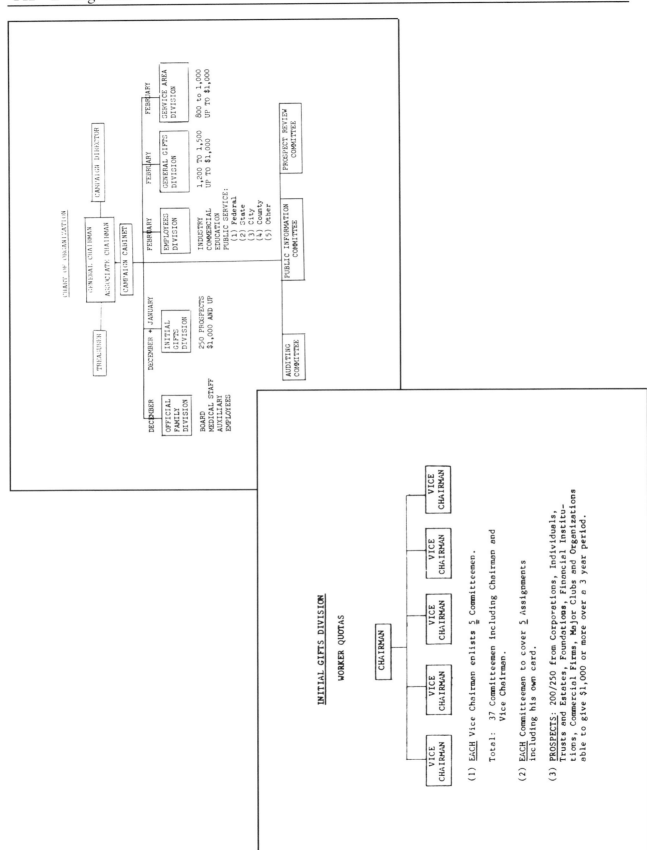

GENERAL GIFTS DIVISION

WORKER QUOTAS

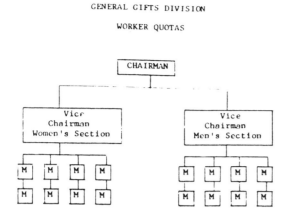

(1) EACH Section Vice Chairman enlists 8 Majors.

(2) EACH Section Major enlists 5 Team Captains (total 40).

(3) EACH Team Captain enlists 5 Campaigners (total 200).

(4) EACH Committeeman to cover 5 to 6 assignments including his own card.

(5) PROSPECTS: 1,200 to 1,500 from Small Business, Individuals, Families, Clubs and Organizations able to give up to $1,000 over a 3 year pledge period.

JOB DESCRIPTIONS - COMMITTEE FUNCTIONS

GENERAL CHAIRMAN

The General Campaign Chairman will occupy the most important position of any individual in the campaign organization. It will be his responsibility, with the aid and cooperation of the Campaign Cabinet to select and appoint each of the Division Chairmen as well as several of the committee heads.

It should be pointed out with pride that the Board of Trustees has selected an outstanding citizen of Greenville to serve in this capacity. Mr. William C. Rhodes, Secretary-Treasurer of American Aggregates Corporation has accepted this important responsibility.

The General Chairman should preside at all meetings of the Campaign Cabinet and either preside or delegate this responsibility at all other Campaign meetings of general character. He should also give counsel and leadership and development and direction of the entire campaign.

OFFICIAL FAMILY PHASE

This is the first step or phase of the campaign.

The average person not closely associated with Wayne Hospital takes it for granted that the board members, professional staff, and those associated directly with the hospital in other capacities, are the best qualified to judge the needs for expanded facilities.

It is therefore important that these best informed persons thus prove the need for the program by working for it and contributing generously.

JOB DESCRIPTIONS - COMMITTEE FUNCTIONS, (con't)

The "OFFICIAL FAMILY", comprised of the Trustees, Executive Committee members, Medical Staff, Auxiliary, nurses, and other employees, have the responsibility in setting the pace or leading the way, thus giving concrete proof of their belief in the need for the enlarged facilities.

The Chairman of this important segment of the campaign will enlist a committee from the hospital to assist him in effectively soliciting investments from the "Family".

INITIAL GIFTS DIVISION CHAIRMAN

The Chairman of this division is in charge of the committee that will seek subscriptions from the corporations, foundations, trusts, and estates, financial institutions, business firms, major clubs and organizations, and individuals who will make the largest contributions.

Committee members will consist of those citizens whose influence is such as they can secure gifts of $1,000 and up. This will be a relatively small committee and the members will undoubtedly be members of the Campaign Cabinet or hold places of responsibility in the campaign organization.

This is the most important solicitation division in the campaign, as the contributors in this group will be prospects so rated as to set the pattern of giving throughout the other divisions. The amount of money raised in this campaign will be in direct ratio to how much is produced in other divisions. There will be approximately 250 prospects in this division.

JOB DESCRIPTIONS - COMMITTEE FUNCTIONS (con't)

The Initial Gifts Division should be completely organized before any of the Chairmen have been selected for the remaining divisions.

All prospects are assigned with those workers accepting as valid the evaluations.

This division should have two reports before it becomes part of the general reporting program of the campaign.

All Initial Gifts cards are specifically assigned. This is generally accomplished by a committee made up of a selected group of the Board, plus the General Chairman, the chairman of the Initial Gifts, and the vice chairmen in this division.

GENERAL GIFTS DIVISION

This division makes our campaign the so-called broad base campaign. It is one of the most important to the campaign as it does much to promote community spirit and total involvement -- "everybody benefits, everybody gives".

There will be approximately 1,500 prospects in this division including small business owners, professionals, individuals, small clubs and organizations, etc.

SERVICE AREA DIVISION

The hospital service area is made up of a number of small communities mostly within Darke County. Each community must be organized with a chairman and campaign organization.

JOB DESCRIPTIONS - COMMITTEE FUNCTIONS (con't)

Organization meetings are held locally, or wherever feasible, combined with neighboring communities.

All prospects that meet the qualification for Initial Gifts are selected for the Initial Gifts Division before cards are distributed to the Service Area group.

EMPLOYEES DIVISION

Employees from all sectors of Darke County will be invited to contribute to the hospital building program. This division will include all industrial, commercial, financial, educational and public service employees in the hospital service area.

As each campaigner (solicitor) is selected for an assignment in this division, he must be able to follow through with his assignment. That is to say, in the case of an industrial plant he will meet with the president or plant manager to secure his cooperation for payroll deduction and in-plant solicitation of employees on company time. He will arrange for an employee kickoff rally within the plant and make arrangements for a 15 minute information program. He will also arrange for a key man (chairman) to be appointed to follow through the in-plant solicitation after he has been trained for the purpose at a key man training meeting presided over by the Campaign director.

NON-SOLICITING COMMITTEES

I.   PUBLIC INFORMATION COMMITTEE

The importance of this committee cannot be overemphasized because it provides a basis for the public to understand and know the reasons for the hospital building program. Unless the public is thoroughly informed, particularly employees, they will not respond.

The Public Information Committee should be divided into three separate subcommittees:

(1) Publicity: This group will be concerned with the promotion of the campaign through newspapers, radio and television; creative programs for radio and TV; securing of billboard space, distribution of posters, store front displays, etc.

(2) Speakers: This group has the responsibility of getting detailed information to the public by means of speaking before all organized groups within the community as well as employee meetings.

The Speakers Committee should be made up of no less than fifteen people, qualified and trained to speak five minutes, ten minutes, or a twenty minute period.

A Speaker's packet including a suggested speech and informational literature will be prepared by the public relations director.

A color slide presentation and a flip chart presentation will be developed along with a script for use by speakers.

NON-SOLICITING COMMITTEES (con't)

The Chairman of this committee should line up speaking engagements with the help and coordination of the campaign director.

(3) Church: This committee will work with ministers, priests and church lay leaders to present the "hospital story" to total membership of all religious groups.

II.   PROSPECT REVIEW COMMITTEE

This is the name for the process of developing suggested amounts for prospect consideration. In its simplest form, it is nothing more or less than an attempt to discover the sources from which the money needed can be raised.

III   AUDIT COMMITTEE

This committee is headed up by the Treasurer of the Wayne Hospital Forward Fund.

In addition to the Treasurer, a committee of two to four men assists him in auditing pledges, with transmittals and bank deposits. These should be audited before the next report meeting. No pre-report meeting audit is made. Reports are taken from campaigners on face value, and scoreboards are posted accordingly. After the report meeting, a bulletin goes to all workers with the scoreboard as filled out at the report meeting. The report envelopes are audited, deposit slips are made out with the name and amount of all cash and checks for easy verification later and all materials pertaining to the pledge is entered on the division card which is the permanent office record.

NON-SOLICITING COMMITTEE (con't)

Making transmittals after each report meeting and transferring them to the treasurer assists the director, for at the end of the campaign he has but one transmittal remaining.

After each report meeting and the audit is made, the scoreboard is then corrected for the next meeting. This is continued until the last meeting, at which time the audit is made before the meeting in order to prevent duplication for the final report.

CAMPAIGN PUBLIC INFORMATION PROGRAM

Informing prospective donors of the plans to up-date
Wayne Hospital to serve the people of Darke County is
essential for the success of the WAYNE HOSPITAL FORWARD
FUND. Information will be disseminated internally (to
members of the "Hospital Family", members of the campaign organizations, selected prospects) through
printed materials, meetings, and bulletins and exter-
nally (general public) through newspapers, radio,
other mass media.

Included in the information program will be a baker's
dozen of projects:

I.   CASE FOR SUPPORT -- A documentation of the
     needs and the financial requirements to meet
     those needs. This will be the basis for all
     communications relative to the WAYNE HOSPITAL
     FORWARD FUND.

II. BROCHURE -- A graphic presentation of the case
     for the Hospital, including suggestions as to
     the type of giving necessary, Memorial Oppor-
     tunities, and a notation of the leaders who
     have accepted volunteer responsibilities in
     the campaign. This is the major piece for
     prospective donors in the lead divisions of
     the campaign and for all workers.

III. QUESTIONS AND ANSWERS -- Questions that have
     been asked and which are anticipated will be
     answered in this piece for use by workers and
     for prospective donors.

CAMPAIGN PUBLIC INFORMATION PROGRAM (con't)

IV.   AUDIO-VISUAL-- A flip chart presentation for
      use with small groups and a slide presentation
      for telling the FORWARD FUND story to larger
      groups.

V.   EMPLOYEE FOLDER -- A concise statement of the
      case and request for support built around the
      "cup-of-coffee a day" concept for distribution
      where employee solicitation is undertaken.

VI.   MEMORIAL FOLDER -- Depending upon the avail-
      abilities, a Memorial Folder will be prepared
      to include an in-depth offering of memorial
      projects which can be subscribed for by donors.

VII. PLEDGE CARDS -- In addition to its function as
      a record of the donor's subscription, the pledge
      card is an informational piece carried by the
      worker in his face-to-face contact with the
      prospect. Pledge cards for the various divisions
      of the campaign organizations and payroll deduc-
      tion authorization cards will be part of the
      printed materials prepared for campaign use.

VIII. WORKER TRAINING SUGGESTIONS -- Techniques for
      successful solicitation and steps to securing
      pledges will be listed and offered in compact
      form for worker use.

CAMPAIGN PUBLIC INFORMATION PROGRAM (con't)

IX. SPEAKER KIT -- Notes and suggestions for
members of the Speaker's Committee are in
preparation and will be available when the
Committee initiates its program.

X. NEWSPAPER, RADIO/TV NEWS RELEASES

XI. PUBLIC SERVICE RADIO AND TV*SPOT ANOUNCEMENTS

XII. The primary written communications among
campaign leaders and workers will be weekly
bulletins after the campaign has been launched.
These are mineographed on attractive bulletin
heads and are educational, informational,
motivational -- designed to give an up-to-the-
minute picture of campaign progress.

Additional printed materials will include
campaign stationery, report envelopes, worker
kits, acknowledgement forms, pledge reminder
forms, Master and Division file cards, transmittal forms, transmittal summary forms,
bulletin heads.

* Efforts will be made to seek TV cooperation.

TENTATIVE CAMPAIGN CALENDAR
October 30, 1972 through March 31, 1973

ADVANCE PHASE

November

November Locate, staff and organize campaign headquarters.
Assemble hospital usage figures and statistics.
Compile list of potential prospects to the campaign. Organize STEERING COMMITTEE. Review and
classify prospects. Plan campaign mechanics.
Outline and develop campaign printed matter and
publicity materials.

November 15 Meeting - Hospital Board to approve Campaign Plan.

November 15 Select and Appoint - Chairman of the Prospect
Review Committee.

November 15 Enlist Chairmen - Hospital Family (Board and
Medical Staff Section, Auxiliary and Employees
Section).

November 24 Meeting - Campaign Cabinet to establish goals
and review potential. (The Campaign Cabinet
should meet regularly, once a week, for the duration of the campaign.)

November 24 Deadline - Completion of Prospect evaluation by
Prospect Review Committee.

November 30 Deadline - Enlistment of Chairmen, Advance Phase
Division (Initial Gifts).

November 30 Meeting - Solicitors, Hospital Employee Section.

```
                    CAMPAIGN BUDGET FOR THE PERIOD
                    OCTOBER 30, 1972 to MARCH 31, 1973

Budget
Account                                        Actual
Number   Account              Allocation       Expenses    Balance

  1.     Duplicating Service   $    300
  2.     Headquarters Equipment    1,750
  3.     Headquarters Payroll      6,000
  4.     Headquarters Rental       1,000
  5.     Headquarters Supplies       500
  6.     Meetings                  1,500
  7.     Postage                   1,000
  8.     Publicity, Printing       5,000
  9.     Telephone & Telegraph       600
 10.     Transportation              250
         Un-allocated Reserve      2,100

                    TOTAL:      $20,000
```

Campaign Schedule

The campaign schedule shows how you are going to accomplish the master plan. You must set up a series of target dates that will lead you toward success in medium-size steps. This schedule will be extremely helpful in programming both staff and volunteer involvement.

When determining the schedule for your campaign, remember that it must have a sense of urgency. A campaign must create the sense that it is aiming to produce gifts *now* and not way down the road.

Russell V. Kohr, writing in the *Handbook of Institutional Advancement*, suggests this year-by-year framework for a five-year effort.

First Year

■ Complete first draft of the long-range plan (involves administration, faculty, staff, trustees, selected friends).

■ Share plan with trustees and selected potential benefactors.

■ Revise plan as necessary.

■ Trustees approve plan and campaign goal.

■ Development office prepares statement of gift opportunities.

■ Development office drafts case statement that is then shared with key people in the organization, trustees, selected friends.

■ Survey various constituencies intensively.

■ Research prospective donors of major gifts in all constituencies.

■ Begin solicitation of major gift, corporate and foundation prospects.

■ Increase annual giving solicitation.

■ A group—such as the president, chairman of the board of trustees and the chairman of the trustee committee on development— enlists a national campaign chairman and members of major gifts committees.

■ Role of the president and other administrative officials in the campaign is determined.

■ Begin solicitation of trustees.

Second Year

- Distribute case statement to national campaign leadership and key prospects.
- Begin solicitation of key prospects.
- Augment staff as necessary.
- Plan major campaign kickoff, other special events.
- Research prospects for special gifts.
- Enlist and train volunteers to solicit special gifts prospects.
- Begin solicitation of special gifts prospects.
- Hold report meetings.

Third Year

- Continue major and special gifts solicitation.
- Research prospects for general campaign.
- Enlist volunteers for general campaign.

Fourth Year

- Distribute case statement to prospects for general campaign.
- Hold campaign kickoff for the local community, if appropriate.
- Hold successive regional campaigns, if appropriate.
- Schedule report meetings, newsletter, public events.

Fifth Year

- Lay plans for post-campaign fund-raising program.
- Complete local community and regional campaigns.
- Hold achievement dinner.

Five years is a long time, and you may not want such a long program. The duration of a campaign fund-raising effort depends on many factors such as: the size and immediacy of your needs, the economic climate at the time, the number of prospects and workers, and the stage of your cultivation activities. For the traditional one-time, large-goal campaign, an oft-tested and seemingly standard schedule is this one:

- Allow nine to 12 months between the decision to "go" and the actual kickoff.
- Take at least one year for major gift solicitations.

- Second-level solicitations start one year after the kickoff and continue until the program ends.
- Then there is a short general solicitation period, preferably the last three to six months of the campaign.
- The average campaign runs 30 to 36 months from kickoff to conclusion, or four years from the decision to "go".

Operating Plan

An operating plan is usually an internal working document that tells who is going to do what, when and how. The format of the capital project is fully detailed, showing all the people involved and how they fit in. The campaign operating plan should be more specific than the campaign master plan because its main purpose is to show how everything fits together and to serve as a working guide for the campaign. Drafting such a plan is a huge job, basically drawing together all key elements of the project into a concise document that everyone can follow.

Timetable

A campaign timetable puts a very specific time framework on the campaign plan. It is prepared to aid both staff and volunteers by showing how elements of the campaign fit together on a time line. A timetable assures that all procedural steps occur in sequence, and it provides a gauge to measure progress. It is much more specific than a campaign schedule.

To create a timetable, it is best to start with the projected date for the end of each stage within the campaign. Then work backward to define necessary steps and how long they will take.

Organizational Chart

An organizational chart pinpoints authority and responsibility in a visual way. One should be drawn up for staff as well as for volunteers, so each person in the campaign knows just where he or she fits in. Organizational charts are usually pyramidal in structure. To create one, start at the top. Look first at your staff. Determine the lines of authority that you want to draw. Will the chief fund-raising officer be the campaign director, or will that be a separate person? If so, how will the staff interact?

Then categorize staff members into levels. It is usually best not to have everyone report di-

rectly to the top unless you have a very small staff. These same points apply to a volunteer organizational chart. And a word of warning: If you have trouble designing your organizational chart, the problem probably rests with the type of organization it is to reflect—not with your artistic abilities.

Figure 21.2. St. Francis Hospital in Wilmington, Delaware, used this campaign timetable.

MONTH	CAMPAIGN	COMMUNICATIONS
June	Establish, equip and staff Campaign Office Prepare Case Statement Start building prospect list Begin printing campaign forms	
July	Prepare Campaign Plan Prepare Advance Gifts Presentation Enlist pro tempore chairman of Campaign Executive Committee Plan Photo Tour Write Announcement of Importance Draft Newsletter series	Announce Campaign
August	Enlist the following: General Chairman Campaign Executive Committee Employee Co-Chairmen Employee Committee Treasurer List Evaluation Chairman Public Relations Chairman Tours Chairman Speakers Bureau Chairman	Article in FC Mail flier to area clubs & organizations Announce Enlistments

MONTH	CAMPAIGN	COMMUNICATIONS
August	Make Advance Gift Presentations Hold Photo Tour Complete forms preparation Prepare Brochure Develop Slide Presentation Prepare View Book	
September	Employee Committee meets Employee Orientation Employee Kickoff Meet with Junior Board Plan Tours Brochure to printer Enlist the following: Major Gifts Chairman/men Medical Staff Chairman/men Speakers Bureau members Executive Committee meets Enlist Medical Staff committee	Mail Announcement of Importance Announce Enlistments Announce Tours Announce Jr. Bd. Gift Report Employee progress Article for FC
October	Enroll list evaluation committee Complete listing Start list evaluation Medical Staff Orientation Medical Staff Kickoff Enlist Major Gifts Committee Medical Staff Report Meetings Executive Committee meets	Mail 1st Newsletter Article for FC Announce enlistments Continue Tours Start Speakers Bureau Mail 2nd Newsletter

CAMPAIGN TIMETABLE

This outline shows activities necessary to maintain orderly progress of the campaign. Exact dates for meetings, events, etc. will be established by committee chairmen as appropriate.

MONTH	CAMPAIGN	COMMUNICATIONS
November	Major Gifts Orientation Major Gifts Kickoff Enlist Special Gifts Chairman/men Executive Committee meets	Article for FC Continue Tours Speakers Bureau Announce Progress
December	Major Gifts Report Meetings Enlist Special Gifts Team Captains Enlist General Gifts Chairman	Article for FC Announce enlistments Continue Tours Speakers Bureau
January	Enlist Special Gifts Teams Special Gifts Orientation Enlist General Gifts Division leaders Executive Committee meets Major Gifts Report Meetings	Article for FC Continue Tours Report Progress
February	Enlist General Gifts Team Captains Enlist General Gifts Team members Special Gifts Kickoff Special Gifts Report Meetings Executive Committee meets	Article for FC Speakers Bureau
March	General Gifts Orientation General Gifts Kickoff Special Gifts Reports Executive Committee meets	Celebrity Speaker? Display Start Radio and TV Spots Article for FC Speakers Bureau Announce Progress

MONTH	CAMPAIGN	COMMUNICATIONS
April	General Gifts Report Meetings Executive Committee meets	Article for FC Speakers Bureau Continue Radio-TV Spots
May	Conclude General Gifts Direct mail to remaining prospects Executive Committee meets Victory Dinner	Victory Announcement
June	Cleanup	Mail Thank you and Final Bulletin

Figure 21.3. This is the volunteer organization chart used by the Lutheran Home for the Aged in Erie, Pennsylvania.

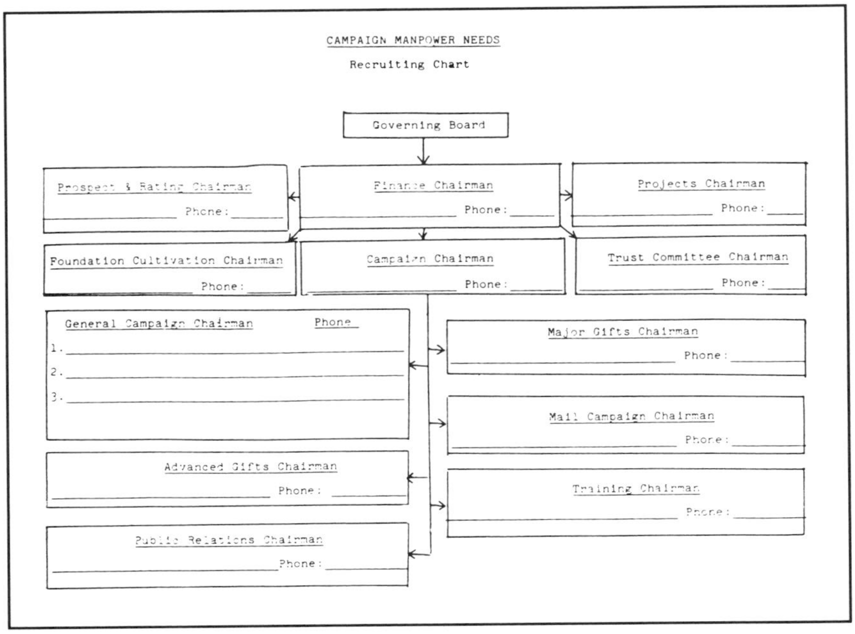

Figure 21.4. These are some excerpts from a Rochester Institute of Technology campaign plan, which includes most of the elements we've discussed so far in this chapter. Detailed job descriptions were also included for the people involved in the campaign.

Rochester Institute of Technology

This document contains a current list of the institutional Capital Campaign objectives to be achieved by Rochester Institute of Technology by 1990. The eventual goal for the Capital Campaign will relate both to the objectives to be achieved and to the fund raising potential. The overall potential will be largely determined by the results of the "Nucleus Fund." The Nucleus Fund is scheduled to take place during 1985 and the first six months of 1986.

Recommended Capital Campaign Projects

On July 16, 1984, the Board of Trustees approved the recommendations of the Strategic Planning Committee concerning the top priority capital campaign projects. These priority items are limited to those considered essential to assuring quality programs and stable or modestly increased enrollment. Physical facilities, building endowment, scholarships, and professorships, equipment, and annual support constitute the recommended project categories.

A market analysis, completed in January 1985, indicated a need to include a facility for Graphic Arts and Photography/Imaging Science in the Campaign. This was accomplished. Elements of the previously identified

CAMPAIGN PLAN

The Campaign not only provides RIT the opportunity to raise funds for these vitally important objectives but at the same time we will win new friends and reinforce relationships with old friends.

Thus, underlying the fund raising objectives are these three long-term advantages:

1. Opportunity to build new enthusiasm and teach/develop new leadership.
2. Opportunity to raise giving sights and broaden the base of support.
3. Provide greater visibility for the development efforts of the Institute--of a long-range nature.

DURATION

The actual planning for the Campaign encompassed 1984. The Campaign will begin January 1, 1985, and will continue through December 31, 1989. Extending the Campaign beyond that date should be done only by action of the Board of Trustees. All gifts and pledges received from December 1, 1983, will count toward the Campaign. A few gifts and pledges made prior to that date concerned with microelectronics will also count because they were made in anticipation of the Campaign.

CAMPAIGN DESIGN

The effort made annually to obtain repeatable gifts from alumni, parents, corporations, foundations, and other friends, which are used for

3

CAMPAIGN PLAN

needs of the College of Applied Science and Technology will be incorporated in the general campaign.

At this time, the estimated project costs for the physical facilities are, in the words of the Strategic Planning Committee, "best guess estimates," based on current data.

Physical Facilities	Estimated Maximum Cost
1. Library Addition	$ 6.5M
2. Microelectronic and Computer Engineering	11.5M
3. Graphic Arts/Imaging Sciences Center	8.5M
4. Campus Life Complex	9.0M
5. RIT City Center Training & Conference Center	4.0M
6. Physical Facilities Endowment Fund	4.5M
7. Endowed Scholarships	9.0M
8. Endowed Professorships	7.0M
9. Equipment	15.0M
10. Annual Support	10.0M
	$85.0M

Many projects of importance have not been included in this top priority list for the campaign. Some of these projects may be fundable through private and government support within or outside the proposed capital campaign priorities.

2

CAMPAIGN PLAN

current educational needs, including student assistance and general budget relief is called Annual Support.

The Capital Campaign is that portion of a comprehensive development program which is devoted specifically to facilities and endowment.

Annual Support is a necessary vehicle to expand the donor base, a market upon which to nurture and build for eventual special level, major, and pace setting gifts.

Annual Support will be "folded into" the overall Capital Campaign in order to preserve continuity and maintain the growth necessary to build for the future. The two fund raising elements are inseparable.

Experience shows that to raise $85 million emphasis must be placed on Major Gifts. While many gifts are to be sought for this campaign, relatively few gifts will comprise the bulk of the funds raised. In other words, approximately 90 percent of the $85 million will come from 1,000 gifts. The following gift table illustrates this point.

4

CAMPAIGN PLAN

GIFT TABLE
$85M

GIFT SIZE	# NEEDED	TOTAL	CUMULATIVE TOTAL
(Top 1/3 of money)			
$ 8M	1	$ 8,000,000	$ 8M
6M	1	6,000,000	14M
5M	1	5,000,000	19M
3M	2	6,000,000	25M
2M	3	6,000,000	31M
(Middle 1/3 of money)			
$ 1M	10	10,000,000	41M
500K	20	10,000,000	51M
200K	30	6,000,000	57M
100K	40	4,000,000	61M
(Lower 1/3 of money)			
$ 50K	100	5,000,000	66M
25K	250	6,250,000	72.250M
10K	600	6,000,000	78.250M
(Lowest 10% of money)			
$ 5K	1,000	5,000,000	83.250M
Below 5K	Many	2,750,000	85M

5

CAMPAIGN PLAN

The Campaign is divided into five phases representing the giving levels:

PHASE I -- Planning, education, involvement (strategy - involve biggest prospects in planning--building "ownership"), leadership recruitment, structuring campaign, market study and temporary setting of campaign goal.

Time Frame: 1984.

PHASE II -- Pace Setting Gifts - to include Nucleus Fund.

Time Frame: Emphasis 1985--through first six months of 1986 With realization this effort will be ongoing throughout the campaign.

PHASE III -- Major Gifts

Time Frame: Category A - 1985--first half of 1986
Categories B & C - 1986
With realization these efforts will also be ongoing for duration of campaign.

PUBLIC ANNOUNCEMENT - Fall of 1986 or when commitments reach 50 percent of goal.

PHASE IV -- Special Gifts
Categories A & B

Time Frame: 1986, 87, 88, 89
With realization this effort will be ongoing throughout the campaign.

PHASE V -- General Gifts
Categories A, B, & C

Time Frame: The focus for seeking capital gifts in Phase V will be 1989. Although this phase is part of the campaign "wrap up," every effort will be made for duration of the campaign to be flexible.

NOTE: 1. Annual Fund will be ongoing throughout each Phase.
2. Equipment Gifts will be sought during each phase.

CAMPAIGN PLAN

Prospects are to be divided into nine giving levels:

A. Pace Setting Gifts--$1,000,000 and above (all Trustees' gifts regardless of size will be counted as Pace Setting Gifts.)

B. Major Gifts

1. $500,000 to $999,999
2. $250,000 to $499,999
3. $100,000 to $249,999

C. Special Gifts

1. $50,000 to $99,999
2. $5,000 to $49,999

D. General Gifts

1. $1,000 to $4,999
2. $500 to $999
3. $1 to $499

The operating theory holds that we want to move from largest prospects down and from closest friends out.

NOTE: Since the Campaign is designed to run five year, the gift's size is based on a five-year payment schedule. For example, a $150,000 gift would be $30,000 a year for five years.

6

CAMPAIGN PLAN

PACE SETTING GIFTS--TO INCLUDE NUCLEUS FUND

Nucleus Fund

The Nucleus Fund represents Trustee giving which is defined as gifts made by Trustees personally or through related business/corporate interests or family foundation, or any combination thereof. This will not include the monies Trustees are expected to raise by virtue of their fund raising responsibilities. Trustees are defined as active, honorary, retired, widows and children of former Trustees. The Nucleus Fund will include the funds raised from the top 16 corporations.

Pace Setting Gifts and Major Gifts

This phase will begin simultaneously with the Nucleus Fund but recognizing serious cultivation must take place in order to prepare these prospects to give at these levels. Therefore, this phase will focus on a select number of pace setting major prospects/donors who are, or will be cultivated so as to be ready for solicitation.

Solicitation of corporations and foundations in the Major Gift category will, of course, be determined by the giving and timing priorities of those organizations.

Cultivation of prospects will not be limited to the year preceding solicitation. Rather, the efforts of staff and volunteers will be focused

9

CAMPAIGN PLAN

primarily on those whose solicitation is scheduled next, but many cultivation activities will involve prospects whose solicitation may not be due for more than a year. However, if any of these reach a readiness for solicitation earlier than programmed, the time of solicitation will be advanced. Solicitation schedules are guidelines not rigid or inflexible timetables.

GUIDELINES FOR SOLICITATION

The following guidelines will be used in developing the strategy for solicitation of Pace Setting/Major Gifts:

1. Only persons who have made their own gifts or pledges will be used as solicitors.

2. Campaign Steering Committee including other key volunteers will be responsible for the solicitation of the Nucleus Fund. The Chairman of the Board will be asked to provide committee leadership with respect to Trustee solicitation. This Committee will be supplemented by a key development staff member or other volunteer leader where appropriate.

3. All donor/prospects with giving potential of $50,000 or more will be solicited by a team of volunteers or a volunteer and staff member.

4. A cultivation-solicitation strategy will be prepared by the Development Officer for each prospect with $50,000 or greater potential.

5. As often as possible, prospects/donors will receive proposals including a "double-ask"; that is, a request for increasing annual

10

CAMPAIGN PLAN

support and a request for a capital gift for a facility or for endowment purposes.

6. Major and Special Donor Prospects (all categories) with giving potential of $5,000 plus will be personally solicited by a team, if possible, or personally by an individual solicitor if necessary.

7. For prospects with $50,000 plus potential, solicitors will be assigned who have the best likelihood of obtaining the gift and without regard to geographical location. For gifts in the $5,000 to $49,999 range, prospects will be assigned to solicitors according to geographic proximity.

8. Prospects will be solicited in descending order of potential, with cultivation efforts and programs focused just on those of greatest potential and gradually extending to other prospects. If a prospect of lesser potential is deemed to be fully cultivated and ready for solicitation, he or she will be solicited when ready, and not delayed until a later time when others of similar potential will be approached. There will also always be "Targets of Opportunity" that will need immediate attention.

9. The highest form of cultivation is personal involvement.

10. Solicitation should occur only after adequate research and cultivation.

GIFTS TO BE COUNTED

A. Gifts of cash, securities, or the equivalent:

11

CAMPAIGN PLAN

1. All contributions made to Annual Support for the period of time from December 1, 1983, to December 31, 1989.

2. All pledges and pledge payments to the Capital Campaign.

3. All Gifts (grants, bequests) to the Capital Campaign made without prior pledges.

4. All gifts and pledges for educational purposes and objectives serving Rochester Institute of Technology not necessarily included as a campaign objective initially.

B. Government Grants

Grants from federal, state, and local governments will be included in the campaign provided they are for facilities, which are objectives of the campaign. Specific projects not now included in the campaign objectives will be added to the campaign goal as funding is realized from government sources. Funding will then be added to campaign totals.

C. Property

Real estate, tangible personal property, works of art, and equipment will be credited at the fair market value as determined by an independent appraisal.

D. Deferred Gifts

1. Life Income Gifts

These gifts will include charitable lead trusts, unitrusts, annuity trusts, gift annuities, and pooled income funds and gifts of real estate where the donor retains life tenancy. These will be credited to the campaign at the full fair market value.

2. Life Insurance

12

CAMPAIGN PLAN

CAMPAIGN CABINET

DESCRIPTION OF RESPONSIBILITIES

Under the direction of the General Chairman of the Campaign, this committee provides the overall leadership for the Campaign. It is responsible for implementing the Campaign, with special emphasis on identification, evaluation, cultivation and solicitation of Major, Special, and General Prospects.

SPECIFIC DUTIES OF THE CAMPAIGN COMMITTEE:

1. To attend the Leadership Committee meetings.

2. To be accessible to the General Chairman of the Campaign, the President of the Institute and the Vice President for Development for counsel on major issues and questions.

3. To use their influence and knowledge to bring other strong leaders into key volunteer positions in the Campaign.

4. To accept assignment of cultivation and solicitation of Pace Setting/Major Gift prospects; counsel, advise and assist in the cultivation and solicitation of other Pace Setting/Major Gift prospects.

5. In selected instances to make appearances at various campus/Institute related meetings.

16

CAMPAIGN PLAN

An actual gift must take place. Typically this will involve an irrevocable assignment of ownership and beneficiary of an existing policy or the writing of a new policy with the Institute as owner and beneficiary.

3. Bequest Expectancies

For persons the age of 65 and over, a "will contract" (life estate notes) must be executed for the bequest to count in the Campaign totals except in a limited number of special cases where a "letter of intent" is accepted from a Trustee or other major prospect/donor.

E. Corporate matching gifts will be credited to the individual donor for internal accounting purposes.

LEADERSHIP

The leadership for the Campaign will focus on a special committee called the Steering Committee. This committee will be chaired by the Campaign General Chairman. The Campaign General Chairman will form a new Leadership Unit—the Campaign Cabinet, composed of the Campaign Divisional leaders and members of the Steering Committee, as well as select members of the Development staff.

The Campaign General Chairman provides overall leadership of the Campaign.

13

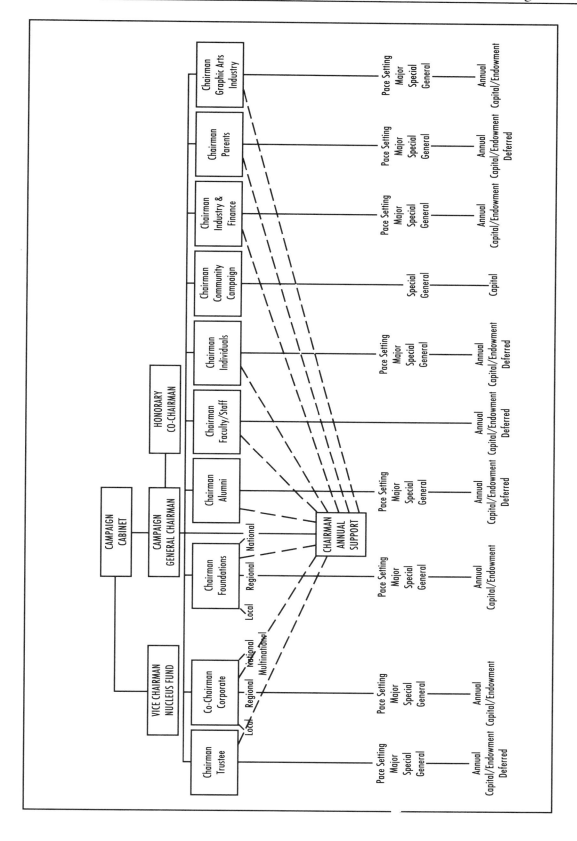

CAMPAIGN PLAN

POSITION DESCRIPTION

GENERAL CHAIRMAN

ROCHESTER INSTITUTE OF TECHNOLOGY

CAMPAIGN

Provides overall leadership of the Campaign.

As General Chairman, he leads the Campaign Cabinet of the Campaign. This Committee is responsible for planning and implementing the Campaign, with special emphasis on identification, evaluation, cultivation and solicitation of the Pace Setting and Major Gifts prospects.

SPECIFIC DUTIES OF THE GENERAL CHAIRMAN:

1. To provide overall leadership and guidance for the voluntary aspect of the Campaign.

2. To preside at meetings of the Campaign Cabinet.

3. To be accessible to the President of the Institute and the Vice President for Development for counsel on major issues or questions.

4. To use his influence and knowledge to help recruit key volunteers as the major division chairmen.

5. To approve appointments of other key volunteers in the Campaign.

6. To bring personal influence to bear on the selected Pace Setting and Major Gift prospects, counsel, advise, assist and actively participate in the cultivation and solicitation of other Pace Setting/Major Gift prospects.

18

CAMPAIGN PLAN

7. To select or concur in selection of the Campaign Cabinet members.

8. To make appearances and speak at meetings.

The Vice President for Development, development staff and counsel are available to provide any support by the chairman or members of the Steering Committee.

19

Gift Policies

Before you start soliciting, you need definite written policies for accepting gifts. You need to establish gift-accounting guidelines and get them approved by the board and the administration. What type of gifts are to be credited to the campaign? When is the gift credited? How much of it? Will any portion or all of annual giving count in the campaign goal?

Decide early on what you are going to do about counting planned gifts in your campaign goals—a tough question. The Fund-Raising Institute polled a number of development officers and came up with varying responses. Most said that they count all planned gifts received during the campaign at full face value, including life-income agreements. (Most of these respondents were colleges and universities.) But some organizations preferred to count only the remainder-interest values of life-income gifts—just the amount the organization can expect to receive, rather than the full value. One university reported that it counts the full face value of all planned gifts, except annuities. For annuities, it uses the remainder value. Few institutions count bequests in capital campaign totals until the donor passes away and the funds are received; wills, they feel, can be changed too easily. This planned gift issue generates considerable controversy within some organizations. So work with your legal counsel to decide on the approach best for you. Among your options are these four:

■ Count all deferred gifts received during the campaign at full face value, regardless of the type of gift.
■ Count only received bequests at full value, using a remainder value for gifts that involve a life-income contract. Do not account pending bequests at all unless the donor has signed an irrevocable note guaranteeing the bequest.
■ Count bequests and all life-income gifts at face value, except annuities—using the remainder value for annuities.
■ For gifts of life insurance, if the policy is paid up, count only the premiums that have been paid, or count the face value. Consider

counting the face value only when the total amount is guaranteed in the policy.

Here's how one experienced practitioner handles it. Robert F. Sharpe, a Memphis-based consultant specializing in planned giving, suggests these guidelines for crediting planned and other gifts.

Gift annuities "When the gift annuity is arranged with the donor, a form is completed showing the actuarial cost and the gift [remainder] portion. I suggest that the gift portion be the amount credited as results for your institution."

Charitable remainder annuity trust "The fair market value of the charitable remainder interest is the amount I would suggest using as credit for results." (Sharpe also recommends the same reporting policy for gifts by *charitable remainder unitrust* and gifts made through a *pooled income fund*.)

Life insurance gifts "There are several ways to count life insurance production. If dividends are given, count the amount actually received. If a paid-up policy is given, use the cash value of the policy on the day of receipt. If a policy is given for which premiums are being paid, use the cash value on the day of receipt. If a new policy is purchased as a gift, credit the cash value as it is available." (For another opinion, see the comments on life insurance earlier in this chapter.)

Gifts in kind "Credit gifts in kind at the fair market value. In the case of real estate, art objects and other gifts needing appraisal, only reports of qualified appraisers should be accepted." (And the donor must find the appraiser.)

Securities "Securities as gifts should be valued at the fair market value at the time the institution has full right of ownership and full right to dispose. The fair market value may be determined by taking the mean value of the high and low on that date."

You must also decide how to handle pledges. You can keep a running total of pledge amounts and show them with cash totals, but it is safer not to add them into the campaign totals until the cash comes in. Some organizations, including the Metropolitan Museum of Art in New York, which once won a court case on the subject, count oral pledges if made to trustees or top administrative leadership. Some organizations also immediately count pledges from trustees because they know the money will come in. But many organizations will not count pledges at all unless they are in writing.

Getting Approval

The act of "officializing" a capital campaign should happen at a board meeting. The actual text of the final resolution to proceed with a campaign might look like this statement from the minutes of a University of Pennsylvania board meeting. This resolution began a $255 million campaign after four years of pre-campaign planning.

"Resolved, That the Trustees affirm their commitment to a major development program over the next five years, with a dollar goal of inspirational size, to support specific academic programs and projects of the highest priority, and to place the University's fiscal structure on firmer, higher ground; and be it further. "Resolved, That the administration be directed to proceed with preparations for public announcement of details of the total program, subject to the approval of the Trustees at that time."

When giving the go-ahead, your board and your administrative leaders should be impressed with the fact that they are also promising to help. Officializing actually takes place twice in relation to capital fund-raising—once when the board authorizes you to plan for a campaign and once when they accept your campaign plan.

If the board doesn't understand the goals of the organization and is not willing to provide leadership in the area of financial support, an institution's campaign is probably doomed. So efforts to strengthen boards of trustees should receive ongoing priority before you even consider a capital campaign.

One purist, a board member himself, puts it this way: "Someone may well ask whether, if a person of means on a board fails to contribute in a measure proportionate to his means, he should be asked to drop off. I think he should, and I have personally participated in a number of such instances. I happen also to find annoying the argument that the contribution of time is the equivalent of money and that this justifies the person of substantial income and means contributing few dollars. We need money as well as time, and money has to come from those who have it." The quote is from Atherton Bean, who has served as chairman and chief executive of International Multifoods Corporation, chairman of the board of the Mayo Foundation, and trustee of Carleton College, addressing the Union of Independent Colleges of Art.

Planning a Budget

A capital campaign is an expensive proposition in terms of needing dollars up front, but not necessarily in terms of the percentage of each dollar spent to raise the funds. Your organization must be told what it will cost to raise the needed capital funds, and it must be willing to foot the bill or to arrange some special financing for the project. The major expense will be salaries and consulting fees. That is why you must determine staff needs at the very beginning.

Many institutions decide to retrain their existing staff for the campaign. This is a good option because the staff members already know the institution. But just because you aren't hiring outside counsel or more staff, don't think that there won't be any extra staff expenses. If you choose this option, you must allow funds for retraining and also for replacing people who move into campaign functions full time.

Staff costs, including hiring consultants, can run 70 to 80 percent of total campaign costs. The next big items—around 10 percent—are promotional materials and cultivation costs (such as entertainment and special events). The final 10 percent of the budget covers everything else.

The larger the goal, the smaller the costs should be in terms of a percentage of the goal. Costs vary according to the scope, length and goal of the program. Remember that most expenses will go toward raising the last 10 percent of the funds—still a profitable enterprise. Many large capital campaigns hold total costs below 5 percent of the amount raised. This seems to be a small-enough cost, but it generally represents only the added costs of tacking a capital campaign on top of your existing fund-raising operation. Be sure you compare your probable costs to those of similar campaigns at similar institutions. Allow for inflation, especially if yours will be a lengthy program. Your budget should have a few cushions and should be subject to review at regular intervals. In preparing your campaign budget, consider the following types of costs:

■ Professional salaries and fees
■ Staff and clerical support
■ Counseling and auditing fees
■ Travel
■ Entertainment and food service
■ Promotional materials
■ Printing and design
■ Postage
■ Audio-visual presentations, videos or films
■ Special events: kickoffs, dedications
■ Office supplies and equipment
■ Copying
■ Telephone
■ Computing equipment or rental
■ Word-processing equipment

Expenses are often taken out of the amount raised, but money must be available up front to get things started. One way to get the money early on is to ask the organization to make a venture capital investment in the campaign. It puts up the budget from reserves, while you create a plan for repayment through proceeds from the campaign.

The costs of a capital campaign depend on such things as the size of the prospect list, how involved the prospects are with the organization, the size of the geographical area to be covered, the length of the program and the organization's fund-raising history. Costs will be higher for a new organization that has no established donors to turn to.

You must keep a careful record of your costs. In the United States, laws increasingly regulate much of charitable fund-raising. Fund-raisers often are expected to know and disclose the percentage of all contributions used for the charitable purpose—after deducting fund-rais-

Figure 21.5. An interim budget report for a $4.1 million Salvation Army building campaign.

THE SALVATION ARMY

CAPITAL CAMPAIGN

MONTH ___ To August 13, 1976

BUDGET REPORT   Not a final budget report

ITEM	BUDGET	PREVIOUS EXPENDITURES	BALANCE LAST MONTH	EXPENDITURES THIS MONTH	BALANCE
Office Equipment	$ 2,000	$ 2,266.59	$ (266.59)	$ 180.00	$ (446.59)
Office Salaries	21,000	22,131.14	(1,131.14)	1,432.44	(2,563.58)
Office Supplies	1,800	1,376.30	423.70	----------	423.70
Duplicating Svces.	2,000	1,455.60	544.40	----------	544.40
Promotional Tools	7,000	9,326.74	(2,326.74)	----------	(2,326.74)
Meetings	3,000	693.04	2,306.96	40.26	2,266.70
Telephone	1,500	1,136.34	363.66	568.76	(205.10)
Postage	2,000	353.37	1,646.63	26.00	1,620.63
Miscellaneous	700	354.00	346.00	----------	346.00
TOTAL	$ 41,000	$ 39,093.12	$ 1,906.88	$ 2,247.46	$ (340.58)

ing, management and general costs. To come up with such figures, you must answer three questions. What costs are really fund-raising costs? How do you calculate them? And, what level of fund-raising costs are ethically and legally acceptable?

The U.S. Council of Better Business Bureaus Inc. has defined three types of fund-raising costs.

■ *Those for a campaign buildup:* recruiting and training volunteer workers, preparing and distributing fund-raising instructions to workers, publicizing the fund-raising drive and producing its special events
■ *Those for solicitation:* preparing and conducting solicitations for bequests, foundation grants and other special gifts; producing campaign material such as worker kits, coin containers, "unordered" items used in mail appeals, and transmittal of mail appeals, including purchase and maintenance of mailing lists, postage, addressing, envelopes
■ *Multipurpose supportive costs:* staff salaries, travel expenses, physical facilities, public relations, telephone—all charged off appropriately as program, administrative or fund-raising expenses. This last breakdown may be difficult because parts of any one cost could fall into all three areas.

And how do you calculate and report these costs? Better Business identifies three ways you can do it: as a percentage of your total gift income, the most common approach; as a percentage of your total expenses, and as a percentage of your direct and indirect income, discounting income from investments and interest.

What is a proper fund-raising cost? Well . . . it all depends. Better Business acknowledges that it depends on at least five variables. 1) The type of fund-raising being done. Mail campaigns, with relatively small gifts, can be much more expensive than personal solicitations for major gifts. 2) The age of the organization. New groups generally have to spend more than older groups. The case for giving must be established and the constituency must be developed. 3) Location of the organization. Groups headquartered in large cities face higher overhead

costs. 4) Scope and public appeal. If the cause is well-known, support will come more easily and less expensively. 5) Competition. If many groups seek support for similar causes from the same constituency, it will mean higher costs per dollar raised.

As a general guideline, you should aim to keep your total campaign costs under 15 percent of the total raised. Some organizations can spend far less and be successful; for others it will cost more.

Should you have a separate budget for a capital campaign, or should its costs simply be reflected in the total development budget? The most common practice probably is to separate the capital campaign costs from the other costs. There is some sense to this because a capital campaign tends to raise funds less expensively than the other forms of fund-raising such as annual giving, which provides the base from which the capital drive is launched. From the viewpoint of your internal politics, especially if you are in a finite-term capital campaign, it's a good idea to maintain a budget that shows the costs of your normal development program and the campaign costs separately. That way, when the campaign is over, you have a continuing, everyday budget base to return to. And your superiors won't expect you to continue raising dollars at the less expensive campaign rate. Remember, the more big gifts you receive, the lower your costs will probably be.

Records

The Wall Street Journal quoted longtime fund-raiser Michael Radock as saying that "modern fund-raising is 90 percent research and 10 percent solicitation." He's right. With this intense emphasis on research comes the necessity to have a good system in which to store and process the collected data. There is no profit in spending scarce budget on researching prospect information, only to find that you cannot produce it again from your records. Most of the records you'll use for a capital campaign are those already existing in any well-organized development office. But for a capital campaign, you must make sure those records are as comprehensive and current as possible for each segment of your constituency: individuals, groups, corporations, foundations etc. And you must make sure that you can retrieve and correlate the information in your records efficiently. Having this information accessible, so you can give it to volunteer and staff solicitors, is vital.

In addition, a capital campaign requires some special information. You need to identify and group each prospect by potential gift level. This will allow you to fire off personal letters and invitations to your highest-level prospects, or to send separate mass mailings to your lower-potential prospects. When the prospect's specific giving potential is rated, that information must appear in your records. You'll want to keep careful track of cultivation progress, documenting each step as the prospect is brought closer to your organization. When a solicitor is assigned and a solicitation strategy is worked out, you'll want to have these items easily accessible, too.

You'll need a record showing the names of each prospect assigned to each solicitor and that solicitor's progress in steering each one of them toward a gift. And when the gift or pledge is made, you'll need a record of that, along with a very accurate record of the dates on which pledge payments are promised and of the payments actually made. Finally, you'll need a running record of total gifts and pledges, so you can know exactly where your effort stands at any given moment.

Different efforts require different records. For example, if your capital campaign has several goals, you'll need to keep a record showing gifts and pledges for each goal.

Some of your capital records will be temporary, and some of these temporary records will duplicate material in your permanent files. One thing is certain though: When your capital campaign is over, your records will be larger and more valuable than ever before.

Your donor and prospect records should be stored in a computer system appropriate for the size of your constituency. You will need a data management system that will allow you to re-

trieve information from those records in a variety of ways. You need the ability to print "hard copy" reports on prospects as well as to retrieve data on a computer screen.

At the University of Pennsylvania, the computer files used during a $1 billion campaign were divided into four screens, so that information could be sorted by a number of variables. The first screen detailed basic biographical information, including home and business address. The second screen included business and professional data such as job title, availability of matching gifts, professional specialty, professional fraternities. The third screen listed family data such as the names of children who are alumni. The fourth was the major prospect screen that included income, net worth, giving ability ratings, inclination to give ratings, interests in the university and staff assignment.

Office Procedures

Development office procedures usually have to be reviewed, refined and streamlined for a capital campaign. Staff members involved in the campaign must keep each other informed about their contacts and successes. Perhaps an extra copy of all campaign correspondence, clippings and reports should be circulated to them on a weekly basis. These same staff members need periodic gift reports. It must also be determined who among them should see gifts as soon as they come in. Clear policies must be set for acknowledging gifts and for handling pledge reminders. Additional staff meetings will be needed to coordinate activities and sometimes to discuss top prospects—one by one.

The aim of your office procedures should be to create a well-oiled campaign effort, where the extra work fits into place easily, where everyone enjoys his or her duties and where the least additional work is created for the person in charge.

Chapter 22
Spreading the Word

Printed Materials

For solicitors, a brochure is an important tool. They may use it during a meeting or leave it behind with the prospect. Although printed materials are an important part of a campaign, don't make the mistake of thinking that they are the most important part. A brochure doesn't raise money; the solicitor does. But the solicitor often feels more comfortable with an effective brochure to refer to, so it is important to have one.

There are two things to keep in mind when printing materials for a campaign. First, you want whatever you print to be appropriate to your organization, both in terms of quality and the amount of money you spend for it. Even if someone donates money to prepare brochures, you don't want them to look too flashy for your organization. You never want a potential donor to be able to say, "If they can print a nice brochure like this, then they don't need my money."

And the second point is to proofread and then proofread again. As you can see in some of the sample materials in this book, mistakes do make it into print. While a typo is not the end of the world, perfect copy still makes the best impression.

Every capital campaign requires printed material such as the case statement, a major campaign brochure, a "how-to-give" brochure, a gift-opportunities brochure, a pledge card, cultivation pieces etc.

The "etc." can include: a "why give" brochure, a capsule case statement, a ways-to-give-securities folder, fact sheets and folders highlighting specific parts of the campaign.

The *case statement* can be an elaborate booklet or merely some typewritten pages. If you opt for the elaborate case statement, make sure of two things: 1) that you keep out of the text anything that is apt to change during the campaign, and 2) that you order more than you think you can use. It is extremely expensive to reprint such booklets.

The *major campaign brochure* is the most important printed piece of any campaign because it is essential to have one document that fully describes the effort. This brochure can either incorporate the case statement completely, or simply be based on its premises. It can list gift opportunities and methods of giving, or be graphically designed to coordinate with separate brochures on those topics. A campaign brochure can be made attractive with art, or it can concentrate simply on effective wording.

Fund-raising consultant Richard S. Henry reviewed the role of major campaign brochures in "The Philanthropic Digest," a bulletin of the consulting firm Brakeley, John Price Jones Inc. Here are excerpts of his key points:

- The major campaign brochure serves as evidence that a campaign or development program is truly in progress.
- It updates the majority of readers on the institution's progress. For some, it's an introduction to the institution or program.

■ It impresses upon all donors the fact that their past gifts have been important. It reminds them that they might consider contributing to this new campaign or program.

■ It stimulates pride in the institution, helping generate a feeling that it deserves financial support.

■ It clarifies hazy impressions of what the institution has been doing in recent years and erases misconceptions.

Figure 22.1. Ohio State used this brochure, which we have excerpted, for its $350 million campaign. It states the needs, gives the personal commitment of university leaders to the campaign and details the areas to be funded.

A CAMPAIGN FOR OHIO STATE

The Ohio State University is part of our lives and achievements — as alumni, parents, professionals, as corporation or foundation executives, as friends of the institution.

For most of us, Ohio State already is significant. At some time, it may have provided the basic intellectual capital by which we gained or measured success. It may have helped fulfill a dream, create a career, establish lifelong friendships, generate an invention, or simply but substantially endow us with the insight to use change to our delight and our advantage. For many, it is alma mater. For some, it already has been the beneficiary of great generosity.

Having survived a period of intense financial pressure, Ohio State is preparing for a new era of achievement. The University is choosing its path deliberately, keeping faith with the past and building on the present to assure its future.

Consistent with its prominence, Ohio State is launching the largest campaign for private support in the history of public higher education. We seek $350 million to greatly increase the endowment, to fund construction of key facilities, to increase financial support for students, and to meet other institutional priorities. Adding substantial amounts of private monies to the public appropriation will provide flexibility to carry out programs, attract scholars, and build facilities which cannot be funded by existing means.

Attainment of these goals is an undertaking of great magnitude requiring intensity, loyalty, and dedication on the part of faculty and staff, on the part of alumni, on the part of all the University's friends and supporters. It is an undertaking that will require continued public assistance as well as a substantial increase in financial support from the private sector.

Private investment coupled with public support is the method through which The Ohio State University will ensure its future. The Campaign provides an unequaled opportunity to preserve the nature and advance the stature of The Ohio State University.

Frederick G. Ruttner, Jr. '50
Chair, The Ohio State University Campaign

A $350 MILLION CAMPAIGN FOR THE OHIO STATE UNIVERSITY

The Arts and Sciences
$65,000,000

The Professional Schools
$65,000,000

Research and Public Service
$75,000,000

The Student Body
$55,000,000

The Athletic Program
$45,000,000

The President's Fund for Emerging Priorities
$15,000,000

A DISTINGUISHED PAST

At every quarter hour, the chimes still ring from the tower of Orton Hall. A gift of eight graduating classes from 1906 to 1915, these 12 bells in the key of E-flat are symbol, tradition, and memory to all who have walked the Oval these many years.

Orton Hall memorializes Edward Orton, geologist, who first presided over the University in 1873. Ohio State, then The Ohio Agricultural and Mechanical College, would combine the classical rigor of the traditional private college with a new utilitarianism born of the industrial revolution.

Founded in 1870, Ohio State would be a true university, enabled by the Land Grant College Act of 1862 to "promote the liberal and practical education of the industrial classes in the several pursuits and professions of life."

Over the last 11 and one half decades, The Ohio State University has achieved an academic stature unrivaled among universities that have maintained universal access, which was the ideal of land grant reform and a uniquely American goal. We remain a university of opportunity, open to all Ohioans who qualify with a high school diploma and a college preparatory curriculum.

It is, some say, remarkable that an academic enterprise of such pervasive quality can exist at an institution so large and so complex. Yet by any measure, Ohio State ranks among the top 20 comprehensive universities in America.

Through The Ohio State University Campaign, we are mounting an aggressive quest for higher educational leadership beyond the status quo. Such leadership will be indispensable to the continuing reemergence of this region in the high technology economy, as it will be crucial to the maintenance of historical perspective, creative ideas, and a social conscience in a time of great and rapid change.

We hope you will join us in realizing the vision of President Orton in his commencement address to the first graduation class of six students in 1878.

"The State University," he said, "properly expanded and equipped, is the summit and the crown."

Leslie H. Wexner '59
Chair, The Ohio State University Foundation

A DYNAMIC FUTURE

One of my first public statements upon coming to The Ohio State University as its 10th president was that this university was one of the most outstanding public institutions of higher education in the nation. That is where I believed we were then, and I firmly believe that is where we are now.

The comprehensive scope of Ohio State is nearly unmatched, with its rich and diverse undergraduate and graduate programs, all organized around our central arts and sciences core. We are one of the major research-oriented, public academic institutions in this nation and, indeed, in the world — in size, scope, and quality.

But we can strive for even more. There is an opportunity here at Ohio State to attain the union of diversity and excellence achieved by only a few truly eminent universities.

We seek to attract private support that will strengthen the academic core of Ohio State, including the areas traditionally viewed as the liberal arts and the institution's complement of professional schools. We seek support that will strengthen and assist the student body of the University.

We will accomplish these goals through a significant expansion of our endowment to support faculty chairs, student financial aid, and research programs; through funds to provide equipment and to bolster the research efforts of the new Cancer Research Institute; and through construction of the most contemporary and far-reaching visual arts facility in the world.

In the public sector of higher education, the margin of excellence is the same as in the private sector: the investment made by people in people, by corporations and foundations who choose to reach out, by alumni prompted by the heart.

The success of The Ohio State University Campaign will make a vital difference between what is acceptable and what is distinctive, what is sufficient and what is exemplary throughout the University.

This is an endeavor for all who care about Ohio State.

Edward H. Jennings
President, The Ohio State University

SETTING THE PRIORITIES

Today, Ohio State students study in 19 colleges, seven schools, the Graduate School, five centers, four regional campuses, and the Agricultural Technical Institute. The University also incorporates Ohio's major medical teaching complex, The Ohio State University Hospitals.

Through our learning centers, educational telecommunications programs, Cooperative Extension Service, and health care programs, the University's impact extends across Ohio and throughout America. We are one of the major graduate research institutions and, therefore, play an important role in the generation of new knowledge and in the preparation of mature scholars. We graduate as many teachers, physicians, dentists, attorneys, veterinarians, optometrists, engineers, nurses, pharmacists, agriculturalists, and architects as virtually any university in the world.

The establishment of priorities for a fund-raising effort of this magnitude has been guided by institutional goals.

❧ To attain uncontested leadership in United States higher education for six to 10 academic departments by 1990.

❧ To demonstrate substantial advances in basic research investigations, including areas considered essential to the economic future of the region.

❧ To attract even more of the best young scholars than the 5,000 undergraduate honors students already here.

❧ To enhance the attractiveness of graduate education to the finest minds in all disciplines.

❧ To recommit in a technological age to the enduring worth of the humanities and the fine arts.

❧ To respond to contemporary demands in intramural and intercollegiate athletics with the necessary facilities.

These goals are realistic given the temper of the Ohio State environment. There is imaginative and solid fiscal management with substantial sums reallocated for selective academic excellence. Faculty morale is high. High school curricula are preparing entering freshmen more thoroughly than in many years. Optimism and positive spirit pervade the University.

For some time, we have been working to increase the overall fund-raising capability of Ohio State. And together we are succeeding.

On an annual basis, gifts already are increasing by 20 percent a year. The Ohio State University Campaign is the logical next step.

THE OHIO STATE UNIVERSITY CAMPAIGN WILL:

- Provide 63 *endowed faculty chairs*
- Fund 21 *endowed professorships*
- Finance a *Center for the Visual Arts*
- Support a *Cancer Research Institute*
- Add to the *Law Building*
- Build an *indoor athletic practice facility*
- Provide $75 million to *support research throughout the University*
- Provide $60 million to *support scholarships and fellowships*
- *. . . and much more*

FOR THE ARTS AND SCIENCES

An abiding respect for the pursuit of knowledge, the ultimate mark of an educated man or woman, is found in the study of the humanities, the fine and applied arts, the social and behavioral sciences, the natural, mathematical, and physical sciences. In total, they form "the liberal arts" or "arts and sciences." For most of recorded history, the arts and sciences incorporated nearly all secular thought.

These many disciplines are diverse as music and microbiology, philosophy and physics, economics and English literature, again are being recognized rightfully by America's leaders as both practical career preparation and the framework for the shared knowledge and values that hold a society together.

The arts and sciences at Ohio State are, first, the basis of the core curriculum for all undergraduates. They are also central to international understanding in a world becoming ever more interdependent, ever more reliant on the knowledge of other languages and cultures.

❧ This portion of The Ohio State Campaign includes 20 endowed faculty chairs and three endowed professorships, which are funds to attract renowned scholars and researchers in varied fields and to help support the administrative costs of their work. Perhaps the quintessential investment that can be made in the world of ideas and innovation is the endowment of such leadership.

Education in the arts and sciences provides a sense of the love of learning for its own sake, a capacity to analyze issues as they come along, ability to place information in a larger context, to identify connections with other fields, and an appreciation of beauty as both form and function.

To quote one of Ohio State's most distinguished professors, the late Edgar Dale, such study helps us "see the forest by means of the trees."

GOAL
$66,000,000

PROGRAM EXAMPLES

Center for the Visual Arts
$26,000,000

Chair in Applied Ethics
$1,250,000

*Chair in Experimental Physical Chemistry, Ohio Eminent Scholar Match**
$750,000

Chair in Molecular Biology
$1,250,000

Chair in Business History
$1,250,000

*Chair in Computer Graphics and Design Technology, Ohio Eminent Scholar Match**
$750,000

*The Eminent Scholar Program matches state funds to private support in selective areas of basic research judged essential to the economic growth of Ohio.

FOR THE ARTS AND SCIENCES

SOME CURRENT HIGHLIGHTS

ARTS . . . The *computer animation* curriculum is considered the finest anywhere . . . Graduate students in this field recently won the grand prize in international competitions both in Japan and Canada . . . "The Insider's Guide to the Colleges" gives an entire page to the *dance* program, calling it "flourishing" with a "well deserved reputation." . . . We were one of the first universities to offer a Ph.D. in *art education* and have one of the largest departments . . . The *Marching Band* recently received the Sudler Trophy as the No. 1 collegiate marching band in America . . . The *Theatre Research Institute* is a resource for students and theatre scholars worldwide.

BIOLOGICAL SCIENCES . . . The *Center for Lake Erie Research* has been instrumental in cleaning up the lake and reviving it for fishing . . . The collection of insects and spiders in *entomology* is one of the world's largest, with 3.5 million specimens . . . The *microbiology* department has educated more minority students than any other in the country, including three graduates who now chair

departments . . . The Borror Laboratory of *Bioacoustics* contains the world's second largest collection of recorded animal sounds. The largest is at Cornell University.

HUMANITIES . . . More than 20 languages are taught in one of the most comprehensive *foreign language* programs in the country . . . The unique *Hilandar Collection of Slavic Manuscripts*, discovered in a monastery in Greece, dates from A.D. 1009; the Slavic and East European languages and literature program is recognized as one of the nation's finest . . . In *linguistics*, computer simulations are analyzing how children learn to talk, a tool that should help improve language skills in the verbally handicapped . . . The *Center for Medieval and Renaissance Studies* is continuing its effort to obtain all records of early English drama . . . Research in the *Department of Black Studies* is examining the role of black political activity in the election of black mayors and the decline of racial consciousness among black college students.

LIBRARIES . . . The William Charvat Collection of *American fiction* is among the strongest in the nation . . . The finest collections of works by *Jack London*, *James Thurber*, and *Nelson Algren* are housed here . . . The University has one of the most advanced *computer based library systems* anywhere, and the *17th largest university collection* in North America with over 3.9 million volumes . . . The Library for *Communication and Graphic Arts* is one of the most comprehensive in the world . . . The Rinhart Collection of early *photographic images* is one of the finest assemblages of daguerrotypes, ambrotypes, and tintypes.

MATHEMATICS AND PHYSICAL SCIENCES . . . *The Institute of Polar Studies*, the foremost research organization of its kind, is the recipient of the papers of Admiral Richard E. Byrd . . . The Alan T. Waterman Prize as the *nation's best young scientist* was awarded to mathematician Harvey Friedman; a Presidential Young Investigator Award, to physicist C. J. Jayaprakash; the British Physical Society's Simon Memorial Prize, to physicist David O. Edwards . . . The *astronomy* department has joined with the University of Arizona in a project to develop the world's largest optical-infrared telescope . . . *Computer and*

information science is one of the fastest growing majors in the university . . . By most surveys, the *chemistry* department is ranked superior among its peers.

SOCIAL AND BEHAVIORAL SCIENCES . . . Two *journalism* graduates are recent Pulitzer Prize winners . . . *The Kiplinger Public Affairs Reporting Program* is one of a few such graduate programs for which working journalists receive leaves of absence to study . . . The *Disaster Research Center* was the first of its kind in the world and helps develop effective plans to cope with group crises . . . Don Scott Field allows Ohio State to offer one of the few degree programs in *aviation* . . . *The Mershon Center* is a leading "think tank" on national security and public policy . . . Findings from *The Center for Human Resource Research* help establish national policy in employment and training.

FOR THE PROFESSIONS

Administrative Science. Agriculture. Dentistry. Education. Engineering. Home Economics. Law. Medicine. Nursing. Optometry. Pharmacy. Social Work. Veterinary Medicine. These are the "professional" colleges at Ohio State which, it is safe to say, have and will continue to provide the nation with a disproportionately large percentage of achievers in all 13 broad degree programs.

The emphasis of The Ohio State University Campaign is in strengthening the academic core of the professional schools through the endowment of chairs and professorships. This mode of philanthropy is especially significant here where, often, the university must compete with lucrative opportunities of the marketplace.

Endowment gifts acknowledge merit and excellence, quality of research, and pioneering enterprise. No other gift to The Ohio State University Campaign can assure the distinction of a program more than endowment, which rewards only the exceptional individual as it pays tribute to the donor.

❧ So prestigious a position as a chair always is named according to the wishes of the donor. A chair at the University is a permanent resource, funded from the income of an endowment gift fixed at this time at $1.25 million.

The gift will finance a distinguished scholar or researcher's compensation and, often, will fund needed office or laboratory support. It both demonstrates the institution's dedication to achievement in a given field and frees existing funds for other purposes, including the base costs of a "named professorship."

❧ A named professorship also will attract or retain educator/researchers of exceptional stature, by producing annual income to supplement institutional salary. A $500,000 endowment funds a named professorship.

GOAL
$68,000,000

PROGRAM EXAMPLES

Chair in Cancer Research
$1,250,000

Chair in Manufacturing Strategy
$1,250,000

Chair in Organ Transplantation
$1,250,000

Chair in Veterinary Surgical Sciences
$1,250,000

Chair in Hospitality Management
$1,250,000

Chair in Agricultural Economics
$1,250,000

Law Building Addition
$7,000,000

CENTER FOR THE VISUAL ARTS

The Center for the Visual Arts is a center, a concept, and a building. As center, it is both the symbolic cornerstone of The Ohio State University and set piece in a new High Street campus entrance. As concept, it is the radical notion of a museum of the 21st century, where the "state of the art" will be but a point of departure for the new and undiscovered. As building, it merges heritage and futurism, its exterior resurrecting traces of the old Ohio State armory in a modern context, its interior encouraging the relationships between the visual arts and technology.

As a national research center in the visual arts, this structure, even before ground breaking, attracted worldwide attention among artists, architects, and art educators. The building will house avant-garde and experimental arts, including new forms involving laser technology, computers, and video. It will be a repository for traditional art and studio for permanent faculty and distinguished visiting artists.

Its four galleries each will highlight a different aspect of the visual arts: The Ohio State Collection, valued at more than $10 million and heretofore undisplayed for lack of a facility; the Experimental Gallery, for mixed media, expanded arts, and high technology events; the Main Exhibition Gallery, for traveling exhibitions and large displays; and the Ohio and Regional Gallery, a showcase for outstanding talent from this part of the country.

A "video wall" will greet entrants to the center, which also will include an arts bookstore, rental gallery, and cafe. A film theater will project video as well as films and multi-media, while a flexible theater space will make the Mershon Auditorium/Weigel Hall/Center for the Visual Arts complex one of the most diverse and complete performing arts centers anywhere.

Projects such as the Center for the Visual Arts first require visionary thinking and innovative design. Its realization as a hub of modern artistic teaching and practice will be the result of gifts from The Ohio State University Campaign.

The construction of this 125,000 square-foot facility will cost $26 million. In addition, the campaign seeks $5 million to create an endowment for an institute that will support the center's activities.

In recognition of a $10 million gift from Leslie H. Wexner toward its construction, the center will be called the Wexner Center for the Visual Arts—a memorial to his father, the late Harry L. Wexner.

- It presents a range of gift opportunities that readers can sample at leisure, while determining which have greatest appeal.
- It is a valuable ally of the campaign organization, in that it prepares the constituency for the visitations of volunteers. In a very real sense, it is the advance force of the campaign.

Figure 22.2. A how-to-give brochure used by Penn State. The main brochure was accompanied by more specific brochures on various gift techniques and a card asking for more information.

OPPORTUNITIES FOR INVESTMENT

It Started with a Gift . . .

1

. . . from General James Irvin, a tract of farmland in Centre County to the Commonwealth of Pennsylvania on which would eventually be built the Pennsylvania State College. With this gift, the tradition of private support for Penn State was born.

Private giving has grown with the University itself. In recent years, private gifts from alumni, friends, and corporations increased at record levels as the need for private funding, and the University's efforts to procure it, also increased. Why give to a state university? While state-related, Penn State is not fully state-supported. The University receives less than 25 percent of its operating budget from that source. Private giving, then, is needed to enhance and support those programs that the Commonwealth cannot, or will no longer, fund.

From the back of Old Main, circa 1910, students walk a diagonal path as they make their way across campus toward Hort Woods.

2

Why People Give To Penn State

Nowhere is it truer that "people give to people" than at Penn State. Here, the tradition of academic excellence is sustained by tens of thousands who, each year, contribute to the University. The small gifts of many combine to meet annual needs, while the large gifts endow the future of the University.

People give to Penn State because of its people — the people who taught yesterday's students, who teach today's students, and who will be attracted to Penn State because of its national preeminence to teach tomorrow's students. To ensure that Penn State has the best of the brightest faculty and students, today *and* tomorrow, it must reach new heights in private giving.

Planned Giving at Penn State

The competition for the private dollar has never been greater. Your decision to support any cause is a personal matter, and once it is made, you must define your support in ways that will best fit your desires and circumstances. For instance, younger donors may find that to maximize tax benefits and participate in a meaningful way in the Annual Giving Program, an outright gift is most appropriate. Older donors who seek to protect their estates and are not in need of large tax deductions, but who wish to make a major gift, may decide that a certain deferred gift is right for them. This booklet out-

3

lines several ways to invest in Penn State. Detailed information is available in separate booklets from the Office of University Development.

OPPORTUNITIES FOR INVESTMENT

Funds for Immediate Use. Alumni and friends of the University can share in its present success by contributing funds for immediate use. Gifts can be made for the general purposes of the University. These gifts are especially appreciated because they allow the President to respond to unique opportunities in a timely manner. Gifts can be designated by the donor for the support of a particular college, program, or other area of interest, including research, faculty development, scholarships, graduate fellowships, equipment acquisition, and the libraries.

Endowments. Donors who create endowments with gifts in certain minimum amounts provide for the future of Penn State. Such funds for a specific purpose, designated by the donors, are held in perpetuity in that only the income it produced is used. Each fund maintains a separate identity but is commingled with the University's endowment to ensure prudent

4

management and investment diversification. The Board of Trustees retains control over the investment strategy for endowment portfolios, seeking to maintain the highest possible investment return and steady growth of the endowment base.

Donors of endowed funds have the opportunity to provide for the future of Penn State while, at the present time, expressing personal affection for the University or honoring the memory of a friend or family member. It is possible to create an endowment to meet any number of needs, including:

— scholarships and undergraduate awards;

— graduate fellowships;

— faculty fellowships, professorships, and chairs; and

— college excellence funds that allow a dean to direct funds where the need is the greatest at the time.

So that the investment return is adequate to meet current needs, minimum amounts are required for establishment of an endowment. The level of spending from endowed funds must strike a balance between the need to support programs and the need to preserve the purchasing power of the endowment base.

5

OUTRIGHT GIFTS

Gifts of Cash. The simplest way to make a gift to Penn State is by giving cash. The date of your gift is the date the check is mailed or delivered. Gifts of cash may be deducted up to 50 percent of adjusted gross income, with a five-year carry-over for any excess.

Gifts of Appreciated Property. If you sell long-term property — that is, property you have owned longer than six months — you are liable for tax on any appreciation. However, if you make a gift of this property to a qualifying charitable organization, you may avoid any tax liability on that appreciation. You also are allowed a charitable deduction for the fair market

Shortly after World War I, Old Main was at the center of a growing campus. Schwab is behind it to the left; McAllister Hall to the right; the old mining building borders College Avenue; across the Mall are Engineering Units A, B, and C; and north of them is the old running track.

Old Main's terrace, a gift of the class of 1913, is shown here shortly after construction was completed.

value of the property on the date it is transferred. (The cost basis must be used for gifts of property held less than six months.)

Securities are a kind of appreciated property often given outright to the University. Suppose you own shares of stock that you purchased in 1970 for $10,000 but that are now worth $50,000. If you were to sell the stock outright and give the proceeds, you would be liable for tax on the appreciation ($40,000) at your maximum individual rate. If instead you transfer the stock to Penn State, you avoid this tax liability. In addition, you are allowed a charitable deduction, based on the mean of the high and the low price on the date of the transfer (the date you relinquish ownership by mailing or delivering the stock). In fact, donors often wait until they feel the stock is at a high price and deliver it by certified mail that day.

After the stock is transferred, the University generally will dispose of it and use the proceeds as you have prescribed. Should the stock rise or fall in price during that period, your deduction will not be affected.

Gifts of long-term appreciated property are deductible up to 30 percent of adjusted gross income, with a five-year carry-over for any excess. An individual may elect to have the contribution of such property come under the 50 percent limit by reducing the total allowable contribution to the cost basis. Such an election

might be warranted if the total appreciation is small. Your tax counsel can best advise you on taking this election.

In certain cases, the appreciation on gifts of long-term property for which an income tax charitable deduction is claimed will be a preference potentially subject to the Alternative Minimum Tax (AMT). You must compute your

6

potential tax liability treating the appreciation as AMT income, and you must also compute your tax the regular way (which does *not* impose tax on the appreciation) and pay the greater amount. As a practical matter, a donor who does not have other tax preferenced items will not be subject to the AMT, unless the donated property is highly appreciated and the donor has a very high income.

Tangible Personal Property. A charitable deduction is allowed for a gift of tangible personal property — art work, books, stamp collections, manuscripts. Tax regulations affecting such gifts held more than six months by the donor should be noted:

— If the University puts the gift to a *related* use — a painting that is accepted by the Museum of Art for its permanent collection, for example — the donor can claim a charitable deduction for the fair market value of that property, and may deduct up to 30 percent of adjusted gross income in the year of the gift.

— If the gift is put to an *unrelated* use by the University — a stamp collection given to the College of Science to sell and use the proceeds — the donor's deduction is limited to the cost basis, which may be deducted up

to 50 percent of adjusted gross income in the year of the gift.

The five-year carry-over may be used for any excess above the prescribed limits. There are strict valuation and reporting requirements which apply to gifts of appreciated property, depending on the type of property given and the charitable deduction claimed. Information on these requirements can be obtained from the Office of University Development.

Bargain Sales. When property is sold to the University for less than its fair market value, the transaction is called a bargain sale. The difference between the fair market value and the sale price is deductible as a charitable gift. If the property has a long-term capital gain, the donor is liable for the proportion of gain attributable to the selling price.

Gifts of Life Insurance. Life insurance may provide a current and future charitable deduction. If the policy is paid up, the deduction is the amount of the replacement value, but not more than the cost basis (usually the total of all premiums paid less dividends received). If premiums are still being paid, the deduction will be roughly equal to the cash surrender value.

10

After the gift of the policy, any additional premium payments may be deducted by the donor so long as the University is named owner and beneficiary of that policy.

Designated Gifts

Many donors choose to designate their gifts for specific programs, projects, colleges, or other academic units within the University. Donors of scholarship funds may establish selection requirements for those receiving the scholarship, provided the established terms fall within the law and do not unreasonably restrict the scholarship.

DEFERRED GIFTS

To encourage certain individuals to make philanthropic gifts to higher education and other qualifying organizations, the federal government allows a number of giving vehicles for making what are called "deferred gifts." In essence, a donor can take a substantial charitable deduction now for a gift that the University will not actually receive until a later date — usually after the death of the donor and selected sur-

11

vivors. The greatest tax benefits of such plans are reserved for older individuals.

When you contribute cash, securities, or real property as deferred gifts, you continue receiving income from the property for your life and, if you wish, the life of others such as your spouse and children. The property is received by the University after the death of the surviving beneficiary.

You are able to take a deduction in the year of the gift or transfer for the value of the property, less the value of the life interest you retain

One-third into their "century of excellence," Penn State gridders draw a good crowd to old Beaver Field, now a parking lot behind Osmond Lab.

OPPORTUNITIES FOR INVESTMENT

(the "remainder value"). The amount of the deduction is based on Treasury tables that take into account the life expectancies of and expected payments to all noncharitable beneficiaries.

The following are brief descriptions of deferred giving instruments.

The Penn State Pooled Income Fund

Gifts made to Penn State for the Pooled Income Fund are "pooled" in a common fund, professionally managed for current income with moderate growth of the assets. Each quarter, the net income from the fund is distributed on a prorated basis to all donors. At the death of a donor or a surviving beneficiary, the units

Summer school teachers shape up in a physical education class held in the Armory, around 1914.

12

OPPORTUNITIES FOR INVESTMENT

assigned to the donor are removed from the fund and the proceeds therefrom are used by the University.

The donor is allowed a charitable deduction for the remainder value of the gift. Readily marketable securities (excluding those exempt from federal income tax) may be used to fund the gift, thus avoiding tax on the appreciation.

The investment strategy of the fund is to produce appreciation of the assets, thus increasing income to donors — a sort of "hedge against inflation." Of course, the assets may depreciate, in which case income decreases.

The advantage of pooled income funds is that the donor may participate at a relatively modest level — $5,000 for the Penn State Fund — using a simple instrument of transfer.

Charitable Gift Annuities

The Charitable Gift Annuity is, in effect, part gift and part purchase of an annuity. An irrevocable transfer of assets is made to purchase an annuity from the University, which promises to pay a fixed percentage of the value of the assets to one or two annuitants for life. The donor is allowed a substantial tax deduction in the year of the gift. The deduction and the percentage of income to be paid are determined from tables that take into account the annuitants' life expectancies.

An advantage of the gift annuity is that a por-

13

14

tion of the payment represents a return of original investment and therefore is not taxable. For many annuitants, the tax-free portion exceeds 50 percent of the transfer.

You may use appreciated property to fund an annuity but, unlike contributors to the Pooled Income Fund, you will realize a part of the gain. However, this liability is only for a portion of the appreciation, reportable not in one year, but rather over the life expectancy of the donor.

For younger donors who do not require additional current income but who want the benefits of a tax deduction, Penn State also offers the Deferred Payment Gift Annuity. Under this plan, the donor makes a transfer now and obtains a partial tax deduction but defers receipt of payments for a period of years. The charitable deduction and the eventual income are higher than an immediate payment gift annuity.

Certain age restrictions apply to both the Charitable Gift Annuity and the Deferred Payment Gift Annuity.

Charitable Remainder Trusts

These trusts differ from pooled income funds in three important ways. First, the trust is created by the donor and its assets consist only of that person's contributed funds or assets. Second, the donor sets the amount of income to be received. Third, the donor selects the trustee to

15

manage the assets — usually a bank, trust company, or lawyer.

This flexibility allows a donor to design an arrangement specifically suited to his or her needs and to use various types of property in its funding. Donors may choose from two types of charitable remainder trusts.

Charitable Remainder Unitrust. A popular choice, the unitrust allows you to select as the income rate a fixed *percentage* of the value of the assets in the trust, as revalued each year. Thus, if the assets appreciate each year, so will your income. Similarly, income will fall if the assets depreciate.

The charitable deduction is determined by the amount transferred, the percentage of income chosen, and the number and ages of the income beneficiaries. The greater the number of beneficiaries and the younger they are, the lower the deduction.

Additional contributions to a unitrust can be made at any time.

Charitable Remainder Annuity Trust. The annuity trust differs from the unitrust in two respects. The donor selects a fixed *dollar* income amount, stated as a percentage of the assets transferred but not less than 5 percent. If the trust does not produce adequate income, the trustee can use principal to meet this payment. The initial tax deduction is generally larger than

OPPORTUNITIES FOR INVESTMENT

for the unitrust (when both pay the same amount at the outset and this amount is less than 10 percent of the assets), since that instrument takes into account the presumable increase in annual income.

It is not possible to make additional contributions to an annuity trust.

Charitable Lead Trust

In a lead trust, the University receives the income rather than the principal. A donor transfers assets to a trustee and provides that income be paid to the University for a period of years, after which the trust principal reverts to the donor or passes to one or more noncharitable beneficiaries. Under the proper circumstances, a charitable lead trust can allow the donor to pass property to family members at a greatly reduced transfer tax cost. A donor can also provide ongoing gifts to the University with no tax liability on the income produced by those assets, or receive a charitable deduction for the University's "income interest."

Gifts of Residence or Farm with Retained Life Estate

Persons who own a home or farm may deed the property to the University and receive the benefit of a charitable income tax deduction while enjoying the continued use of the property for life. Such a plan is appealing to many donors because it allows them to continue to

16

OPPORTUNITIES FOR INVESTMENT

live in their homes with the knowledge that they have saved taxes and made a major gift to Penn State. Under such a plan, the donor is still obligated to maintain the property and pay any real estate taxes.

Certain limitations apply, and valuations must be made in order to claim a charitable deduction when making such a gift.

Bequests

A charitable bequest is a popular way of making a deferred gift to Penn State, expressed in terms of either a specific sum or a percentage of the residuary estate. The University may be the recipient of an outright bequest, or named as a contingent beneficiary in the event that certain individuals predecease the testator. Suggested wording for including a bequest to Penn State in your will can be provided by the Office of University Development.

Unlike the plans just described, a charitable bequest provides no immediate tax benefits.

17

CHARITABLE
REMAINDER TRUSTS

Giving to Penn State in Trust

A GIFT TO
PENN STATE
THROUGH
YOUR WILL

Including The Pennsylvania
State University
in Your Estate Plans

GIFTS THAT MAKE
A DIFFERENCE

Ways to Provide Academic
Assistance Funds
at Penn State

THE PENN STATE
POOLED INCOME
FUND

A Life Income Plan from
The Pennsylvania State Uni...

THE PENN STATE
CHARITABLE GIFT
ANNUITY PROGRAM

A Life Income Plan from
The Pennsylvania State University

GIFTS OF
APPRECIATED
PROPERTY
TO PENN STATE

HOW TO GIVE
APPRECIATED
SECURITIES
TO PENN STATE

■ It is the one communication that reaches the majority of prospects in most campaigns.

You must spend some money on the major campaign brochure. It should be well-designed, well-written—the best and most appropriate you can produce. It is a professional explanation of your most pressing needs.

A *how-to-give brochure* details how a prospect can go about making a gift, once he or she has decided on doing so. This should be an easy to understand guide, covering the tax advantages and the mechanics of making outright and planned gifts of cash, securities or property.

A *needs brochure* explains in detail exactly what the objectives of the campaign are. This information should be in the main campaign brochure, but you might also want to break it out in a simpler form. Here are some sample pages from a very detailed needs brochure by Ohio State.

Figure 22.3. Excerpts from the Ohio State campaign needs brochure

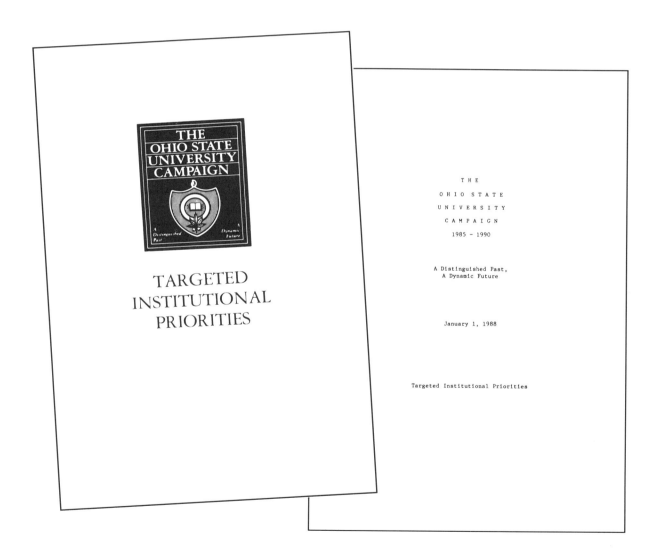

The
Targeted Institutional Priorities
of
The Ohio State University

proceed from

1. The concept of selective enhancement of strong academic programs in the liberal arts and the traditional land-grant disciplines.

2. Research and public service aspects of the University's mission and the way in which these items reinforce selective enhancement.

3. The role of financial aid in attracting outstanding undergraduate and graduate student scholars to the top academic departments, thereby contributing to a "critical mass" of intellectual competence.

4. The University's commitment to quality education and equal educational opportunity and to international understanding and cultural exchange.

2

Dollar Equivalents
Targeted Institutional Priorities

Endowed Chair	equals	$ 1,250,000	
Eminent Scholar Endowed Chair	equals	$ 500,000	state funds
		750,000	university
		$ 1,250,000	matching gifts
Named Endowed Professorships	equals	$ 500,000	

3

The Ohio State University Campaign

Strengthening the Academic Core of the University	$ 231,000,000
–Liberal Arts	$ 67,500,000
–Professional Schools	$ 68,500,000
–Research and Public Service	$ 80,500,000
–President's Endowment for Emerging Priorities	$ 13,500,000
–Regional Campus Priorities Fund	$ 1,000,000
Strengthening and Supporting the Student Body of the University	$ 74,000,000
Strengthening the Athletic Programs of the University	$ 45,000,000
Total	$ 350,000,000

The Ohio State University Campaign

Strengthening the Academic Core of the University	$ 230,777,000
– Liberal Arts	$ 67,500,000
–Chairs & Professorships	23,000,000
–Werner Center for the Visual Arts	31,000,000
–Arts/Libraries Projects	10,500,000
–Mershon Center Programs	3,000,000
– Professional Schools	$ 68,250,000
–Chairs and Professorships	60,250,000
–Law Building Addition	7,000,000
–Law Library Endowment	1,000,000
– Research and Public Service	$ 80,352,000
–Faculty Research Support, Labs and Equipment	58,852,000
–Arthur G. James Cancer Hospital and Research Institute	21,500,000
President's Endowment for Emerging Priorities	$ 13,425,000
Regional Campus Priorities Fund	$ 1,200,000
Strengthening and Supporting the Student Body of the University	$ 74,150,000
Strengthening the Athletic Programs of the University	$ 45,000,000
Total	$ 349,877,000

The Ohio State University Campaign

Strengthening and Supporting
the Student Body of the
University

Unit	Title	Amount
General Scholarship Fund	Undergraduate Scholarships	
-College of the Arts		$ 1,000,000
-College of Biological Sciences		$ 1,000,000
-College of Humanities		$ 2,000,000
-College of Mathematical and Physical Sciences		$ 2,000,000
-College of Social and Behavioral Sciences		$ 1,000,000
-College of Social Work		$ 500,000
-University College		$ 1,000,000
Office of Academic Affairs	Endowment for University Honors Program	$ 5,000,000
Office of Student Affairs	General University Scholarship Endowment Fund	$ 4,000,000
General Scholarship Fund	University Family Scholarship Fund	$ 1,000,000

19

The Ohio State University Campaign

Strengthening the
Athletic Programs
of the University

Woody Hayes Athletic Center	$ 10,600,000
Maintenance Facility	$ 270,000
Intercollegiate Athletic Center	$ 8,430,000
Main campus weight training center (addition to French Field House)	$ 1,624,000
Sports Park Development	$ 2,000,000
-Softball and Baseball Fields 2 softball fields 2 baseball fields	$ 404,000 860,000
-Practice Field Complex	$ 60,000
-Cross Country Course	$ 100,000
-Tennis Facilities	$ 264,000
Sports Pavilion	$ 13,300,000
Facility Renovation	
-Ohio Stadium	$ 4,500,000
-St. John Arena	$ 600,000
-French Field House	$ 400,000
-Golf Course	$ 1,000,000
-Ice Arena	$ 500,000
-Other Priorities	$ 88,000
Athletics - Total	$ 45,000,000

23

A *gift-opportunities brochure* highlights two things: specific needs within a campaign that an individual might find attractive, and opportunities to name facilities or funds by making a gift. By breaking down facilities and endowment needs into small pieces, you can make participation in, say, a $20 million campaign feasible for even the average constituent. And it lets donors put gifts where their strongest interests are.

Figure 22.4. These are some pages from a New York University Medical Center gift-opportunities brochure.

Table of Contents

Philanthropy and NYU Medical Center

NYU Medical Center is one of the nation's foremost biomedical institutions, enjoying a reputation for excellence in patient care, medical education and research. The rise of the Medical Center to its present position of preeminence can be attributed in large measure to the generous philanthropic support it has received throughout its history. The commitment of trustees, patients, alumni, friends, corporations and foundations has made possible the creation of an institution that serves as a health care resource for all the world.

Today, private philanthropy continues to be essential to carrying out the mission of NYU Medical Center. Many donors choose to support the Medical Center's record of achievement by funding programs in teaching, research, student financial aid and patient care. Others choose to purchase hospital equipment or to fund the building or renovation of facilities. Gifts may be made in a broad range of amounts and may be pledged over a period of two or more years.

The following pages suggest many opportunities for you to link your name with the NYU Medical Center tradition of excellence. All of these gifts, from the smallest to the largest, help to insure the ultimate goal of our programs—shaping a better future for humanity.

2

Opportunities for the Major Benefactor

Significant opportunities exist for the major donor to make a gift of particular importance to the growth and future leadership of NYU Medical Center.

Naming Gift Opportunities:

The Medical Center	$150,000,000
School of Medicine	100,000,000
University Hospital	50,000,000
Clinical Sciences Research Building	25,000,000
Intensive Care Pavilion	25,000,000
Medical Science Building	10,000,000
Diagnostic Research Pavilion	6,000,000
Alumni Hall	5,000,000
Kips Bay Residence Hall/ Administration Building	5,000,000
Geriatrics Center	3,500,000
Department of Medical and Molecular Parasitology Building	3,000,000
Graduate Student Housing (26th Street)	3,000,000
A Basic Science or Clinical Department	3,000,000
Cooperative Care Pavilion	2,500,000
Alumni Hall Breezeway	2,000,000
Mayfair South Residence Hall (34th Street)	2,000,000
Sports Medicine Pavilion	1,500,000
Diagnostic Research Pavilion Entrance	1,500,000
Emergency Room	1,500,000
Division of Pediatric Neurosurgery	1,500,000
A Permanently Endowed Professorship in the School of Medicine	1,250,000
Blood Donor Center	1,000,000
Magnetic Resonance Imaging Suite	1,000,000

3

The Arnold and Marie Schwartz
Health Care Center

Bold innovations in care for ambulatory patients were introduced in 1979 with the opening of the Arnold and Marie Schwartz Health Care Center. The unique Cooperative Care Unit of the Center introduced a new concept in hospitalization that combines patient education and family participation in medical care while substantially reducing costs. The Center also houses the Day Surgery Unit, the first ambulatory surgical unit on the east coast, and the clinical practice offices of School of Medicine faculty.

Naming Gift Opportunities

Cooperative Care Pavilion	$2,500,000
Patient Recreation Pavilion	1,500,000
Magnetic Resonance Imaging Suite	1,000,000
Patient Dining Room	1,000,000
Blood Donor Center	1,000,000
Therapeutic Center	750,000
Radiology Pavilion	750,000
Day Surgery Recovery Room	350,000
Patient Laboratory Waiting Room	350,000
Elevator	100,000
Nursing Reception Area	100,000
Operating Room	50,000
Patient Suite	50,000
Treatment Room	40,000
Patient Room	30,000
Consultation Room	25,000
Administrative Office	25,000

6

Endowed Professorships and
Faculty Support

As an academic medical center with a fully integrated program of teaching, research and clinical services, the future of NYU Medical Center revolves around the character and ability of its faculty. Endowed professorships enrich the School of Medicine immeasurably by insuring its continued success in attracting exceptional faculty. The professorships support faculty who embody the model of the teacher/physician/scientist, and who will maintain and extend the Medical Center's high standards of leadership.

Naming Gift Opportunities:

Permanently-Endowed Professorship	$1,250,000
Three-Year Associate Professorship	150,000
One-Year Associate Professorship	50,000
Faculty Teaching and Research Fellowship	40,000

Fellowship Support

NYU Medical Center has long been recognized as a leader in biomedical research. To maintain this momentum, the Medical Center must provide financial support for innovative and pioneering scientific investigators. This support allows the Medical Center to attract and encourage exceptionally gifted individuals and to permit them the freedom to realize their full potential unfettered by financial pressures.

Naming Gift Opportunities:

Fellowship Fund for Senior Faculty Members	$600,000
Four-Year Fellowship Fund	350,000
Two-Year Fellowship Fund	200,000
Fellowship Fund for Clinical Faculty	150,000
Fellowship Fund for Biomedical Science Faculty	150,000
Fellowship Stipend Fund for M.D.-Ph.D. Candidates	150,000
Postdoctoral Fellowship Fund	150,000

17

Student Scholarships
and Loans

It is a proud tradition of the School of Medicine that no student has ever been forced to withdraw for lack of funds. Today, however, eighty percent of the students require financial assistance to complete their educations, and after exhausting all other sources of public and private aid, the majority of these students must turn to the School of Medicine for assistance. The creation of new student scholarship and loan funds is of the utmost importance to the School of Medicine, therefore, if it is to continue to attract the most qualified and talented students and to prepare them for leadership roles in medicine.

Naming Gift Opportunities:

Endowment of a medical education providing tuition, fees, books and equipment	$200,000
Tuition, fees, books, equipment and a stipend for four years	79,200
Tuition, fees, books and equipment for four years	57,200
Tuition, fees, books, equipment and a stipend for one year	19,800
Tuition, fees, books and equipment for one year	14,300

Student Life

To enhance the quality of student life and to offset the rigors of an exceptionally demanding curriculum, the School of Medicine has established the Student Life Fund and is seeking to upgrade existing recreational facilities.

Naming Gift Opportunities:

Student Lounge	$300,000
Student Life Fund	250,000
Student Athletic and Recreational Facility	100,000
Fund for Residence Hall Programs	15,000
Student Room	10,000

18

Figure 22.5. This is a letter of intent form used by the Saint Joseph Medical Center Foundation in Burbank, California

Campaign Providence
Saint Joseph Medical Center Foundation

LETTER OF INTENT

In consideration of the Capital Expansion needs of **Saint Joseph Medical Center;** I (we) intend to give the sum of $__________ payable over the next ______ years, on the basis of $________ each ________ beginning ________

THIS GIFT IS:

__________ Undesignated Within the Capital Expansion Program

__________ Designated to __________

__________ An initial contribution of $__________

toward my commitment is enclosed with this letter I understand that future payments are to be made to the **Saint Joseph Medical Center Foundtion** at the address below

Dated ________ Signature __________

Name __________

Address __________

City __________ Zip ______

Telephone __________

The *pledge card* or *subscription form* or *letter of intent* is the graphic moment of truth for any capital campaign. But it actually comes after the real moment of truth. First, the prospect decides on a gift. Second, the pledge card is signed. Sometimes this card becomes a legal document, taken to court to collect the gift. Most often, though, it is simply considered the sign of a strong moral commitment. The wording will vary from group to group, but it generally names the organization to receive the gift, tells how much the donor plans to give, on what schedule and for what purposes. There is a place for the donor to sign and to enter a date.

In a way, all campaign printed pieces are *cultivation pieces.* But what we are referring to here are publications that are not aimed directly at fund-raising. Rather, they are aimed at a preliminary step: cultivating the prospect's interest in the institution. They don't explain the case or ask for money directly. Instead they keep prospects up to date on what is happening at the institution. You could include newsletters in this category. Even when a campaign is under way, you shouldn't stop sending prospects general information about your organization.

Many other types of publications can be helpful in raising major gifts during a capital campaign. Here are some examples that may give you ideas for your own campaign.

Figure 22.6. An employee pledge card used by St. Francis Hospital in Miami Beach, Florida

NAME __________ **DEPT.** ______

ADDRESS __________ **APT. #** ______

CITY & STATE __________ **ZIP** ______

In support of the Modernization Program for St. Francis Hospital and in consideration of the gifts of others, I hereby authorize my employer to deduct from my bi-weekly pay and to remit to St. Francis Hospital:

$ ________ per pay period

for 60 months beginning ________

OR

I subecribe the total of $ ______ to be paid in installments and upon receipt of reminder statements from the Office of Financial Development:

☐ **Monthly** ☐ **Quarterly** ☐ **Semi-Annually** ☐ **Annually**

beginning ________ and over the next 60 months

or cash (enclosed) $ ______

Signature: ________

This pledge will remain in effect only while I am empl[...] terminated in case of prolonged illness or my demis[...]

—Over Please—

St. Francis HOSPITAL

Employee Pledge Guide
Bi-Weekly Pay Period
contributions are deductible for income tax purposes.

Deduction Bi-Weekly	Total Pledge 5 Years
$ .50	$ 65.00
1.00	$ 130.00
2.00	260.00
3.00	390.00
4.00	520.00
5.00	650.00
6.00	780.00
7.00	910.00

ST. FRANCIS HOSPITAL, INC. MODERNIZATION PROGRAM

Receipt

Date ______ Dept. ______

Name __________

Address __________

Pledge ....$ ______

Paid ....$ ______

Balance ....$ ______

Cash Gift ......$ ______

REMEMBRANCE OR TRIBUTE DESIGNATION

This gift is being made: **In HONOR of** __________

In Memory of: __________

Donated by: __________

IN HONOR OF are contributions at times of celebration — birthdays, anniversaries; in thankfulness for recovery or other special occasions; or appreciations.

IN MEMORY OF are contributions in memory of departed ones.

Figure 22.7. Here are excerpts from a solicitor's packet used by Mercy Hospital in Miami, Florida. It includes a pledge card and a report form for solicitors

Table of Contents

Solicitor's Guide

Solicitor's Guide

This guide is designed to assist you, the volunteer, in preparing for your personal visits with prospective donors to Mercy Hospital.

We encourage you to become familiar with the information contained herein along with the other components included in your solicitor's packet:

• The Scale of Gifts Needed to Achieve Success
• The Organization Chart
• The Pledge Card and Report Envelope
• The Brochure
• The Commemorative Gifts Folder

We ask that you carefully review all materials in order to:

1) Become familiar with the basic campaign plan, time-table and the organizational structure.

2) Become conversant with the many services and benefits this health care facility will provide our community.

3) Become properly informed in the procedures for a successful solicitation call.

Please remember, the majority of prospects on whom you will call are "good community citizens." They readily recognize the importance of good health care institutions. Your best sales tools are your own sincerity, interest and enthusiasm.

That is why you have been asked to represent Mercy Hospital in this fund-raising program.

The Solicitation Call

Preparation

1. Planning your approach to the prospect:

   a. The Mercy Hospital Foundation, Inc. will have supplied background information on each prospect, where such data was available. This will include information pertaining to the prospects' usage of the hospital; what gifts, if any, they may have made in recent years to the hospital; what volunteer participation they may have had with the hospital; any other pertinent information.

   b. A gift category has been suggested for each prospect. This procedure is scientifically inexact, hence we suggest you relate the gift category to the knowledge you may have of this prospect—adjusting upward or downward the suggested "gift potential." Feel free to discuss this with the foundation's Executive Vice President if you wish to reinforce your thinking.

   c. Refer to the commemorative gifts folder in order to support your decision relating to the gift category. Often, the idea of honoring a person, a family, or an organization will provide "emotional impact" in support of a larger gift.

2. Setting the appointment:

   a. All solicitations should be conducted face-to-face. A phone call is the most appropriate method of establishing a personal visit.

   b. The home, with the husband and wife present, is the best place to hold your initial meeting with the prospect. The office, with the Chief Executive Officer and the responsible contributions officer present, is best when your prospect is a business or corporation. With organizations (civic and fraternal) the presentation is most often made to the Board.

   c. To assist you, the solicitor, even more fully, we established a conference center at the foundation where you may bring your prospects for a review of our movie and a discussion with our staff. Similarly, the movie is available for loan to you, in case you want to take it with you on your initial call.

The Call

   a. Determine the degree of knowledge the prospect possesses—regarding the Replacement and Modernization Project for Mercy Hospital. Fill in any important voids that you feel exist.

   b. Confirm any past or previous relationship between the prospect and Mercy Hospital.

   c. Establish the importance of the hospital as an important community asset—appeal to the prospect's sense of community pride and citizenship.

   d. Stress the importance of participation of all residents within the greater Miami community.

   e. Show examples of needed financial support. (Refer to Scale of Gifts in Solicitor's Packet)

   f. Explain to prospects how their gift, when added to those already received, will encourage others.

   g. Close your gift decision by completion of the pledge card or letter of intent.

   h. If unable to close at the initial meeting, obtain a firm date for a follow-up meeting.

   i. If you are encountering difficulty in closing at a reasonable gift category level (in your mind) suggest that the prospect consider the matter further before deciding. You can then seek counsel with the campaign leadership.

Suggestions for Solicitors

Mercy Hospital Needs You:

You have accepted the responsibility of personally calling on a few prospects to secure the "private sector" financial support needed for the successful completion of this promising community health care facility.

Know Your Story:

Carefully read the promotional items furnished you—the brochure, the commemorative gifts folder, and the items in your solicitor's packet. Each was carefully designed to provide you the essential background so you could speak with confidence, courage and conviction. If you feel the need for additional clarification or assistance, please consult with the members of the foundation staff and/or the campaign leadership.

Know Your Prospect:

Your knowledge of the prospect is important. We hope you will have chosen prospects who are somewhat known to you and that you may have even broadened your knowledge of the prospect by consulting with others. By doing so, each of you will be more comfortable and your results enhanced.

Make Your Own Commitment:

It will be immeasurably easier for you to represent this program effectively if you have already made a commitment—before you contact any of your prospects. Often prospects will ask you what you have done and then relate that to what you are asking them to do.

Make Your Calls Now:

This campaign has been carefully planned and solicitations properly scheduled. Advance preparations and publicity have been provided. It is extremely important that you proceed immediately as your section of the campaign moves out.

Personal Visits Are A Must:

You, the volunteer solicitor, will greatly influence your prospect by a personal visit. You compliment the prospect—you can present the story in a proper forum emphasizing the value of his or her contribution.

Take and Maintain the Initiative:

Always bear in mind that most everyone wants to be supportive of essential community projects. The manner in which you present the story should be positive and forceful to a degree. Speak out, listen carefully, meet all questions or objections with proper answers and thoughtful replies.

Ask For The Gift:

Obtaining a commitment on the first visit is not always possible. With such a large dollar objective, it has become necessary to seek much higher gift levels from each of our prospects—probably higher than they have ever been asked to consider before. Therefore, a second visit—even a third—may be necessary.

The extended pledge period should enable most to budget their payments over a three-year period. The gift can be larger while the annual payments are smaller and less apt to be burdensome.

Suggest A Down Payment:

After a prospect has agreed to pledge a certain amount, suggest to him or her the possibility of making a down payment.

Do Not Overstress Tax Benefits:

While our government encourages philanthropy and provides tax incentives for giving—most will give because of the meritorious appeal of the project, their sense of community pride and sharing.

Acknowledgement:

Thank all prospects for their time and commitment. Feel free to do so by letter as well—if you choose. All gifts, large and small alike, will be properly acknowledged by the foundation.

Acknowledgement/ Pledge Follow-up

Every contribution, regardless of size, will be officially acknowledged by Ralph Di Santo, Executive Vice President. Usually the acknowledgement follows within one week of the date after the official pledge card has been received at the Mercy Hospital Foundation, Inc.

A follow-up procedure will apply in the case of all pledges. The terms indicated by the donor will be properly recorded. Official reminder notices will be mailed thirty days prior to the specified payment dates.

In the event changes become necessary, Mr. Di Santo will be happy to consider those adjustments that seem most appropriate.

6

Costs Funding Sources

Listed below is a capsule account of the costs and needed funding for the Replacement and Modernization Project.

New construction	$20,184,000
Renovation	2,816,000
Total construction	23,000,000
Moveable equipment	835,500
Professional fees	2,144,000
Construction contingency	907,500
Administrative expenses	350,000
Total project cost prior to financing expenses	$27,237,000

Construction Schedule

Construction is scheduled to begin in Spring, 1982 with remodeling to be completed in Fall, 1984.

Summary of Space Development in the Proposed Project

Department/Service	New	Remodeled
Medical/Surgical Units	82,000	—
Critical Care Unit	7,000	—
Food Services	10,000	11,000
Normal Newborn Nursery	—	5,000
Labor/Delivery Suite	—	8,000
Main Lobby	2,000	
Mechanical, including new Energy Center	20,800	—
General Circulation links, elevator core, etc.	22,200	—
Total New Building	**144,000**	
Total Remodeling		**24,000**

Donor Recognition

Mercy Hospital provides a broad range of commemorative gift opportunities for subscribers who wish to establish an enduring living tribute or a permanent memorial to an individual, family or organization.

Names will be displayed in an architecturally appropriate manner in a suitable public area depending upon the nature and location of the facility.

In addition, the following gift categories will be used:

Humanitarian	$1 million plus
Benefactor	$500,000 to $999,999
Founder	$100,000 to $499,999
Patron	$ 50,000 to $ 99,999
Sponsor	$ 10,000 to $ 49,999
Friend	$ 1,000 to $ 9,999
Good Samaritan	$ 75 to $ 999

Donor names will be properly recorded in perpetuity. The list will recognize all present donors and serve as an example to others, especially the young whom we must look to, in years to come—to build similar fine community institutions.

Sample Letter of Intent

(For those donors who do not wish to use the standard pledge card.)

Date (

Mr. Ralph Di Santo
Executive Vice President
Mercy Hospital Foundation, Inc.
3663 South Miami Avenue
Miami, Florida 33133

Dear Mr. Di Santo:

It is presently my intention to contribute $_____ to Mercy Hospital, Inc.

Payments will be in the form of cash and/or securities, on a flexible basis, over the next three years.

Please be advised that this is merely a statement of intent and may not be construed as legally binding on me or my estate.

Sincerely,
(To be signed)

10

MERCY HOSPITAL, INC.

GROWING TO SERVE AN INTERNATIONAL COMMUNITY

Total Pledge $	2,500
Paid Herewith $	500
Balance $	2,000
1982 $	500
1983 $	500
1984 $	500
1985 $	500

Solicitor _____

Name _____
Address _____
City & State _____ Zip _____

In support of the Replacement and Modernization Project for Mercy Hospital, and in consideration of the gifts of others, I/we subscribe the sum of

Twenty-five hundred _____ Dollars ($ 2,500.00)

To be paid: annually X Semi-annually ☐ Quarterly ☐ Monthly ☐ or as follows _____

Date Payment to Start December 1, 1982

Signed Mr and Mrs John E. Davis Date September 1, 1982

Please make checks payable to Mercy Hospital Foundation, Inc.
3663 South Miami Avenue, Miami, Florida 33133
(If payment is made in stock, please endorse in blank and send to Ralph Di Santo, Executive Vice President.)
For more information, contact: Ralph Di Santo, 305 285-2711.

This gift is tax deductible as provided by law

over please

Example: Pledge Subscription

Donor's subscription consists of September 1, 1982 payment, and balance to be paid over the next three years.

8

9

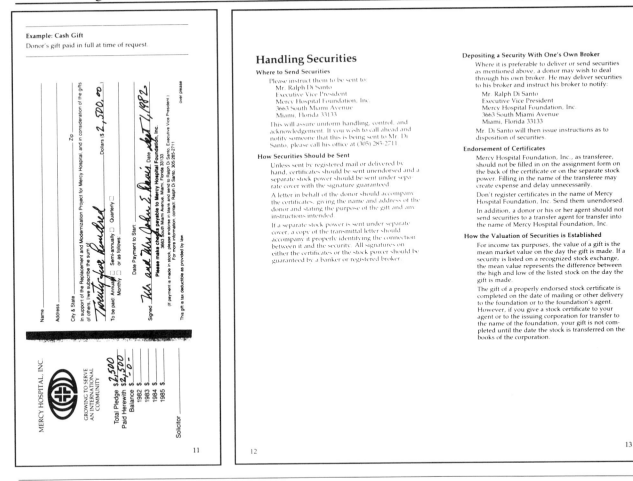

Figure 22.8. The front side of this prospect information card was filled in by the development office at Centre College in Danville, Kentucky; the back side by the volunteer

Figure 22.9. Washington University in St. Louis prepared regular campaign bulletins to report to participants on the progress of its $300 million campaign, which received more than double its goal in donations.

Fall 1987   Number Thirteen

Bulletin

A Periodic Report to Participants in the ALLIANCE FOR WASHINGTON UNIVERSITY

ALLIANCE Campaign Surpasses $575 Million

With less than two months remaining until its scheduled conclusion on December 31, 1987, the ALLIANCE FOR WASHINGTON UNIVERSITY keeps rolling up record numbers. Campaign chairman George H. Capps has announced that total commitments to the campaign have reached $575.8 million.

The latest total exceeds the original $300 million goal for the campaign by 92 percent and continues to be the largest amount raised by any single university fundraising campaign. The ALLIANCE was the first university campaign ever to reach the half-billion-dollar mark.

Capps, president of Capitol Coal and Coke Co., said that gifts for capital purposes now total $422.4 million, and gifts for operating purposes total $153.4 million.

The present totals have been achieved through more than 220,000 gifts from some 59,000 donors, and through the efforts of more than 5,500 volunteers, Capps said.

"The credit for these outstanding results is due not only to the generosity of our donors," he said, "but also to the volunteers who committed themselves so strongly to the University's goals, and who spoke so convincingly on behalf of Washington University."

Continued on page 5

Endowed Chairs—Legacy of Greatness

The history of Washington University is recorded in the names associated with it, in the men and women who have contributed to its quality and stature. Its achievements are the harvest of a stimulating blend of skillful teachers and talented students—and of those special friends whose beneficence has made possible the evolution from a local institution serving the St. Louis region to a national institution of worldwide distinction.

Abundant testimony of the generous spirit of benefactors to Washington University is found in the endowed chairs and in the discoveries and contributions to learning of the renowned scholars appointed to these chairs.

Were it not for the vision of Wayman Crow, a leading public-spirited citizen of the city, and the dedication of William Greenleaf Eliot, a Unitarian minister and firm believer in the importance of education, Washington University might never have been conceived and developed into a vibrant institution. Today it lives, and the memories of Eliot and Crow live with it. They are perpetuated in the first endowed professorships established well over a century ago: the Eliot Professorship in Chemistry, created in 1856, and the Wayman

Continued on page 2

Figure 22.10. This campaign review appeared in a University of Pennsylvania employee newspaper. It gave insiders the what, why and how of the campaign.

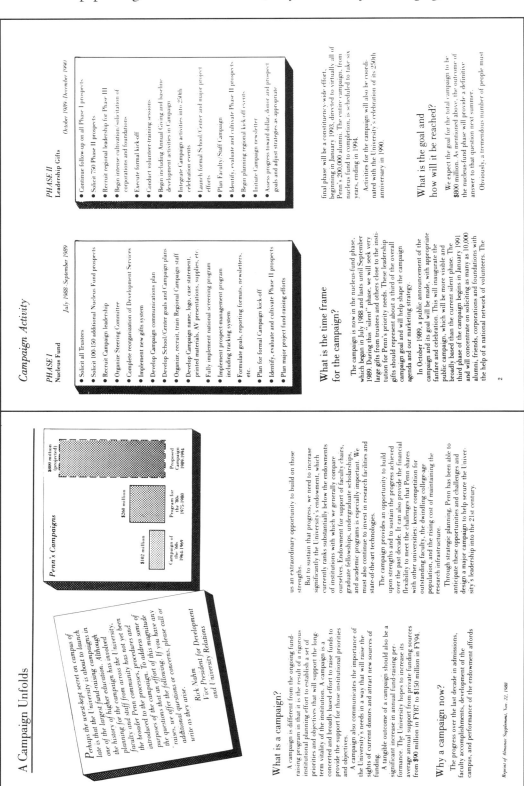

Gift Stratification Scenario for an $800 Million Campaign

Gift Level	Number of Prospects Required	Number of Gifts Required	Average Gift	Dollar Yield Subtotal	Dollar Yield Total
$ 20 mm +	6	3	$ 22 mm	$ 66 mm	$ 66 mm
$ 10-25 mm	12	6	$ 12 mm	$ 72 mm	$138 mm
$ 5-10 mm	35	20	$ 6 mm	$120 mm	$258 mm
$ 1-5 mm	280	105	$ 1.75 mm	$184 mm	$442 mm
$.5-1 mm	350	130	$600,000	$ 78 mm	$520 mm
$250,000/$500,000	430	150	$300,000	$ 45 mm	$565 mm
$100,000/$250,000	1,125	375	$150,000	$ 56 mm	$621 mm
$ 50,000/$100,000	1,800	600	$ 60,000	$ 36 mm	$657 mm
$ 25,000/$50,000	4,500	1,500	$ 30,000	$ 45 mm	$702 mm
Under $25,000		(over 100,000 gifts)		$ 98 mm	$800 mm

The campaign is an extremely ambitious undertaking, but the continued vitality of the University depends on its success. Over the course of the next several years, we will require the best efforts of not only our volunteers and staff, but the Penn faculty and staff, and we hope you will enthusiastically join us in this enterprise.

principally for professorships, student financial aid, and academic programs; and raising more than $250 million for construction and renovation of facilities.

Essentially, it is these priorities that will drive our fund-raising efforts and the success of the campaign will be measured by how well we were able to raise monies to support them. The challenge will be to match the interests of our potential donors to those priorities. Most donors, as would be expected in any population, have very specific areas that concern them and that they are willing to support. Therefore, we don't expect that at the end of the campaign there will be a large pool of unrestricted funds to devote to ventures not already established as among the University's priorities.

How will the money be used?

Through the campaign, gifts will be sought to support the priorities established by the academic leadership of the University, which are faculty development, student financial aid, research, and undergraduate education. Over the course of several years, these four central priorities were identified through ongoing planning processes in each of the University's schools and centers. They are described in more detail in *Strategic Investments in Academic Excellence* and *Choosing Penn's Future*, but can generally be described as follows:

● endowed chairs to retain and recruit nationally ranked faculty;

● enrichment of the undergraduate experience, both within and outside of the classroom;

● continued development and expansion of state-of-the-art research facilities as complements and incentives to recruiting and retaining faculty;

● student aid for graduate, professional and undergraduate students.

In order to support these academic priorities, the goals of the campaign include increasing the University's endowment by $500 million (including growth through investment of existing and new funds),

4

PHASE III
Major Gifts/Regional Campaign
January 1991-December 1992

● Continue follow-up on all Phase I and Phase II prospects

● Solicit 3000 Phase III prospects through regional kick-offs followed by committee work and reunions

● Begin faculty staff solicitation

● Complete national screening and prospect identification programs

● Develop strategies for Phase IV to conduct primarily of direct mail and telemarketing

● Assess progress toward goals and adjust strategies as appropriate

PHASE II
Constituency-wide Campaign
January 1993-June 1994

● Continue follow-up on all Phase I and Phase II prospects

● Following up on previously solicited Phase III prospects

● Solicit an additional 5000 Phase III prospects

● Conclude corporate and foundation solicitations

● Execute Phase IV constituency-wide solicitation

● Hold final Campaign celebration

● Develop final public report

● Formulate procedure for internal evaluation of results and preparation of final internal report

● Establish plan for continued stewardship beyond Campaign

participate in Penn's campaign, including alumni, trustees and friends as well as corporations and foundations, if we are to meet that goal. As the chart on page 4 illustrates, we will require some 400 top gifts of $250,000 to more than $20 million; close to 2,500 gifts of $25,000 to $250,000; and thousands more gifts of smaller amounts to meet the campaign goal of $800 million.

As a rule, one-third of the goal for a campaign should be met before a public announcement of the campaign is made. This means we will need commitments of $267 million during the nucleus-fund phase we are now in if we are to announce an $800 million goal next October. The funds raised during this period represent the endorsement and commitment of those who know the University best, and their gifts serve to raise the sights of the rest of the constituency.

Such an ambitious undertaking will require the dedication and hard work of a well-organized corps of several hundred volunteers. Leading the effort is the Campaign Steering Committee, composed of trustees and other alumni leaders and friends. The Steering Committee will meet quarterly to assess campaign policies and strategies.

In addition to the Steering Committee, there are School/Center and Project Committees for each of the University's schools and resource centers, seven Regional Committees, a Corporate Committee, Annual Giving and Class Reunion Committees, and

Oversee Committees in most of the schools and centers.

To provide professional support for the efforts of all of these volunteers, Penn's Office of Development has expanded its services and activities in a number of areas. To identify prospects capable of giving $25,000 or more, Development has assembled a staff team that conducts in-house research, and organizes review, or screening, sessions with alumni groups across the country.

A Development Information Systems unit has been established to provide ongoing services to central, school and center fund-raising staff. The Development Office has also established new procedures to coordinate outreach to alumni and institutional philanthropies.

The Office of Planned Giving, reorganized three years ago, provides education and support on planned-giving instruments (e.g., charitable-lead trusts, gift annuities) to field staff, University administrators and volunteers. This office also works with donors on financial and tax planning for their gifts.

A Campaign Marketing and Communications staff has been assembled to design a comprehensive campaign communications program and produce materials to motivate and educate volunteers and potential donors.

Film and Video Presentations

Prospects are increasingly sophisticated in terms of media exposure. Television, cable TV, VCRs and personal computers have revolutionized how we think about cultivating prospective donors. Film and video presentations are an excellent way to capture the real feeling of your organization and expose others to it. But remember, we are all used to very well-produced films and videos, so it can be costly and difficult to produce something that will impress the viewer.

Films and videos can be used during a campaign to:

- Reintroduce the audience to the organization
- Train volunteers in the process of asking
- Take the organization and its leaders to a far-flung geographic constituency
- Inspire prospects by showing people helped by the organization

Films and videos can be very effective, but they can also be very expensive. Before producing such a product, be sure you have its purpose clearly in mind. Also be sure that it can be used in multiple ways.

When seeking vendors to supply the creative and technical backup for these items, be sure to check them out with satisfied clients. Find someone who has done similar projects for similar organizations.

Once you produce a film or video project, be sure to put it to good use. Too often, organizations want to produce these items just because they are trendy.

Using Publicity

Basically, your publicity for a campaign should aim at highlighting the key events—the kickoff, volunteer appointments, major gifts received, progress and, finally, success in reaching the goal. Publicity should be used to support any capital fund-raising effort—a campaign or a continuing program.

We have listed some of the high points that publicity can be used to underscore. As you read them, don't think simply in terms of media publicity—newspaper, magazine, radio and TV reports. Think in terms of the full range of activities that can publicize something—that can change human attitudes and behavior. Think of letters, reports, mailings, calls, meetings, films, books.

The need. Long before you announce your plan to raise $250 million over the coming three years, make sure you've made the need for such a fund-raising effort a blazing reality in everyone's mind—blazing brightest, of course, in the minds of the people you've quietly identified as your major prospects. Write to them. Call them to meetings. Ask their advice. Let them read about it in their local newspaper, see it on TV, hear it on the radio, have friends discuss it with them at parties. Talk about it in all your publications and communications. Don't raise money; raise understanding of the need first.

The announcement. Publicity must be sequential. When your prospect's colleagues tell him they heard an announcement of your campaign on TV last night, you want him to respond, "Oh yes, the president called me about that last week and gave me full details." First the prospects—then the public. Tell people you're going to launch a drive. Tell them why, what good will result and how much you seek. But do this only when your program is completely firm. This announcement is the button you push to make it go.

The people. Like thunderclaps, one rolling slowly after the other as a storm passes over and then drifts away, announce your volunteer personnel. The major thunderclaps—the telegrams, phone calls, front page stories—should be reserved for the major volunteers and your top leadership. Finally, as the storm is about out of range, come the dim echoes announcing the minor people—several per release at this point. But always remember there's an audience for news of every volunteer, no matter how minor in your scheme of things: his wife, her husband, the parents (a copy of the news release from the president), the home-town newspaper, a trade publication, the alumni magazine of the volunteer's college. If used right, publicity can hook volunteers into an obligation to perform. People important to them know that if your effort flops, they may have been part of the cause. If it succeeds . . .

The features. These can appear in the press or in your own publications or both. They can be seminars or films. Spread continuing publicity that reinforces your need and keeps alive an awareness of the fund-raising effort.

The gifts. When the incredible gift finally arrives, make sure word gets around—fast and in a big way. You can usually do the story again by turning the gift into a ceremony—a presentation or dedication. The people you called or wrote to about the gift are now your guests at the dedication or luncheon. The press that reported it is now covering it.

The reports. When things get quiet, focus on totals, report meetings—anything that shows progress. Keep the action going and visible. Maintain awareness of the need.

The end. You have two purposes here. One is to reward your volunteers and donors with recognition. The other is to get things lined up so your next capital campaign will be well-received—by both volunteers and donors.

Throughout all of this work, remember that the publicity is not a separate program. It is something you mesh carefully with the many other activities that make up a capital campaign. It's a complex business. Publicity shots that go off at the wrong time usually do you little good. They use up budget, and they also leave you with an empty cannon when you may need it the most.

Figure 22.11. A news release announcing Worcester Polytechnic Institute's $52.5 million campaign

WPI

NOV 11

Worcester
Polytechnic
Institute

(617) 793-5616
793-5604
100 Institute Road
Worcester, MA 01609

FOR IMMEDIATE RELEASE   November 11, 1986
                               Contact: Michael Dorsey

WPI Launches $52.5 Million "Campaign For Excellence;"
Four-Year Capital Campaign is First in a Decade

WORCESTER, Mass. — On the anniversary of the dedication of its first building 118 years ago, Worcester Polytechnic Institute today launched a $52.5 million Campaign for Excellence, the school's first full-scale capital fund campaign in a decade.

The Campaign for Excellence will seek resources to stengthen the "WPI Plan," the school's renowned undergraduate program; to enhance opportunities for faculty scholarship and expand the graduate research program; and for a new information sciences building and other improvements to WPI's academic and athletic facilities.

The target date for completing the campaign is November 11, 1990. November 11, long observed as "Founders Day" at WPI, is the anniversary of the dedication of Boynton Hall, the college's first building which was named for its founder, John Boynton. The year 1990 will also mark the 125th anniversary of the legal birth of WPI.

In a letter sent to the college's 17,000 alumni, Howard G. Freeman, chairman of the WPI Board of Trustees, announced that $10.5 million has already been raised toward the campaign goal.

"Ours is a challenging goal," Freeman said in the letter. "Yet it is an attainable goal. It is an objective that must be met if WPI is to remain preeminent among the nation's major institutions of engineering, science and management."

-more-

WPI/Campaign for Excellence 222

According to WPI President Jon C. Strauss, one thrust of the campaign is raising the funds needed to continue the school's primary emphasis on high-quality undergraduate education.

"WPI has an extraordinary undergraduate program in its nationally recognized WPI Plan," Strauss said. "This project-oriented, competency-based academic program was far ahead of its time when it was conceived and implemented by the WPI faculty 16 years ago. Through the campaign, WPI will strengthen and enhance The Plan."

This enhancement will include a new resident project center in London, opening in the spring of 1987. Modeled after a highly successful center in Washington, D.C., the center will allow undergraduates to complete projects in cooperation with British government and private agencies. Campaign funds will be used to gradually expand this center and the Washington, D.C. center, which has hosted more than 500 students and more than 40 faculty in residence since opening in 1976.

In addition to the Washington and London centers, WPI operates several non-resident centers in the Worcester area in conjunction with local governments, health agencies and industries through which undergraduates complete two required major projects? one in their field of study and one which relates science or technology to a larger social context. Another aim of the campaign is creating new opportunities and strengthening the support for these undergraduate projects.

-more-

WPI/Campaign for Excellence 333

The undergraduate program will also be enhanced with new equipment for undergraduate laboratories, a major increase in funds for financial aid, improved access for students to the college computer network and the establishment of thematic learning centers within the residential centers. These "theme centers" will allow small groups of sophomores, juniors and seniors to study special subjects within their own living areas, continuing the learning experience beyond the classroom and laboratory environments.

The second thrust of the campaign, Strauss said, will be a renewed emphasis on excellence in scholarship. This will be achieved, in part, Strauss said, by financial support (equipment, library resources, released time) to faculty for conducting new avenues of scholarly investigation.

"It is the faculty who determine the vitality and stature of every educational institution," Strauss said. "One role of the faculty is to create new knowledge through their own research and scholarship and to communicate that knowledge through effective teaching and publication. A major objective of the campaign is to enable our faculty to achieve their full potential as scholars and teachers."

Toward this end, WPI will create six new endowed faculty chairs, bringing the total at WPI to 11. The endowed chairs will serve to recognize continued excellence by WPI's best scholars and also attract high quality faculty candidates, Strauss said. The chairs will also elevate the quality and recognition of the academic departments which host them, Strauss noted.

In addition to the faculty chairs, WPI will establish six graduate student fellowships and six graduate teaching assistantships to help attract the ablest candidates for graduate study, Strauss said.

—more—

WPI/Campaign for Excellence 444

The campaign will also raise seed money to support faculty who are developing research programs in new and emerging fields of study. This seed money will help primarily junior faculty acquire needed equipment and supplies, develop professional and industry contacts and obtain outside funding for their work. Most recently, WPI has supported the development of new programs in such areas as biotechnology, biomedical engineering, laser holography, materials science, firesafety and manufacturing.

"In such rapidly changing areas as science and technology, it is essential that WPI have funds available to allow faculty to move into new areas expeditiously," Richard H. Gallagher, vice president and dean of the faculty, said.

Another major goal of the campaign is the creation of new centers which will provide links between WPI and industry. WPI's existing Manufacturing Engineering Applications Center (MEAC) and Management of Advanced Automation and Technology (MAAT) Center provide faculty and students "real-world" laboratories for work in robotics and advanced manufacturing technology. WPI expects to develop other partnerships with industry in such areas as biotechnology, materials science and artificial intelligence.

Other goals aimed at improving opportunities for scholarship include the creation of new, specialized collections in WPI's Gordon Library and the enhancement of the college's computer facilities. The continued "computerization of WPI" will include new computer equipment and a comprehensive communications network to link the university's buildings and programs, an enhanced computer support staff and programs to assist faculty in incorporating computers in their teaching and research.

—more—

WPI/Campaign for Excellence 555

The primary "bricks and mortar" program to be funded by the campaign will be a new Information Sciences Building. The first new academic building to be constructed at WPI in over two decades, it will house the campus's computer facilities and Computer Science Department and will include a 400-seat auditorium. The building will be located adjacent to the Atwater Kent Laboratories, which the Computer Science Department now shares with the Electrical Engineering Department.

Campus improvements will also include the renovation of Alden Memorial Hall. Built in 1939 as a 700-seat assembly hall for the full student body, its role as an auditorium has been superceded by Harrington Auditorium, which can hold 3,500. Alden will be turned into a performing arts center with classrooms, offices and rehearsal spaces for courses and activities of the Humanities Department.

By locating the Humanities Department in Alden Hall, space in the Salisbury Laboratories Building will be freed up for the expansion of classroom, laboratory and office space for the Biology and Biotechnology Department and Biomedical Engineering Program. Both of these relatively new programs have seen a steady increase in enrollment and research over the past decade.

Additions and renovations to Goddard Hall and the Higgins Laboratories will provide badly needed space for, respectively, the Chemical Engineering Department and the Department of Mechanical Engineering. Also included in the campaign goal are funds for the recently renovated outdoor athletic facilities, which included the installation of a synthetic surface on the football field and track. Another $400,000 is still to be raised for this project, completed this past summer.

NOTE: A DETAILED BREAKDOWN OF THE CAMPAIGN OBJECTIVES IS ATTACHED.

-30-

CAMPAIGN FOR EXCELLENCE
Worcester Polytechnic Institute
November, 1986

Objectives

Resources for the Undergraduate Program

Enhancement of the WPI Plan through the addition of more undergraduate project centers, including a residential center in London, strengthening the faculty advising program, creation of new project opportunities and support of ongoing institutional evaluation of the Plan. $1,650,000

Funds for new equipment for undergraduate teaching laboratories, including procurement of expensive one-of-a-kind units.   2,000,000

Financial aid for undergraduates. WPI currently admits students on a "need blind" basis and hopes to continue the practice of providing access to WPI to all admitted students.   2,000,000

Development of residential college programs to extend the learning experiences within the living environments.   1,500,000

Extension of computer network and expansion of computer facilities for substantially growing undergraduate learning applications.   2,250,000

     /9,400,000/

Additional Faculty Resources and Funding for New Program Development

Seed funding to develop academic opportunities in new and emerging areas of technology. In fields such as science and engineering, targets of new opportunity occur with unpredictable frequency. WPI desires to continue to be in a position to respond to selective opportunities, consistent with its mission.   3,500,000

Six endowed special professorships to be awarded to nationally recognized scholars to permit WPI to move rapidly into new areas or to coalesce diverse campus resources with strong leadership.   6,000,000

Figure 22.11 Continued

Six endowed research assistantships and six endowed teaching assistantships to attract outstanding graduate students in desired areas or new fields, capitalizing on the strength of the graduate program and assisting in teaching. 2,100,000

Additional Industry/WPI Centers to further integrate the real world of industry and commerce with the project and research opportunities at WPI in science, engineering and management. 4,000,000

Enhancement of computer network and facilities for faculty research and scholarship. 2,250,000

Development of additional library collections in new subject areas that will enhance teaching and research in new areas. 605,000

/18,455,000/

Physical Plant Development

New building for Information Sciences to provide needed space for Department of Computer Science, the Campus Computer Center and hub of campus computer network, and an all campus 400 seat lecture hall. 6,045,000

Renovation of outdoor athletic facilities including synthetic surface on football field and track, six tennis courts, and a reorientation and resodding of the baseball and softball diamonds. (Project completed in 1986) 1,900,000

Property acquisition to meet future needs for student residential facilities and offices for WPI's support functions, and continuation of campus beautification program. 2,500,000

Redevelopment of interior of Alden Memorial to create a center for the humanities with a performing arts theater, performance areas, rehearsal spaces, classrooms and offices for the Department of Humanities. 2,500,000

Completion of renovations in Salisbury Laboratories to permit use of the entire building for programs in Biomedical Engineering and in Biology and Biotechnology. 1,000,000

Addition to Goddard Hall to meet space needs of Department of Chemical Engineering for additional laboratories for teaching and research. 2,200,000

Continuing Renovation of Higgins Laboratories of Mechanical Engineering. First major work since Higgins was built in 1941 will retrofit the structure to adapt interior space to modern needs of instruction, including some new space. 3,500,000

/19,645,000/

Unrestricted Giving

To be used in development of WPI's annual budget to provide the 2% margin for excellence that permits WPI a degree of flexibility to respond rapidly to unforeseen opportunities. Such funding also has been used to keep deferred maintenance of the physical plant at a minimum in recent years. /5,000,000/

Campaign for Excellence Goal $52,500,000

Fiigure 22.11. Continued

Chapter 23
Going After the Gifts

The Nucleus Fund

Probably the most important early task in a capital campaign is defining the way prospects are going to be cultivated and solicited. This is particularly important for donors to the nucleus fund. The nucleus fund includes all early gifts to the campaign. Usually those closest to the organization—board members and other major regular donors—are asked to make gifts that are bigger than they have ever given before. The nucleus fund then sets the pace for the rest of the campaign. Usually at least a quarter to one-half of the total campaign goal is raised during the nucleus fund stage. And this is before the campaign is announced publicly. If it proves difficult to raise the funds anticipated for the nucleus fund, this says something very important about the whole campaign effort and may lead to a reassessment of the goal or of the campaign's timetable.

The most vital initial solicitor for the nucleus fund is the CEO of the organization. He or she asks the board chairman to give. Then the board chairman asks other board members. Once other board members commit, they can then also become solicitors. It is usually the job of five to six very carefully selected and trained solicitors to raise the nucleus fund. This group can include the CEO, the chief development officer and board leadership. The most successful board solicitor for the nucleus fund is probably the best candidate to chair the entire campaign.

Special Cultivation Activities

In addition to managing the nucleus fund stage of the campaign, the staff must also develop prospect management policies that will hold throughout the campaign. For large organizations, such as universities that have development officers in various schools, setting priorities on prospect management is vital. Everyone should know which prospects are being solicited, by whom and when. The aim should be to avoid overlapping solicitations that could turn off the prospective donor. It may help to create prospect lists for every major asker such as the president, board members and deans. And then only the assigned solicitor should pursue a prospect during a given time period. If the initial assignment does not seem to produce results, a new solicitor might be chosen.

You might consider having a prospect evaluation committee to help define appropriate assignments once prospects are carefully rated. Including top volunteers in this process can help since volunteers, especially board members, can often advise which solicitation scenario will lead to the maximum gift.

Your prospect management plan should aim at just that—seeking the maximum gift from each prospect. All in-house research data must be pooled with staff expertise and volunteer insights to seek the best path to follow with each prospect. And remember that it really takes an individualized plan to seek the biggest gift from each prospect.

Prospect cultivation goes on before, during and after a capital campaign. Cultivation is a continuous process. But a capital campaign offers many exciting opportunities that would not arise without such a special effort being under way.

Prior to a major capital campaign, organizations often hold a series of cultivation events to bring prospects to the site and update them on current activities. Once a campaign begins, there are many cultivation event opportunities. A campaign kickoff event followed by a series of dinners might be in order. If an organization's constituency is spread out geographically, there might be a series of regional kickoff events.

A campaign kickoff event can accomplish the following:

■ It announces the campaign broadly to all constituents.
■ It introduces the campaign's volunteer leadership.
■ It serves as a cultivation event for major prospects.
■ It celebrates past organizational accomplishments and looks forward to a new future.
■ It builds momentum for the campaign—starts the bandwagon effect.
■ It recognizes major donors to date.

When large commitments are received during a campaign, you have additional opportunities to recognize donors through dinners and social events. These events to commemorate major gifts often encourage others to think about big pledges. By inviting top prospects to campaign events, you can give them a real sense of the organization's movement and progress.

Your continuing cultivation program during a capital campaign might include some of these traditional elements:

■ Progress reports
■ Invitations to major events
■ Personal visits from institutional leaders
■ Meetings, luncheons, dinners or parties
■ Asking prospective donors for advice
■ Preparation of printed materials
■ Doing anything that makes a person feel special, such as providing parking privileges, tickets to events, access to materials
■ Films or slide presentations

What are the objectives of all these cultivation activities?

■ To build a viable and powerful constituency
■ To increase public interest
■ To develop new volunteer leadership
■ To provide a broad range of information to those who can help
■ To construct a lasting foundation for raising private funds—now and later

During a capital campaign, cultivation activities actually have two major objectives. First and foremost is to attract gifts for the campaign. But often campaign cultivation actually encourages prospects to have a long-term interest in the organization that might lead to even bigger gifts later on.

Keys to Soliciting Big Gifts

The basic key to soliciting large gifts from individuals, as we have already mentioned, is finding the right person to ask the right prospect for the right amount in the right way for the right reason at the right time. This of course involves some luck and the careful pairing of prospects and solicitors.

Capital campaigns provide an air of expectation that often aids the solicitation process. But your solicitor still needs to be on the same wavelength as your prospect, so that a natural relationship can develop. Solicitors are most effective if they are truly interested and exude an aura of confidence in the institution.

Solicitation contacts must be recurrent. Very few large gifts result from a single solicitation. Large gift solicitations should start with those closest to the institution and proceed through top prospect groups out to the wider constituency, following this wise fund-raising advice given by Benjamin Franklin: " . . . in the first place, I advise you to apply to all those who you know will give something; next to those whom you are uncertain whether they will give anything or not; and show them the list of those who have given; and lastly, do not neglect those who you are sure will give nothing; for in some of them you may be mistaken."

The development staff has a large—in some cases increasing—role to play in the solicitation process, especially during a campaign. With the growing complexity of methods of giving, especially planned gifts, trained staff members have become more and more involved in soliciting. But an influential volunteer is still instrumental in setting the stage and getting entry to the prospect.

The staff is also responsible for establishing the volunteer solicitor organization. Timetables and goals are structures the staff gives the soliciting effort. The staff must prod the volunteer to do his or her job on schedule. This is a delicate task. You cannot overload a volunteer solicitor and then expect all work to be done on time. A series of report meetings where volunteers know they will be asked to outline their progress is a good way to keep activities on track.

Two types of printed pieces usually are associated with soliciting: the pledge card that the prospect signs and some sort of booklet that tells the solicitor how to solicit. This booklet generally contains instructions basic to almost any solicitation, and it sometimes also has information specific to one campaign or program.

Thus far, we've been talking primarily about individual prospects. In addition, corporations and foundations are usually solicited for major gifts during a capital fund-raising program. The procedures for soliciting foundation or corporate gifts do not change from the usual during a capital fund-raising campaign, except that you can usually involve more key members of your constituency in the actual solicitations. Most nonprofit institutions and agencies are always on the lookout for grants from these sources, so procedures should already be fairly well-established prior to a campaign.

Also keep in mind that corporations and foundations will rarely give just because you're having a campaign. They need to see a demonstrated case for support and a relationship to their giving interests.

Creative Follow-up

Getting the gift is by no means the end of the line. First a contributor must be thanked and sent an acknowledgment or receipt. Then he or she should be kept informed about use of the gift and the progress of the fund drive, and be included in campaign events. Also, depending on the size of the gift and its purpose, thought should be given to a dedication or testimonial honoring the donor or someone named by the donor.

For major capital gifts, individual approaches to follow-up should be worked out. Every donor requires something different in the way of recognition. Some want to remain anonymous, while others seek a public expression of gratitude. Often the terms of the gift stipulate official recognition such as the placing of a plaque on a facility. Don't delay in carrying out such wishes; they often lead to another gift. The more personal and individualized the follow-up, the better. All donors of major gifts should receive a personal letter from at least the top administrative officer of the organization.

A word of warning: In capital campaigns, the development officer tends to focus on the prospects who have not yet given; they remain "on the list." There is a natural tendency to stop thinking about the donors whose gifts have been made; they are no longer on the list. Common sense tells you this could be a grave mistake. The donor is your known friend; the prospect is a question mark. Don't neglect your friends in your pursuit of the question marks. Make sure your program has a niche built into it for donors, who are now practically members of the team. Keep them posted on what others are doing—possibly as a result of their generous examples. Keep inviting donors to your special events, your cocktail parties, your dinners with the president. Their presence there will create a good effect on the prospects. They will be positive about your project because they have invested in it themselves. In fact, they will be anxious to help you raise money. Consider sending them some of your insider reports on the fund-raising project. If they are big donors, keep sending them personal letters on what's happening—in advance of the announcement to the masses. Keep telephoning them.

Why all this effort? Well, first of all, it is polite. But more importantly, you are setting the scene for your next campaign. And maybe your donors will give again to the current effort.

Analyzing the Results

Your analysis will vary depending on the type of capital campaign you have used. You can reflect very specifically on the various stages of a campaign or on the effort as a whole. Here are some important points to consider when analyzing the results of any capital fund-raising program.

■ Was the effort a success or a failure?
■ Was the program on the whole well-received?
■ Which expenses proved the most beneficial? Which expenses were least effective?
■ Which promotional materials and events were the most effective?
■ What was the best method of solicitation?
■ Which procedures should be repeated and which ones should be abandoned?
■ What conditions should be changed before more capital fund-raising is done?
■ Did key leadership develop during the campaign?
■ Did key prospects appear for the future?
■ Have you recorded all of the data that turned up during the solicitations?
■ Should you publish a final report on the effort?

Many organizations publish final statistical reports on capital campaigns. But few take the time to critically and honestly analyze the actual effect of the effort on the organization. You should reflect on the important gains and failures of the capital drive. This type of analysis will prove invaluable in organizing future fund-raising programs. Remember, the process of raising major private gifts never ends if a nonprofit organization intends to remain financially stable. There must be a continuous series of funding programs accompanied by reappraisals of needs, prospects and procedures.

After your campaign is over, what do you do next? Craig W. Stewart, director of development at the Lakeside School in Seattle, Washington, suggests these steps:

■ At the same time that you announce the success of your campaign, be sure to recognize and thank your volunteers.
■ Ask for feedback from your volunteers.
■ Do a post mortem on the campaign. Why were you successful or unsuccessful? What could you have done differently? Record your findings for future reference and learn by your successes and mistakes.
■ Update information on your constituents, particularly on volunteers and on any major prospects you may have uncovered.
■ Examine your staff. If any performed exceptionally, can you promote them? Are any of them burned out? Are you, yourself, ready to take on more responsibility? If you used consultants, evaluate their performance, and give them the results.
■ Don't forget your annual giving program; turn capital gift donors into annual donors.
■ Decide how you will continue to raise major gifts. Will it be through a new campaign or through a long-term major gifts program, which is not campaign-oriented?
■ Take a look at your long-term planning and research. Does it need reassessment, revised goals? What about your gift policies? Are you doing all you can with planned giving? Is your research turning up all of your major gift prospects?

These comments suggest, as we have said in this book, that major gifts fund-raising never ends. A capital campaign can give your organization a real boost in funding, but the real benefit is in increasing fund-raising sights for the future.

Figure 23.1. Excerpts from the final report on the Deerfield Campaign at Deerfield Academy in Massachusetts

Assuring Excellence: Deerfield Academy's Next Decade

A Statement by Headmaster Robert E. Kaufmann

As early as 1982, I began to visualize what I considered the important needs of Deerfield as we entered the last decade of our second century. The people at Deerfield were paramount in these images. I traveled across the country for two years speaking with alumni and friends of the Academy to see if this emphasis was correct. The encouragement I received from virtually every source led to the creation of a detailed plan to raise $31.5 million. Everyone thought it was ambitious. Some people thought it was impossible.

Since the official beginning of The Deerfield Campaign in April 1985, we have seen the financial markets rise dramatically and then fall precipitously. We have seen significant changes in tax law. At the same time, we began this effort at a time when many other institutions to which Deerfield alumni, parents and friends have loyalties were also embarking on major capital campaign programs.

As we finished this campaign in June 1988, it was clear that we had done extremely well, and credit for our success can rightly be given to the thousands of Deerfield alumni, parents and friends who have responded to our requests for support.

In my discussions before and during the campaign, I referred to Mr. Boyden's objectives as he built this school. His need to create new teaching spaces and new dormitories left Deerfield in the early 1980's with an endowment that was significantly smaller than that which existed at comparable schools. The school had been successful in large measure because of the extraordinary success of Annual Support. It was clear, however, that we needed to put Deerfield on a firm, long-term financial footing through the growth in our endowment in order to remain competitive with the best boarding schools in New England. Faculty salaries had to be raised. Professional development funds were essential. Enhanced scholarship resources were critical in order to keep Deerfield diverse and open to the best students. These objectives could not be achieved through tuition resources alone. In addition, we needed to consolidate the physical circumstances of an excellent program in the arts and to refurbish and renovate the two buildings which serve as the center of the campus.

How have we done and how will we compare with the other fine New England boarding schools at the end of this decade?

A summary of our accomplishments is easy to construct. For the year 1988-89, average faculty salaries at Deerfield will be in the top 10% when compared with other boarding schools in New England. Faculty salary levels have made significant progress in *real* terms during the decade of the '80's and much of that progress is the direct result of The Deerfield Campaign.

Deerfield now has in place a program for professional development which is the envy of most schools. The academic year 1988-89 will see the third Deerfield faculty member leave campus for an entire year of sabbatical and, at the same time, we have enlarged our resources for those faculty members who need support for academic opportunities during the summers. Scholarship resources have grown and expenditures for financial assistance in 1988-89 will represent approximately 16.4% of total tuition revenue, an increase from 14.7% in 1983-84.

Construction has begun on the dormitories which will replace Plunkett. Included in the process is the construction of seven new faculty apartments, each of which will be significantly larger and more liveable than any of those in Plunkett. The former corridors of 22 students will give way to smaller, more manageable units of 15. We will have, by the fall of 1989, newly constructed music facilities, a new theater; and a fully renovated and integrated arts facility which will be as good as any school our size can rightfully expect. At the same time, we will have created exciting new teaching locations by utilizing spaces that were previously poorly utilized or used for other purposes. In addition, the Main School Building and the Arms Building will have undergone renovation and refurbishment, eliminating a long list of deferred maintenance on those two buildings and establishing them as functional entities for the 1990's, while guaranteeing their usefulness and beauty for another 30 or 40 years. With the exception of the gymnasium, the school is now in a circumstance where its overall physical plant is as good as that of any other secondary school. Further specific details of each of these accomplishments are presented in other reports in this document.

As a result of the rise in financial markets combined with the added resources generated by The Deerfield Campaign, our endowment per student has risen from approximately $66,000 in 1984 to approximately $116,000 today. This enhancement helps to guarantee a stable financial future while allowing us the opportunity to invest in new programs and new learning opportunities.

As the campaign has proceeded, a great deal has also transpired in the life of the Academy. The most visible and momentous decision was that which was made in January of this year when the Board of Trustees voted to admit girls to the student body as of September 1989. The combination of the enhancement of our financial circumstance and the exciting challenge of making Deerfield a truly coeducational environment augers well for this school as we approach our 200th Anniversary. Deerfield has a strong faculty which is well paid and will continue to be well educated. We have scholarship resources to welcome the best students we can find into our student body. And, we have a physical plant which offers myriad opportunities for young people to grow and learn and for faculty to live and work. In a word, we are well positioned for the future.

None of this would have been possible without the generosity, seen in terms of time, effort, and financial contribution of many members of the

Deerfield family. We now have combined the best of Mr. Boyden's plans for the growth and development of a unique school with strong financial management and adequate endowment resources to keep us on an equal footing with the very best schools in New England. With your continued support and commitment I am optimistic that those of us who work at this Academy will continue to make you proud of the heritage that we share.

Assuring Excellence: Deerfield Academy's Next Decade

A Statement by Gilbert H. Lamphere '70
President, Board of Trustees, and
National Chairman, The Deerfield Campaign

By any measure, The Deerfield Campaign was an overwhelming success and a rewarding achievement for both volunteers and donors alike. While the numbers are staggering—$86.2 million, 2,290 gifts, an average of $83,000 in gifts per day—they cannot begin to suggest the multitude of ways in which life at the Academy on a personal level will be enriched. In sum, the campaign has ensured that the people of Deerfield—faculty and students alike—will be characterized by the excellence of which our alumni, parents, grandparents and friends have said the Academy is worthy.

Let us begin to outline the impact of the campaign by starting with its effect on the faculty. Most importantly, from a financial point of view, we have elevated teaching at Deerfield to a true profession. Moreover, we have taken the lead and set the pace among New England boarding schools in setting goals related to faculty compensation and development. Among the highlights:

1. Deerfield has boosted faculty salary levels by 10%, 15% and 12% respectively over the last three years.

Our faculty, *on average*, are now within 10% of the highest paid boarding school faculty in New England. For all distinct age categories, Deerfield ranks first or second in average compensation among its peer schools.

The overwhelming response to the McGlynn Teaching Chair was yet another vivid and moving example of our alumni and parents' commitment to teaching. Over $830,000 was raised from 654 gifts and pledges in response to the McGlynn Challenge.

We will continue to be aggressive in the area of faculty compensation.

2. Deerfield now also has the permanent capital to *each* year provide two faculty members and their families with a one-year sabbatical to study, reflect and research areas of interest. This time of renewal is not only vital but also provides the entire faculty community with a focus and an expectation—and reinforces both trustee and alumni commitment to the faculty,

and our perception of Deerfield as a learning, educational and academic community in its fullest sense.

3. Faculty housing has been expanded and enhanced. An integral part of Deerfield's distinctiveness is the close interaction of faculty, on a full-time basis, with the students. Our new dormitories will provide a total of seven semi-attached faculty residences of three to four bedrooms, allowing for a Deerfield faculty member to be fully involved in corridor life, while providing suitable accommodations for family time as well.

In so doing we have not only reduced the size of the corridors, but have also provided top quality housing that responds to today's faculty circumstances.

All three of the above areas will be critical in attracting, retaining and developing a faculty body whose current average tenure is a robust 14 years.

Let us now move to what the campaign has meant to the *students*:

1. Deerfield must continue to be able to provide financial aid to all qualified students who require scholarship assistance if it is to remain in the top ranks of educational institutions. This means we must continually increase the amounts we provide for scholarship aid. Thirty percent of the student body is now receiving some sort of assistance.

2. The Deerfield Campaign's endowment giving not only ensures ample scholarship aid, but also enables us to avoid *being forced* to raise tuition at accelerating rates. The implication is clear. With reasonable tuition and sufficient financial aid we will continue to be able to attract a cross section of students from all walks of life and economic circumstances. This is critical to the health and vitality of the school.

In addition to providing for important human needs, the campaign has also had a significant effect on the Academy's facilities. Teaching and learning require facilities that support and encourage these activities. Mr. Boyden and Deerfield have always believed in building things right—with quality and an aesthetic sense of belonging to and in the historic Village of Deerfield. We have not given in to the temptation to sacrifice quality for short-term, "penny wise-pound foolish" cost savings.

1. Our three new dormitories, which will replace Plunkett, are being built as "35-year" facilities—i.e., they will outlive many of us. These new dormitories will provide reduced corridor size, enhanced opportunity for student/faculty interaction, and faculty family living space that is consistent with today's educational and teaching realities and challenges.

2. The new Greer School Store is a further reflection of this commitment to quality. Used by hundreds of boys every day, it provides a relaxing but vibrant quality to the students' interaction and learning.

3. The Reed Arts Center will be one of the finest arts facilities in New England. It is an endorsement of the students and faculty whose accomplishments in the arts have already made their mark on Deerfield life in the last fifteen years. The opportunity for drama, art, music, and now dance, to combine in a coherent interdisciplinary manner is an exciting prospect.

Although expensive, the cultural tone and awareness it brings to the campus is exciting and invigorating, Mr. Boyden would have been pleased that the funds were committed to build this facility in a thoroughly first class manner:

4. The new teaching and administrative space opened by extensive renovation in the Main School and Arms Buildings is equally exciting and worthy of note. The renewal of these facilities is important for effective teaching, whether it be the humanities, language, or science. The computer will be another beneficiary of this renovation as its use spreads as a learning device in all disciplines.

Where do we go from here? We feel we are well prepared for the next many years, but the educational world of which Deerfield is a part will not stand still. Our alumni, parents and friends are our partners in this process of change. Annual Support will provide the near-term catalyst as we plan new objectives and goals. Of course, The Deerfield Campaign has greatly strengthened our alumni body's knowledge of the school. We will continue to develop the wonderful appreciation and understanding that our alumni have for Deerfield's people and their work. Promoting that understanding is, to me, the core of the development process.

On a concrete level, our athletic plant deserves a hard look, and likely, some hard dollars in the near future. Coeducation will provide some new challenges and costs. But fortunately the ship has been well maintained over the last 25 years – there are no hidden surprises or holes at the waterline.

You have all given not just from your abundance but I feel have stretched to a level of real sacrifice. I trust you have experienced the satisfaction of giving back to Deerfield in proportion to what Deerfield may have given to you.

Recently, Robert Morgenthau '37, District Attorney of Manhattan and the 1985 recipient of the Deerfield Heritage Award, was asked by New York Magazine "Who Really Counts" in the future of the community. Each of the other 40 or so notables, besides Morgenthau, who were asked the same question, named a well-known person of established reputation. But, Morgenthau's response seemed to me to be the best. Morgenthau said the most important person is "a sixteen-year-old boy or girl who's got the most important decision to make about whether and how they are going to contribute to society."

In my mind, Bob Morgenthau just put his finger on what our alumni, parents and friends and their response to this campaign have been trying to say. Bob Morgenthau may have just summed up the underlying philosophy of The Deerfield Campaign.

Enthusiastic Volunteers Assure Campaign's Success

by David G. Pond, Director of Development

The Deerfield Campaign began unofficially in the New York office of Garry Bewkes '44, the former head of our Development Committee, in July 1983. It was agreed that a campaign should be conducted on a national basis over three years. A "needs" list was also in the process of being completed. A good portion of that meeting was spent identifying a number of people who might serve as national chairman or assist in various leadership roles. We also traveled extensively across the country and sought the advice of many alumni and parents who had been involved in earlier Deerfield campaigns.

Gil Lamphere '70, a member of our Board of Trustees, was asked to serve as national chairman. He had demonstrated considerable leadership skills not only as a member of Deerfield's Board of Trustees as head of its Investment Committee, but also as a volunteer for his college capital efforts. His volunteer work, coupled with his extensive experience in the New York financial community, suggested that he was the logical choice.

Shortly after Gil's selection, our office began to identify individuals across the country who would be asked to assist in the solicitation of leadership gifts. This National Campaign Committee, comprised of 41 alumni and parents, was organized for this purpose. The list included alumni and parents primarily from the Northeast, but an attempt was made to have at least one National Campaign Committee member from each of the fifteen locations where we planned to have an area campaign. Along with the Headmaster and the National Chairman, the National Campaign Committee was charged with the collective responsibility of the solicitation of 250 alumni and parents who it was felt were in a position to make leadership gifts. Because the sizes of the requests ranged from $25,000 to over $1 million, several visits were often required with each prospective donor. The National Campaign Committee had an extremely high completion rate with the number of solicitations that it was assigned. Whether the solicitation included writing a letter, or making a phone call, or travelling across the country to visit with a prospective donor, each member of the committee completed his or her assignments on time and with style. This group provided The Deerfield Campaign with good early momentum (better than $10 million had been raised prior to our public kickoff), and contributed to the ongoing momentum throughout the three-year effort. Their early enthusiasm and frequent successes were contagious.

We also sought to make this campaign a truly national one. It was therefore decided that we should organize thirteen area committees across the country. These campaigns ranged in size from 75 volunteers (in New York City) to fewer than 10 volunteers in several locations outside the Northeast.

Area efforts were also initiated less formally in Texas, St. Louis, Atlanta, Orlando, Hilton Head, Cincinnati, Cleveland and Denver. All together, approximately 250 volunteers assisted in the area campaigns. The range of gifts which were sought in each of the area campaigns generally were from $5,000-$25,000; however, smaller and larger gifts were also solicited. The area campaigns were launched over a three-year period at the rate of about five per year. Each campaign included an area chairman who, in turn, recruited vice-chairmen and other key volunteers. Each person was asked to approach not more than five individuals for gifts. Therefore, over 1,200 individuals were personally contacted by members of the various organizations. All area campaigns were given ambitious but manageable goals, and I am pleased to report that all have *exceeded* their original goals and one has even exceeded its goal by over sixty percent!

Several benefits have been derived from the nearly 1,500 personal solicitations which occurred during the campaign. First, over 300 donors who had not participated in the Annual Support program in recent years supported this special campaign. We are hopeful that the interest of these individuals in the Academy has been revitalized and that they will continue to be donors for many years into the future. Second, a stronger feeling of cohesiveness has developed. Each area organization had a genuine pride in itself and its accomplishments. Following many years of exclusive reliance on class organization, the area organizations now complement our strong class system which has been the hallmark of Deerfield volunteerism in the past. Third, there was a broad-based campaign participation. An awareness developed at the "grass roots level" for The Deerfield Campaign. We "took the campaign to the people," and each of our workers did a wonderful job of being certain that a gift or pledge was considered. Overall, in excess of 2,250 gifts have been made or pledged toward the capital objective of The Deerfield Campaign. This is an extremely high rate of participation for a capital campaign.

No statement about the volunteers of The Deerfield Campaign would be complete without mention of our class agents. Under the masterful leadership of David Preston during the years of the campaign, the class agents continued their Annual Support efforts. Many class agents also stepped forward to help as members of various area campaign committees. (Deerfield opted for the "single ask" approach of having a separate capital organization rather than the "double ask" approach whereby class agents would ask for the Annual Support gift and a capital gift at the same time.) Virtually all of our alumni and parents understood the need for both Annual Support dollars and capital dollars, as well as the need for making separate requests during the life of The Deerfield Campaign. Without the patience, follow-through, and overall dedication which was demonstrated by David Preston and the 75 individuals who serve as class agents, we would not have had such successful Annual Support years during The Deerfield Campaign.

Finally, this campaign could not possibly have been successful without an extraordinary Board of Trustees. During the years of The Deerfield Campaign, we were blessed with three very able Development Committee chairmen – Garry Bewkes, Gil Lamphere and Isabel Wilson – who provided wonderful leadership and inspiration not only for me but for the entire board as well.

Clearly The Deerfield Campaign's tremendous success was due to the enthusiasm of its volunteers across the country. Over 300 individuals serving in a variety of volunteer roles have spent the past three years strengthening our ties with alumni and parents. Their efforts have left behind a strong organization which should serve Deerfield well for years to come. The class agent organization has been strengthened with new agents uncovered in the area campaigns. Many area workers decided that this was a good way to continue to serve in some volunteer function. The area organizations have also established an identity of their own. We now have 13 areas which have cohesive groups of people who stand ready to assist in whatever fashion might be helpful. It will be the special challenge of those of us who are working at Deerfield following this campaign to channel the enthusiasm and wisdom of these volunteers into meaningful assistance for Deerfield.

Louis Marx, Jr. '49P with Fran L'Esperance '49

The Deerfield Campaign
Table of Gifts Report

	Number of Gifts/Prospects		Dollar Value of Gifts		
Size	Goal	Gifts/Pledges	Table of Gifts Goal	Gifts/Pledges	% of Goal Realized
$2,000,000 +	3	2	$ 4,000,000	$ 6,602,000	165.1
$1,000,000 +	4	7	$ 6,000,000	$ 8,928,176	148.8
$ 500,000	7	2	$ 3,500,000	$ 1,000,000	28.6
$ 250,000	8	8	$ 2,000,000	$ 2,440,288	122.0
Leadership Gift Total	22	19	$15,500,000	$18,970,464	120.5
$ 100,000	25	25	$ 2,500,000	$ 3,351,458	146.1
$ 50,000	35	41	$ 1,750,000	$ 2,420,473	138.3
$ 25,000	75	50	$ 1,875,000	$ 1,472,257	78.5
Major Gift Total	135	116	$ 6,125,000	$ 7,244,188	123.2
$ 10,000	150	103	$ 1,500,000	$ 1,393,459	92.9
$ 5,000	250	182	$ 1,250,000	$ 1,031,304	82.5
Special Gift Total	400	285	$ 2,750,000	$ 2,424,763	88.4
$ 1,500	300	249	$ 450,000	$ 593,083	131.8
$ < 1,500	1000	1616	$ 175,000	$ 426,131	243.5
General Gift Total	1300	1865	$ 625,000	$ 1,019,214	163.1
Campaign Totals	1857	2285	$25,000,000	$29,658,629	118.6
Annual Support			$ 6,500,000	$ 6,575,000	101.2
			$31,500,000	$36,233,629	

63

Chapter 24
Profiles of Four Successful Capital Campaigns

Now that you have learned how to run a capital campaign, let's see what one really looks like. Although these examples come from four very different nonprofit organizations, you will see that the basic principles of major gift fund-raising run throughout these campaigns. The case histories show how the basic concepts of capital campaigns can be applied to varying situations and how the same elements can be combined into different packages, individually tailored to specific organizations.

Culver Military Academy and Culver Girls Academy

Culver, Indiana **Goal: $47 million**
Amount raised: $60.1 million

The capital campaign conducted for Culver Military Academy and Culver Girls Academy is an interesting one for many reasons. First, the campaign involved soliciting major gifts from alumni who at one time had been given a written guarantee that they would never be asked to contribute to the school. Second, the goal of $47 million was arrived at by comparing the number of alumni in Culver's pool to the number of alumni from selected major universities who had participated in recently completed campaigns at those universities. After gathering

data from those schools, a formula was applied to Culver and a goal was set. Third, the extraordinary success of the Culver campaign helped raise the fund-raising sights of all private secondary schools across the country.

Culver conducted no formal feasibility study prior to the campaign. Professional fund-raising counsel was not hired until two years into the five-year campaign and then served on an advisory basis for only a year and a half.

The Culver campaign took two years to plan and was conducted over a five-year period in the mid-1980s. The Culver Educational Foundation, which operates the two academies, actually conducted the campaign. The professional development staff was increased from three to seven at the peak of the campaign, and the development budget averaged about $400,000 a year.

J. Frederick Lintner, director of development at Culver, reported that the most effective solicitation approach was to pair a volunteer with the president. The development staff did many initial visits to prospects, but these were seen primarily as cultivation visits.

The Culver campaign raised a total of $60.1 million and became the most successful fund-raising effort in the history of American private secondary education. Culver Military Academy and Culver Girls Academy are, first and foremost, academic institutions. Culver's military system is designed for the orderly, disciplined and cooperative achievement of constructive and creative goals, not to prepare students for combat. The Girls Academy is a separate institution, organized in the preparatory school tradition. The schools enroll approximately 700 students, and the campus includes an airfield and the largest indoor riding hall in the country.

The largest single gift to the campaign ($5 million) was made anonymously and came from a family that had connections with the school. There were 14 other gifts of $1 million or more and 96 of $100,000 or more. Obviously Culver found significant wealth among its alumni body and elsewhere. Over half of the money raised was added to the school's endowment. In addition, funds were used to support faculty salaries and to provide student financial aid. A new library built after the campaign was also funded by the effort.

The success of the Culver campaign was based on the combined efforts of President Ralph Manuel, the development staff and a few very involved trustees. The board of trustees was key to the success of this campaign. Twenty-eight members of the board gave over 38 percent of the total raised. Jim Henderson, the trustee who led the campaign, has said, "The people who gave were convinced that their education at Culver was one of the most meaningful experiences—in some cases the most meaningful experience—in their lives."

The campaign zeroed in on the 8,700 alumni of Culver. The development staff felt that the competitive spirit engendered by the school's extensive sports program helped push donors to give bigger gifts. The competitive urge during the last days of the campaign helped spur Culver alumni to give more to position Culver's effort as the largest campaign for a secondary school in the country.

Here are some of the printed materials used during the Culver campaign.

Figure 24.1: Excerpts from the case statement. This was used early in the campaign, but priorities changed during the course of the campaign.

The Choices People Make

In the lives of every one of us, it is ultimately the sum of the many choices or decisions we have made along the way that determines the quality of our existence. Perhaps to a greater extent even than most individuals realize, we, each of us, choose the kind of person we will be, the kind of work we will perform, the goals or achievements we will strive for, the things and people we will love, and, if need be, those values and ideals we will die for. In the end, whether we have been finally judged good, successful, happy, fulfilled, whether we have been judged failures, evil, miserable, and disappointed—or whether, like most people, we fall somewhere in between—the choice will have been ours. Only ours.

So it is with institutions. The choices their directors and patrons make today will determine just as surely the quality of that organization's future as choices made by others in the past have determined its stature now.

And always the choices, both for individuals and institutions, seem somehow to be the same: freedom versus dependence, love versus hate, hope versus despair, growth versus decline, good versus evil, excellence versus mediocrity, constancy versus indifference. And more than intelligence, more even than timing or heredity or luck, the distinguishing mark of the good man or woman—of the quality organization—is courage. Those who dare to make the tough decisions when not to decide is easier, who persevere when it is right though not necessarily most expedient to do so, who look far ahead when to be short-sighted is in vogue, whose decisions, in short, events, not popular opinion, prove good and correct—it is

those individuals and institutions we come eventually to identify as great . . . as admirable . . . as leaders.

Choices for Culver: 1894-1968

In the world of private secondary education, Culver has achieved leadership standing—perhaps precisely because it has never abandoned its guiding founder's purpose. In an age just returning to the realization that scholarship alone is no virtue, Culver has never abandoned its traditional, tripartite emphasis on academics, character-building, and leadership.

In this respect, Culver is indeed unique in our contemporary society. For, in an age and a world suffering for the lack of men and women of values and qualities of the leader, Culver continues to turn out young adults who have been taught as much of integrity, initiative, self-discipline, manners, and respect for self, others, and authority as they have of calculus, history, foreign languages, and physics. As time and events have eroded those traditional American beliefs that combined to make our society great, Culver has refused to take refuge, as some others have done, in the "brain game," admitting only the brightest applicants as measured by I.Q. or standardized tests. Culver has not forgotten that a majority of our nation's leaders traditionally have not come from the ranks of those only who were once most brilliant in the classroom.

For almost a century, then, Henry Harrison Culver's ideal of nurturing the

In the lives of every one of us, it is ultimately the sum of the many choices or decisions we have made along the way that determines the quality of our existence. So it is with institutions.

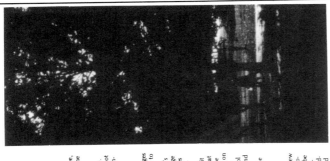

whole individual has been the immutable core of the school's philosophy. This "first choice for Culver" has endured. It prevailed in 1938, when a team of progressive educators from Harvard recommended, after a lengthy period of observation on campus, that the school move to limit its offerings in the future to a terminal academic program, one designed to prepare students immediately for business careers, without any thought of further education. The Culver faculty voted overwhelmingly to reject this suggestion. In fact, the school resolved finally, instead, to become a college-preparatory institution exclusively. And the result today is that virtually every Academy graduate goes on to university studies.

Inherent in this choice, this landmark decision, was the determination that Culver be known, first and foremost, as an outstanding academic institution and that every effort be made to strengthen its programs of instruction in the basics of English, mathematics, science, history, foreign languages, and the fine arts.

So successful was the effort that resulted from this decision that by the early 1960s, Culver had become one of the country's most vigorous participants in the operations of the College Entrance Examination Board, the Culver faculty had grown to include authors of nationally-respected textbooks and several leading participants, as well, in the creation and preparation of College Board Advanced Placement materials, and TIME Magazine had by then reported that Stanford University rated Culver Military Academy among the top five private secondary schools in the nation and that Yale University included Culver in a list of twelve U.S. prep schools it recommended to parents of high-school-age youngsters.

This tradition of excellence in the classroom continues today, under the direction of current superintendent Dean Ralph N. Manuel, former dean of Dartmouth College. With four to six

faculty members serving each year, Culver currently ranks among the top six prep schools in the country in providing readers for College Board Advanced Placement Examinations.

Average class size has been kept to under sixteen. And Culver is now one of only twenty-six American and ten British prep schools which participate annually in the prestigious Morehead Scholar Program of the University of North Carolina, a distinction shared by only one other school in the entire Midwest. Culver's distinguished faculty has been bolstered even further in recent years by the addition of several foreign-born instructors, bringing yet another important dimension to the Academies' educational offering.

Other important choices, of course, have been made along the way in establishing Culver's uniqueness, not the least of which was the decision back in 1897 to institute and maintain what is now an unparalleled secondary school horsemanship program. The most recent appearance of the Culver Black Horse Troop as the lead unit behind the U.S. Marine Corps Band in President Ronald Reagan's 1981 inaugural parade not only reminded Culver alumni everywhere of the school's many proud traditions, but brought Culver national attention as well.

Also far-reaching was the decision in 1902 to initiate and, over time, expand a summer school and camping program at Culver, one of the results of which is that today Culver's facilities and campus are used year-round, with summer programs involving more than 2,000 youngsters annually. No other preparatory school in America can claim such intensive year-round use of its physical plant.

Also significant was the decision in the 1960s to establish a special scholarship program for minorities, funded by gifts from alumni, which helped accomplish the smooth and complete integration of minorities on the Culver campus.

basics of English, mathematics, science, history, foreign languages, and the fine arts—in the belief that these are the solid, timeless cornerstones of a truly effective college-preparatory program. Culver's directors and faculty chose not to follow the pied pipers of experimental education into peripheral or "far out" course offerings in response to contemporary pressures.

In response to institutional challenges elsewhere, Culver chose not only not to abandon but, in fact, actually to redouble its efforts, through the school's unique America's Democratic Heritage Program, to teach students the virtues and strengths of the American democratic free-enterprise system. Culver chose also to continue to require (as it does to this day) student attendance at church services. Finally, Culver chose not to abandon, either, its emphasis on courtesy, respect, manners, and personal appearance. In short, the school maintained its emphases on values and discipline in the face of enormous pressures of the time on young people to "do their own thing" and avoid responsibility.

To be sure, these were not easy times, and there were more than a few difficult moments. But so it is that today student leadership continues to be emphasized still in both Culver Military Academy and Culver Girls Academy—despite the fact that fewer and fewer, it seems, of the country's secondary schools today any longer even attempt to develop leadership ability directly.

But this has always been a strength of Culver. Former Dean of the Faculty John Edgell is fond of reminding patrons and alumni that when Who's Who in America last kept track of such information, there were more Culver graduates listed in its rolls than those of any other preparatory school in the country. Culver is known world-wide for the quality of its graduates: men and women of uncommon courage and directness, marked by their quiet con-

1968-1983: The Era of Difficult Choices

Perhaps the most difficult choices of all for Culver, however, have occurred within the last decade and a half.

The late-Sixties and early-Seventies, as we all know, were a particularly difficult era for all educational institutions in this country. The war in Vietnam triggered great unrest among all segments of American youth, leading eventually to their questioning of all authority. Unfortunately, in response to this challenge, many secondary schools, colleges, and universities relaxed all but their most minimal standards of behavior and academic achievement.

The military establishment was a special target of youthful unrest at this time. Those schools with a military organizational framework came under severe pressure, and many of the most prestigious simply closed their doors or dropped the military entirely—Staunton, Kentucky Military Institute, Shattuck, and McCallie, among them.

Culver felt the same pressures, yet managed to come through this period relatively intact. There is no question, however, that the choice to establish Culver Girls Academy in 1971 made a significant difference in maintaining enrollment figures at a level sufficient to enable Culver to retain its outstanding faculty and to maintain its extensive physical plant in reasonable condition.

Equally important was the decision to keep admissions standards high, despite operating, even with the influx of girls, at below-capacity enrollments.

Perhaps most crucial, however, Culver chose to weather this storm without compromising those principles which it firmly believed then, as it continues to believe now, are vital to the education of young men and women. Thus, the academic curriculum maintained its position as focal point of the Culver Experience, still rooted in the

fidence and constructive competitiveness bred through the Culver ethic of achievement, and distinguished by their loyalty to those ideals that made their school and country great.

Culver, of course, has been fortunate that during this period Dean John R. Mars, a stalwart member of the faculty since 1941, was here to provide that strength of character and moral suasion that helped guide Culver through the latter half of the Seventies and into the Eighties. He brought to an enlightened, forward-looking term as superintendent a much-needed sense of historical continuity, one grounded in his firm understanding of Culver's traditional strengths.

Now we have in Dean Ralph N. Manuel, Culver's eleventh superintendent, an educator who brings a proven record of successful college administrative experience to the superintendent's office. And Culver appears poised on the brink of yet another golden era.

The Cost of Difficult Choices

Culver's determination to stand fast against the storms of a decade and a half ago came not without its price. At a school functioning smoothly in the early-1960s as one of the recognized leaders among American preparatory schools, the war in Vietnam exacted a terrible toll. Public confidence in matters related to all things military had plunged deeply and rapidly by the end of that decade, and qualified applicants to Culver Military Academy dropped suddenly to about forty percent of 1965 levels. Enrollment declined.

Fortunately, the Culver administration and board of directors had already been studying for some time the option of adding a girls school to the campus, believing that such a step would provide a more natural educational environment for boys and girls alike. The

founding of Culver Girls Academy in 1971, therefore, helped to make up for some of the loss of qualified applicants experienced during this period by the boys school. In fact, it might be said that the establishment of Culver Girls Academy at this particular time actually saved Culver as a quality educational institution.

The continued loss of tuition income, however, despite the admission of girls, along with the need to add staff for girls and the almost simultaneous impact of runaway inflation through the early-1970s, had put Culver's operating budget into a loss position by 1975. And, despite the best efforts of board and administration, losses could not be stopped.

In the ensuing, continuing effort to "break even," faculty salaries were allowed to fall behind rates of increase being won by teachers in Indiana's best public schools. Scholarship funds were actually cut. And maintenance funds, too, were reduced, thus allowing the physical plant to fall behind a proper maintenance schedule.

Happily, in the last seven years, the enrollment decline has been reversed; and Culver is once again operating at or near capacity levels. However, inflation has continued throughout most of these years; and, while Culver has recently stopped the gap from widening between faculty/staff compensation here and elsewhere in Indiana, that gap has not been narrowed, either. And, while scholarship funds have also risen again since 1979, Culver's funds still are only half those of the leading Eastern schools. Finally, despite major tuition increases since 1975, inflation still has prevented the board and administration from balancing the annual budget.

Quality, however, has not suffered yet.

Culver is known worldwide for the quality of its graduates: men and women of uncommon courage and directness, confidence and constructive competitiveness, loyalty to their school and country.

Choices for Culver, 1983: Why $47 Million?

In the face of the realities mentioned above, Culver's board of directors two years ago undertook a careful, thorough, and long-term study of Culver's needs in order to project a detailed plan that would chart the course not only toward rectification of immediate deficiencies but toward achievement of an altogether firm structural and financial footing for the future, one which would ensure Culver's vital and increasingly unique role in American society into the Twenty-First Century.

Out of that study, which included an exhaustive, detailed structural analysis of the campus by the prestigious Houston firm of Caudill Rowlett Scott, Inc., one of the most outstanding architectural firms in the country (with extensive experience on more than 200 American campuses, including Harvard and Duke), the following needs eventually became evident:

• Endowment at Culver must be increased to $40 million (from its current $17 million level) and Annual Giving more than doubled (from its current $400,000) in order to provide the additional annual income necessary to properly compensate our faculty, provide scholarships, continue to enhance our program offerings, and gradually reduce Culver tuition rates in comparison with other leading prep schools.

• Culver's physical plant, constructed for the most part between 1900 and 1920, while fundamentally sound, needs major rehabilitation and renovation. A master plan of campus development has, therefore, been prepared for this purpose to include, as well, conversion of one dormitory complex (Chateau-Thierry and Argonne Barracks) to a girls dormitory complex in order to bring the ultimate Culver enrollment mix to 500 boys and 300 girls.

• Finally, an engineering study has

identified approximately $3 million in deferred maintenance that now demands immediate attention.

Endowment ($23 Million)

The principal long-term need for Culver is to increase endowment. According to the 1979-80 Report of Annual Giving to Private Education, Culver's $17 million endowment now ranks a respectable twelfth among U.S. secondary schools but still significantly below those of the top five, which include: Andover ($73 million), St. Paul's ($55 million), Exeter ($46 million), Lawrenceville ($29 million), and Hotchkiss ($27 million).

On average, the return on the endowments of these five schools toward their operating budgets exceeds $3.5 million each annually, more than $2 million above Culver's. Because of this difference in annual return, Culver's faculty and staff are paid less than their counterparts in other leading preparatory schools, scholarship funds available at Culver are less, and student tuition is higher.

In seeking to raise, out of a total campaign goal of $47 million, $23 million for endowment alone, Culver seeks an endowment total that will enable the school to achieve its desired goals while utilizing only the first five percent of endowment return toward the operating budget. As additional $23 million in endowment would, therefore, add over $1 million annually to the budget, thereby erasing the average $250,000 deficit experienced in each of the last six years, while, at the same time, meeting competitive compensation levels for faculty and staff, whose salaries now run more than twenty percent behind those of their public school counterparts. Equally

The choice Culver's guardians must make today is: Will they determine to ensure Culver's vital and increasingly unique role in American society into the Twenty-First Century—or not?

significant, by instituting the procedure of applying only a five percent return on endowment to the operating budget, the endowment itself will continue to grow with inflation, an important, far-reaching step in maintaining the endowment's earnings potential in the future.

Faculty Salaries

In an effort, therefore, to provide the adequate salaries that will ensure a stable faculty and a flourishing academic program into the next century, various levels of support are being requested of alumni, parents, and friends in making *their* "Choices for Culver":

• to endow an entire program in Fine Arts or Horsemanship or Athletics, gifts of one million dollars each;
• to endow sixteen academic chairs, gifts of $500,000 each;
• to endow sixteen instructorships (to ensure recruitment and retention of outstanding young faculty members), gifts of $250,000 each;
• to endow ten Summer School instructorships, gifts of $50,000 each.
• Culver seeks contributions in addition toward a $1 million faculty enrichment fund to be used for the continuing improvement of Culver's faculty through advanced studies, sabbaticals, and in-service training.

Student Scholarships

The continued excellence of these Academies and Summer Schools depends, as well, on the matriculation of a steady stream of able, earnest, and motivated youngsters, regardless of their parents' or guardians' ability to pay full tuition costs. Scholarships help many outstanding students to come to Culver who, in many cases, set examples of achievement the rest of the student body may emulate. Generous scholarship and financial aid programs, therefore, are vital in the effort to guarantee that such students are able *to choose Culver* in the future.

In order to bring Culver up to a level compatible with its desire to join the country's leading college-preparatory schools in this regard, Culver seeks:

• gifts of $250,000 each to endow five full Winter School scholarships;
• gifts of $100,000 each to endow ten partial Winter School scholarships;
• gifts of $25,000 each to endow ten full Summer School scholarships;
• and contributions in addition toward a $1 million general scholarship fund.

Facility/Equipment Endowment

Finally, to complete its endowment for the future, Culver seeks $3 million in facilities and equipment endowment.

Facilities ($17 Million)

Due to recent financial constraints since 1968, Culver's physical plant has not had proper care in recent years. And in order to determine just exactly what priority each of those needs should have, the board of directors commissioned development of a Master Plan for Culver, prepared by Houston's Caudill Rowlett Scott, Architects, Planners, and Engineers, in order to arrive at a detailed long-term survey of Culver's facility needs into the next century. This study addressed the long-term physical development of the Culver campus. In addition, a Facility Maintenance Plan addressed the matters of maintenance, minor safety and structural problems, as well as several important cosmetic improvements to the campus.

As a result of these studies, Culver has identified three major areas of concern which require immediate attention: barrack/dormitory renovation, modernization of energy systems, and deferred maintenance.

Barrack and Dormitory Renovation

Barrack and dormitory renovation is the major facilities item. Included in this category are:

• the conversion of CT and Argonne Barracks into the central girls dormi-

tory ($2.3 million);
• renovation of West Barrack ($800,000);
• renovation of Main Barrack ($1.3 million);
• and renovation of other living units ($200,000).

Also scheduled for repair, remodeling, or renovation are the Culver **Memorial Chapel**, Eppley Auditorium's **Little Theatre**, the **Admissions Office**, and the **South Entrance** to the campus. Culver seeks, as well, $3.8 million toward the creation of a modernized **Learning Center** on campus, with $1.5 million earmarked for renovation of the Culver Legion Memorial Building and $2.3 million for construction of a Memorial Building addition.

Included also within this facilities improvement category are $1.5 million for repair and replacement of steam lines on campus and installation of distributive boilers with an eye toward lowering energy costs in the future.

Deferred Maintenance

Finally, Culver seeks contributions to accomplish maintenance deferred in the following areas: Academic ($500,000), Horsemanship ($500,000), Recreation ($400,000), Barracks ($600,000), Lodgings ($300,000), Service ($300,000), and Campus ($400,000).

Annual Giving ($4.5 Million)

Undesignated annual giving—that is, gifts to Culver specifically for support of the annual budget but not specified for purposes that would not otherwise appear in the budget—will be counted in the campaign, as well. This, in order to emphasize its vital importance to the welfare of the school.

Undesignated annual giving at Culver in 1979 was $290,000. By 1981, it had climbed to over $400,000. During the course of the campaign, it is the board of directors' goal to nearly triple the 1979 annual total in order to reach $850,000 by 1987.

Culver's campaign goals for Annual

Giving are:
• 1982, $525,000;
• 1983, $575,000;
• 1984, $625,000;
• 1985, $675,000;
• 1986, $750,000;
• 1987, $850,000.

Finally in this area, Culver seeks an additional $500,000 in program support—proceeds not applied to endowment but designated specifically for academic or scholarship support in the annual budget—from foundations and corporations.

And so, once again, there are choices to be made. And, in making those choices, alumni, patrons, and friends everywhere are asked to reflect on the fact that what Culver has striven to become as a school is not only rare today, it is actually unique on the American educational landscape: coordinate, private, secondary boarding schools (whose facilities and traditions happen also to support one of the largest, most extensive summer recreational programs in the nation), whose ambitious commitments to the development of the finest programs and facilities anywhere, in academics and athletics and extracurricular opportunities and character training and leadership development, has been matched over the years only by the talent and the resources implementation of such a vision requires.

Culver was not built—no great school is built—in a day. And, having once been built, only a few are insulated—financially—from disaster, much less erosion. But, if Culver is as vital to America today and as unique within our society as examination of contemporary circumstances would seem to suggest, then it is eminently important that the school's guardians choose to ensure that position and service for the future.

For if, as we believe, America's young men and women need Culver now, they will need her even more in the uncertain decades to come.

In the 1980s, alumni, patrons, and friends everywhere will be asked: If America's young men and women need Culver now, won't they need her even more in the uncertain decades to come?

Choices for Culver
Campaign Needs

ENDOWMENT $23,000,000

Faculty Improvement 16,500,000
  Three Endowed Programs (1,000,000) 3,000,000
  Sixteen Academic Chairs (500,000) 8,000,000
  Sixteen Academic Instructorships (250,000) 4,000,000
  Ten Summer School Instructorships (50,000) 500,000
  Faculty Enrichment Fund 1,000,000

Student Aid Improvement 3,500,000
  Five Full Winter School Scholarships (250,000) 1,250,000
  Ten Partial Winter School Scholarships (100,000) 1,000,000
  Ten Full Summer School Scholarships (25,000) 250,000
  Additions to Scholarship Funds 1,000,000

Facility/Equipment Endowments 3,000,000

FACILITIES $17,000,000

Master Plan, Phase I 10,000,000
  Energy Steam Line Replacement 600,000
  Barrack/Dormitory Renovation 4,600,000
    CT/Argonne Conversion (2,300,000)
    West Barrack Renovation (800,000)
    Main Barrack Renovation (1,300,000)
    Other Renovation (200,000)
  Learning Center 3,800,000
    Library Renovation (1,500,000)
    Library Addition (2,300,000)
  Chapel Repair 300,000
  Campus Entrance Construction (South) 500,000
  Auditorium Lecture Hall Renovation 100,000
  Admissions Renovation 100,000

Deferred Maintenance Projects 3,000,000
  Academic 500,000
  Horsemanship 500,000
  Recreation 400,000

FACILITIES (Continued)
  Barracks 600,000
  Lodgings 300,000
  Service 300,000
  Campus 400,000

Master Plan, Phase II (Selected from the Following) 4,000,000
  Energy/Distributive Boilers 900,000
  Dining Hall Renovation 1,600,000
    Renovation, Dining Hall Proper (750,000)
    Student Center Conversion (850,000)
  Barrack/Dormitory Renovation 1,600,000
    North, East Renovation (1,400,000)
    Other Renovation (200,000)
  Music and Arts Complex 600,000
    M&A Renovation (200,000)
    Band Hall Addition (200,000)
    Art Center Conversion (200,000)
  Recreation Building Renovation 500,000
  Horsemanship Additions 1,000,000
  Woodcraft Classroom Building 1,000,000
  Infirmary Renovation 300,000
  Hotel Renovation 500,000

UNDESIGNATED ANNUAL GIVING $4,500,000
  Goal, 1982 525,000
  Goal, 1983 575,000
  Goal, 1984 625,000
  Goal, 1985 675,000
  Goal, 1986 750,000
  Goal, 1987 850,000
  Foundation/Corporation Support, 1983-87 500,000

CAMPAIGN EXPENSE $2,500,000

TOTAL $47,040,000

Figure 24.2. The portion of the campaign for the dining hall/student center became very important. A family connected with Culver put up a challenge grant for the renovation, and this brochure was produced to sell that part of the campaign.

Choices for Culver is a major campaign to raise the endowment, facilities, and annual funds which will sustain the Academies as one of this nation's premier institutions of private secondary education. The capital program will affect every one of the Academies' renowned educational and extracurricular programs.

The campaign seeks to further Henry Harrison Culver's vision of a unique school at which attention is paid to the development of the whole individual. Through it, the ideal of a great private institution maintained by generous private-sector support will be continued. The ultimate success of the program depends on unstinting assistance from benefactors who believe strongly in the conceptual foundation upon which Culver has been built.

The Culver Educational Foundation
Culver, Indiana 46511
(219) 842-8230

Illustrations: Duane A. Greisness 11-83-2.5M

Offering the Best Possible Campus Life

The year 1986 marks the 75th anniversary of a seemingly timeless Culver landmark. The great Dining Hall building was dedicated on April 15, 1911. Since those honored ceremonies, the building has served the entire campus community continuously.

A principal asset of campus life and architecture, the Dining Hall building has always been the place where the largest number of students come together on a regular basis. Generations of alumni remember taking their meals—morning, noon, and evening—in the grand expanse of the main-floor dining area. For many decades too, families and friends of students have visited campus and departed with the indelible memory of the building's impressive towers and facades.

Three-quarters of a century and constant use have taken their toll on the Dining Hall. The original luster of the building's finish has faded. The kitchens and operating systems are severely outmoded.

A key objective of the Academies' $4,300,000 Choices for Culver campaign is the complete renovation and restoration of the Dining Hall building. The dining area itself will be renewed, up-dated, and upgraded. Potentially attractive space on the building's lower level will be refurbished as a brand new Student Center.

Total funding needed to realize plans for a new Dining Hall Student Center is $2,200,000. This is a capital expenditure which Culver cannot make without the philanthropic assistance of alumni, parents, and friends.

Deeply committed to the future of the Academies, the Lav family of Dallas has chosen to give a very generous memorial gift of $1,300,000 toward building revitalization. This benefaction stands as a campaign challenge to other interested donors. Your gift is needed now to help meet this challenge, which will assure that this and future generations of Culver students enjoy the best possible campus facilities during their pivotal years of learning and growth.

The regiment marches to mess in this early photograph of Culver's historic Dining Hall. Completed in 1911, the building offered modern facilities in a setting hailed for its architectural beauty. The Dining Hall has become an essential campus structure, revered by generations of students and visitors to the Academies.

Now, the Lav family of Dallas has made a major commitment which has launched the Dining Hall/Student Center Challenge. With the Lavs' gift and matching funds from Culver alumni, parents, and friends, the Academies will undertake a $2,200,000 renovation of the Dining Hall building. A new Student Center will be created, and all other Dining Hall facilities will be restored and updated for the fullest current and future use.

Renewing for Today and Tomorrow

When the Dining Hall building was dedicated, Indiana Governor Thomas Marshall and officials from several universities came to celebrate one of the real wonders of its day.

The new facility was declared the finest of its kind in the world and an architectural achievement. A steel-trussed roof provided a large, unobstructed dining area with a seating capacity of 1,000. Walls were paneled with green and white marble and trimmed with special woodwork. High up, large murals were set into alcove frames. The kitchens were state-of-the-art of the day.

Eventually, the building's lower level came to be used as an informal student center. Today, however, a basement atmosphere limits use of the area, and it offers no real facilities for more than casual conversation and informal meetings.

Students spend their leisure hours at The Shack in the Inn, Beason Hall, or the Student Social Center in the Humanities Building. None of these facilities substitute well for a campus-wide Student Center.

Culver is fortunate that the Dining Hall building exists today as a sturdy, still-elegant landmark that can be restored and renovated according to contemporary and future needs of the Academies. To build a totally new structure fulfilling the same demands would require an expenditure many times that needed to revitalize the Dining Hall. Moreover, a great and historic feature of the campus would be lost.

$2,200,000 in Critical Initiatives

In response to student needs and perpetual use of the facilities, plans for Culver's Dining Hall/Student Center are based on three initiatives for building renewal:

1. Creation of a new student-life center, converting underused space to active space and making the Dining Hall building more specifically a center of campus activity.

A staircase will be built between the building's main dining area and the brand new Student Center on the lower level. Within the center will be the QM bookstore, game and television rooms, meeting and quiet rooms, and the new Shack offering popular food items and beverages. All interior finishing will be geared to make the center a lively, inviting, and spacious facility—a major improvement in campus life at the Academies.

2. Modernization of the main Dining Hall area to enhance its historic architectural beauty.

Self-service food lines will be recessed into part of the kitchens to regain the full dimensions of the dining area. These service lines will be screened by a short wall with a new salad bar and beverage counter, which in turn will create a distinct separation between main food service and dining. An unsightly tray conveyor system will be replaced by

Culver's new Student Center will bring life and activity to underused space in the Dining Hall building.

tray drops near exits. A new private dining room for special guests will be built on the current mezzanine. New furniture, trophy cases, and a general renovation of the dining area will revive much of the room's original quality.

3. Renovation of the kitchens to upgrade them to contemporary standards and to improve their efficiency.

A major reorganization of kitchen space will increase the cost-effectiveness and efficiency of operations. Staff will supply food items to the serving lines directly from portable heating and cooling equipment, and a new elevator will more efficiently move stock and meals between floors. Appliances and central operating systems will be improved and upgraded.

The main-floor dining area will be restored and updated, making a Culver landmark handsome once again.

What Your Support Can Do

Recognizing the immediacy of the need for renovation of the dining center, the Lay family of Dallas has made a $1,300,000 challenge gift to Choices for Culver.

The gift is a memorial to Herman W. Lay, late founder of Frito-Lay, Inc. and a much-revered Culver benefactor, and to H. Ward Lay III. Mr. Lay's grandson, a 1984 Culver alumnus who died tragically three weeks after graduation. Young Ward Lay's father, H. Ward Lay, '64, is a member of the Board of Trustees of the Culver Educational Foundation. Both father and son were elected President of their graduating classes, a unique occurrence in Culver history.

Within the $2,200,000 Dining Hall/Student Center project, there are attractive opportunities for named memorial and commemorative gifts, such as major funding for

the Shack, the private dining room, the QM bookstore, the television room, and the meeting room. Every gift, however, will help Culver meet the Lay family challenge and will provide a better student life for this and future generations at the Academies.

The spirit of urgency of this special campaign is symbolized by the first gifts to the challenge, which have come from the students of the Class of 1985 and which total $10,000.

Pledges to the Dining Hall/Student Center Challenge may be fulfilled over three to five years. All donors of capital gifts of $2,500 or more will be recognized on a special plaque in Culver's new center. Your support is essential.

Help Meet the Center Challenge

To meet the Lay family challenge and fund the new Dining Hall/Student Center, all friends of Culver are invited to lend their support. A number of significant gifts are needed, and their donors may name important center facilities. Smaller gifts, too, will help take this special program to its goal.

Total Program Goal	$2,200,000
Lay Family Gift	1,300,000
Named Gift Opportunities	
Private Dining Room	$200,000
QM Bookstore	200,000
Television Room	100,000
Reading/Meeting Room	100,000
Goal for Parents Association	
The New Shack	$300,000

Figure 24.3. The Jack C. Vaughn family made a $1 million challenge grant to Culver. The Vaughn Challenge brochure was mailed to alumni who had been involved in Culver's horsemanship program.

The Vaughn Challenge

On the Cover: The Culver Black Horse Troop first drew national attention in 1904 when it appeared at the Louisiana Purchase Exposition in St. Louis. The organization attended its first Inaugural Parade in 1913, and has since received nine additional invitations, including one to the cancelled (In augural Parade of 1985.

Horsemanship at Culver

Early educators at Culver Military Academy, recognizing that patience, self-discipline, and concentration were benefits that could be attained through a sound equestrian program, in 1897, just three years after the founding of the school, authorized the purchase of 66 horses for a CMA Black Horse Troop.

Ninety years later, horsemanship remains an integral part of the school's educational program, providing unexcelled opportunities for thousands of young men, winter and summer, to learn the joys of riding, while at the same time inculcating the high ideals of the U.S. Army Cavalry.

That rich tradition was augmented in 1971 by the introduction of a horsemanship program for girls. And so, today, Culver Military Academy and Culver Girls Academy offer comprehensive instruction for young men and women at all levels of equitation and training of the horse, from basic to advanced, while offering those with previous horsemanship experience opportunities to participate as well in varsity polo or jumping or to become members of the prestigious CMA Lancers or CGA Equestriennes.

Facilities

Culver's 130 horses are stabled today in the largest riding hall/stables complex in the United States. Built in 1917, the indoor arena measures 300 feet long by 90 feet wide, with spectator seating for 700 people. Outdoor facilities include five show rings, a complete hunter-training area, cross-country courses, dressage ring, and more than five miles of groomed riding trails.

The Riding Hall and Stables, however,

The *Lancer Platoon* is the honor organization of the Black Horse Troop, which is the largest individual cavalry unit in the United States. Members are selected on the basis of strong academic standing, proficiency in riding, demonstrated leadership potential, and good citizenship.

THE VAUGHN CHALLENGE

Total Program Goal	$3,000,000
Endowment	2,000,000
Facilities	1,000,000
Vaughn Family Gift	**1,000,000**
Additional Gifts Received	**525,000**

NAMED GIFT OPPORTUNITIES

Endowments

• Director of Horsemanship	$500,000
• Horse Replacement Fund	300,000
• Instructorship	250,000
• Polo Program	200,000
• Jumping	200,000
• Summer Horsemanship Program	150,000
• Troop/Lancers	100,000
• Equestriennes	100,000
• Instructor-in-Residence	100,000

Facilities

• Renovation of Main Arena and Gallery	450,000
• Construction of Outside Ring	150,000
• Grandstands for Outside Ring	50,000

Polo is a major varsity sport, which has long enjoyed a rich tradition at Culver. Elementary instruction in polo is provided for those without previous experience. Junior varsity and varsity polo teams are fielded, with the varsity competing normally against college and adult polo clubs.

Jumping Boys and girls elect to participate in any one or all seasons, fall, winter, and spring, in which jumping is offered. Varsity jumpers represent the Academies at away shows at least once a month during each season.

Clinics. Noted horse authorities frequently visit Culver to conduct clinics. Jean Froissard, Robert Egan, Jack Fritz, Paul Wimert, and William Gutierrez have been the most recent.

Summer Equitation Programs

In addition to equitation programs during the academic year, Culver conducts a Horsemanship Camp for Boys, ages thirteen to seventeen, for six weeks during the summer. The campers can avail themselves of other parts of Culver's widely-varied summer offerings in addition to learning or polishing their equitation skills through equitation classes, polo, and jumping. High-point of the camp is the six-day, cross-country hike, during which Troopers live outdoors and care for their animals in the fashion of the old U.S. Cavalry.

Girls enrolled in Culver's Summer Camp may also take instruction in equitation and jumping. Girls enrolled in these classes may also choose to take a three day, cross-country hike, which many feel is a particular highlight of the summer.

The Equestriennes, honor organization of Culver Girls Academy, perform intricate precision drill maneuvers, to musical accompaniment, at some of the country's leading horse events.

PHOTO BY GARY W. LEWALLEN

have suffered from heavy usage and age. Two years ago, the roof over the Stables had reached such a point of deterioration that it was considered unsafe.

Consequently, during the fall of 1985, at a cost of $450,000, the old roof was replaced with a pre-cast, pre-stressed concrete roof. And, while additional repairs, maintenance and upgrading continue to be done to put the fences, jumps, pastures, and rings in good condition, much work yet remains to restore the entire facility to top-flight condition.

The Vaughn Challenge

Recognizing the immediate need to renovate the entire horsemanship center, as well as the chance to create an endowment for the horsemanship program, members of the Jack C. Vaughn family of Dallas, Texas, have made a $1,000,000 challenge gift to the Choices for Culver Campaign. And in recognition of their generosity, Culver's horsemanship facilities will hereafter be known as the Jack C. Vaughn Equestrian Center.

Jack C. Vaughn, CMA Class of '43, was a longtime advocate of the Academy and supporter of the Troop. A talented sportsman who shared his love of horses with his children, Mr. Vaughn was a member of Battery B at Culver, before going on to receive his bachelor's degree in business administration from the University of Texas at Austin and joining Vaughn Petroleum, Inc., a family-owned oil and gas exploration and production company. In a business career that eventually saw him serve as an officer or director of some fifteen corporations, the impact of Jack C. Vaughn's activities, in radio and television, petroleum, insurance, banking, printing, ranching, and real estate, was seen and felt throughout the state of Texas and, indeed, throughout the Southwest.

Giving this generous gift to Culver in his honor were Mr. Vaughn's sons, Jack C. Vaughn Jr. '72 and Robert C. Vaughn '74, both former leaders of the Black Horse Troop at Culver and now chairman and president, respectively, of Vaughn Petroleum, Inc.; and David C. Vaughn; his daughter, Mrs. Sharon Vaughn Gallivan '76; and his widow, Mrs. Mary Jo Vaughn Rauscher, all of Dallas.

The Vaughn family, recognizing the dual importance of facilities and endowment, has asked that their gift be divided between these two needs. Culver seeks an additional $2,000,000 to meet the overall challenge in these areas. Of this amount, $1,350,000 is designated for endowment, in order to ensure the program's excellence in the future. And $650,000 is earmarked for facilities improvement, including renovation of the Riding Hall Arena and Gallery (which dates back to 1917) and construction of an outdoor riding ring with grandstands between the Stables and the Armory.

What You Can Do

With escalating costs, the high quality of Culver's horsemanship program cannot be maintained without the direct support of alumni who have shared in that special experience which comes from being a member of the Troop or the Equestriennes. Therefore, to meet the Vaughn Challenge, all friends of Culver are urged to lend their support. A number of significant gifts are needed, and their donors may name important facilities or endow different aspects of the program which are of special interest. Smaller gifts, too, will help take this special program to its goal.

Figure 24.4. The final financial report on the campaign

CHOICES FOR CULVER

12-31-88

GIFT SIZE	NUMBER NEEDED	TOTAL NEEDED	NUMBER RECEIVED	TOTAL RECEIVED
		LEADERSHIP GIFTS		
$5,000,000	1	$ 5,000,000	1	$ 5,016,853
2,000,000	2	4,000,000	5	14,811,118
1,000,000	12	12,000,000	10	11,971,244
750,000	2	1,500,000	3	2,610,000
500,000	10	5,000,000	8	4,290,424
250,000	24	6,000,000	20	5,817,518
100,000	45	4,500,000	49	5,865,973
	—		—	
	96	$ 38,000,000	96	$50,383,130
		MAJOR GIFTS		
50,000	50	$ 2,250,000	24	$ 1,415,051
25,000	60	1,350,000	37	1,001,620
10,000	60	550,000	58	742,495
5,000	80	350,000	44	235,685
Under 5,000			34	39,204
	—		—	
	250	$ 4,500,000	197	$ 3,434,055
Annual Giving	- -	$ 4,500,000	18836	$ 6,306,082
TOTAL		$ 47,000,000	19061	$60,123,267

Total $47,000,000

Total Pledges and Gifts. $60,123,267*

Total Needed . . . . $ 0

Percent of Goal Completed 128%

* Of this amount $49,222,991 has already been received in pledge payments and outright gifts

Figure 24.5. This end-of-campaign report was an insert in Culver's Alumnus Magazine. *"We chose to go this direction," said J. Frederick Lintner, "as a way of rather inexpensively getting the message to all our alumni and friends. Also, we did not want to make such a big deal of the end of the campaign that it gave the impression that all our needs had been met. For, in fact, we have already begun planning for our next campaign."*

A SPECIAL END-OF-THE-CAMPAIGN REPORT

SETTING THE RECORD

What Does $60 Million Buy?

Text by Mary Ellen Hamer, Editor
Culver Alumnus Magazine

Photos by Gary Mills (South Bend, Ind.)

RECENTLY a Culver faculty member, the kind that no school can afford to lose, was offered a position at a prestigious day school in a large city. After a weekend of wrestling with the decision, on Sunday evening he called and refused the offer. "What kept nagging at my wife and me was the feeling that Culver is an important place," he says, "although we didn't articulate it in quite that way. I guess I was afraid I'd end up at a school where I'd have a good idea, and there'd be no money to implement it."

Culver is now in a position to afford not only good ideas, but great ones as well, thanks to the generosity of its graduates. On December 31, 1988, the Academies closed the books on a five-year capital campaign, "Choices for Culver," which netted $60.1 million, making it the single most successful fund drive in the history of American private

LEFT: David Sampson, fine arts department chairman.

We went back to people who had earlier said, 'I'm not in a position to help now,' and they gave. Others, especially board members, came back and gave for the second, sometimes even the third, time."

Good old-fashioned school pride and competitiveness (and a lot of hard work) raised over $15 million in a little over two months. Henderson, Dicke, President of the Academies Ralph N. Manuel, and members of the development staff were on the road, making calls through Christmas and right up to New Year's Eve. The largest gift of the campaign, an anonymous family donation of $5 million, came in on December 22, pushing the total past the $60 million mark.

It was a herculean effort by a nucleus of committed board members and the Academies

BELOW Jeanne Cunningham '91 (North Judson, Ind.)

development staff, headed during the campaign by current director J. Frederick Lintner and Channing E. Mitzell, now assistant to the president for external affairs. Over five hundred prospects were researched, nearly three hundred people were visited (some as many as half a dozen times), countless letters were written and phone calls made, and hundreds of thousands of miles were traveled (Ralph Manuel accumulated 170,000 bonus miles with Piedmont Airlines alone).

But most of all, it was an overwhelming vote of confidence, a tremendous show of support by Culver alums—a putting-their-money

ABOVE Matt Canlis '90 (Bellevue, Wash.)

ABOVE Language chairman Thomas Thornburg with Chuck Eller '89 (Cleveland Heights, Ohio) and Eric Sheeler '90 (Wooster, Ohio)

secondary schools. The previous record holder, Phillips Academy of Andover, Mass., had raised $52 million in 1979 as part of its centennial celebration. Not only did the $60.1 million figure exceed Andover's record by fifteen percent, but it also exceeded Culver's own original campaign goal of $47 million by twenty-eight percent.

The accomplishment was noted by no less than the *New York Times*, the *Chicago Tribune*, and the *Chronicle of Philanthropy* (a recent companion to the *Chronicle of Higher Education*) and by countless other papers nationwide. James A. Henderson '52, CEF board president and chief operating officer of Cummins Engine, Inc., of Columbus, Ind., says: "What really excites me is that it has given Culver publicity in the world of education—publicity that we usually don't get since we don't sit on one of the two coasts where educators talk among themselves."

It wasn't clear until the October board meeting that Culver would reach its $47 million goal and, in fact, had a good chance of breaking the Andover record: at that point, the tally stood at a little over $45 million. "Then there was the tremendous confluence of the end of the tax year, the end of the campaign, and the opportunity to break the record," recalls James F. Dicke II '64, national campaign chairman and president of Crown Equipment Corporation of New Bremen, Ohio. "The Culver constituency was galvanized by the idea that we could go past Andover's $52 million."

BELOW On the lower level of the dining hall, Culver's newly created student center

can. If a Harvard or a Princeton shriveled up and blew away tomorrow, America would not have lost anything unique or irreplaceable as it would if Culver did. Culver gives young people not only a superior college-preparatory education, but also leadership training and the experience of living with an honor code."

Another alum, who contributed $2 million to the campaign, bringing his giving record over the years to $4.5 million, wrote a letter some time ago to his father, recalling an incident that had happened twenty-five years before: "I will never forget a foggy, cold morning in September when you dropped me off on the shores of that lake. I wondered what I had done to make a wonderful pair of parents treat a wonderful person like me in this way. I now know you gave me something I couldn't have gotten anywhere else."

What makes the success even more exciting, and perhaps surprising, is that Culver has been a "Johnny-come-lately" in the fund-raising arena. It was 1958 before the school began a formal annual-giving program, and 1961 before it ran a capital campaign. In fact, "Choices for Culver" was only its third capital campaign; the earlier two, one in the early '60s and another in the '70s, had netted $5 and $18 million, respectively.

In contrast, most of the country's other leading independent schools have been in the fund-raising business for fifty years or better. Phillips Exeter Academy (Exeter, N.H.) has had an annual fund since 1924. Choate (now Choate Rosemary Hall, Wallingford, Conn.), since 1943. Lawrenceville School (Lawrenceville, N.J.), since 1939. Deerfield Academy (Deerfield, Mass.) ran its first capital campaign in the late '20s. Northfield Mount Hermon School (Northfield, Mass.) had its first annual appeal in 1904 and opened a development office in 1909.

That's why it seemed particularly ambitious (perhaps quixotic) five years ago when the Academies announced a campaign for $47 million, at the time the second and most ambitious fund-raising effort in the history of secondary education. But the funds were desperately needed the '70s had exacted a heavy price on the Academies—spiraling inflation, falling enrollment in the boys school due to a Vietnam backlash, all the start-up costs involved in creating the girls school and pursuing a system of coordinate education, runaway energy costs, and a deteriorating physical plant— resulting in

BELOW: Interior, the Herman W. Lay Dining Center

BELOW: The Herman W. Lay Dining Center

ABOVE: Interior, H. Ward Lay III Student Center

where-their-hearts-are—the likes of which had never been seen before in private secondary education. It was a campaign of "megagifts" and "megagivers": ninety percent of the $60.1 million was contributed by less than five percent of the givers. There was one gift of $5 million, two of $4 million, thirteen between $1-$3 million, and eighty between $100,000-$750,000. Thirty-seven percent of the total was contributed by board members alone.

What causes people to step forward with that level of commitment to an institution? In his book Megagifts, Jerold Panas, one of the country's leading fund-raising consultants, asserts: "To those who make the really large gift, there has to be an unswerving belief in the objectives and the mission of the institution. This takes precedence over any other factor. No matter how tantalizing the project, no matter how persuasive the caller, no matter how distinguished the organization, a dedicated belief in the work and role of the organization is quintessential."

Culver's mission has remained unchanged over the years: to be a first-rate academic institution, but one that is equally committed to the development of moral and spiritual values and the teaching of leadership through hands-on experience. And its graduates obviously buy that mission with a zeal.

The campaign's largest donor ($5 million) explains: "Culver is in a position to make an impact on young lives in a way that no college

ABOVE: Jack C. Vaughn Equestrian Center

a deficit of approximately $200,000 for several years running and a program of deferred maintenance.

As the school's needs were assessed and reassessed during the planning stages, the campaign goal leapfrogged from seventeen to twenty-seven to thirty-seven to forty-seven million dollars. The board decided to stop at forty-seven, not because it would meet all the needs, but because everyone felt it represented the outer limit of what was possible. Deciding that Culver alums could and should support their school at the same level as graduates of leading universities in the country, trustees took the campaign goals of Princeton, Yale, Stanford, and Dartmouth, divided each goal by that school's number of alumni, arriving at an average alumni contribution. That number was then multiplied by Culver's 9,000 graduates. The result: $47 million.

At the time, the number sounded incredible. Chan Mitzell, then director of development, describes his reaction in one word, "fear." "Fred Lintner, current director, says, "Only one person really thought it was possible, and that was Jim Henderson." Paul C. Gignilliat '49, annual-fund chairman for the past three years and vice-president at Kidder Peabody Company, Inc., of Chicago, Ill., says, "It looked impossible . . . . no, perhaps I should say like a very aggressive goal."

Ralph Manuel, who at the time had been recently selected as Superintendent John Mars' successor and was completing his tenure as dean of the college at Dartmouth, recalls saying to his wife, only half in jest, "I have to get out there and stop these people." Even Jim Henderson concedes, "Forty-seven million looked so large at the time that we all had concern, concern that if we didn't work hard we couldn't succeed. We didn't want to fail."

The campaign turned out to be an act of faith, faith on its organizers' part in the loyalty and generosity of Culver alums and faith on its graduates' part in the institution and its mission. Henderson explains: "Fund-raising counsel would say that we should have done a survey before ascertaining a goal, but I never felt the need. My dad (the late Dean John Henderson) knew Culver families for forty years as dean of admissions, and I had known another couple of generations worth myself. I was confident of two things: that to a surprising degree Culver alumni are successful people and that they value highly the training they received here."

He was right on both accounts.

Now, with money in hand (more than eighty-

RIGHT: *Exterior view of the Vaughn Equestrian Center*

LEFT: *Benson Hall Lounge*

financial aid, faculty salaries, and academic support, enabling the school to operate deficit-free and to slow down tuition increases. At the start of the campaign (when CGA and CMA had different tuition rates), CGA ranked second, and CMA fourth, in tuition costs among the country's ten leading college-prep boarding schools. Today, the Academies rank fifth.

Sixty-point-one million means Culver is once more able to compete for the best students and faculty. When the campaign began, $700,000 was being spent a year on financial aid. This year $1.7 million was spent; next year, $2.1 million will be spent, and the investment is paying off. Five of the top six students in this year's graduating class were financial aid recipients; two of the top seven in the junior class; three of the top four in the sophomore class; and two of the top three in the freshman class.

Culver now ranks among the top five independent schools in the country in financial

ABOVE: *A Remington sculpture, inside the Vaughn Equestrian Center*

LEFT: *Inside the H. Ward Lay III Student Center*

five percent of the total has already been received in pledge payments and outright gifts, an unusually high percentage so soon after the close of a campaign). Culver is in a position to answer the question: What does $60.1 million buy for a school these days? What does it mean for the future of the institution?

Perhaps most important, $60.1 million means Culver is once more on steady financial feet. Fifty percent of the campaign funds, $30 million in all, went to strengthening the endowment, tripling it over the past five years—from $17 million in 1984 to $51 million (and growing) today. It is impossible to overstate the importance of a school's endowment. It is the rock upon which great schools are built; it is the anchor which steadies them through rough times. The 1987-88 CFAE (Council for Aid to Education) Report ranks Culver number eleven in endowment among U.S. independent schools.

Of next year's estimated operating budget of $16.4 million, $2.4 million will come from interest earned on the endowment (according to board policy, only half of the interest earned annually on the endowment can be used for annual expenses; the remainder is added to the endowment to ensure further growth).

Also vital to that financial steadying has been annual giving, which, under the direction of Paul Gignilliat, added $6.3 million to the campaign funds for ten percent of the total. This past year alone, annual giving contributed over a million dollars to the operating budget. Like endowment interest, annual funds are used each year to meet current expenses, such as aid awarded. Today, one in three Culver students receives financial assistance; five years ago, just under one in five did. The average new student award for the 1988–89 school year was almost $8,000 (tuition: $12,750).

And over the course of the campaign, the number of endowed scholarships grew by forty-six percent, from fifty-eight in 1984 to eighty-four in 1989.

Faculty salaries have increased by some fifty percent over the same period of time. Five years ago, Culver salaries were not only far below other leading private schools but fifteen to twenty percent behind average salaries in Indiana's better public schools. Although still not in a leadership position, Culver salaries are once more competitive. The median salary for a full-time instructor in 1984 was $18,256, today it is $25,200. Six academic chairs have also been added in support of faculty salaries, bringing the total number of endowed chairs at Culver to twenty-two.

Sixty-one million means the physical plant is being systematically reclaimed and upgraded, improving dramatically the quality of life on campus, and that ground will be broken in May for a new $6 million library. Some forty percent of the total campaign funds, $24 million in all, has been targeted for facilities. Of that sum, almost $16 million has already been spent, with the remainder being held for designated projects.

The dining hall (The Herman W. Lay Dining Center) has been renovated from top to bottom, including even the murals, and a student center (the H. Ward Lay III Student Center), complete with snack bar, bookstore, and reading, game, and meeting rooms, has been created on its lower level. Student living quarters have been updated, re-furnished, made more comfortable and attractive. Argonne and CT for coeds (thanks to the William A. Moncrief Jr. '37 family of Fort Worth, Texas) and Main Barrack for cadets (thanks to Courtenay C. Davis '20 of Horse Creek, Wyoming).

The riding hall (The Jack C. Vaughn Equestrian Center) has a new stable roof and stalls; after graduation, work will begin on the masonry of the south towers. The interior of the infirmary has been redone, from wiring to wallpaper to air conditioning, and the exterior is in process. The Henderson House (former residence of Dean John Henderson) has been renovated and redecorated as home to the Montgomery Lecture Series. Eppley Auditorium has a modern lecture hall, the Eileen Dicke Theater, formerly known as the Little Theater.

The Music & Arts Building has been re-roofed, and its exterior rehabilitated. The Woodcraft dining hall has a new roof, as does the Fleet/Viersen gym. Repairs have been made to the Chapel, the armory, and North and East Barracks. As energy conservation measures, regional boilers have been installed around campus and steam and water lines replaced. Trees and flowers are being planted, curbs are being installed, company streets are being re-paved.

Sixty-one million means Culver can afford to encourage and support innovation, creativity, new ideas. It means that in the history department, Rich Davies' World Religion class now sits around tables, discussing the relationship between the historical and risen Jesus, rather than back-to-back in desks (two more rooms in the department will be outfitted in a similar manner by September); that the Academies' Dancevision troupe has a new floor in its studio; that Eppley Auditorium has a new sound system.

It means that two mobile language labs have been purchased for the language department at a cost of $13,000 each, to be used until space can be created for a permanent lab; that $50,000 has been spent on computing in academic areas over the past three years; that the math department has two complete classrooms of Macintosh SE computers, enabling it to pilot a course being written at the University of Chicago and that the English department will have a writing center by this fall, equipped with twenty-four word processors, staffed by a full-time director, and available for student use during the class day and in the evenings.

It means that over the past few years, through the Montgomery Lecture and Affiliate Artists Series, students have had the chance to listen to, learn from, and visit with experts in various fields—from an ex-Presidential spokesman to the editor of Forbes magazine, from a world-class cellist to an authority on Afro-American gospel music.

It means that CGA finally has its own suite of offices, giving the girls, according to Dean Trudy Hall, "a sense of identity"; that Culver can run a comprehensive drug/alcohol education program, staffed by a full-time professional; that a part-time

ABOVE Anne O. Duff, fine arts instructor

BELOW Snack Bar inside the H. Ward Lay III Student Center

BELOW Inside renovated Main Barrack

ABOVE The Herman W. Lay Dining Center

Catholic chaplain has been hired; that a department of leadership has been created.

Sixty-one million means that Culver has been revitalized, "re-founded" in the words of Ralph Manuel, once more secure in its leadership position among the top private schools in the country, once more able to aggressively pursue excellence in all its programs. As Jim Dicke says: "Culver is now in a position to take significant initiatives to put it at the forefront of secondary education, something which was not an option at the beginning of the campaign."

Six months after the close of the campaign, the question is inevitable: What next? Although Culver has no immediate plans to launch another capital campaign, the board has already identified some short and long-range financial goals for the Academies.

Perhaps first is to raise the remaining money for the library—approximately $3 million more for construction costs and several million more for furnishing and equipment.

Longer-range goals include moving the school from a competitive to a leadership position in the area of faculty compensation; putting the school among the top ten independent schools in the country in terms of endowment (one of the campaign's original goals); and perhaps most important of all, increasing annual-giving participation by fifteen to twenty percent.

Over the course of the campaign, alumni participation in annual giving rose by six points, from twenty-two to twenty-eight percent. Re-establishing a class-agent system and having an active annual-fund chairman (Paul Gignilliat) helped. However, many of Culver's competitors approach or surpass the fifty percent mark (Phillips Exeter Academy: fifty-four percent; St. Paul's School of Concord, N.H.: fifty percent).

As President Manuel points out, "Everyone who has ever attended Culver was on scholarship. Tuition alone has never met the full cost of a student's education. Today it covers only sixty-one percent, the remainder coming from alumni contributions and endowment, which, of course, were built by those who came before. Culver graduates have the continuing responsibility to ensure that this institution is here for succeeding generations as it was for them."

Where will the major donors to future campaigns come from? In *Megagifts*, Panas says he never met a "megagiver" who started out that way, that giving is a habit, a learned behavior, acquired over time. The $50 or $100 annual givers of today are often the million-dollar

givers of tomorrow.' This was certainly true in Culver's recent campaign.

Not one of the million or million-plus donors was a first-time giver. Each had had a solid history of giving to the school, a record which had grown stronger over time. "I remember making five and ten dollar gifts to the Academy as a student," recalls one donor. "Even as a seventeen-year-old kid, I knew that I wanted to do something special for Culver someday for what it had done for me and my brother." He did—to the tune of $5 million.

That there are many other alums who wanted to and did, do something special for Culver, as well, was made evident in the recent campaign. Their "Choices for Culver" came through loud and clear. A quotation from Elton Trueblood, a former chaplain at Stanford University, was used to preface an early campaign piece: "A man has made at least a start on discovering the meaning of human life when he plants shade trees under which he knows full well he will never sit."

Over the past five years, more than five hundred trees have been planted across campus. □

"A man has made at least a start on discovering the meaning of human life when he plants shade trees under which he knows full well he will never sit." (Elton Trueblood)

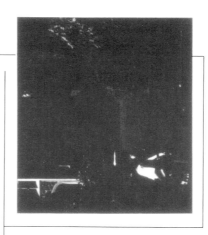

Planned Parenthood Southeastern Pennsylvania

Philadelphia, Pennsylvania

Goal: $4 million
Amount Raised: $3.9 million

The Planned Parenthood organization in Philadelphia spent three years assessing the feasibility of selling its physical facility and raising funds to construct a new building in the center of the city. Once a new location and a buyer for the existing facility were found, the Planned Parenthood group announced a three-year capital campaign to raise $5 million. While the initial plans for the campaign included raising funds for regional centers as well as the Center City Philadelphia facility, as the effort progressed, emphasis was placed primarily on raising approximately $4 million for the new building.

The Southeastern Pennsylvania chapter is one of the largest Planned Parenthood affiliates in the United States. The new facility, which it now occupies as a result of this successful campaign, is the only structure in the whole organization to be designed and built specifically to service the clients of Planned Parenthood. Therefore this project has become a showcase for other affiliates. The new building has also repositioned how the mission of Planned Parenthood is seen in the community. With a medically well-equipped facility that provides a far more hospitable atmosphere for clients, Planned Parenthood in Philadelphia is now seen as a mainstream medical facility.

This campaign was also interesting because it was conducted at the same time that a number of major capital campaigns were under way in Philadelphia, and there was much overlap among prospects for these various causes. Most of the large gifts to Planned Parenthood came from individual donors, with some support from foundations and corporations.

The campaign was called Design for Progress. Paul Blanchard Associates of Bucks County,

Figure 24.6. The text of this case statement was prepared by the consulting firm of Steege/Thomson.

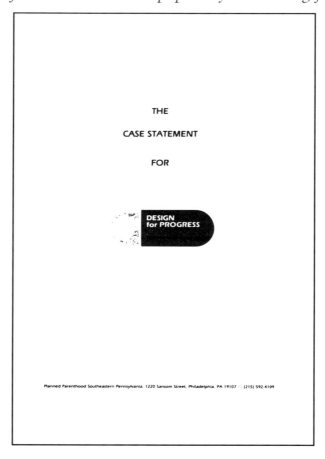

THE

CASE STATEMENT

FOR

DESIGN for PROGRESS

Planned Parenthood Southeastern Pennsylvania, 1220 Sansom Street, Philadelphia, PA 19107 :: (215) 592-4109

Pennsylvania, provided resident counsel during the early stages of the campaign. The John F. Rich Company of Philadelphia conducted a feasibility study to test Planned Parenthood's ability to raise $1 million during a campaign. The study was done at a time when the plan was still to renovate the original site instead of building a new facility. Fifty-two interviews were conducted with members of the board, staff, the advisory committee and donors.

The study found that Planned Parenthood Southeastern Pennsylvania was highly regarded, with a dedicated staff and board. There was concern about the narrowness of the base of major donors. Seventy-three percent of those interviewed favored the capital campaign and 33 percent felt $1 million could be raised. An important issue addressed in the study was whether $1 million could be raised without reducing needed annual support.

When a new facility became a possibility, the goal for the campaign had to be raised significantly. The new goal was never really tested on the constituency.

Two committees of the Planned Parenthood board were key to the success of the campaign. First, a building committee negotiated the sale of the existing property and the purchase of the new one. Second, a steering committee led the fund-raising effort. The chairman of the steering committee devoted a great deal of time and effort to the campaign, and it was her leadership that really kept solicitations moving.

This case statement was prepared in the early stages of the campaign, when the goal was $5 million and included regional needs. It is very straightforward and shows that you don't need a fancy four-color brochure to be effective.

DESIGN FOR PROGRESS

Today our right to choose if and when to have a family is a reality that most of us take for granted. This right, however, has been hard won in a 70-year struggle by Planned Parenthood and its sister organizations.

Today, Planned Parenthood is recognized as the leading advocate for reproductive freedom and an outstanding resource for the finest women's health services and thoughtful, professional family education programs. Planned Parenthood Southeastern Pennsylvania now encompasses 12 family planning centers throughout the area. New and important constituencies, ranging from the city's medical schools, prestigious law firms, seek its educational programs and depend on its resources. And today, while it has won many of the battles for reproductive freedom, Planned Parenthood must lead the struggle against a small but vocal group of extremists who would destroy our critical reproductive rights.

1

THE LEADER IN FAMILY PLANNING

A corporate executive takes time from his work to persuade legislators of the importance of Medicaid funding for family planning services. A young woman looks to her nurse practitioner at Planned Parenthood to help her examine options in the face of a problem pregnancy. As part of Project MARCH (Men Acting Responsibly for Contraception and Health), North Philadelphia teenagers gather in a community center to talk with a Planned Parenthood educator about the trials and tribulations of growing up. At work in our Resource Center, an historian studies newspaper accounts of the controversies surrounding early birth control clinics. A Planned Parenthood educator meets with an Episcopal church youth group to discuss human sexuality.

Planned Parenthood is many things to many different people in all corners of our community. This wide range of services all began with the courageous efforts of Margaret Sanger and other early advocates of family planning, outraged that many poor and desperate women had no choice but to try to induce their own abortions or seek the services of back-alley abortionists. In 1916, Sanger, a nurse, opened the first birth control clinic in the United States and aided thousands of women despite police raids, imprisonments, and fines. Her work spearheaded a nationwide effort to seek legislative reform, to create more birth control clinics, and to educate people about family

3

In the face of these trials and triumphs, Planned Parenthood Southeastern Pennsylvania has taken a hard look at its programs and services. It has developed a new plan for the organization, management, and staffing of its health care centers. It has taken stock of its physical facilities and determined that it needs a new, prominently located headquarters building. This will house a model center for family planning services, offer ample space for its growing educational programs, and provide a strong, symbolic center for its on-going crusade for reproductive rights. Also pressing is the need to improve the facilities at three of its centers in Delaware and Montgomery Counties.

To make these important projects possible, Planned Parenthood Southeastern Pennsylvania is now launching Design for Progress, a $5 million capital campaign that will support its continued central role in family planning advocacy and service to our region.

2

planning — building toward the dream of a society in which all children would be wanted.

In 1929, her supporters in Pennsylvania opened the Maternal Health Center, the state's first contraceptive clinic, in Upper Darby. Ever since, Planned Parenthood Southeastern Pennsylvania has provided family planning services to generations of area women and men, and these services have expanded with each passing decade.

Delaware Valley's Largest Family Planning Program

Today Planned Parenthood Southeastern Pennsylvania provides more contraceptive and reproductive health care services than any other private agency in the area. Its full complement of women's health services ranges from breast cancer screening to diagnosis and treatment for sexually transmitted diseases. Planned Parenthood is now the primary or sole health care source for many of the 26,500 patients who come to its 12 centers located throughout the Delaware Valley. These centers now serve men, too, who come with their partners for counseling on birth control, for treatment of sexually transmitted diseases, or for vasectomies.

With the 1973 Supreme Court ruling making abortions legal, Planned Parenthood Southeastern Pennsylvania moved to ensure this right by offering first trimester abortions. Today Planned

4

Parenthood is the largest such center in Philadelphia and serves the greatest number of women who cannot afford to pay for the procedure. More than 2,500 women seek abortions through Planned Parenthood each year.

A Unique Educational Resource

From the time of Margaret Sanger, education has been a critical facet of Planned Parenthood's mission. In constant demand by community groups of all kinds, Planned Parenthood educators last year conducted 440 programs at over 300 schools, religious institutions, and community organizations. The focus of these programs ranged from human sexuality to relationships between parents and teenage children.

In 1965, the federal government declared its support for family planning, and Planned Parenthood soon became a center for professional training as social workers sought information to educate their clients about birth control. Today, Planned Parenthood's Education and Training Department has grown to offer training to 1,200 professionals a year in many fields. Its educators address issues of human sexuality, birth control, and teenage parenthood with medical students, nurses, and other health care students who have traditionally received little or no training about human sexuality. Teachers, another critical professional group, sought Planned Parenthood in record numbers

5

last year with the approval of Planned Parenthood's new course, "Planning and Implementing Classroom Human Sexuality Courses," for teacher certification credits.

More specialized educational projects include Project MARCH, where Planned Parenthood educators work with young men, ages 13 to 19, in a pioneering program to educate them about their roles and responsibilities in sexuality, contraception, and parenthood. In less than two years, Project MARCH has reached 3,000 young people in 64 sites ranging from YMCAs to church groups to shelters for runaways.

At Planned Parenthood's Resource Center, some 2,800 people a year come to seek information on a wide range of family planning issues. High school students looked for information for school papers on such topics as teen pregnancy. Teachers used resource materials to develop sex education courses, and parents came for appropriate materials to introduce the subject of sexuality to their children.

The Leading Advocate For Reproductive Rights

On a national level, Planned Parenthood's role as advocate for reproductive freedom has won us the rights we take for granted today. Just 20 years ago, Planned Parenthood was instrumental in the Supreme Court decision to make contraceptive devices legal.

It supported the legal battle leading to the 1973 decision making it a right to choose an abortion. The political and religious extremists who battled to deny these basic human dignities are now at work again, this time to dismantle these legal rights. In the past few years, they have strengthened their political attempts to destroy family planning programs, eliminate funding for services, and deny fundamental reproductive rights, to say nothing of their terroristic assaults on staff and patients of family planning clinics. Thus Planned Parenthood's role as an advocate requires even greater commitment and resolve.

Last year Planned Parenthood used its broad network for advocacy to block every anti-choice initiative in the Pennsylvania General Assembly and won three significant victories in the budgeting process, including a line item increase in family planning funding. In Washington, it defeated attempts by Senator Hatch and Representative Kemp to destroy the national family planning program and protected access to safe legal abortions by blocking "riders" attached to unrelated funding bills.

These national efforts depend on Planned Parenthood affiliates for support of many kinds, from financial to lobbying legislators to letter-writing campaigns. As the affiliate in the fifth largest urban area in the country, Planned Parenthood

Southeastern Pennsylvania makes a vital contribution to every success and every right defended at the national level.

The Commitment Of Volunteers

All of Planned Parenthood's programs are possible only because of its intensely committed staff and scores of equally committed volunteers. Volunteers serve the agency in every possible way — from working in family planning centers and speaking to community groups to pressing Congressional leaders for legislative reform. Planned Parenthood's volunteer Board of Directors provide leadership to the organization and hundreds of supporters give generously of their financial resources to make this important work possible.

A Plan For The Future

In the late 60s and early 70s, Planned Parenthood Southeastern Pennsylvania recognized that the legislative climate and public opinion made it an important time for strong growth in its programs. Thus it developed a series of centers to provide family planning services throughout the region and expanded its services to include breast cancer screening, abortion services, and other new programs. In the early 80s on the heels of this growth, the Board carefully considered Planned Parenthood's physical facilities while a new management team studied its services. Out

8

of this critical evaluation, Planned Parenthood came to several important conclusions:

—— Planned Parenthood must offer the finest quality, most professional, most accessible services in the area.

—— Each center needs to be developed as a strong, independently managed program working to reach a maximum of 5,000 patients.

—— Planned Parenthood is firmly committed to serving all women, regardless of their ability to pay for its services. At the same time, it will develop strategies to increase the number of women who can afford to pay so that its centers can sustain a greater share of the cost for those who cannot.

—— The Education and Training Department must have better and more appropriate space for its training programs.

—— The physical facilities for several programs, most notably those housed in its Sansom Street building in Center City, no longer meet the standards of a dignified, professional and attractive environment to which Planned Parenthood must aspire for its patients and its educational clients in the 90s and beyond.

New Initiatives For Management

The Board and staff of Planned Parenthood Southeastern Pennsylvania have already moved to address several of these issues. First, they closed three centers that were in

9

unprofessional or unattractive locations or whose services were available only for a limited number of hours each week.

At the Center City service, Planned Parenthood's 12,000 patients often waited weeks to get an appointment and then had long waits to see their clinicians. To relieve this overcrowding, the administration responded to patients' needs and developed a new center in a very visible location in Market East and created an environment where more women who work and shop in the area would seek health care and family planning services.

The Planned Parenthood administrative team also changed the management of the centers dramatically by shifting responsibility from the central administration to the managers in each center. It also set standards for longer, more convenient center hours and established a model to increase staffing as its patients grew in number. In a single year, these changes have brought about a 25 percent increase in the number of patient visits to Planned Parenthood.

A Headquarters For Planned Parenthood

The decision to create a new center for Planned Parenthood Southeastern Pennsylvania in a prominent site in Center City will take Planned Parenthood to its next and most exciting step. The center will contain model clinical facilities. It will offer

10

ample, professional spaces for educational programs and the Resource Center, and it will provide adequate administrative offices. Above all, the new headquarters will stand as a powerful symbol to the agency's detractors that Planned Parenthood is thriving, is planning for its future, and is here to stay to lead the fight for reproductive freedom.

The Board and staff have chosen a highly visible corner in the center of Philadelphia at 12th and Locust Streets. They have engaged the architectural firm of George Yu Associates and charged them with creating a light, airy, friendly building that fits well with the stately brick structures in the surrounding area. The ample site will enable Planned Parenthood to create a warm, caring, professional environment for its patients and clients. It will become comfortable for all and marketable in a climate where a great deal more is expected of the environment for health care services.

Before the decision to create a new headquarters was reached, Planned Parenthood's Board and staff carefully considered renovating their existing building, but found this old diamond factory on Sansom Street wanting in several important ways. First, Planned Parenthood, by its very mission, could not justify being part of a multi-tiered health care system in which those who cannot afford to pay receive health care in less dignified

11

surroundings. Nor could it meet its financial mandate for expanding services to working women without more attractive, professional facilities. Second, its location would always position it on a narrow back street, which no longer gives the image that Planned Parenthood strives to create for family planning services. Third, the building would need entirely new and expensive mechanical and energy conservation systems to solve the costly and uncomfortable environmental problems.

For the many visitors that come to Planned Parenthood, the new headquarters will not only offer ample, comfortable meeting areas, but will create an entirely different image of Planned Parenthood Southeastern Pennsylvania. This, Planned Parenthood's leadership believes, is critical to its role as the nation's leading advocate for reproductive rights.

Model Facilities For Service, Education And Advocacy

The new Philadelphia Center, which will be built around a small courtyard with flowers and trees, will house surgical services on the ground floor, separate from the comings and goings of other Planned Parenthood visitors. On the street level above will be the women's health services, also removed from the flow of staff and visitors. The layout of the examining rooms, bathrooms, and labs in both of these facilities has been designed to offer private surroundings for each patient and her clinician.

12

Comfortable waiting areas for patients and their families or friends are connected to both services. And the surgical services area was designed so that the recovery room is suffused with light from the courtyard.

Planned Parenthood's Institute for Family Planning, which now works from a crowded oblong room that seats only 20 and suffers from real problems with temperature control, will soon have a 100-seat conference room on the corner of the new building with natural light from two sides. Not only will this space work for large groups, but it is also designed to be divided to provide a more intimate space for a maximum of about 30 people, or a larger space to accommodate 70.

On the street level below, the Resource Center will be housed in a large, airy room with adequate space to meet the needs of its growing collection, both now and in the future. Entered through the green court and a handsome lobby, this Center will clearly position Planned Parenthood as a dignified professional information resource with an emphasis on quality and permanence.

The top two floors of the building will provide offices for Planned Parenthood's central administration -- the Executive Director's offices, public affairs, development, personnel, and finance. This space has been planned with an eye to efficiency and to the future growth that Planned Parenthood projects. The

13

building, will offer model clinical facilities and fine meeting spaces to which Planned Parenthood's leadership and volunteers will be pleased to bring key politicians and community leaders to show the quality of Planned Parenthood's programs.

To build and furnish this new building will require $3.9 million.

Strengthening the Centers

Another high priority for Planned Parenthood is to offer the same attractive, dignified environment for patients in centers throughout the region.

In Chester, where youth unemployment and despair are legendary, Planned Parenthood has hired a center manager to define the needs of the area and develop the kind of program that will have the greatest impact. She will consider such alternatives as a women's health service and a teen center with some employment training along with health care. The manager's assessment is expected to be completed early next year, at which point she will move to acquire the space needed for such a program and begin the necessary renovations.

Planned Parenthood's program in Norristown is growing in response to strong community need and demand. In 1985 its three staff members offered family planning and women's health services to 3,794 patients. It has also developed a pilot program with the

Family Planning Council and Montgomery County Hospital to provide prenatal care in an area with a very high rate of adolescent pregnancy and infants at risk. Unfortunately, the facilities for these services, both traditional and innovative, are woefully inadequate. The center is too small; it is not in a good location for the people it wants to serve; and it does not offer an appealing, professional environment. Thus Planned Parenthood now needs to purchase and renovate a new facility for Norristown.

Another growing program is Planned Parenthood's center in Media. Here the number of patient visits has grown to 3,307, and the staff now numbers three. Unfortunately, there is no room for growth at the present center while the number of patients seeking Planned Parenthood services there is increasing. Thus Planned Parenthood is now planning to relocate and renovate its Media facility.

To strengthen these three key facilities, Planned Parenthood is seeking $750,000 to purchase or renovate these facilities.

Finally, Planned Parenthood needs a modest endowment of $350,000 to underwrite some of the costs of operating and maintaining its many facilities. This would permit a greater share of its operating funds to go directly to providing more educational and patient services, the heart of Planned Parenthood's programs, and would offer it resources for maintenance in lean years as well as strong ones for decades to come.

16

A POWERFUL SYMBOL FOR THE FUTURE

Clearly, Planned Parenthood Southeastern Pennsylvania has earned its place as an exemplary leader in family planning. Its role as our advocate has won important freedoms for every single woman and man in America. Its tradition of service and advocacy is more viable than ever after almost 60 years in the Delaware Valley. Planned Parenthood is what it is today because of the commitment of many people, as volunteers, as staff, as supporters.

Planned Parenthood Southeastern Pennsylvania turns to these loyal friends today to join in creating the resources for its future. With everyone's help, new clinical facilities will enable Planned Parenthood to offer dignified, personal services to all of its patients and will invite new people to seek its programs. Its new headquarters will stand as a powerful symbol of strength, warmth and endurance to those who would tamper with our hard won reproductive rights.

Please join us with your gift to help Design for Progress meet its goal of $5 million to make a stronger Planned Parenthood Southeastern Pennsylvania.

17

Figure 24.7. Campaign kickoff news release

Planned Parenthood Southeastern Pennsylvania   1220 Sansom Street, Philadelphia, PA 19107, (215) 592-4100

FOR IMMEDIATE RELEASE   CONTACT: Louise Axon
                                      Public Relations
                                      Coordinator
                                      (215) 592-4100

**PLANNED PARENTHOOD LAUNCHES $5 MILLION CAPITAL CAMPAIGN TO
BUILD NEW CENTER CITY HEADQUARTERS**

Planned Parenthood Southeastern Pennsylvania has launched Design For Progress, a capital campaign to raise five million dollars over the next three years. The money will be used to build a new agency headquarters in Center City Philadelphia and to renovate several contraceptive centers in Delaware and Montgomery Counties.

Located at the corner of 12th and Locust Streets, Planned Parenthood's new headquarters will house clinical services, administrative offices, a library/bookstore, and meeting spaces for community educational programs. The architectural firm, George Yu and Associates, has designed a light, airy, three story building surrounding a courtyard garden which complements the historic structures of the neighborhood. The building successfully combines a welcoming environment for clients with a functional, cost-effective administrative headquarters for the non-profit agency.

"This beautiful new building will not only help us serve the community better," says the Rt. Reverend J. Brooke

Mosley, Chairman of the Board, "but it will serve as testament to Planned Parenthood's continued strength and growth. Sixty years ago, we were the first organization to provide family planning services to the Philadelphia community. Today, we continue to lead the movement to guarantee reproductive freedom."

Founded in 1929, Planned Parenthood Southeastern Pennsylvania is one of the largest and oldest of the 187 Planned Parenthood affiliates in the country. In 1986, the agency served over 60,000 women and their families, making it the largest private provider of reproductive health care in the Delaware Valley. Planned Parenthood's present facilities in an old diamond factory at 1220 Sansom Street have proved inadequate to the burgeoning demand for its services, which has more than doubled over the past decade.

Throughout its history, Planned Parenthood Southeastern Pennsylvania has received outstanding support from the greater Philadelphia community, with over one third of its four million dollar operating budget coming from individual, corporate and foundation gifts. Mrs. Charles D. Dickey, Jr., of Devon and Mr. Paul F. Miller of Gladwyne co-chair the capital campaign – the agency's largest community fundraising effort to date. Board members and volunteers have already raised $2.3 million towards the five million dollar goal. The City of Philadelphia has demonstrated its support by making redevelopment authority land available, thereby helping the agency to maintain a prominent presence in Center City Philadelphia.

(more)

The Design for Progress campaign is an excellent example of a community-based effort, spearheaded by dedicated volunteers. The total raised included $2.67 million in gift commitments, $1.1 million received from the sale of the original building and accumulated interest. This campaign made possible a dramatically improved level of service and created a broad new community awareness of Planned Parenthood's services. The materials for this case study were provided by Anne Adriance, who was director of development for Planned Parenthood Southeastern Pennsylvania during the campaign.

Figure 24.8. The case statement was turned into a mailing piece. It details the needs, includes a gift table and shows the leadership for the campaign.

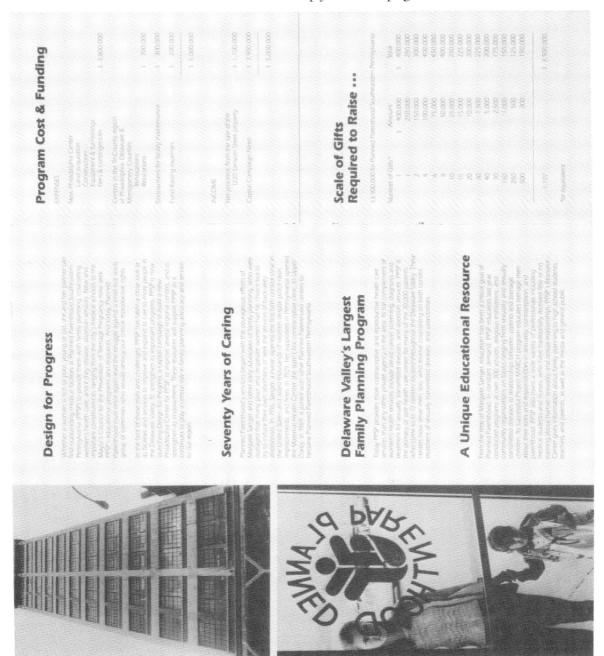

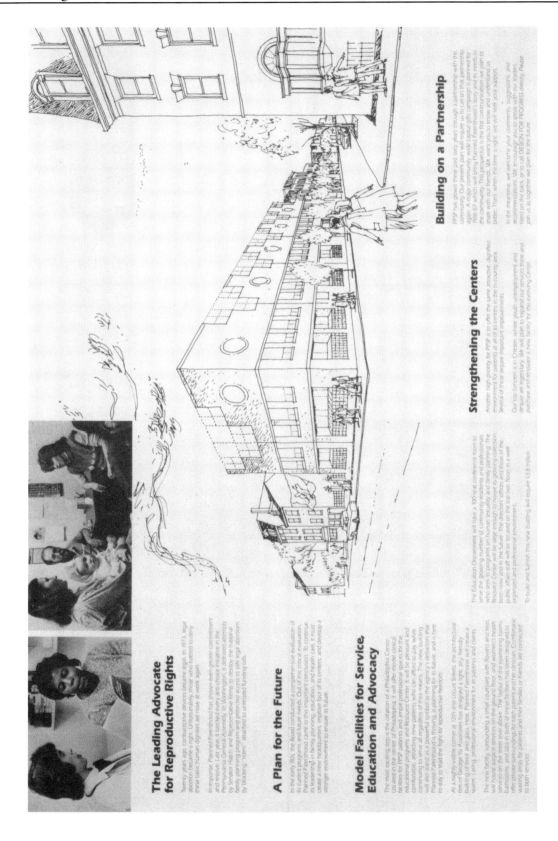

A Prospectus

Leadership

Board

Figure 24.9. A question-and-answer brochure

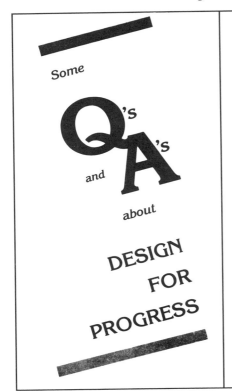

Some Q's and A's about DESIGN FOR PROGRESS

Q. WHO WILL BE ASKED TO GIVE?

A. Some 2,500 select individuals, corporations and foundations will be given the opportunity to participate in this important and critical project for PPSP.

Q. HOW CAN I PARTICIPATE IN 'DESIGN FOR PROGRESS'?

A. Many ways. By making a personal gift/pledge. Interest family and friends to participate. By becoming involved as a solicitor.

Q. I'D LIKE TO MAKE A LARGE GIFT, BUT MUST I DO IT IN ONE LUMP SUM?

A. A gift/pledge can be spread out over a three to five year tax period.

Q. ARE THERE SPECIAL GIFT OPPORTUNITIES?

A. There are many commemorative gift opportunities available in **DESIGN FOR PROGRESS.** If you are interested, please contact the **DESIGN FOR PROGRESS** Campaign office, (215) 592-4109.

Q. WHERE CAN I SEND MY GIFT?

A. All gifts, regardless of size, are needed and welcome. All gifts are tax deductible. You can send your gift/pledge to:

DESIGN FOR PROGRESS
1220 Sansom Street
Philadelphia, PA 19107
call for additional information:
(215) 592-4109

Q. WHAT IS 'DESIGN FOR PROGRESS'?

A. 'DESIGN FOR PROGRESS' is a major capital campaign to support:

(1) construction of a new Philadelphia center for PPSP;
(2) facility improvements at selected PPSP neighborhood centers;
(3) establishment of a modest facility endowment fund.

Q. WHAT DOES THIS MEAN FOR PPSP?

A. DESIGN FOR PROGRESS will help to support PPSP's continued central role in family planning advocacy and service to our region.

Q. HOW MANY USE PPSP's SERVICES ANYWAY?

A. Last year, nearly 60,000 individuals took advantage of the contraceptive, family planning, surgical and educational services offered by PPSP; 18,000 alone at the Center City facility.

Q. WHAT DOES THIS MEAN FOR THE PRESENT FACILITY ON SANSOM STREET?

A. The Heublein Building — affectionately known as '1220' — has been sold. PPSP will now lease space in the building until the new facility is completed.

Q. WHY IS PPSP MOVING FROM '1220'?

A. Because '1220' does not meet PPSP's needs. The building's design will not permit proper space configuration nor efficient, cost-effective service delivery.

Q. WHY RELOCATE IN CENTER CITY?

A. Since 1933, PPSP has maintained a presence in Center City. To withdraw would curtail services to thousands of people who live and work in Center City. Additionally, it would signal a symbolic retreat in the minds of the anti-choice forces.

Q. WHY BUILD?

A. Ownership means PPSP can control its destiny, affirm the value of programs and services being offered and make patient security easier to assure.

Q. WHAT WILL BE IN THE NEW BUILDING?

A. The new building will house the agency's two busiest patient centers, its resourse center and all administrative and support services.

Q. WILL THIS NEW BUILDING BE ANOTHER OF THOSE 'STATUS SYMBOL' IVORY TOWERS?

A. Absolutely not! Every effort is being made to keep the design simple, functional and inexpensive to operate.

Q. WILL THE NEW CENTER INCREASE COSTS FOR USERS OF PPSP's SERVICES?

A. No one can predict for certain what the economic climate will be in the years ahead. Fees for services may increase because of inflationary factors, but not because of the new building. That is why we have the **DESIGN FOR PROGRESS** Campaign.

Q. WHICH NEIGHBORHOOD CENTERS ARE PART OF THE 'DESIGN FOR PROGRESS' CAMPAIGN?

A. The Chester, Media and Norristown centers have been earmarked as part of **DESIGN FOR PROGRESS.**

Q. WHY ARE IMPROVEMENTS NECESSARY AT THESE SITES?

A. A priority of PPSP is to offer the same attractive, dignified environments for patients in centers throughout PPSP's service area as it will provide at the new Center City locations.

Q. HOW WILL PPSP PAY FOR ALL OF THIS?

A. Proceeds from the sale of '1220' and the **DESIGN FOR PROGRESS** Campaign are earmarked for these projects.

Q. WHY A CAPITAL CAMPAIGN WHEN THERE IS ANNUAL GIVING?

A. The capital campaign is a special campaign for restricted giving, in this case, for the construction of the new building, and for some neighborhood centers. The Annual Giving Campaign, the life blood of non-profit organizations, is that form of unrestricted giving which helps PPSP operate from day to day.

Q. HOW MUCH IS PPSP EXPECTING TO RAISE WITH 'DESIGN FOR PROGRESS'?

A. The new building is projected to cost $3,800,000. The Campaign is committed to raising as much of this total cost as possible.

Figure 24.10. This brochure was given directly by solicitors to major prospects. It includes basic data on the needs and a line drawing of the new building.

We urge you to support Planned Parenthood's DESIGN FOR PROGRESS Campaign.

The campaign is for more than a building fund. It is about helping people, about providing one superior level of care and service to all who turn to us regardless of ability to pay. The building is a contraceptive clinic and surgical center.

The campaign is about educating young women and men so they can act responsibly in their sexual lives. The building is a resource for learning and research.

The campaign is about better stewardship of resources. The building, custom designed for Planned Parenthood, will be state-of-the-art in energy efficiency.

The campaign is about a more effective use of personnel. The building promotes better management because it brings people together.

The campaign is about taking a stand in our community for the freedom to choose how we will manage our reproductive lives. The building will be a beacon of independence and strength for all to see.

These are the reasons we are committed to the success of the DESIGN FOR PROGRESS Campaign.

Please join us and hundreds of others who are setting a generous example of support for this vital community project.

Your gift will make a valuable difference.

Rogie Dickey
Co-Chair

Paul F. Miller, Jr.
Co-Chair

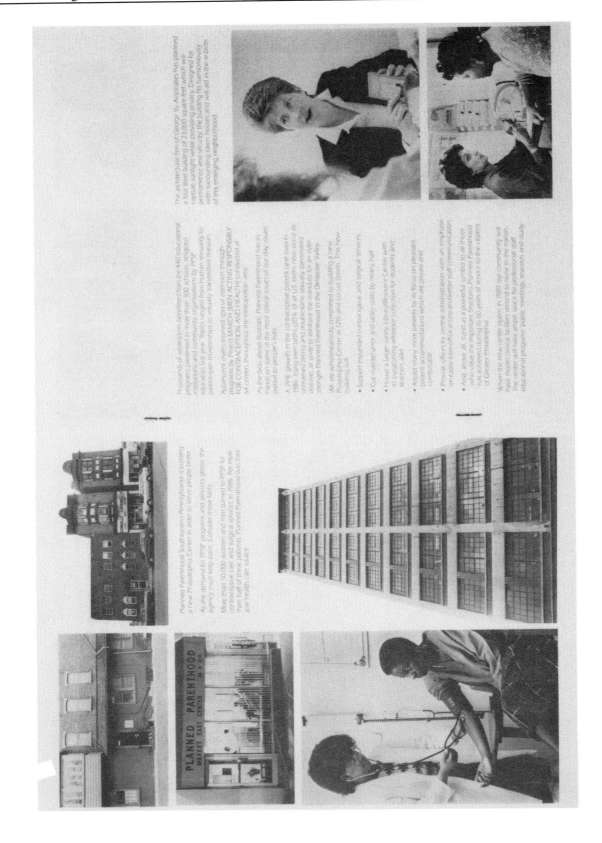

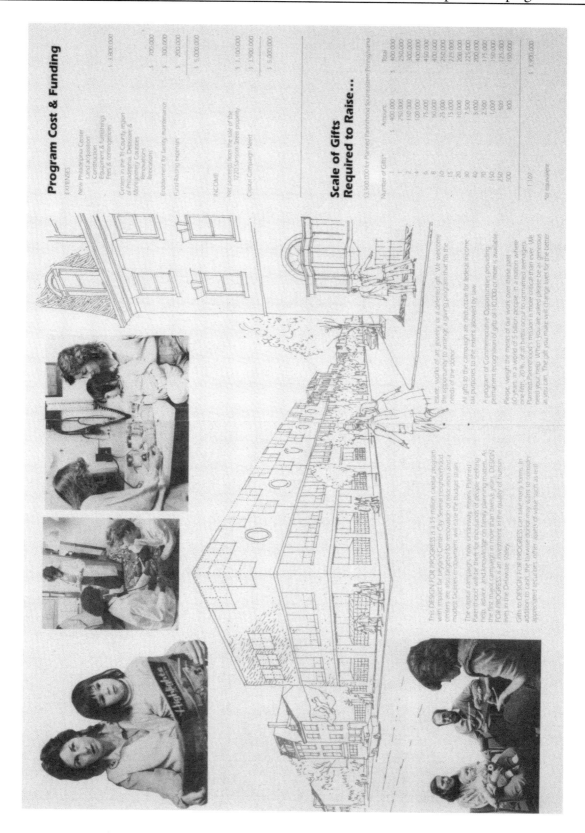

Figure 24.11. These excerpts are from a brochure called Design for Remembering that lists opportunities for commemorative giving.

The commemorative gifts described in this brochure present a wide range of giving opportunities.

For many, the occasion to memorialize a loved one, a friend, a family or simply to recognize the good work of an organization adds immeasurable pleasure to a charitable gift.

If you are planning a significant gift to DESIGN FOR PROGRESS, the capital campaign for Planned Parenthood Southeastern Pennsylvania, you may be interested in a memorial.

Gifts ranging from $10,000 and up may receive permanent recognition in a public area of the new building. Pledges are payable over a three to five year period at the convenience of the donor, and are fully deductible for income tax purposes.

For additional information or questions regarding this program, or to reserve a commemorative unit, please contact the DESIGN FOR PROGRESS Campaign Office, (215) 592-4109.

Thank you.

TERRACE LEVEL

Unit 1	Floor Dedication	$500,000
Unit 2	Surgical Services Clinic	$300,000
Unit 3	Reception Area	$ 50,000
Unit 4	Interim Waiting Room	$ 45,000
Unit 5	Surgical Waiting Room	$ 45,000
Units 6-10	Counseling Room (5)	$ 12,000 each
Units 11-14	Procedure Room (4)	$ 25,000 each
Unit 15	Surgical Lab	$ 30,000
Unit 16	Manager's Office	$ 15,000
Unit 17	Physician's Office	$ 15,000
Unit 18	Kitchenette	$ 12,000

Figure 24.12. Gift-report formats

PLANNED PARENTHOOD SOUTHEASTERN PENNSYLVANIA
CAPITAL CAMPAIGN DESIGN FOR PROGRESS
GIFT REPORT   22-Jul-88

CAPITAL CAMPAIGN GOAL: $4,000,000

DIVISION	# DONORS	AMOUNT PLEDGED	AMOUNT PAID	%
BG Board of Directors' Gifts*	104	892,879	615,109	68.8
LG Leadership Gifts	52	826,628	513,243	62.0
SG Select Gifts	201	359,965	226,987	63.0
FD Foundation Gifts**	24	258,250	178,250	69.0
CO Corporation Gifts	8	63,500	43,500	68.5
EG Employee Gifts	66	18,170	6,657	36.6
CG Community Gifts	17	7,850	6,200	78.9
	472	$2,427,242	$1,589,946	65.5

Sale of 1220 Sansom $1,100,000

RAISED: $3,527,242

LEFT TO RAISE: $472,758

* Includes Allen M. Johnson Fund
**Includes Lesley F. Craig Trust verbal pledge: $50,000

ALLAN M. JOHNSON FUND

Lang Smith Challenge Grant $30,000.00
Pledged to date $59,300.00
        $89,300.00

ERNESTA'S GARDEN

Challenge grant to be matched: $30,000
Raised (176 Gifts): $21,685
        $51,685.00

CAPITAL CAMPAIGN GIFTS AS OF AUGUST 12, 1987

CATEGORY	DONORS	PLEDGED	PAID
Board Gifts:			
$5,000 and up	27	$ 725,964	
$2,000 - $4,999	10	31,428	
$500 - $1,999	32	30,697	
less than $500	20	3,100	
TOTALS	89	$ 791,189	$ 405,884
Leadership Gifts:			
$5,000 and up	15	$ 386,550	
$2,000 - $4,999	0	0	
$500 - $1,999	7	8,325	
less than $500	6	925	
TOTALS	28	$ 395,800	$ 126,618
Select Gifts:			
$5,000 and up	2	$ 25,000	
$2,000 - $4,999	21	143,685	
$500 - $1,999	58	55,864	
less than $500	45	8,145	
TOTALS	126	$ 232,714	$ 139,137
Employee Gifts:			
$2,000 - $4,999	1	$ 2,300	
$500 - $1,999	9	8,375	
less than 500	55	6,369	
TOTALS	65	$ 17,044	$ 6,154
Community Gifts:			
payment on pledges	16	$ 17,650	$ 4,950
Foundation Gifts:			
payment on pledges	9	$ 138,100	$ 84,767
Overall Campaign:			
$5,000 and up		$1,137,514	
$2,000 - $4,999		177,413	
$500 - $1,999		103,281	
less than $500		30,189	
Foundations		138,100	
TOTALS	333	$1,586,497	$ 691,220

Figure 24.13. The volunteer organization included chairmen for various gift levels and for various constituencies. These included: select gifts, board gifts, leadership gifts, employee gifts and community gifts. Here are two letters used by volunteers to set the stage for solicitations.

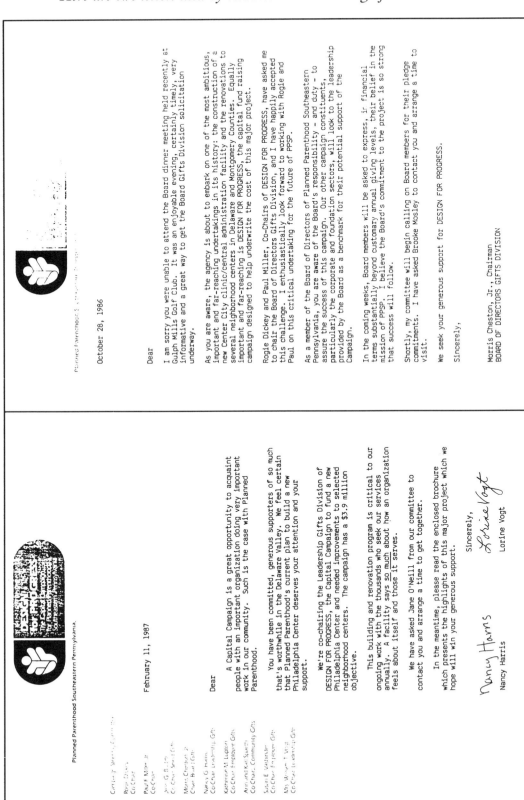

Planned Parenthood Southeastern Pennsylvania.

October 28, 1986

Dear

I am sorry you were unable to attend the Board dinner meeting held recently at Gulph Mills Golf Club. It was an enjoyable evening, certainly timely, very informative and a great way to get the Board Gifts Division solicitation underway.

As you are aware, the agency is about to embark on one of the most ambitious, important and far-reaching undertakings in its history: the construction of a new Center City clinic/central administration facility and the renovations to several neighborhood centers in Delaware and Montgomery Counties. Equally important and far-reaching is DESIGN FOR PROGRESS, the capital fund raising campaign designed to help underwrite the cost of this major project.

Rogie Dickey and Paul Miller, Co-Chairs of DESIGN FOR PROGRESS, have asked me to chair the Board of Directors Gifts Division, and I have happily accepted this challenge. I enthusiastically look forward to working with Rogie and Paul on this critical undertaking for the future of PPSP.

As a member of the Board of Directors of Planned Parenthood Southeastern Pennsylvania, you are aware of the Board's responsibility - and duty - to assure the success of this campaign. Our other campaign constituents, particularly the corporate and foundation sectors, will look to the leadership provided by the Board as a benchmark for their potential support of the Campaign.

In the coming weeks, Board members will be asked to express, if financial terms substantially beyond customary annual giving levels, their belief in the mission of PPSP. I believe the Board's commitment to the project is so strong that success will follow.

Shortly, my committee will begin calling on Board members for their pledge commitments. I have asked Brooke Mosley to contact you and arrange a time to visit.

We seek your generous support for DESIGN FOR PROGRESS.

Sincerely,

Morris Cheston, Jr., Chairman
BOARD OF DIRECTORS GIFTS DIVISION

Planned Parenthood Southeastern Pennsylvania

Campaign Steering Committee

Rogie Dickey
Co-Chair

Paul F. Miller, Jr.
Co-Chair

Joan G. Butler
Co-Chair, Leadership Gifts

Morris Cheston, Jr.
Co-Chair, Board Gifts

Nancy G. Harris
Co-Chair, Leadership Gifts

Katherine M. Lupton
Co-Chair, Employer Gifts

Ann and Karl Summ
Co-Chair, Community Gifts

Susan E. Vashinder
Co-Chair, Employee Gifts

Mrs. William T. Vogt
Co-Chair, Leadership Gifts

February 11, 1987

Dear

A Capital Campaign is a great opportunity to acquaint people with an important organization doing very important work in our community. Such is the case with Planned Parenthood.

You have been committed, generous supporters of so much that's worthwhile in the Delaware Valley. We feel certain that Planned Parenthood's current plan to build a new Philadelphia Center deserves your attention and your support.

We're co-chairing the Leadership Gifts Division of DESIGN FOR PROGRESS, the Capital Campaign to fund a new Philadelphia Center and needed improvements to selected neighborhood centers. The campaign has a $3.9 million objective.

This building and renovation program is critical to our ongoing work with the thousands who seek our services annually. A facility says so much about how an organization feels about itself and those it serves.

We have asked Jane O'Neill from our committee to contact you and arrange a time to get together.

In the meantime, please read the enclosed brochure which presents the highlights of this major project which we hope will win your generous support.

Sincerely,

Nancy Harris

Lorine Vogt

Figure 24.14. Two actual solicitation letters

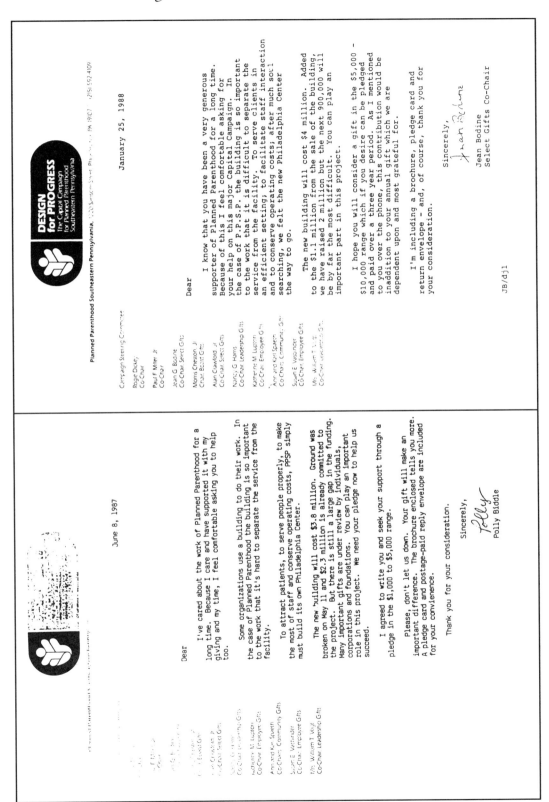

Letter 1 (June 8, 1987)

June 8, 1987

Dear

I've cared about the work of Planned Parenthood for a long time. Because I care and have supported it with my giving and my time, I feel comfortable asking you to help too.

Some organizations use a building to do their work. In the case of Planned Parenthood the building is so important to the work that it's hard to separate the service from the facility.

To attract patients, to serve people properly, to make the most of staff and conserve operating costs, PPSP simply must build its own Philadelphia Center.

The new building will cost $3.8 million. Ground was broken on May 11 and $2.3 million is already committed to the project. But there is still a large gap in the funding. Many important gifts are under review by individuals, corporations and foundations. You can play an important role in this project. We need your pledge now to help us succeed.

I agreed to write you and seek your support through a pledge in the $1,000 to $5,000 range.

Please, don't let us down. Your gift will make an important difference. The brochure enclosed tells you more. A pledge card and postage-paid reply envelope are included for your convenience.

Thank you for your consideration.

Sincerely,

Polly Biddle

Letter 2 (January 25, 1988)

Planned Parenthood Southeastern Pennsylvania, 1220 Sansom Street Phila., PA 19107 (215) 592-4109

January 25, 1988

Campaign Steering Committee

Roge Dickey,
Co-Chair

Paul F. Miller, Jr.
Co-Chair

Jean G. Bodine
Co-Chair, Select Gifts

Morris Cheston, Jr.
Chair, Board Gifts

Alan Crawford, Jr.
Co-Chair, Select Gifts

Nancy G. Harris
Co-Chair, Leadership Gifts

Katherine M. Lupton
Co-Chair, Employee Gifts

Ann and Karl Speoth
Co-Chair, Community Gifts

Susan E. Valander
Co-Chair, Employee Gifts

Mrs. William T. Vogt
Co-Chair, Leadership Gifts

Dear

I know that you have been a very generous supporter of Planned Parenthood for a long time. Because of this I feel comfortable asking for your help on this major Capital Campaign. In the case of P.P.S.P. the building is so important to the work that it is difficult to separate the service from the facility. To serve clients in an efficient setting; to facilitate staff interaction and to conserve operating costs; after much soul searching, we felt the new Philadelphia Center the way to go.

The new building will cost $4 million. Added to the $1.1 million from the sale of the building, we have raised 2 million but the next 900,000 will be by far the most difficult. You can play an important part in this project.

I hope you will consider a gift in the $5,000 - $10,000 range which if you desire can be pledged and paid over a three year period. As I mentioned to you over the phone, this contribution would be in addition to your annual gift which we are dependent upon and most grateful for.

I'm including a brochure, pledge card and return envelope - and, of course, thank you for your consideration.

Sincerely,

Jean Bodine
Select Gifts Co-Chair

JB/djl

Figure 24.15. Invitation to the ground-breaking

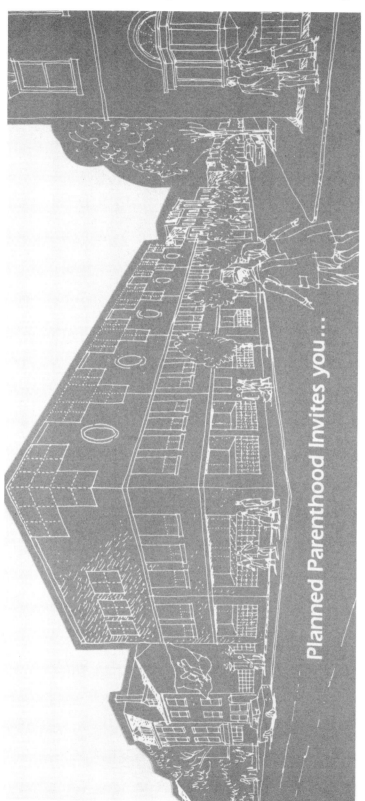

Planned Parenthood Invites you....

To celebrate
the ground breaking for
our new Philadelphia Center. Come
to the first picnic of the season! Help
us launch the community support phase
of our campaign!

Monday, May 11, 1987
11:00 a.m.
on the site.... 12th & Locust Streets, Philadelphia
RSVP by May 1st

Free parking at the Allright Parking Lot, 12th & Locust Streets

Figure 24.16. Pledge reminder

Planned Parenthood Southeastern Pennsylvania, 1220 Sansom Street, Philadelphia, PA 19107 ☐ (215) 592-4109

Campaign Steering Committee

Rogie Dickey
Co-Chair

Paul F. Miller, Jr.
Co-Chair

Jean G. Bodine
Co-Chair, Select Gifts

Morris Cheston, Jr.
Chair, Board Gifts

Alan Crawford, Jr.
Co-Chair, Select Gifts

Nancy G. Harris
Co-Chair, Leadership Gifts

Katherine M. Lupton
Co-Chair, Employee Gifts

Ann and Karl Spaeth
Co-Chairs, Community Gifts

Susan E. Vasbinder
Co-Chair, Employee Gifts

Mrs. William T. Vogt
Co-Chair, Leadership Gifts

REMINDER OF PAYMENT
PLANNED PARENTHOOD SOUTHEASTERN PENNSYLVANIA
DESIGN FOR PROGRESS

SECOND NOTICE

August 11, 1988

Dear

According to our records, your payment for June of
1988 has not come in. If our information is
incorrect, or you would like to change your
payment schedule, please contact the Development
Office at 351-5530.

If this notice has crossed your check in the mail,
please accept our apologies.

Sincerely,

Bettina Lauf
Campaign Manager

enclosure

BL/rg

Figure 24.17. Letter to donors detailing a challenge offer to meet the final goal

Planned Parenthood Southeastern Pennsylvania, 1220 Sansom Street, Philadelphia, PA 19107 □ (215) 592-4109

November 21, 1988

name
address
city, state zip

Dear :

You have built a beautiful building on the corner of 12th and Locust.

Finished on schedule and on budget, Planned Parenthood's new Headquarters/Family Planning Center has exceeded our dreams. It has made a remarkable difference in our ability to serve clients, facilitate staff interaction, and conserve operating costs. The building is a magnificent statement of your belief in the rights of women and their families to quality health care and educational programs. It is also *your* home, and we hope you will visit and enjoy what you made possible.

The Capital Campaign, DESIGN FOR PROGRESS, has been very successful--we are at the end, with only $300,000 of our $4 million goal left to raise. You belong to a very special group of friends who gave early, generously and without hesitation. Your gifts and unflagging belief in our mission led the way in inspiring others to give. Now, an exciting new challenge grant has been created by one of our Board members to encourage you to give again and lead the way to closing this campaign by year's end. Every dollar given will be matched up to $50,000.

We hope you can help us. We would be pleased to meet with you or answer any questions. A pledge card and postage-paid return envelope are included for your convenience. Thank you in advance for your generosity.

Gratefully,

Rogie Dickey   Paul Miller
Co-Chair   Co-Chair

Figure 24.18. Letter to prospects about the challenge offer

Planned Parenthood Southeastern Pennsylvania.   PA 19107   (215) 592-4109

November 21, 1988

name
address
city, state zip

Dear :

 We care very deeply about Planned Parenthood's Capital
Campaign, DESIGN FOR PROGRESS. Because of our commitment,
we have supported it with our giving and our time. Now we are asking for
your help.

 After three years of careful planning and the support of our
friends, we have raised all but $300,000 of our $4 million goal. Finished
on schedule and on budget, the new Philadelphia Headquarters/Family
Planning Center on the corner of 12th and Locust has exceeded our
dreams. The building has already made a remarkable difference in our
ability to serve clients, facilitate staff interaction and conserve operating
costs.

 We are pleased to announce a new challenge from one of our
Board members. He has pledged up to $25,000 to be matched by new
gifts received before the end of the year. Your gift now, payable over two
years, will help us secure this challenge grant. Won't you help us achieve
our $300,000 goal by the end of 1988?

 A pledge card and postage-paid reply envelope are included for
your convenience. We thank you in advance for your generosity.

Sincerely,

Paul F. Miller, Jr.   Rogie Dickey
Co-Chair   Co-Chair

Figure 24.19. The Annual Report for Planned Parenthood Southeastern Pennsylvania, excerpted here, details the opening of the new facility.

A New Foundation For Growth

Planned Parenthood Southeastern Pennsylvania has a very special mission: we provide reproductive health care, education and advocacy for the people of Philadelphia, Delaware and Montgomery Counties to help them improve the quality of their individual and family lives. In 1988, over 38,000 people used our services, and we expect an even greater number to do so in 1989.

We have a responsibility to the Delaware Valley community to continue providing quality medical services, accurate information, and legislative support of reproductive rights, despite a changing health care climate and looming financial and political challenges. To that end, we believe that the best plan to strengthen our position is to reinforce and expand those services and programs that have helped establish Planned Parenthood's high standing and fine reputation, and put them to work to the best advantage of the organization and our clients.

We have four major focal points to report on from 1988, the completion of our new headquarters, contraceptive and surgical services, community and professional education and training, and advocacy. The following pages of this report will explain why each of these areas is considered a significant force within our organization. This year we laid a handsome and solid foundation of bricks and mortar on the corner of 12th and Locust Streets, and repositioned our core services to ensure that Planned Parenthood will continue to thrive in the years to come.

"We at Jefferson salute you, Planned Parenthood, as our neighbor and partner in fostering the concept of informed decision making in women's health care issues. Like you, we know that the wisest decisions come from those women who are well informed about their own and their family's health care. We look forward to serving this goal with you for many years to come."
Stephanie W. Naidoff,
Vice President and University Counsel,
Thomas Jefferson University

We are also proud to report that we were recertified this year by our national organization, the Planned Parenthood Federation of America. In preparation for the Federation review, a complete and consolidated patient services Policy and Procedures Manual was produced for use in all of our centers. The review team was impressed by the thoroughness and clarity of the manual and recommended that we market it to other organizations. We received approval to carry the Planned Parenthood trademark for an additional four years, the highest approval rating Planned Parenthood Federation of America awards.

The quotations throughout this report from friends, clients and staff attest to Planned Parenthood's leadership in the community and personalized health care.

5

We are extremely excited about our new teen program, called RESPECT, at our Market East Center Fundext through the William Penn Foundation. RESPECT programs encourage teens to discuss their concerns and questions about sexuality with staff. We always welcome parents and friends to these meetings. We're also training teens to be "Peer Educators" for their friends in schools and communities. This is a powerful means of teaching young people about sexuality and its consequences—teens listen to their peers!

While we endeavor to help people prevent unintended pregnancies, we need to protect the right to safe, legal abortions. A serious threat to legal abortion has been posed by the Webster v. Reproductive Health Services case, currently in the hands of the U.S. Supreme Court. For the first time since the Roe v. Wade decision of 1973, there is a strong possibility that legal abortions could be eliminated, or made a states' rights issue.

Since the Roe v. Wade decision was made, the health and welfare of millions of women has improved. People are now able to have their families when they are most able to provide love and support. Making abortions illegal would not prevent women from having them. However, abortions would be difficult to obtain, often life threatening, and expensive. And, as history has shown, poor women would bear the brunt of the overturned law. Legal abortion must be upheld as a constitutional right for all women.

Our tasks are laid out before us, and with your continued support, we pledge to work with you and our community in the common cause of upholding reproductive freedom of choice for all.

Yours truly,

Pamela A. Gallimore
President, Board of Directors

Carol Carter Wall
Executive Director

A New Foundation For Growth

Planned Parenthood Southeastern Pennsylvania has a very special mission: we provide quality medical services, education and advocacy for the people of Philadelphia, Delaware and Montgomery Counties to help them improve the quality of their individual and family lives. In 1988, over 38,000 people used our services, and we expect an even greater number to do so in 1989.

We have a responsibility to the Delaware Valley community to continue providing quality medical services, accurate information, and legislative support of reproductive rights, despite a changing health care climate and looming financial and political challenges. To that end, we believe that the best plan to strengthen our position is to reinforce and expand those services and programs that have helped establish Planned Parenthood's high standing and fine reputation, and put them to work to the best advantage of the organization and our clients.

We have four major focal points to report on from 1988: the completion of our new headquarters, contraceptive and surgical services, community and professional education and training, and advocacy. The following pages of this report will explain why each of these areas is considered a significant force within our organization. This year we laid a handsome and solid foundation of bricks and mortar on the corner of 12th and Locust Streets, and repositioned our core services to ensure that Planned Parenthood will continue to thrive in the years to come.

"We at Jefferson salute you, Planned Parenthood, as our neighbor and partner in fostering the concept of informed decision making in women's health care issues. Like you, we know that the wisest decisions come from those women who are well informed about their own and their family's health care. We look forward to serving this goal with you for many years to come."
Stephanie W. Naidoff
Vice President and University Counsel
Thomas Jefferson University

We are also proud to report that we were recertified this year by our national organization, the Planned Parenthood Federation of America. In preparation for the Federation review, a complete and consolidated patient services Policy and Procedures Manual was produced for use in all of our centers. The review team was impressed by the thoroughness and clarity of the manual and recommended that we market it to other organizations. We received approval to carry the Planned Parenthood trademark for an additional four years, the highest approval rating Planned Parenthood Federation of America awards.

The quotations throughout this report from friends, clients and staff attest to Planned Parenthood's leadership in the community and personalized health care.

Our Headquarters: A Symbol of Progress

In 1929 our first contraceptive center opened its doors in Upper Darby and offered family planning services to women in need. Since then, Planned Parenthood has moved to several buildings in Philadelphia, always increasing our size and the number of people we care for. In May of 1988 we completed construction and moved into our proud new headquarters building.

As a structure, our building is a fine example of contemporary architectural mastery. It is handsome, warm and welcoming. As a city landmark, it adds physical stature and grace and sets an example for a neighborhood in the midst of growth. Our home also tangibly represents sixty years of service and positions us for a strong future in reproductive health care.

You will discover the entrance to our headquarters on Locust Street, protected by an elegantly crafted wrought iron gate and the Ernesta Drinker Ballard shade garden, which welcome visitors. Once inside, on the first floor, you find an expanded Library/Bookstore dedicated to Christopher Heublein Perot, open to the public, with books, periodicals, and informational materials on sexuality and reproductive health. Tables and comfortable chairs are at hand for those who wish to read or study.

It is extremely appropriate that a medical building, housing an organization dedicated to choice and freedom in reproductive health care for all people, is now in a residential and commercial area in the midst of change and growth, helping to create the ideal urban neighborhood.

Eugene B. Letevre:
Partner, Growth Properties

Just beyond the Library/Bookstore is our S. Emlen and Lydia B. Stokes Contraceptive Center with numerous counseling and examination rooms and a floor plan allowing for an increased and more efficient patient flow. On the lower level is our Lesley F. Craig Surgical Center for abortions and vasectomies. A spacious waiting room, additional counseling and procedure rooms, and a recovery area with a garden view comfortably accommodate more patients than ever before. Patients receive quality care at an affordable cost in a pleasant and professional atmosphere.

The second and third floors house the departments of education, public affairs, patient services, finance, development and administration. Both floors are thoughtfully laid out with a sympathetic balance of privacy, open space, natural lighting, and several small meeting and conference rooms — dedicated to Brooke Mosley, Elaine Smith, and Allan M. Johnson — all of which contribute to work efficiency and communication among staff.

Also on our second floor is the large and sunny Dora Butcher Hillman Board Room for educational trainings and programs, conferences and meetings. We are now able to offer more programs for a larger number of public participants and staff in a comfortable environment conducive to effective training.

Caring for Our Patients

Planned Parenthood Centers: Bringing Affordable Services to the Community

The staff in our ten Philadelphia, Delaware, and Montgomery County centers are expert in giving patients accurate information, skilled medical care and support in decision making. Counselors educate patients on the sensitive and personal topics of sexuality, contraception, fertility and pregnancy, and prevention of AIDS and other sexually transmitted diseases. In confidential counseling sessions, our trained staff build relationships based on trust with men and women and help them make informed and responsible choices about their reproductive health—choices that will affect the course of their lives.

Medical practitioners provide pelvic exams, birth control methods, screening tests for anemia and diabetes, testing for and treatment of sexually transmitted diseases, PAP smears, breast exams, pregnancy testing, and referrals as indicated. Patient fees are on a sliding scale based on each person's ability to pay. Each year we strive to provide care to more people in need of affordable reproductive health services, especially low-income women and teenagers.

In 1988 several new clinical services and programs were introduced.

☐ An exciting new pilot program called RESPECT was launched at our Market East Center. Weekly orientation programs are offered for adolescents, who gather for group discussions to explore their concerns and questions about sexuality and birth control. Parents, friends and partners are welcome.

☐ Teen Peer Educators were trained through the RESPECT program to pass along accurate information about sexuality, birth control and sexually transmitted diseases to their peers in schools, communities and the RESPECT orientation sessions.

☐ We conducted the AIDS Risk Assessment Survey, in conjunction with other Pennsylvania Planned Parenthood affiliates and the Centers for Disease Control. Based on the survey results, we increased our emphasis on teaching patients about safer sex and began providing risk assessment counseling. Testing for the Human Immuno-deficiency Virus (HIV is the virus that causes AIDS) was introduced at three centers.

The building, opened for service in May 1988, houses the contraceptive and surgical centers on the ground floor, with administration and education on the upper floors.

☐ Screening became available at all ten centers for women considering intrauterine devices (IUDs) as birth control, with four centers once again offering IUD insertion on a regular basis.

☐ Blood-screening tests for syphilis are now routinely offered at three centers.

Surgical Services: Supporting Personal Decisions

The Surgical Center in our new headquarters offers first trimester abortion services. Counselors work closely with each woman to explore all possible options, and then support the patient in her own personal decision.

We also offer vasectomies for men. Our trained staff counsels each man considering a vasectomy and gives him the information he needs to make an informed decision.

At left: Board President Pamela Gallimore greets Sandra Numair M.D. at the celebration of our new building.

...in Our Community

Education and Training: Empowering Today's Youth

While the provision of clinic services is the backbone of our mission, education is an equally vital component. Philadelphia's high rates of unintended pregnancy and sexually transmitted disease testify to the urgent need for a broad range of sex education for all ages.

We cannot afford to risk the futures of our youngest citizens. Adolescents and children are particularly vulnerable to unplanned pregnancies and disease. They lack information and channels of communication because of society's discomfort with discussing sexuality and its ramifications.

In a 1988 Planned Parenthood survey conducted by Louis Harris and Associates, Inc., 89% of Pennsylvania parents polled, with children ages seven and eight, agreed that parent-child discussions would reduce unintended pregnancies. However, only 50% surveyed felt comfortable talking with their children about sex and the issues surrounding the subject. In addition, nine out of ten adults in Pennsylvania supported the notion of sex education in schools, but the majority of schools do not provide comprehensive programs on values, sexuality, contraception, pregnancy and disease prevention.

"... that the programs that Planned Parenthood provides ... I can't imagine where women, particularly women of color, would help. More and more young people today need to know about their bodies and sexuality ... and then can protect themselves."

Emma C. Chappell,
Vice President, Continental Bank

At Planned Parenthood we reach out to young people, their parents and other care-givers with community programs. Educators provide teens, parents and community groups with accurate information and room for discussion about relationships, sexuality, disease prevention, and fertility control in a context of values and attitudes. Young people are given the essential tools that they need to make informed decisions about their bodies and a head start on taking responsibility for their actions. Community education programs include: "Parents and Teens Together;" "Parents as Primary Sexuality Educators;" and "Values and Decision Making," which all address important sexuality issues.

Training is also available for professionals—teachers, social workers, family planning providers, medical practitioners, clergy, and our own staff and volunteers. Through such courses as "Sexual Attitudes Reassessment" and "Planning and Implementing Human Sexuality Courses," professionals explore their own feelings about sexuality and learn new and effective teaching techniques.

In 1988 we developed a number of new and exciting programs in education.

☐ Formal programs on AIDS were introduced for professionals, students, members of the community, and staff. The results of our "AIDS Risk Assessment Survey" in

At left: RESPECT Coordinator works with teen "Peer Educators"
At right: An in-service training brings Planned Parenthood staff up-to-date on contraceptive methods

Pennsylvania showed that one in seventeen clients engaged in behavior that risked HIV infection. A growing number of Delaware Valley residents are encountering illness and loss of partners, parents, and loved ones from AIDS. Because the disease is preventable but not yet curable, education remains the single most effective weapon in the fight against the disease.

AIDS programming ranges from "Teens and AIDS" and "Risk Reduction Counseling" to "Exploring Issues of Grief and Loss." Clinic staff are now trained in counseling techniques geared toward facilitating the discussion of sensitive, highly personal information around HIV assessment and promoting safer sex practices.

☐ Two programs for professionals were established that focused on communication with pre-adolescents (ages nine through twelve). This new initiative was designed to give professionals the tools needed to help this age group focus on their life goals and potential and provide them with preventive sexuality education *before* they become sexually active.

☐ An "Open Enrollment/Registration" program was instituted for professionals and was held at our new headquarters. In the spring we offered five registration workshops on a range of human sexuality topics and in the fall we offered another nine. These new training opportunities encourage professionals to explore sex education issues with guest lecturers from the Delaware Valley and Planned Parenthood's own experienced educators.

One of the greatest assets of the [new ...] is the staff who are on hand to answer questions and help people make choices ...

Library/Bookstore: Resources for Learning

The Library/Bookstore, located in our headquarters building, is open to the public and houses the most comprehensive collection of current information on sexuality, reproductive health and family planning in Philadelphia. We provide resources to an increasing number of people each year, including professionals, students, parents, and our own staff and volunteers.

The new location has given us space to add more material on topics related to sexuality, ranging from reproductive health, family life, and international family planning to curricula on sexuality education for grades K-12.

By the end of 1988 our library collection included:

☐ 2,250 library books
☐ Over 100 professional journals, magazines and newsletters
☐ 36 linear feet of material including pamphlets, news clippings and article reprints
☐ 100 videos, films, and other audio-visual aids available for rent

Design for Progress

Dear Friends,

In May of 1988, Planned Parenthood moved its headquarters from 1220 Sansom Street to 1144 Locust Street. This is a dream come true! Truly, the new Headquarters/Centers building is a symbol of the strength of the organization. The significant gains that have been made over the years, culminating in this success, have come from your belief in our work. The permanence of the building speaks to the wide acceptance of family planning values and practices.

We deeply appreciate the generosity with which you have supported our Capital Campaign. Your gifts of time, funds and personal commitment have made this achievement possible. Many of your contributions were made as challenges or matching gifts. Three challenges enabled us to reach our goal: one honored Allan M. Johnson, the second raised funds for Ernesta's Garden, and the third was an Anonymous Challenge pledged in the final segment of the campaign.

We were inspired by the more than eighty volunteers who called, wrote letters, visited and gave tours of the site, and later, the building. We thank you all for your untiring efforts. Your responses were a testament to your caring. Your willingness and unfailing enthusiasm were echoed by our many friends in the Delaware Valley and beyond.

We can only begin to express our gratitude by taking this opportunity to tell you what a remarkable and positive effect the new facility has had on our clients, service delivery operations and the public's appreciation of our work.

Our best work is yet to come!

Sincerely,

Rogie Dickey

Rogie Dickey
Co-Chair

Paul F. Miller, Jr.

Paul F. Miller, Jr.
Co-Chair

*Members of the
Campaign Steering
Committee*

Rogie Dickey
Co-Chair

Paul F. Miller, Jr.
Co-Chair

Jean G. Bodine
Co-Chair: Select Gifts

Morris Cheston, Jr.
Chair: Board Gifts

Alan Crawford, Jr.
Co-Chair: Select Gifts

Nancy G. Harris
Co-Chair: Leadership Gifts

Katherine M. Lupton
Co-Chair: Employee Gifts

Ann and Karl Spaeth
Co-Chairs: Community Gifts

Susan E. Vasbinder
Co-Chair: Employee Gifts

Mrs. William T. Vogt
Co-Chair: Leadership Gifts

16

A Successful Campaign

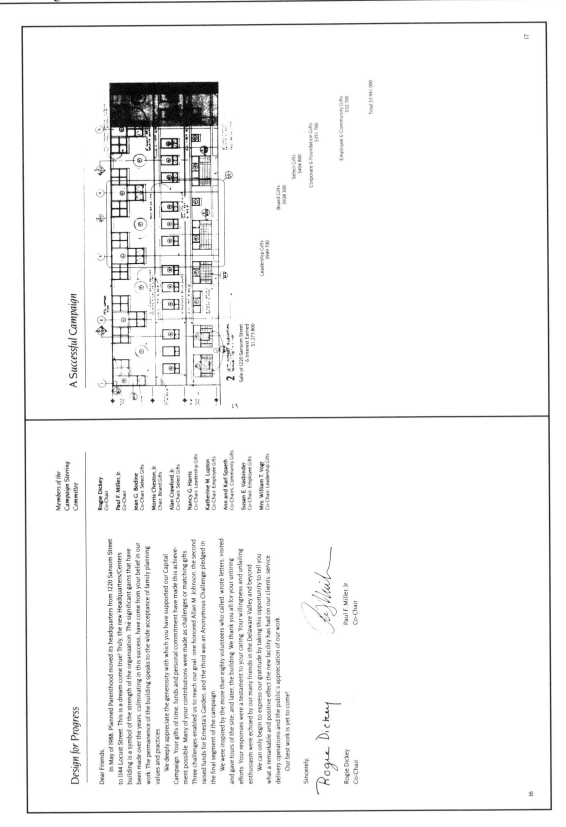

2 1st FLOOR ELEVATION

Sale of 1220 Sansom Street
& Interest Earned
$1,273,800

Leadership Gifts
$949,700

Board Gifts
$928,100

Select Gifts
$404,800

Corporate & Foundation Gifts
$351,700

Employee & Community Gifts
$32,700

Total $3,941,000

17

Roger Maris Cancer Center

Fargo, North Dakota

Goal: $6.8 million
Amount raised: $5.8 million
and continuing to grow

A $6.8 million capital campaign was organized to fund the construction of the Roger Maris Cancer Center. The center is part of the St. Luke's Hospitals group in Fargo, North Dakota. This group includes three hospitals—a general hospital, a children's hospital and a neuroscience hospital. St. Luke's is directly linked through the MeritCare marketing group and by contract to the Fargo Clinic, which is a proprietary organization of 244 physicians. (Proprietary means the clinic is a for-profit organization owned by the physicians who work there.)

Roger Maris, a well-known baseball hero, was a native of North Dakota and long-time resident of Fargo, who died of cancer. The linking of his name to the facility has helped market the cause.

George J. Lukac, executive director of the St. Luke's Foundation until 1990, was directly responsible for mounting the campaign. The foundation was established as the recipient organization for private funds, an effort made specifically to differentiate the hospitals group from the proprietary Fargo Clinic.

The doctors at St. Luke's Hospitals declared publicly in the spring of 1987 that a cancer center was to be built. One year of negotiations between the hospitals and the clinic followed. Once plans were firm, internal planning for a fund-raising program began.

George Lukac initially interviewed 12 fund-raising consulting firms to conduct a feasibility study. Three finalist firms were then screened by a special committee of the hospital board and Fargo Clinic board. Jerold Panas, Young & Partners of Chicago was selected.

The firm conducted a feasibility study during July of 1988. About 50 people were interviewed. The study revealed that St. Luke's was highly regarded and considered an integral part of the Fargo community. People felt positively about the plans for the Roger Maris Cancer

Center. Although the goal was one of the largest ever attempted in the area, it was considered doable. The necessary volunteer leadership was there, as was the concern about fighting cancer. The study suggested a series of steps to reach the campaign goal.

The Panas firm then was named to help with the campaign, and a full-time resident counsel was on hand for 36 weeks. The active solicitation period of the campaign ran from November 1988 to July 1989, with the resident counsel answering to the executive director rather than vice versa.

This campaign was unusual because it was aimed largely at employees, though external groups and individuals were also solicited. Separate goals were set for various groups within the hospital's constituency:

Physicians	$800,000
Hospital Employees	$300,000
Hospital Trustees	$200,000
Clinic Employees	$100,000
Auxiliaries and other volunteers	$100,000

Local corporations and community leaders also made sizable commitments. George Lukac reports that in many ways the campaign for the cancer center really broke ground for other fund-raising activities in the Fargo area. The community contains substantial wealth, but this funding potential had never before been pursued as part of an organized, professionally run capital campaign. The professional approach led to much larger gifts than normal.

Most of the major solicitations were done by a volunteer, accompanied either by a staff member or the resident consultant. The total professional staff for the campaign numbered three (one full time and two part time), plus the consultant and two secretaries. Pledges to the campaign were solicited over an eight-month period and were payable over five years.

The campaign for the Roger Maris Cancer Center shows that a small group of people can mount a successful campaign that has an impact even beyond the cause itself. This campaign crystallized philanthropic interests in the Fargo community and introduced the concept of a professionally run campaign. It also showed that a hospital in the area could raise funds successfully.

Another unusual characteristic of this campaign was that it would be used to build a continuing annual fund-raising program into the hospital's agenda. Usually annual funding efforts are well under way before a campaign begins. However, in this case, the entire program was new, so it was done in reverse.

Here are the printed materials that were used during the Roger Maris Cancer Center campaign.

Figure 24.20. Case statement

"JOIN IN THE CARING...
CAMPAIGN FOR THE ROGER MARIS CANCER CENTER
CASE STATEMENT

"Join in the Caring..." The campaign for the Roger Maris Cancer Center is a program to raise $6.8 million to construct this new facility at St. Luke's Hospitals--MeritCare in Fargo, North Dakota. The Roger Maris Cancer Center is being built for the benefit of the greater community of North Dakota, western Minnesota and northeastern South Dakota.

In simple terms, the Roger Maris Cancer Center will be an outpatient facility combining all cancer screening, diagnosis, therapy, prevention, education and research activities in one building.

The Center is named for Roger Maris, the former major league baseball great, home run record holder and North Dakota hero. He grew up in Fargo, where he got his start in professional baseball. Roger Maris died of cancer, and this will be a fitting memorial to a Fargo favorite and a national hero.

Page 2

"Join in the Caring..." has many meanings --- the community has an opportunity to join hands with the medical professionals who have a reputation for expertise combined with deep concern and care for their patients; to join in the special attention for the patients who, perhaps above all others, need extra care because they suffer with one of the most dreaded diseases; and join in mobilizing the caring which the people of the Northern Plains have for their fellow man, in creating this new community cancer center.

RESPONDING TO URGENT NEEDS

The Cancer Program identifies the illness and treats cancer patients from a large geographic area--all of North Dakota, western Minnesota and northeast South Dakota. In an average year, St. Luke's Hospitals cares for approximately 1,200 to 1,300 new patients with cancer. This program is conducted by two organizations which are separately owned and operated. St. Luke's and Fargo Clinic are physically connected but are legally and financially separated. However, in their joint efforts they have enormous medical capabilities and provide the following:

---Four board certified oncologists/hemotologists specializing in care of adults with cancer and blood diseases.

Page 4

Cancer requires the support and involvement of many members of a professional team. The St. Luke's Cancer Program uses such a multi-disciplinary team approach to care for cancer patients. In addition to the physicians, this includes oncology nurses, social workers, clinical dietitians, clinical nurse specialists, chaplains, home care personnel and physical, occupational and speech therapists.

The Cancer Program is a member of the Association of Community Cancer Centers, the Oncology Nursing Society and the American Society of Clinical Oncology. The program also is accredited by the American College of Surgeons as a Community Cancer Program and receives support from the National Cancer Institute.

Since 1983 St. Luke's Cancer Program has been designated by the National Cancer Institute as a Community Clinical Oncology Program. One of only 52 such funded programs in the country and the only one in North Dakota, St. Luke's has received grant funds from the National Cancer Institute in excess of $1.5 million to conduct CCOP. This federal funding is used to support research, patient/family education, professional education, public education and medical outreach.

Page 3

---One pediatric oncologist who cares for children with the disease, and one or two others to be added.

---Two radiation oncologists who are physicians specializing in the use of radiotherapy to treat cancer in adults and children. Approximately half of all cancer patients receive radiotherapy during the course of their treatment.

---More than ten highly-trained surgeons who perform surgery, a treatment which is a widely used method of fighting cancer. They include general, orthopedic, pulmonary, plastic, otolaryngologic, gynecologic, dermatologic, and maxillo-facial surgeons.

---Under the direction of physicians, specially-trained staff who administer close to 6,000 chemotherapy treatments each year. Chemotherapy is the use of medicines to treat cancer.

St. Luke's has a 36-bed cancer inpatient unit staffed by nurses specially trained to meet the complex needs of cancer patients and their families. In addition, children with cancer are admitted to Children's Hospital-- MeritCare located in the St. Luke's Hospitals building. The Pediatric Intensive Care Unit is available when necessary.

In its Tumor Registry Office, St. Luke's maintains computerized records of every inpatient cancer victim it treats. This is for patient follow-up and for research purposes. The Registry now contains records on nearly 15,000 inpatients who have been treated for cancer at St. Luke's.

Page 5

Through the Community Clinical Oncology Program, St. Luke's has a relationship with the National Cancer Institute which provides St. Luke's with access to the newest drugs and therapy techniques. This may include drugs available only to NCI Cancer Programs. This affiliation also permits physicians and nurses to interact with national leaders in cancer care.

A PROUD TRADITION

This Cancer Program is part of an institution with a long history and earned reputation of quality and caring. St. Luke's Hospitals, founded in 1908, includes a general hospital, children's hospital and a neuroscience hospital, with a total of more than 400 beds. St. Luke's is designated a Trauma Center II; is a multi-specialty hospital for the greater Fargo, North Dakota/Moorhead, Minnesota area; and is a referral hospital for complicated and special cases for all of North Dakota, western Minnesota and northeastern South Dakota. Services are enhanced by 'LifeFlight', which consists of a helicopter and a fixed-wing aircraft to transport emergency cases from outlying rural areas.

A comprehensive program of surgical procedures is available at St. Luke's, encompassing virtually all types of surgery. Same-day surgery is performed

Page 6

in a separate facility. The Hospitals also have a full service rehabilitation unit. Relationships exist with other medical organizations, including, for example, the Mayo Clinic through the CCOP program. St. Luke's is the largest nongovernmental employer in North Dakota, with nearly 1,900 employees and is the largest medical center between Minneapolis-St. Paul to the east and Seattle to the west. The Fargo Clinic, with which it has a contractual relationship, has 244 physicians between its main facility next to the Hospitals and its 30 regional and satellite clinics throughout the greater Red River Valley region. St. Luke's Patient/Community Education program is nationally recognized, and the Hospitals is financially sound and viable. Other oncology-relevant programs at St. Luke's, which is a teaching hospital, are a Senior Health Services program and Psychiatric Consultation Service.

St. Luke's Hospitals--MeritCare is private and voluntary. Voluntary Hospitals of America, a national health care system comprised of the 800 most highly respected hospitals in the country, chose St. Luke's as one of only 29 owners/shareholders. VHA provides access to group purchases, research and program development and permits St. Luke's to work closely with other prestigious hospitals. St. Luke's is completely self-sustaining, receiving no support for its operating budget from any organization or government entity. No funding or support is received from United Way or other federated giving program.

Page 7

MEETING THE CHALLENGE

The St. Luke's Cancer Program is unique to the region because of the comprehensiveness of its services and the extensiveness of its outreach capabilities. Since the program began, it has grown to meet the new and ever-changing needs of cancer patients and has responded to technological advances and maximized existing resources. However, the Cancer Program is now at the point where its growth potential is restricted. The program of such importance to a large geographic region and to a population of one million people is facing certain limitations of its cancer services.

The Cancer Program is now split between the Hospitals and Fargo Clinic. The Roger Maris Cancer Center will create a regional center under St. Luke's ownership for people with cancer. The Center will provide them with some of the finest medical talent and the latest in equipment and technology for diagnosis, care and treatment. This will be in one organized, cohesive, coordinated program.

The Center will concentrate in one location all of St. Luke's and Fargo Clinic's current outpatient cancer services which are now spread throughout the Hospitals' and Clinic buildings.

Page 8

The problem of insufficient space will be overcome by expanding current cancer medical care from its approximately 11,000 square feet to 31,000 square feet. This will accommodate the many services mentioned, as well as provide space for services such as social work, education, pharmacy, laboratory and x-ray within the Center. Thus, the new Roger Maris Cancer Center will provide:

-centralized coordination of both St. Luke's and the Clinic's cancer programs.

-combination in one location of those services which now exist in multiple locations.

-opportunity to expand cancer education and prevention activities, including on an outreach basis.

-elimination of the necessity for patients to move from location to location during multi-dimensional treatment.

-complete accessibility for handicapped patients.

-increase in patient comfort.

-creation of a separation between ill and bedridden patients on one hand and mobile and healthier patients on the other.

-increase in the number of examination and treatment rooms so more patients can be treated and, when needed, more cancer physicians added to the staff.

Page 9

-upgrading in state-of-the-art cancer treatment and research, both now needing more space and new equipment.

-providing more space to relax for patients undergoing chemotherapy.

-meeting all national cancer program standards regarding a comprehensive program.

The Roger Maris Cancer Center will house the departments of Medical, Pediatric and Radiation Oncology; the Community Clinical Oncology Program; and the staff members of the multi-disciplinary cancer team. It will be connected to the main Hospitals building for easy back-and-forth access. Additionally, the new facility will allow for an emphasis on prevention and early detection of cancer and an expansion of current programs.

The cancer center concept allows for the centralization and coordination of the full range of services and care required to meet the very involved needs of cancer patients and their families. Comprehensive cancer care services will become readily accessible to cancer patients and will be coordinated under a central administration. This cancer center approach will increase the opportunity to better plan the care of cancer patients over extended periods and will help care to be delivered in a more cost effective manner.

Page 10

The main items of equipment needing to be purchased are a part of this campaign: one of two linear accelerators, a simulator and a hypothermic unit.

There currently are two linear accelerators at St. Luke's. One will be moved into the new Cancer Center and will be replaced in the future. The other also will be replaced--by a new state-of-the-art accelerator purchased for installation in the Roger Maris Cancer Center. This machine will be compatible with the simulator, meaning that patients can be treated by either the new or existing machine--something presently not possible.

The simulator plans the course of radiation treatment for cancer patients. The current simulator is outdated and will be sold at the time the new simulator is purchased.

The hypothermic unit is a piece of equipment totally new at St. Luke's. It is state-of-the-art in radiation therapy and treats cancer by using heat therapy. It may be used by itself or in conjunction with radiation.

All other items to be bought are basic medical equipment and furnishings and are not included in the goal of this campaign.

Page 11

GROWING TO SERVE MORE

All current cancer medical space amounts to approximately 11,000 square feet. Upon construction of the Roger Maris Cancer Center, total square footage will nearly triple--to 31,000 square feet. The building will be one-story high and built at the northeast corner of the St. Luke's Hospitals building. It will be connected to the Hospitals and situated between the Hospitals building and 4th Street North. The Cancer Center building will be owned by St. Luke's Association, the parent corporation of the Hospitals which represents the community. Space will be rented to Fargo Clinic to provide appropriate medical services, and the Hospitals also will utilize certain areas. The programmatic aspects of the Roger Maris Cancer Center will be governed by St. Luke's Foundation and the Foundation Board of Directors. This $6.8 million campaign is being conducted by St. Luke's Foundation, the resource development and fundraising arm of the St. Luke's medical complex.

The building will be divided into several major functional areas. It will contain a Pediatric Oncology Treatment Area and a Medical Oncology Treatment Area. Another large portion of the building will be for research, and one-third of the building will be devoted to Radiation Oncology, where the major pieces of equipment will be housed. Space will be available for cancer education specialists. Areas currently not available will be

Page 12

located in the Cancer Center, such as an administrative area for an Executive Director, Medical Director and Community Clinical Oncology Program. There will be a large entry-reception-waiting area and common space for the pharmacy, nursing services, basic laboratories, meeting rooms, regular x-ray and employee facilities.

The total cost of the Roger Maris Cancer Center is $6.8 million. Of this, $4.9 million is for construction. The remaining $1.9 million covers the following: the new accelerator will cost $1.2 million and the simulator $300,000. The cost of the hyperthermic unit is close to $100,000 and other related medical equipment will require $300,000.

PLAN FOR PROGRESS

The entire cost of the Roger Maris Cancer Center--$6,800,000--will be raised through this capital campaign, which is being sponsored and conducted by St. Luke's Foundation--MeritCare.

The approach to this funding effort has been very serious and has involved extensive investigation and deliberation. A feasibility study, during which 38 Fargo-Moorhead area community leaders were interviewed, was conducted before the decision was made to proceed with this fundraising effort. The well-done feasibility study, showed, without question, that strong support

Page 13

exists for a community-directed and oriented Cancer Center in the Fargo-Moorhead and Red River Valley area. This support includes the readiness to provide volunteer fundraising assistance and major financial commitments. Analyses have shown that funding also will come from other sources, such as Minneapolis-St. Paul and from throughout St. Luke's medical services region. Likely commitments from national corporations and foundations concerned with cancer treatment and research -- possibly also the federal government -- help to seal the $6.8 million goal as attainable.

Under the auspices of St. Luke's Foundation, an extensive campaign is being organized. The financial commitments of the MeritCare family will be among the first sought, that is, from St. Luke's Board of Trustees, Foundation Board of Directors, the administrators and employees of St. Luke's Hospitals, the physicians affiliated with Fargo Clinic and Fargo Clinic employees.

St. Luke's Auxiliary--MeritCare, in its determination to launch the campaign and prove the MeritCare family's commitment, has made the first major pledge of $100,000. An additional $100,000, to be used in the research area of the Roger Maris Cancer Center, has been paid by the Women's Auxiliary of the North Dakota Veterans of Foreign Wars. The major commitment from the MeritCare family towards the success of the campaign is from St. Luke's Association. This parent of the entire Hospitals organization represents

Page 14

the community through the constituent churches. The Board of Trustees on behalf of the Association has pledged $2 million from reserve funds to the construction of the Roger Maris Cancer Center. This pledge has been made because of the firm belief by St. Luke's Association--MeritCare that such a facility is necessary for the people of Fargo and of Moorhead...of the Red River Valley...of North Dakota, South Dakota and Minnesota.

Excavation for the Roger Maris Cancer Center began in September 1988. Work is scheduled for completion over a period of two years time, that is, by the summer of 1990.

YOUR SUPPORT IS CRITICAL

St. Luke's turns to the public to build the Roger Maris Cancer Center for a number of reasons. St. Luke's Association, as shown through its own promised $2 million pledge, believes this facility is absolutely essential to the welfare and the very lives of the residents of the Northern Plains area of the United States. This belief is so strongly held, that the Board of Trustees, on behalf of the public, will use these funds from reserves. The Fargo-Moorhead area is the center for much human activity -- educational, cultural, agricultural, financial, mercantile, distribution, economic, health, religious and more. This attracts people from throughout the region to Fargo. People have come to Fargo for years from nearby and

Page 15

from throughout the region to find out if they have cancer and to be treated by all possible means if they have this disease. When the Roger Maris Cancer Center is completed, they will come with even greater hope and confidence about their treatment and the caring help they will receive.

While research has been a regular element of the Cancer Program, it will become even a larger part of the St. Luke's Cancer Program. For the first time, a building with adequate space and equipment for research will exist. One of the reasons that the Cancer Program will be answerable to and through St. Luke's Foundation is that the Foundation will have the capability to raise private and government money for research. Funds also will be sought in support of the Center's prevention and education programs offered to the entire regional community.

St. Luke's could attempt to build the Cancer Center by committing reserves together with a bond issue to borrow money. However, digging deeply into reserve funds could threaten the stability of this region's most important medical complex. To borrow funds to build the facility, even in part, would greatly increase its cost, because of years of interest payments to be paid on the borrowed funds.

St. Luke's is a voluntary hospital, which means it always takes all patients regardless of ability to pay. This will be the case with the Cancer Center.

Page 16

The Roger Maris Cancer Center is the epitome of a community project. It is a North Dakota, South Dakota, Minnesota project. It is a St. Luke's project only because of the Hospitals' concentration of expertise to create, manage and operate such a center. No hospital in this day and age can prudently provide the funds necessary to build such a facility no matter how necessary it is. It can only be created with the caring support and dedication of the people of the region.

JOIN IN THE CARING

With significant gift investments from the citizens of our region, the Roger Maris Cancer Center can and will become one of the finest in the nation--a center for the alleviation of cancer and a major partner in worldwide research to eradicate the disease.

North Dakotans and all Midwesterners have a history of generously supporting important endeavors to aid those suffering and dying from cancer. We again have the opportunity to be a part of this vital step to win the fight against cancer.

GJL
11/27/88

Figure 24.21. Campaign plan

ROGER MARIS CANCER CENTER

"JOIN IN THE CARING"

CAMPAIGN PLAN

Table of Contents

	Page
Introduction	1
Campaign Organization	2
Campaign Cabinet	2
Family Division	3
Major Gifts Division	4
Key Gifts Division	5
Community Gifts Division	5
Prospect Review Committee	6
Standards of Giving	7
Sources of Support	8
Standards Chart	9
Campaign Budget	10
Campaign Timetable	11

November 29, 1988

JOIN IN THE CARING

A $6,800,00 Campaign for the
Roger Maris Cancer Center

Tentative Campaign Plan
November 1988 - June 1989
INTRODUCTION

The following plan is based on tested campaign procedures employed by the firm of Jerold Panas Young and Partners, Inc., in the successful direction of many hospital campaigns over nearly three decades.

Successful execution of this plan, and consequently the success of the campaign itself, hinges on the presence of these fundamental prerequisites:

- There must be a need and a plan to feel that need. This need must be felt by the Trustees, the medical staff, the employees of the Hospitals and Clinic and the people of Fargo-Moorhead and the region.

- There must be sufficient contributable dollars available to meet this need.

- Finally, and above all, there must be hard working, dedicated leadership - men and woman who will lead the effort through to a successful conclusion.

The leadership exists but must be developed to a point of extreme effectiveness. A campaign of this magnitude is a task for the "first team". Men and women who are deeply interested in the welfare of the community must

-1-

be enlisted to take important leadership positions in the campaign organization. It is vital that our leadership be nothing less than the best.

It is important that members of the Hospital Trustees and medical staff leaders serve in important capacities. If Trustees and medical staff do not readily become involved in this campaign, there is little chance of interesting others.

We must state at the beginning that only by soliciting "gifts fully commensurate with ability to give" over the next three to five years can we hope to be successful. We will not be successful with one time cash "out-of-pocket" contributions. This must be emphasized at all levels of giving ability.

CAMPAIGN ORGANIZATION

As a successful business is built, so is a capital campaign organized. The selection of its leadership is paramount.

It is recommended that the campaign be organized into four soliciting divisions under the leadership of the Campaign General Chairman. The Chairman will first form the Campaign Cabinet. This committee will set the overall policies for the campaign. The Campaign Chairman will head this group which will include as members the chairman of St. Luke's Board of

-2-

Trustees, the Hospital's President/CEO, the Clinic's Chief Executive, and the Chairman of each soliciting division as well as the St. Luke's Hospitals Medical Chief of Staff and the President of the Fargo Clinic Board of Directors.. The Foundation's Executive Director and the Campaign Director will serve as ex-officio members. Additional members can be added at the discretion of the General Chairman.

SOLICITING DIVISIONS

I. FAMILY DIVISION

The Family Division will be organized in four sections. These are:

Hospital Trustees -
Approximately twenty-five present and past members of St. Luke's Hospitals Board of Trustees.

Hospital Medical Staff -
Approximated 275 members of the Hospitals' medical staff.

Hospital Employees -
Approximately 1800 full and part-time employees of the hospitals.

Clinic Employees -
Approximately 600 employees of the Fargo Clinic.

The Family Division Campaign will be "PEER" solicitation. Trustees will call on their fellow Trustees, medical staff on other medical staff and employees on fellow employees.

The impetus for any successful capital campaign must come from the "Family". Those closest to the need for the building program must be the first to demonstrate their belief in the project with a worthy and challenging commitment to work in the campaign and to give to the best of their ability. This must be done at the outset of the campaign to set proper high standards for the rest of the community. The overall success of the campaign will be placed in serious jeopardy if the Family does not respond in a timely and generous fashion. A detailed campaign plan and timetable will be developed for the Family Division.

II. MAJOR GIFTS DIVISION

This division will include the top 60 to 75 prospects (corporations, foundations, financial institutions and individuals) judged to have the ability to commit more than $50,000 over the three to five year payment period.

Organization Requirements:

1 - Division Chairman
3 - Vice Chairman
15 - Campaigners
Major Gifts Division Goal $1,700,000

Although small in number, this division is most important to the success of the campaign. The Major Gifts Division, together with the Family Division will set the standard for others to follow. The giving pattern established at the outset with outstanding pacesetting gifts will have a great influence on the quality of support received in other divisions that will kick off at later dates.

Central to the success in the Major Gifts Division is volunteer leadership. Only those willing and able to ask for high five and six figure gifts can be considered.

III. KEY GIFTS DIVISION

Key Gifts Division will have approximately 150 prospects judged to have the ability to support the Roger Maris Cancer Center Capital Campaign with gift investments from $10,000 to $50,000 over the three to five year payment period. To solicit Key Gift Prospects the following organization will be developed:

```
1 - Division Chairman
6 - Vice Chairman
30 - Campaigners
```

Key Gifts Goal - $1,320,000

IV. COMMUNITY GIFTS DIVISION

Community Gifts Division leadership will have the responsibility to solicit gift investments from $1,000 to $10,000 payable over three to five years. Community Division leaders must have the ability to make gifts at this level and the willingness to actively enlist and solicit others for like amounts.

-5-

Approximate number of prospects - 300. Organization Requirements:

```
1 - Division Chairman
3 - Vice Chairman
15 - Captains
75 - Campaigners
```

Community Division goal - $380,000

V. In addition to the Soliciting Divisions there needs to be one additional committee formed:

Prospect Classification and Review Committee

This behind the scenes committee will aid the campaign leadership by using their knowledge of the community to classify and rate the giving ability of prospects so that they can be properly assigned within the campaign structures. Separate groups will be formed: one to rate the prospects in the Family Division and another to rate and classify prospects in the other three "public" soliciting divisions.

-6-

STANDARDS OF GIVING NECESSARY FOR SUCCESS

In a major capital fund campaign, it is essential that a scale of pledging be projected in line with the objective. From a wealth of experience, certain very usable data is available regarding the giving patterns that must emerge to assure success.

Analysis of hundreds of successful hospital capital campaigns with objectives of more than $3 million indicates that there should be a top investment in the realm of 10 to 20% of the objective. Study also shows conclusively that 90% of the funds raised in successful campaigns comes from less than 10% of the donors. These basic findings, therefore, must be adhered to in projecting the number and size of gifts needed for success.

Further study shows that, in the aggregate the top ten gifts must produce 45 to 55% of the objective, with the balance coming from everyone else.

-7-

ROGER MARIS CANCER CENTER--MERITCARE
JOIN IN THE CARING
CAMPAIGN

SOURCES OF SUPPORT

$6.8 MILLION GOAL

From St. Luke's Association--MeritCare Reserves		$2,000,000
From St. Luke's "family"		
Board of Trustees	$200,000	
Medical Staff	800,000	
Hospital Employees	300,000	
Clinic Employees	100,000	
Auxiliary	100,000	
		$1,500,000
From Public Campaign		$3,300,000
Need and Goal		$6,800,000

-8-

LOCAL CAMPAIGN BUDGET

The Campaign Director is responsible for operating within the authorized campaign budget of $40,000. The budget categories may be overspent without authorization but the budget total may not be exceeded without the approval of the Foundation Executive Director.

Expenditures will be accounted for by the Campaign Director and approved by the Foundation Executive Director.

BUDGET

Printing	$ 16,000
Office Supplies	$ 1,000
Postage	$ 2,000
Telephone (long distance)	$ 1,000
Public Relations	$ 3,000
Meetings/Meals	$ 6,000
Travel & Expenses	$ 3,000
Training Material	$ 2,000
Contingencies	$ 6,000
TOTAL:	$ 40,000

-10-

PUBLIC CAMPAIGN

$3,300,000 GOAL

Number of Gifts	In the Range of	Cumulative Total
1	$ 500,000	$ 500,000
1	$ 250,000	$ 750,000
3	$ 150,000	$1,200,000
5	$ 100,000	$1,700,000

Top 10 gifts = 53% of goal

Number of Gifts	In the Range of	Cumulative Total
10	$ 50,000	$2,200,000
16	$ 25,000	$2,600,000
32	$ 10,000	$2,920,000
42	$ 5,000	$3,130,000

Top 110 gifts = 95% of goal

LESS THAN $5,000		$ 170,000
GOAL		$3,300,000

-9-

CAMPAIGN TIMETABLE

(1) Week of November 14, 1988

-Start to write Campaign Plan

(2) Week of November 21, 1988

-Complete Campaign Plan
-Develop case for support

(3) Week of November 28, 1988

-Case for Support approved
-Start to develop employee formula/goal
-Begin prospect research - public phase
-Campaign plan approved.

(4) Week of December 5, 1988

-Continue prospect research - public phase
-Continue to develop employee formula/goal

(5) Week of December 12, 1988

-Prospect research complete- Trustees
-Decide employee formula/goal
-Enlist Hospital Employee Section Vice Chair (1)
-Public Phase Prospect Research continues

(6) Week of December 19, 1988

-Enlist Employee Section Steering Committee
-Continue Research-Public Phase

-11-

(7) Week of December 26, 1988

-Start to enlist Employee Section Group Leaders
-Continue Research Public Phase

(8) Week of January 2, 1989

-Complete enlistment of Hospital Employee Section Group Leaders (35)
-Start enlistment Clinic Employees Section Group Leaders
-Continue Prospect Research & Public Plan

(9) Week of January 9, 1989

-Information Meetings Hospital Employees
-Continue Prospect Research - Public Phase

(10) Week of January 16, 1989

-Information Meetings with Hospital Employees
-Mailing to all Hospital Employees
-Enlist Campaign Chair (1)
-Enlist Prospect Review Chair (1)
-Enlist Trustees Chairman (1)
-Prospect Research completed

(11) Week of January 23, 1989

-Hospital Employee solicitation begins
-Enlist Prospect Review Committee (6)
-Enlist Major Gifts Division Chair (1)
-Enlist Trustees Committee (6)

(12) Week of January 30, 1989

-Prospect Review Committee meets
-Hospital Employee solicitation continues
-Enlist Major Gifts Division Vice Chairs (3)
-Campaign Cabinet meets
-Kick Off Trustee Solicitation

(13) Week of February 6, 1989

-Prospect Review Committee meets
-Hospital Employee solicitation completed
-Start to enlist Major Gifts Division Campaigners
-Report Meeting - Trustee Committee

-12-

(14) Week of February 13, 1989

   -Prospect Review completed
   -Complete enlistment of Major Gifts Division Campaigners (15)
   -Enlist Key Gifts Division Chair (1)
   -Report Meetings - Trustee Committee

(15) Week of February 20, 1989

   -Kick Off Major Gifts Division
   -Enlist Key Division Vice Chairs (6)
   -Campaign Cabinet meets
   -Trustee solicitation complete

(16) Week of February 27, 1989

   -Start to enlist Key Division Campaigners

(17) Week of March 6, 1989

   -First Report Major Gifts
   -Complete enlistment of Key Division Campaigners (30)
   -Enlist Community Division Chair

(18) Week of March 13, 1989

   -Kick Off Key Division
   -Enlist Community Division Vice Chairs (3)
   -Campaign Cabinet meets

(19) Week of March 20, 1989

   -Second Report Major Gifts
   -First Report Key Division
   -Enlist Community Division Captains (15)

(20) Week of March 27, 1989

   -Start to enlist Community Division Campaigners

(21) Week of April 3, 1989

   -Third Report Major Gifts
   -Second Report Key Division
   -Complete enlistment of Community Division Campaigners (75)
   -Campaign Cabinet Meets

(22) Week of April 10, 1989

   -Kick off Community Division

(23) Week of April 17, 1989

   -Final Report Major Gifts
   -Third Report Key Division
   -First Report Community Division

(24) Week of April 24, 1989

   -Campaign Cabinet meets

(25) Week of May 1, 1989

   -Final Report Key Division

(26) Week of May 8, 1989

   -Campaign Cabinet Meets

(27) Week of May 15, 1989

   -Third Report Community Division

(28) Week of May 22, 1989

   -Final Report Community Division

(29-30) Weeks of May 29 and June 5, 1989

   -Campaign Clean-up and Final Report
   -VICTORY CELEBRATION

Figure 24.22. A brochure mailed to employees at their homes was accompanied by a letter from the hospital president.

St. Luke's Association
MeritCare

5th St. North at Mills

Fargo, North Dakota 58122

701 234-5104

St. Luke's
Hospitals of Fargo
Regional
Neuroscience
Children's

Ambulatory
Surgical Center,
Inc

HealthCare
Accessories, Inc

Health
Enterprises, Inc

Imaging Dynamics,
Inc

St. Luke's
Foundation

January 20, 1989

Dear St. Luke's Associate:

St. Luke's needs and asks for your help. As you know, construction of the Roger Maris Cancer Center is underway east of the hospital. Many people, companies and organizations in the area have indicated they wish to contribute to help build the Center. Our goal is to raise $6.8 million to build the Cancer Center and to buy the major equipment it needs.

St. Luke's Association has committed $2 million toward the project; the physicians and employees of Fargo Clinic have pledged $900,000, and St. Luke's Auxiliary has pledged $100,000. The MeritCare family has so far donated or promised a total of $3 million. Other gifts put the total over $3.1 million.

We are asking the more than 2,000 employees of St. Luke's Association to consider a combined pledge of $300,000 or more. Your commitment, together with the other gifts pledged or received, will bring us to more than half of our goal. Once we reach that halfway point, we will have a major public announcement emphasizing the support the MeritCare family has to this project.

This fund drive provides an excellent opportunity to examine what St. Luke's means to each of us and to respond with financial support to this very worthwhile project - a project that will benefit St. Luke's, our community, and every one of us individually.

The volunteer leadership of this campaign, including the Steering Committee of your co-workers, has come up with an excellent way to help you make a contribution toward this project. Your gift will help us reach our $300,000 Association goal.

Join your associates in supporting this marvelous new facility. You have my personal thanks for joining in this fight against cancer and for helping to improve the quality of life for all the people of the greater Red River Valley.

Sincerely yours,

Lloyd V. Smith
President and Chief Executive Officer

lb

Roger Maris Cancer Center
MeritCare

"Join In The Caring"

You may know Connie, Sanford, Florence or Bonnie. Or, you may know other associates, friends and family members who have had to deal with cancer.

In the weeks ahead, hundreds of MeritCare associates will be pledging their financial support to the Roger Maris Cancer Center. In fact, many associates have already volunteered to help reach our goal of $6.8 million. They'll be encouraging you to help build the Roger Maris Cancer Center, too.

Your financial support is **very** important. As a member of the MeritCare family, you can be very proud of the care and compassion you show to your associates and our patients. You can continue that tradition and "Join In The Caring" to help the many patients and families who are dealing with cancer.

"Join In The Caring" with enthusiasm! Then, in the years ahead, the Roger Maris Cancer Center can be a very special place, where many people can find hope, comfort ... and a cure.

"Join In The Caring!"

The Roger Maris Cancer Center is being built next to St. Luke's Hospitals–MeritCare. It is designed as an outpatient facility and will be completed in the summer of 1990.

The Roger Maris Cancer Center will have adult and pediatric cancer areas, examination rooms and staff offices. It will house all of the most advanced equipment for chemotherapy, radiation therapy, cancer screening, diagnosis, prevention, education and research.

"It will be wonderful to have everything under one roof," says Connie Hatlelid, LPN. Connie is a nurse in the Family Birth Center and realizes first-hand how much the new Roger Maris Cancer Center will mean. Connie was diagnosed with cancer and had surgery and one year of chemotherapy.

"I strongly believe that early detection gave me a better chance of surviving cancer," says Sanford Albertson. Sanford works in Environmental Services and underwent surgery for cancer. His father also had cancer.

A dedicated team of MeritCare associates helps patients deal with the physical and emotional aspects of cancer. Each year, 1,200 **new** cancer patients are diagnosed and treated by MeritCare's oncologists/ hematologists, radiation oncologists, surgeons, nurses, social workers and support staff. When the Roger Maris Cancer Center is completed, these associates can work even closer together to provide the best possible care.

Florence Anderson, who works in AM Admitting, recalls the support she received from the cancer team. "I am grateful for the support I received, especially on that first day when I found out I had cancer." Florence now has a new outlook on life and appreciates every moment.

The Center will serve people from North Dakota, South Dakota and Minnesota — people who are determined to find hope, comfort ... and a cure.

Bonnie Kennelly, who works in Medical Education, recognizes how important our cancer program is. She underwent cancer surgery and six weeks of radiation therapy. "A positive attitude is very important," says Bonnie, "but I couldn't have made it without the support of my associates. They helped me every step of the way."

Figure 24.23. Pledge form for employee gifts. The PTO or Paid Time Off concept allowed employees to convert unused sick time and vacation pay into cash for the campaign.

COPY

Campaign For
Roger Maris Cancer Center
MeritCare

St. Luke's Foundation

720 4th Street North

Fargo, North Dakota 58122

701 234 6620

_____
Solicitor

So that I can be a vital part of the St. Luke's Hospitals--MeritCare employee campaign to help fund the Roger Maris Cancer Center:

☐ I pledge one vacation day or ☐ _____ vacation days per year for the next five years and authorize St. Luke's Hospitals to take the vacation day(s) from my Paid Time Off (PTO) account each March (1989 through 1993).

☐ I pledge one day's pay per year for the next five years, to be paid through payroll deduction.

☐ I prefer _____

_____

_____

_____
Signature

_____
Date

Join In The Caring...

Figure 24.24. A brochure used by volunteers seeking gifts from employees

Roger Maris Cancer Center
MeritCare

"Join In The Caring"

Your Gift is Tax-Deductible

All gifts are fully tax-deductible on your state and federal tax returns as a charitable contribution. Each year, you will receive an acknowledgement and receipt of your gift from St. Luke's Foundation—MeritCare for tax purposes.

Other Ways to Give

Your gift of one PTO day will go a long way to help those who are determined to fight the dreaded disease of cancer.

If you decide to give the suggested amount of one day's pay but would like to not use a PTO day, you may request that a set amount be deducted from each of your pay checks over the next five years.

Here is an example to help determine this:

1. Your hourly wage $10.00
2. Multiplied by 8 hours $80.00
3. Divided by 26 pay days equals
   your gift per pay period $3.08

In this example, $3.08 would be deducted from each pay check as a tax-deductible gift to the Roger Maris Cancer Center.

A third option is to give to the "Join In The Caring" campaign by personal check. You can do this quarterly, semi-annually or annually for five years.

Recognition for your Generous Support

For those who choose to give the suggested minimum amount, or more, there will be a special permanent St. Luke's associates plaque listing names and recognizing this important support. The pledge of one day's pay per year, regardless of amount, will result in the donor's being listed. This is an important project for our community and the MeritCare family. Your support will be sincerely appreciated.

A Closing Thought

As the Roger Maris Cancer Center becomes a reality, it is the hope of many cancer patients that their loved ones, their neighbors and their fellow associates will "Join In The Caring" to help them fight this dreaded disease.

And in the years ahead, the Roger Maris Cancer Center will be a very special place, where many people are determined to find hope, comfort ... and a cure.

Please "Join In The Caring."

A Place of Hope and Comfort

The Roger Maris Cancer Center is being built next to St. Luke's Hospitals–MeritCare. It is designed as an outpatient facility and will be completed in the summer of 1990.

A Name Symbolizing Success

It is an honor to have the name, Roger Maris, associated with the Cancer Center. For those who knew Roger while he was growing up in Fargo, or knew of him during his baseball days, it is fitting that his name and all that it represents — courage, honor, sensitivity and success — be a part of this project.

A Team of Dedicated Associates

Each year, 1,200 *new* cancer patients are cared for by a team of dedicated MeritCare associates. When the Roger Maris Cancer Center is completed, this team can work even closer together to provide the best possible care for cancer patients and their families.

You may know one of the patients. It may be a loved one, a neighbor, a fellow MeritCare associate or a child. Or, it may be you.

It is much too easy to find someone whose life has been affected by cancer. But, our nation has a goal. The goal is to reduce the deaths from cancer by 50 percent by the year 2000. It is an ambitious goal, but one that the Roger Maris Cancer Center is proud to be a part of ... a goal that you can be a part of, too.

Providing the Best Possible Care

Your donation to the Roger Maris Cancer Center will mean that more patients throughout North Dakota, South Dakota and Minnesota will be able to receive state-of-the-art cancer care. It will mean that there will be a facility that takes into account the special needs of their families.

It will mean that more education will be available to help people prevent cancer and more research to discover better ways to treat cancer.

It will mean more people will survive cancer and return to productive, healthy lives. Someday, it will mean a cure.

For MeritCare associates, the Roger Maris Cancer Center will mean all of this ... and more.

■ We will be able to continue to improve the care we provide to our patients.

■ We will be a part of a more secure work force.

■ We will be even more efficient in what we do best... delivering quality, compassionate health care to the people of our region.

"Join In The Caring"

A quality, up-to-date cancer center is a top priority of our community. Financing such a facility is the responsibility of all of us.

The Roger Maris Cancer Center will be made possible by funds from the MeritCare family of trustees, medical staff, Hospital and Clinic associates and volunteers, businesses and corporations, financial institutions, clubs and organizations, responsible citizens, foundations and trusts.

What is needed for success is an outpouring of enthusiastic support from all of these segments of the community. "Join In The Caring" is a $6,800,000 campaign for the Roger Maris Cancer Center. It is truly the most important and vital community investment of our time.

The Roger Maris Cancer Center will improve the quality of life for thousands of men, women and children for generations to come ... and will join in the worldwide research efforts to fight this dreaded disease.

Please "Join In The Caring" with determination and enthusiasm in this important community effort. With everyone uniting together, the campaign will be a $6.8 million success!

How You Can Help

Each MeritCare associate plays an important part in the success of the Roger Maris Cancer Center, because it is the hope of many cancer patients and their families that this Center become a reality.

You can help. Each MeritCare associate is asked to consider pledging a minimum of one day's pay per year for the next five years. Your gift can be paid by authorizing Payroll to withdraw from your Paid Time Off (PTO) account one or more vacation days. They will donate this amount to the Roger Maris Cancer Center in your name.

Here is the formula for this type of pledge:

1. Your hourly wage . . . . $ _____
2. Multiplied by 8 hours
   equals one days pay . . . . $ _____
3. Multiplied by 5 years
   equals your total pledge . . . . $ _____

For those associates who are part time, weekend or flex status, simply divide your weekly hours by five (days) and multiply your hourly wage by that figure to determine one day's pay.

Here's an example for a person who works 32 hours per week, making $10.00 an hour:

1. Number of hours per week 32
2. Divided by 5 days equals 6.2
3. Multiplied by $10.00
   equals one day's pay $62.00

When this amount is divided by 26 pay days, your gift per pay period would be $2.38.

Special thanks to those associates who are participating on the Steering Committee for this project:

Paul Swanson, Chairman
Material Services

Bernie Kieselbach, Finance
Business Office

Mary Jo Kroshus, Ancillary and Support Services
Radiation Oncology

Lyle Lamoureux, Executive Division and Officers
Quality Assurance

Gary Lee, Ancillary and Support Services
Cardiopulmonary Services

Mary Jane McNeal, Corporate Services
Dietary

Ev Quigley, Nursing
Administration

Kathy Scheibe, Nursing
3 Main

Patty Warne, Nursing
4 East

Roger Maris Cancer Center
MeritCare

St. Luke's Foundation–MeritCare
720 4th St. N.
Fargo, ND 58122

Int 189/2M

Figure 24.25. Campaign instructions for volunteers soliciting gifts in the top two external groups—major gifts and key gifts. The major gifts category included individuals and other prospects who might give more than $50,000 over three to five years. The key gifts category was made up of prospects with the potential to give $10,000 to $50,000.

Campaign For
Roger Maris Cancer Center
MeritCare

St. Luke's Foundation

720 4th Street North

Fargo, North Dakota 58122

701 234 6620

CAMPAIGNERS INSTRUCTIONS
About Successful Campaigning

As a Campaigner for the Roger Maris Cancer Center Capital Campaign YOU are the key to success.

You are giving unselfishly of your time and energy for this vital endeavor. In order that your talents may best be used, we suggest you use the following procedures that have been proven successful in hundreds of similar campaigns.

1. Study the Case Statement

    A review of the Case Statement and the other campaign literature is basic preparation for effective solicitation. If you have any questions get them answered before you make your first contact.

2. Know the ways of giving

    Encourage your prospects. to make three to five year pledges because one time out-of-pocket gifts will not achieve our objective. If a prospect offers a gift of securities or property, contact the campaign office. We have experts in these areas available to assist in these areas.

3. Be your own first prospect

    Your support is an essential first step in the effective salutation of others. You must be convinced of the Roger Maris Cancer Center's worth and have demonstrated your own conviction through a generous gift before you can convince others. Decide on your own pledge before you seek the pledges of others.

Join In The Caring...

4. See your best prospect first

Concentrate your first efforts on your most promising prospect, one who you feel will be the most receptive. Your enthusiasm is the key ingredient of success and securing your first generous gift is a great way to maintain your enthusiasm!

5. See your prospects in person

You can only obtain the best results from face-to-face contact. The fact that you are willing to make personal visits to explain the Campaign will help your prospect realize the importance of the Roger Maris Cancer Center Capital Campaign. Phone conversations invites delay and substandard gifts.

6. Plan for two visits

Your first visit should be designed to gain your prospects' interest and to briefly explain the vital need for the Roger Maris Cancer Center. Give your prospect the Campaign material and set up another appointment in a few days. Generous gifts will be required to make this a success and your prospect should have time for thoughtful consideration. On your second visit ask your prospect if he has any questions, answer them and then present the pledge form for signature.

7. Suggest a Memorial or Living Tribute

Naming opportunities are available in the Roger Maris Cancer Center. A pamphlet, included in your campaign kit, gives many choices. Discuss these opportunities with your prospects. They may wish to receive recognition for these gifts or honor a loved one or friend.

8. Discuss tax advantages

Your prospects often will give more when they are made aware of the tax savings for charitable deductions. Gifts to the Roger Maris Cancer Center are fully deductible on your Federal and State income tax returns.

9. Never leave the Pledge Form

Pledge forms left with prospects are seldom seen again or, if returned, usually have smaller than expected gifts on them. Most successful volunteers, in fact, do not take the pledge form with them on their first visit. Each pledge form, whether they show a gift or not, must be returned to the Foundation office.

10. Make sure the Form is properly filled out

Each pledge form must be signed and dated. Be sure the terms are clearly marked. Three or five years? Month of payment?

The success of the Roger Maris Cancer Center is dependent upon your enthusiasm and your ability to convince your fellow employees to make a significant pledge investment in the program. The Center will provide the best possible care for our family and friends suffering from cancer and will make a major contributions through research toward the inevitable cure of this dreaded disease.

Funding the Roger Maris Cancer Center is important -- It's worthy of our best effort.

Figure 24.26. Why conduct a public fund-raising campaign to build the Roger Maris Cancer Center? When a local corporation president raised that question early in the campaign, this sheet was written to prepare one of the trustees to meet with him. Then the feeling was that this information was so important that it should be provided to all volunteers who were dealing with the public.

Campaign For

Roger Maris Cancer Center
MeritCare

St. Luke's Foundation
720 4th Street North
Fargo, North Dakota 58122
701 234-6620

THE ROGER MARIS CANCER CENTER

Why Conduct a Public Fundraising Campaign to Build It?

1. In 1987, Americans contributed almost $94 billion to charitable non-profit institutions, that is, churches, colleges and universities, hospitals, social welfare agencies, cultural organizations, etc. Non-profit health care received about 15% of the total of all contributions , or $13.65 billion, and much of this amount was donated to hospitals.

2. St. Luke's Hospitals is a non-profit corporation, a "charity", qualified by IRS to seek and accept tax-deductible gifts and donations.

3. St. Luke's is a voluntary hospital; it accepts all patients regardless of ability to pay.

4. Unlike private business and industry, St. Luke's is not in business to make a profit; it exists for the public good.

5. Most surplus funds realized are put back into the hospital for modernization, new and replacement equipment, new public programs for patients, etc. Some surplus, though not a large proportion, is retained as reserves for contingencies.

6. While "private" by definition, that is, it is not owned by government, St. Luke's mission is totally public, meaning that it operates for the benefit of the people of the region.

7. While cost of construction of the Cancer Center and major equipment is $6.8 million, if funds were borrowed to build it, the final cost could be as high as $21 million because of interest on the debt.

8. St. Luke's operates at three levels--as a primary health provider for the Cass-Clay area; a secondary or extended health care institution for a radius of 150 miles; and as a specialized medical center for all of North Dakota, western Minnesota and northeastern South Dakota. The Roger Maris Cancer Center will serve the approximately 1,000,000 people of this large region.

9. Of the $6.8 million needed for the Cancer Center, St. Luke's Association, which represents the public and is the parent organization, has committed $2 million from reserves to the project. Therefore, $4.8 million is being sought directly from the public through this campaign.

10. In addition, all groups part of the total St. Luke's Family have contributed to this campaign out of their own pockets -- $800,000 from the physicians, $300,000 from St.Luke's employees, $100,000 from employees of the Fargo Clinic and $100,000 from St.Luke's Auxiliary, that is, the volunteers. Present and former trustees are now being solicited, and $200,000 is expected from them.

11. If the Roger Maris Cancer Center is not built by public contributions, St. Luke's would have to borrow most of the money to build it. This would greatly increase the cost, part of which would have to be passed on to all patients in their medical bills.

Join In The Caring...

-2-

Figure 24.27. A naming gift-opportunities brochure used with external constituencies

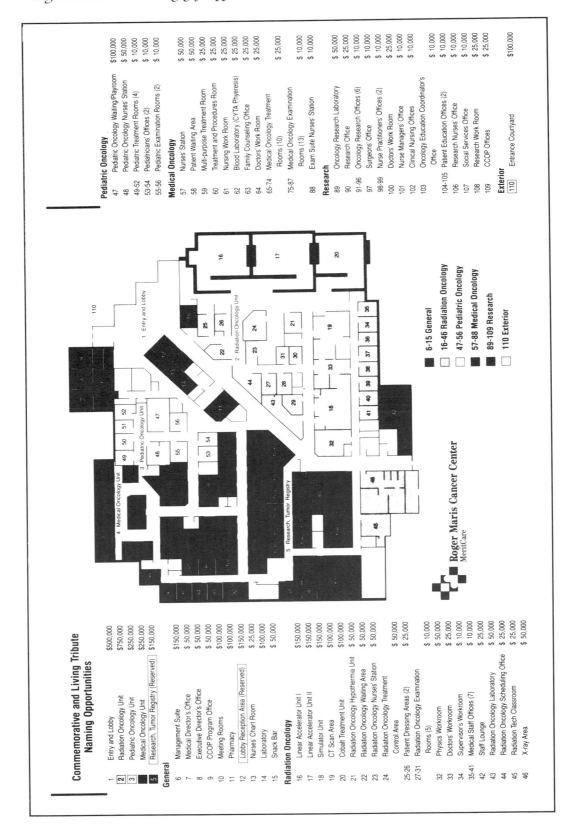

Figure 24.28. The primary campaign brochure

A Place of Hope and Comfort

The Roger Maris Cancer Center is being built next to St. Luke's Hospitals–MeritCare in Fargo, North Dakota. It is designed as an outpatient facility and is scheduled to be completed in the summer of 1990.

In its 31,000 square feet, the center will include a pediatric cancer area, an adult cancer area, examination rooms and staff offices. It will house all of the most advanced necessary equipment for chemotherapy, radiation therapy, cancer screening, diagnosis, prevention, education and research.

A Name Symbolizing Success

It is an honor to have the name, Roger Maris, associated with the Cancer Center. For those who knew Roger while he was growing up in Fargo, or knew of him during his baseball days, it is fitting that his name and all that it represents — courage, honor, sensitivity and success — be a special part of this project.

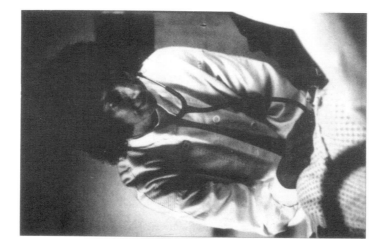

A Group of Dedicated Individuals

Each year, 1,200 new cancer patients are cared for by a team of dedicated individuals. Board-certified oncologists/hematologists, pediatric oncologists, radiation oncologists, surgeons, nurses, social workers and support staff work as a team. When the Roger Maris Cancer Center is completed, these team members can work even closer together to provide the best possible care for the patients and families they serve.

You may know one of their patients. It may be a loved one, a neighbor, a classmate or a child. Or, it may be you.

It is much too easy to find someone whose life has been affected by cancer.

But, the National Cancer Institute has a goal. The goal is to reduce the deaths from cancer by 50 percent by the year 2000. That is an ambitious goal, but one that the Roger Maris Cancer Center is proud to be a part of . . . a goal that you can be a part of, too.

A Gift of Health

Your donation to the Roger Maris Cancer Center will mean that more patients throughout North Dakota, South Dakota and Minnesota will be able to receive state-of-the-art cancer care. It will mean that there will be a facility that takes into account the special needs of their families.

It will mean that more education will be available to help people prevent cancer, and more research to discover better ways to treat cancer.

It will mean more people will survive cancer and return to productive, healthy lives. Someday, it will mean a cure.

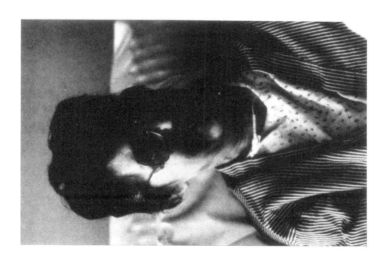

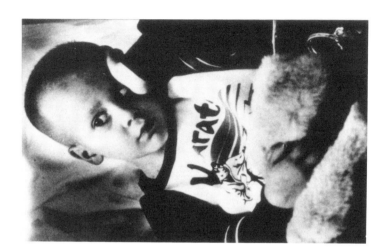

"Join In The Caring"
A Capital Campaign for Everyone

A quality, up-to-date cancer center must be a top priority for any community . . . a center like the Roger Maris Cancer Center.

What is needed for success is an outpouring of enthusiastic support from all segments of the community. Funds will come from: the MeritCare family of trustees, medical staff, Hospitals and Clinic associates and volunteers, businesses and corporations, financial institutions, clubs and organizations, responsible citizens and foundations and trusts.

"Join In The Caring" is a $6,800,000 campaign for the Roger Maris Cancer Center. It is among the most important and vital community investments of our time. The Roger Maris Cancer Center will improve the quality of life for thousands of men, women and children for generations to come . . . and will join in the worldwide research efforts to fight this dreaded disease.

Please "Join In The Caring" with determination and enthusiasm in this important community effort. With everyone uniting together, the campaign will be a $6.8 million success! And in the years ahead, the Roger Maris Cancer Center will be a very special place, where many people are determined to find hope, comfort . . . and a cure.

"Join In The Caring"

Figure 24.29 A corporate proposal

St. Luke's Foundation
720 4th Street North
Fargo, North Dakota 58122

701 234-6620

Campaign For
Roger Maris Cancer Center
MeritCare

COPY

February 28, 1989

Dear

St. Luke's Foundation is conducting a capital campaign for $6.8 million to build the Roger Maris Cancer Center.

So far, half the money has been raised from within the family -- physicians, Hospitals employees, Fargo Clinic employees, volunteers and St. Luke's Association -- the "parent" corporation.

We are now in the early stages of taking this effort to the community and are writing to you to request the support of IBM's Fargo office. Enclosed is a complete proposal detailing the case for support and our request to IBM. Also enclosed is a brochure about the capital campaign.

Bruce Furness, Systems Engineering Manager, is a member of the Board of Trustees of St. Luke's Association and a member of the Board of Directors of St. Luke's Foundation. He can answer many questions about the Cancer Center and the capital campaign. If there is any further information or material I can provide, please let me know. I also would be happy to discuss this request with you in person.

Sincerely,

George J. Lukac
Executive Director
St. Luke's Foundation

Enclosures

Join In The Caring...

PROPOSAL
ON BEHALF OF
the Capital Campaign
for the Roger Maris Cancer Center,
St. Luke's Hospitals--MeritCare
Fargo, North Dakota 58122

This proposal requests your consideration of a gift of $10,000 to the capital campaign for the $6.8 million Roger Maris Cancer Center. This commitment may be payable over as many as five years if your policy permits.

We are submitting this proposal to the IBM Fargo branch office for several reasons. On a national level, IBM strongly supports health and welfare projects and organizations in its corporate philanthropy. Specifically, the company assists hospitals and has a major orientation toward community projects. The new Cancer Center falls squarely into all these categories, and we believe IBM in Fargo has similar priorities in its charitable activities.

In a recent IBM annual report, it was stated that "IBM's philanthropy is founded in the corporation's self-interest." This is understandable and is a wise policy. In fact, it adds yet another reason for IBM's support of this capital campaign, that is, the strong business relationship between IBM and St. Luke's Hospitals. St. Luke's mission is to provide its patients with the highest quality health care -- to cure illness, ease pain and save lives. Nevertheless, it is also a major corporation, with a $100 million annual budget. The future of American business is closely tied to the stability of the non-profit sector, especially medical institutions. If IBM supports this project at the requested level, the company would receive permanent recognition of its generosity in the new Roger Maris Cancer Center in several ways.

St. Luke's has a long history of caring for cancer patients. Every year, in fact, St. Luke's physicians diagnose and begin treatment on approximately 1,300 new cancer patients, besides those whom we are already treating. They are not just from Fargo, North Dakota-Moorhead, Minnesota, but from throughout North Dakota, western Minnesota and parts of South Dakota.

-2-

St. Luke's Hospitals is undertaking a major construction program--one costing $17 million. This includes total renovation and expansion of the emergency medicine department--a department where the number of cases has been and is increasing dramatically. Emergency medicine is being hampered by lack of space and must be expanded and updated.

This multi-faceted building project also will include a new surgical suite with ten new operating rooms. This is a necessity dictated by the fact that the current ten operating rooms are in two locations, six floors apart, and have not been expanded or remodeled in fifteen years.

The primary element in this construction project is the new Cancer Center. It will be an outpatient facility dedicated to testing, diagnosis, therapy, screening, prevention, education, and research activities. The Center will not provide patient beds, which will continue to be housed in the existing hospital building. These functions are not new at St. Luke's, but they have been hindered by insufficient space and disjointed locations.

The Cancer Center will be named for Roger Maris, the former major league baseball great. He grew up in Fargo, got his professional baseball start locally and returned to Fargo often. Roger Maris died of cancer, and his name on the Cancer Center will be a fitting memorial to a Fargo favorite and national hero.

By the summer of 1990 those afflicted with the dreaded disease of cancer will begin coming to the Roger Maris Cancer Center for their treatment. For the first time in St. Luke's history, all medical services needed by cancer patients will be provided in one location.

Patients will continue to benefit from the outstanding medical knowledge and experience of our physicians, nurses and other staff members. In the Roger Maris Cancer Center, however, these professional abilities will be magnified and strengthened by new equipment and by all oncology services of both the Fargo Clinic and St. Luke's Hospitals -- being in one place. The Fargo Clinic is a physicians' corporation, separate from the Hospitals, but which functions together with St. Luke's under contract. The St. Luke's cancer program is the only one in North Dakota designated by the National Cancer Institute as an NCI Community Clinical Oncology Program. Of more than 50 CCOPs nationwide, the program at St. Luke's has recently been identified by NCI as

-3-

probably the strongest in the country. The program makes possible the newest drug and therapy techniques. It allows our physicians and nurses to interact with national leaders in cancer care and works closely with organizations such as the Mayo Clinic. St. Luke's Hospital has received cancer research funding in excess of $1.5 million through NCI.

Until fairly recently, sophisticated cancer diagnoses and treatment were available at the largest medical centers in only a handful of major urban areas. Today, St. Luke's is an outstanding example of a relatively new phenomenon in American healthcare: A sophisticated, diversified, state-of-the-art regional cancer center in a smaller metropolitan area, which also will service an extensive rural area. The Roger Maris Cancer Center at St. Luke's will soon be the focal point of specialized oncology services in this life-and-death struggle and will be one of only about six such facilities anywhere in the United States. Cancer patients will have the finest medical care available to them in Fargo and will not have to travel to a large city hundreds of miles away.

St. Luke's could attempt to build the Cancer Center by committing reserve funds together with a bond issue to borrow money. However, digging deeply into reserve funds could threaten the stability of this region's most important medical complex. To borrow funds to build the facility, even in part, would greatly increase its cost through interest payments.

No hospital in this day and age can prudently provide the funds necessary to build such a facility no matter how urgently needed. It can only be created with the caring, enthusiastic support and dedication of the people of our region and of others elsewhere in the United States concerned about cancer care, education and research.

St. Luke's Hospitals, founded in 1908, encompasses a general hospital, children's hospital and neuroscience hospital with a total of 404 beds. St. Luke's is designated a trauma center II and is the primary care hospital for the greater Fargo-Moorhead area and the tertiary care facility for all of North Dakota, western Minnesota and eastern South Dakota. Services are enhanced by "Lifeflight", which consists of a helicopter and a fixed-wing aircraft to transport emergency cases from outlaying rural areas.

All surgical procedures are available, including same-day surgery in a separate facility. We have a full-service rehabilitation

-4-

unit and maintain relationships with other medical organizations, for example, Mayo Clinic in the federally-funded Community Clinical Oncology Program (CCOP); Magnetic Resonance Imaging (MRI) with United Hospitals, Grand Forks, North Dakota; lithotrypsy with Metropolitan Medical Center in Minneapolis, Minnesota; and contractual with Fargo Clinic including its thirty regional and satellite clinics throughout the Red River Valley region. St. Luke's is the largest non-governmental employer in North Dakota (nearly 1,900 employees) and is the largest medical center between Minneapolis-St. Paul to the east and Seattle to the west. The Fargo Clinic, with 244 physicians, is one of the nation's largest doctors' corporations and also has 1200 non-physician employees.

St. Luke's Hospitals--MeritCare is a quality institution, and the staff and physicians have solid commitments to the community. "Community" has a definition in the Northern Plain states different from many other locales. It takes in entire states and parts of states - a service area of thousands of square miles and about 1,000,000 people. St. Luke's is an anomaly--a combination of a sophisticated, diversified, hi-tech regional medical center situated in a smaller metropolitan area located in the heart of one of America's largest rural areas. Simultaneously, it is a personal, caring institution where people are neighbors and valued as individuals. St. Luke's is strong in many specialties, particularly oncology, emergency medicine, pediatrics, neuroscience, cardiology and cardiac surgery.

We are pleased to report that over $3.4 million has already been pledged to the program. Included in the amount is $2,000,000 from St. Luke's Association, which represents the community and is the "parent" corporation. St. Luke's staff physicians have pledged $800,000 and the Fargo Clinic employees have committed $100,000. Also, the Hospitals' Auxiliary has promised $100,000 and the North Dakota VFW Auxiliary has paid $100,000.

St. Luke's employees have launched a campaign with a goal of $300,000 and are close to attaining the goal, and the Hospitals' Board of Trustees is seeking $200,000 from its current and past membership. This will increase the total to at least $3.6 million, or 53% of the goal, almost all of which will have come from the St. Luke's--Fargo Clinic family. Public announcement of the capital campaign is scheduled for March.

-5-

We now seek commitments from interested individuals, corporations, foundations and organizations to successfully complete this campaign. We ask your thoughtful consideration of this request.

Should you have any questions, please contact the offices of St. Luke's Foundation at (701) 234-6246.

Figure 24.30. A newsletter report on the campaign

FOUNDATION REPORTER

SPRING

The publication of St. Luke's Foundation MeritCare

The Roger Maris Cancer Center: It's all about heroes

The Roger Maris Cancer Center is about heroes. Baseball great Roger Maris is the obvious hero. Then there are the less obvious heroes: the patients, including the 1,300 new patients, who will be treated at the center each year; and the employees', who expertly and compassionately care for patients with cancer. They're heroes because of their great courage in facing cancer, one of the most dreaded diseases.

Roger Maris: Baseball hero

Roger Maris is a former major league baseball great and homerun record holder. He grew up in Fargo, graduated from Shanley High School, and got his start in professional baseball here. Four years ago, he died of cancer. The Roger Maris Cancer Center, which will open in 1990, is a fitting memorial to this North Dakota and national hero.

Though it will not open until 1990, the cancer program at Merit-Care has been in place for a number of years and has developed as much as possible with its current resources. Dr. Paul Etzell, medical director of the center, explained: "We have a cancer program that's unmatched by any in the region because of the comprehensiveness of its services and the extensiveness of its outreach capabilities. The program has grown as much as it could with the resources available, and it's now at the point where its growth potential is restricted. This center is needed."

The Roger Maris Cancer Center will be an outpatient facility, with almost everything a patient would need: the most advanced equipment for chemotherapy, radiation therapy, cancer screening, diagnosis, prevention, education and research. The center will have adult and pediatric cancer areas, examination rooms and staff offices. Only a few such centers exist in the country.

The employees: A reputation for excellence

When it comes to cancer care, MeritCare has already built its reputation for excellence. The reasons are many, and include top quality staff, a team approach and involvement in research.

Treating cancer requires knowledge and experience. On staff at MeritCare are four board-certified oncologists/hematologists who specialize in the care of adults with cancer and blood diseases; two radiation oncologists, who are physicians specializing in the use of radiotherapy to treat cancer in adults and children (approximately half of all cancer patients receive radiotherapy during the course of their treatment); more than ten highly trained surgeons (surgery is a widely used method of fighting cancer); a specially-trained staff who administer close to 6,000 chemotherapy treatments each year. Also on the cancer staff is a PhD pharmacist, of which there are few in the country. And soon to join will be a pediatric oncologist.

Caring for patients with cancer takes knowledge, experience and compassion. "Working with cancer patients is rewarding, but tough. It's not an easy thing to do," said Terry Miller, coordinator of the Community Clinical Oncology Program at MeritCare. "Often the staff sees patients over a long time and they become like family to us."

Nurses who are specially trained to meet the complex needs of cancer patients and their families work in St. Luke's 36-bed cancer inpatient unit. In addition, children with cancer are admitted to Children's Hospital MeritCare. (Even after the cancer center is built, hospitalized patients will continue to be hospitalized at St. Luke's and Children's Hospital, though they will go to the cancer center for some of their treatments.)

"Cancer requires the support and involvement of many members of a health care team. When the Roger Maris Cancer Center is *(Back page, Column 1)*

Foundation Reporter 1

The University of Miami

Coral Gables, Florida

Goal: $400 million
Amount Raised: $517.5 million

During the 1980s, the University of Miami in South Florida conducted what was to that point one of the largest capital campaigns in history for a university. A new president came to the university in 1981 and began a strategic planning process. A fund-raising consulting firm conducted a feasibility study in 1982. Planning for the campaign began in 1982, and solicitations for the nucleus fund began on June 1, 1983.

The nucleus fund brought in $82 million, and the campaign was formally launched in December 1984 with a five-year time frame. One of the early key gifts came from a trustee in the form of a charitable lead trust that will yield $56.25 million for unrestricted purposes over 30 years. This was soon followed by a foundation commitment of $27.5 million for capital purposes, operating endowment and faculty support. It is the largest complete gift ever made to the university, generating more than $72 million over 30 years. Later in the campaign, the foundation added $5 million to its commitment.

The goal of this major capital campaign was to strengthen the university academically. The most significant factor in its success, according to Rita Bornstein, vice president for development at the time of the campaign, is that 75 percent of the funds came from the South Florida community. The campaign became an effort for the betterment of the entire region, with most of the major donors being people who had moved to Florida from other states.

The University of Miami is one of the youngest major universities in the United States. It was founded in the 1920s. Half of its alumni have graduated since 1972. Therefore it was essential for the community to get behind the campaign—and it did in a major way.

Because of the newness of the Miami constituency, a great deal of time and effort was spent throughout the campaign on prospect identification. Donor recognition also became a priority.

The chairman of the board of trustees and the university president were the key solicitors. Luckily for Miami, these two leaders had a "real appetite for asking," according to Rita Bornstein. During the campaign, the existing development committee of the board was eliminated, and a campaign steering committee operated under the office of the chairman. Initial attention was given to $1-million-and-up prospects, and within the last year of the campaign, emphasis was placed on separate school and division campaigns. Faculty and staff were solicited as well as alumni. Alumni provided only 10 percent of the totals, but the campaign doubled the number of alumni donors.

Resident campaign counsel was in place for a total of three years, through the first 18 months of the public campaign. A separate consulting firm was hired to run a phone campaign aimed at alumni.

The campaign brought to the University of Miami a number of intensified changes in the way fund-raising was done. New cultivation activities were organized in large numbers. The prospect research staff was expanded from one to eight. A tracking system to monitor progress with prospects was installed. A major gifts program was started and staffed. The planned giving program was redesigned and strengthened. During the period of the campaign, the president of the university moved toward consolidating development within a central staff.

The campaign for Miami exceeded its $400 million goal by raising $517.5 million. This campaign was a prospect-focused effort rather than a need-focused one. Much time and effort went into plans that would maximize gift potential from individual donors.

The following materials were made available by Rick Schuster, director of development communication during the campaign.

The campaign for the University of Miami shows very well how a fund-raising campaign can rally new constituencies around an organization that is vital to a community. It had big goals and broad vision but its success was based on hard work identifying, cultivating and soliciting major prospects.

Figure 24.31. Here are some excerpts from the case statement for the campaign, which was attractively done with four-color illustrations. In most cases, we have not reproduced the photographs referred to in the captions at the bottom right of some pages.

A CONFLUENCE OF INTERESTS

Such a world will need educated men and women and especially its great universities.

It is the mission of the University of Miami, as the only major private research university in this region, to quicken and prepare eager minds and to conduct research to increase the understanding of ourselves, our planet and beyond. A great university must not only educate its students. It must improve life by expanding knowledge.

The Campaign for the University of Miami is the cornerstone of our plan in this passage of history. Through this campaign, we will reinforce the curricula, strengthen support for the faculty and students and provide the facilities necessary to meet our obligation as the primary intellectual resource for our region. This campaign will make possible that confluence of energies, ideas, hopes and achievements characteristic of great crossroads at historic moments. It will insure the building of a great university in a great city.

EDWARD T. FOOTE II
President
University of Miami

JAMES W. McLAMORE
Chairman, Board of Trustees
Chairman, The Campaign for
the University of Miami

James W. McLamore, left, Chairman of the University of Miami Board of Trustees, and Edward T. Foote II, President of the University.

2

A CONFLUENCE OF INTERESTS

The world's great cities share at their core vibrant cultures fostering both intellectual ferment and lively commerce. This mix of greatness has electrified such cities as Athens, Cairo, Hong Kong, London, Madrid, Paris, Rome, New York and San Francisco. The life of great cities transcends the provincial to embrace the world; indeed, transcends even the limitations of time itself.

Each of those centers of civilization became, as South Florida is today, a "land of verges," of constant creative encounters among different peoples and ideas. Each grew to preeminence as crossroads of travel, trade and of innovation. Each shaped the future.

As the 21st century approaches, the turning point is more significant than even the arrival of a new millennium. People have never confronted so sweeping a transition of eras. Fundamental change explodes around us. From science to political alliances, electrons to infinity, and the building blocks of life itself, our knowledge expands now exponentially. So do our problems. The century we leave to our grandchildren will be fundamentally different.

They will live in a world where the fortunes of the United States will be locked to those of developing nations, especially our neighbors in this hemisphere. They will be forced to compromise with nature rather than attempt, as we have in the past, to dominate it. Our children's children will live in cities more polycultural and multilingual than at present. The world will remain a dangerous place, for increasing millions a potentially desperate place, as technology races with starvation and dwindling energy reserves.

PROGRESS REPORT IN A DEADLY BATTLE

THE PUBLIC NEED

Four times as many Americans die each year from cancer as from automobile accidents, and statistics indicate one of every four Americans will contract cancer. While these figures are frightening, the outlook in Florida is even more ominous: the state leads the nation in the incidence of new cancer cases—4,500 new cancers per million people. Ironically, hope has never been brighter for those charged with battling this dreaded killer, both in Florida and the nation. The rate of cure per six cases of cancer has risen from two in 1900 to four in the mid 1980s. And, when cancer is diagnosed early, cure rates of 80 percent are not uncommon. However, much remains to be done, both in laboratory and clinical research. The state of Florida, with a major cancer problem, has an opportunity to offer major cancer-cure leadership.

THE PRIVATE RESPONSE

Established a decade ago as an integral part of the University of Miami/Jackson Memorial Medical Center, the University's Comprehensive Cancer Center is having a substantial impact on the treatment and prevention of cancer in the Southeast United States. One of only 21 like it in the country, this Center has established a reputation for pioneering clinical and laboratory research and patient care—especially in the area of chemotherapy. Explains veteran cancer researcher Dr. Edward Beattie, who came to the Center in 1983 after eighteen years at Memorial Sloan-Kettering Cancer Center in New York. "We take an interdisciplinary approach to the most common cancers—breast, lung, colon and gynecological—so that Florida patients can have the best treatment close to home."

Dr. Edward Beattie, Professor of Surgery, in a University of Miami/Jackson Memorial Medical Center operating suite.

6

THE REALITY OF ARTIFICIAL INTELLIGENCE

THE PUBLIC NEED

A technological explosion in our society has permitted us to produce and move knowledge in more ways than ever before. This explosion has been keenly felt in South Florida, an area that depends on a smooth and accurate flow of information to keep its high-technology, international trade and banking, travel and service industries viable and profitable. The key to future development in this area is the so-called "fifth generation" computers, machines that can think and plan for other computers—artificial intelligence. All the world's industrial nations are working to lead in this challenging and vital field.

THE PRIVATE RESPONSE

"Any change in the way knowledge is handled is a matter of concern for the academic community," declares David Bendel Hertz, Director of the Intelligent Computer Systems Research Institute (ICSRI) at the University of Miami. Professor Hertz defines artificial intelligence as "the use of computers to do difficult tasks that ordinarily require intelligence, and to do them faster and more elegantly than is possible for a human being." During its first months of operation, the Institute secured several research projects, and already has developed an artificial intelligence system for the largest computer manufacturer in Florida.

David B. Hertz, Director of the Intelligent Computer Systems Research Institute at the University of Miami, in the Dade County traffic control room.

4

CREATION OF NEW TRADITIONS

THE PUBLIC NEED

C hange and growth may be the only lasting traditions in South Florida. Adaptation and innovation have always been necessary to accommodate the different peoples and cultures that populate and distinguish the region. Recently, local pride in achievement has grown not only for the physical rejuvenation of areas such as Biscayne Bay, downtown Miami and the Gold Coast but for South Florida's successful adaptation to the complex realities that characterize a modern, multi-cultural society. Legislative and cultural changes have had to keep pace with populations that shift day by day. The acceptance of differences that is becoming a hallmark of South Florida marks the beginning of a new tradition that will set an example for the rest of the country to follow into the next century.

THE PRIVATE RESPONSE

B ecause South Florida's is a young culture, amenable to change, a great deal can be achieved in a short time," points out Whittington Johnson, a University of Miami professor of history, nationally-known historian, and a recent student choice for *Professor of the Year*. "The University of Miami has been the prime regional forum for the exchange of cultural ideas and viewpoints among South Florida's various populations, facilitating the continuing vital process of understanding and accommodation. One of my graduate students, Arthur Chapman, is now completing his Doctor of Arts project on the evolution of Miami's black police force from 1925 to 1980, a period of considerable progress for Miami. The progression to a unified law enforcement system may seem like a small step, but it is a point of pride for all South Floridians that we have accomplished this and many other comparable societal transitions in a few years."

Whittington Johnson, left, Associate Professor of History, and Arthur Chapman, a University doctoral candidate, at City of Miami Police Headquarters.

8

THE GLOBAL IMPLICATIONS OF MIAMI BUSINESS

THE PUBLIC NEED

I n *The Book of America*, authors Neal Pierce and Jerry Hagstrom point out that "so many (international) business decisions came to be made in Miami that in 1979 Ecuadorian President Jaime Roldos proclaimed at a hemispheric conference that Miami has become 'The Capital of South America.'" Indeed, South Florida has become a hub for international banking and business so rapidly that, since 1969, more than 100 banking entities of various types have been established in Miami, and more than 105 multinational corporations have established offices in Coral Gables. What is not so easily illustrated is the impact this surge has had on the overall economic and human development of the region, and it is difficult to gauge the long-range results of the region's dependence on what is essentially a single commercial base.

THE PRIVATE RESPONSE

U niversity of Miami international business experts Duane Kujawa and Robert Grosse insist that it is no longer possible for the United States to take Latin American and Caribbean business for granted. "Recent headlines have forcibly called our ignorance of this region to our attention," notes Kujawa. South Florida is uniquely positioned to help the nation understand the implications of the surge in international business, and the University of Miami's International Business and Banking Institute, which Professors Kujawa and Grosse helped found, is part of a broad research, conference and publication effort designed to address important issues both for Latin Americans doing business in America and Americans doing business in Latin America.

Duane Kujawa, left, Professor of General Business, Management and Organization, and Robert Grosse, Associate Professor of General Business, Management and Organization.

10

THE REQUIREMENTS OF QUALITY

INCREASED REVENUE FROM ALL SOURCES

The University has several major sources of revenue to fund present operations, as well as new ventures.

With the exception of private gifts, each of these revenue sources has considerable growth limitations. *Tuition and fees*, which provided 29.4 percent of the 1984 budget, cannot increase dramatically without affecting the number of prospective students who can afford to study at the University. *Government grants and contracts* for research, etc., 20 percent, has been limited in recent years. *Auxiliary fees* for services, 8 percent of the budget, are in exchange for activities which cost as much as the revenues. *Gifts* provide 7 percent. *State support* for the School of Medicine, 2.8 percent, consists primarily of a capitation grant to help the University defray the costs of medical education for Florida residents. *Income from Hospitals and clinics*, 30.2 percent, is fees-for-services-rendered which match out the revenue. *Income from endowment*, while it has grown over the years through philanthropy and careful management, still provide only 1.4 percent of the University budget and will always be limited as long as the University's financial reserves are relatively small (see table on this page). *All other sources* are responsible for 1.2 percent.

Thus, in the implementation of the Strategic Plan the Trustees and administration concluded that only *a major infusion of new funds*, with particular emphasis on endowment, would provide a sound financial base.

Consider the University's Endowment. Endowment income is the mechanism through which great private universities have become preeminent. Endowment funding is both permanent and flexible. As a reserve, it allows institutions to ride out bad times, and by wise investment it

allows institutions to benefit from good times. In this regard, the University has been especially diligent: over the five-year period ending May 1984, the University's endowment and annuity fund benefited by a 13.4 percent compound annual rate of return, compared to a 6.9 percent rise in the Consumer Price Index.

Yet even given top returns on investment, the endowment corpus is not yet of a size to make endowment a substantial source of revenue. The University must seek to increase its endowment by $150 million if it is to move to the front rank of private universities.

Comparative Endowments of Major Private Universities

Harvard Upiversity	$2,451,290,000
University of Chicago	539,500,000
Northwestern University	490,987,000
Washington University	460,759,000
Emory University	403,388,000
University of Pennsylvania	314,654,000
Johns Hopkins University	313,033,000
Duke University	206,097,000
Case Western Reserve	201,187,000
Carnegie-Mellon University	173,434,000
Boston University	93,152,000
St. Louis University	77,100,000
Syracuse University	73,480,000
University of Miami	66,342,000
Tufts University	61,502,000

Source: Chronicle of Higher Education, May 9, 1984

Endowed scholarships often make it possible for outstanding students to attend the University, including from left, Eleanor Knight, Christopher Lawdy and Michael Enkerlin.

28

THE REQUIREMENTS OF QUALITY

A PLAN FOR EXCELLENCE

Since the 1981 inauguration of Edward T. Foote II as fourth President of the University of Miami, the institution has been looking at the future with a special focus: what innovations in teaching and research could it provide in asserting its commitment to its global responsibilities while responding to the needs of its own region.

The University has undergone a period of self-examination and analysis. This process has included:

An *intensive two-year review* of the strengths and weaknesses of the University, with each school, college and division probing its potential and forecasting its requirements for the next decade.

An *objective assessment* of the University's schools and colleges, the libraries, and student services by 14 Visiting Committees, each chaired by a Trustee and composed of outstanding civic, professional and academic leaders.

A *Strategic Plan*, developed according to the rigorous standards of the corporate world, which matches the internal analysis of the schools to the recommendations of the Visiting Committees.

As the Strategic Plan was developed, it attracted national attention. George Keller, an authority on academic strategic planning, called the document "the finest strategic plan done by a major research university to date." Among the plan's key points are:

The University of Miami must strive for the highest quality in its teaching, research and public service.

The University must pursue a balanced course between a quality liberal arts education and the most innovative graduate and professional school curricula.

The University will stabilize enrollment, but will steadily increase the quality and diversity of its students.

The University will expand the faculty by 100–125 members to strengthen the student-faculty ratio.

The University will seize a unique opportunity to use its gateway position between two continents and a subcontinent to serve all of these geographic areas—as a Global University.

Because of its location, the University is in a position to pursue special research opportunities particularly in the areas of international studies, health, marine sciences, finance, international business and law, engineering, and relationships with a multi-ethnic community.

The University will strengthen its position among research universities and seek to increase the support it has received during the past two decades in research funding which has placed it in the top two percent of American institutions.

With the development of the Strategic Plan came a growing awareness of the University's unique position: a bold, energetic, visionary president; a committed Board of Trustees; a clearly defined plan of action; a developing and financially sound region; a quality faculty; and a geographic position as the only institution of its kind in the nation—and perhaps the world.

The exceptional possibilities inherent in the University's position are limited only by its small endowment. If the University is to move ahead as it should in preparation for the 21st century, its capital resources must be increased dramatically.

The Otto G. Richter Library is the intellectual focal point for all the schools and colleges of the University.

26

THE REQUIREMENTS OF QUALITY

INCREASED ENDOWMENT: $150,000,000

Here are some areas of endowment most in need of support.

New Endowment Funds for Faculty $75,000,000
Endowed chairs, lectureships, visiting professorships, lectureships, named professorships and research positions, all serve to invigorate and strengthen a faculty. They attract and retain renowned teacher-scholars and provide valuable incentives for younger faculty.

Increased Endowment for Student Assistance $50,000,000
The cost of an undergraduate education has soared. Many families must borrow to finance their children's education. Students who continue in graduate and professional school often graduate with large debts. Every effort has been made at the University of Miami to contain tuition increases, but the total costs, including room and board, now surpass $10,000 a year. More than 70 percent of our students receive assistance in some form.

Graduate students play a vital role in a research university. As scholar-apprentices, they work under the guidance of senior faculty, often devoting years to their work with little remuneration. In addition, most share with undergraduates the difficulty of financing their education, and most are independent of family support. These funds are to be used to assist these young scholars throughout the University. More financial assistance must be available both on a need and a merit basis to assist the University in attracting the most able students.

Increased Endowment for Research Support, Library Support and Program Development $25,000,000
The University has increased its annual funding for faculty research from all sources from $21.8 million to $33.5 million over the past 10 years. But not all research is immediately fundable from outside sources; some require support from University funds until it can gain attention of federal or other agencies or organizations; some can occur *only* with University funds. Young scholars often need assistance in establishing themselves and getting their work recognized.

The library collections at the University are strong, but each of the principal libraries has need for special collections to support teaching and research. These are in addition to acquisitions obtained with current operating budget funds.

Programs must constantly be refreshed if the University is to serve its students' interests and society's needs.

THE REQUIREMENTS OF QUALITY

FACILITIES AND EQUIPMENT: $125,000,000

While increased endowment is the most pressing campaign need, some new facilities and equipment are required in some areas if the University is to attain the excellence envisioned in the Strategic Plan.

Among the University's most urgent facilities needs are:

Physical and Geological Science Laboratory and Classroom Building: As a companion facility to the James M. Cox, Jr., Science Center.

Library Additions: Facilities at the Otto G. Richter Library and the Baron deHirsch Meyer Law Library are now at capacity, and expansions are needed for future acquisitions.

Music Studio/Office Building: The success of the School of Music has caused overcrowding of its facilities. Appropriate studio and office space to complete the School of Music complex is needed.

Graduate School of International Studies/North-South Center: The University plans to erect a facility to house GSIS faculty and students and provide a common meeting ground for international research and symposia. Given such a facility, the University can provide world leadership in this discipline.

Student Residential Colleges: In fall 1984, the University established an Honors Residential College for integrated academic, living and extracurricular activities. This concept has proven successful, and renovation and construction will provide four more residential colleges.

Convocation Center: The largest assembly hall on the Coral Gables campus is Maurice Gusman Concert Hall, which accommodates fewer than 600 persons. The University plans to construct a multi-purpose facility which would accommodate large events from athletics to commencement.

School of Medicine Research Buildings: Successful recruiting of talented new faculty has created an urgent need for 250,000 square feet of new research facilities, including Diabetes Research and Neurological Science Research centers.

Training and Administration Building, School of Medicine: The School of Medicine plans to construct needed classroom and administrative space, freeing areas to expand research.

Campus Master Planning and Beautification: To improve and enhance the campus environment by upgrading signage, parking and landscaping.

College of Engineering Addition: Growth of the College of Engineering requires laboratories, classrooms and faculty offices.

School of Business Administration Lecture Hall/Classroom Building: New programs in international business and information management require seminar classrooms and computer laboratories.

Art Museum/Arts Teaching Center
A new, more visible and centrally located Museum of the Arts on the Coral Gables campus with related teaching space is needed.

Drama and Theater Arts Building: The famed Ring Theater, one of the oldest buildings on the Coral Gables campus, should be replaced to serve the University and community with a broader range of cultural programs.

THE REQUIREMENTS OF QUALITY

THE CAMPAIGN STRATEGY

In developing the Campaign for the University of Miami, the Board of Trustees and administration have made certain key assumptions. These include:

The goal of $400 million is among the largest ever conducted by a major private research university in the nation and the largest in the history of the University. It will require an unprecedented effort and will have lasting impact on the University.

The Campaign is designed to seek major gifts for endowment, facilities and equipment and operating support.

Announced in December 1984, the Campaign runs for five years until the end of calendar year 1989.

All gifts are vital to the Campaign and the University.

All gifts from private sources, including research grants and documented bequest expectancies, will count toward the Campaign goal.

Because of the University's long-standing record of service to its region, the largest portion of gifts to the Campaign will come from individuals, corporations and foundations in the South Florida area which have reason to respect the University's achievements and its potential. But the Campaign will be far broader in scope and will involve every member of the University community—including those outside the United States.

Although donors will be encouraged to make their gifts unrestricted as to use (that is, to be applied as the Trustees and administration judge appropriate), there will be numerous opportunities for—and expectations of—gifts restricted to the special interests or concerns of the donor. There will be many named gift opportunities within the Campaign at a University that already lives with names such as Calder, Cox, Glasser, Hecht, Jenkins, Knight, Leach, Mailman, McArthur, McKnight, Meyer, Palmer, Richter, Rosenstiel and many others.

During the course of the Campaign for the University of Miami, annual giving solicitation will continue unabated, with an effort made to encourage donors to upgrade their annual support to the University even as they consider a capital gift to move the Campaign forward.

The key strategy for success of the Campaign is to create as much involvement as possible among friends and alumni who perceive the opportunity the Campaign raises for the entire University to take a giant step ahead in quality.

Considering the University of Miami's private character, relatively brief history and substantial funding requirements, participation at all levels is essential.

Drs. Karl Magleby and Owen McManus, both Associate Professors of Biophysics in the School of Medicine, study the function of muscle membrane. Their basic research work in ion transfer helps bring about better understanding of diseases of the nervous system.

36

THE REQUIREMENTS OF QUALITY

SUSTAINED AND ENHANCED GIVING FOR CURRENT OPERATIONS: $125,000,000

The major source of private funds for the University of Miami has been the support received through alumni and friends in annual giving to maintain current operations. These are the gifts which help fill the gap between tuition and what it actually costs to provide a university education.

Over the last five years, current operations support has ranged from $12 million to $20 million annually with the majority of these funds designated for specific purposes. Now the University has set a target amount of $25 million to be raised each year in the course of the Campaign for the University of Miami.

This ambitious goal will require that members of the University community not only make a gift to the Campaign for the University of Miami, but also their annual gift. In similar institutions, alumni often have been asked to increase significantly their annual contribution during a campaign. This goal also will require that those who have not previously given, begin to do so on a regular basis.

It is important to recognize that these monies support ongoing activities at the University and will be utilized directly to increase the quality of instruction, research and student financial assistance.

The Growing Willingness of Donors to Support the University of Miami
(Private Cash, Gifts and Grants in Support of Current Operations, 1978–79 to 1983–84)

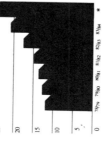

25

20

15

10

5

0

78/79 79/80 80/81 81/82 82/83 83/84 *

* Campaign Goal

Across the University, professors like Georgie Labadie, School of Nursing, make every effort to know and understand the goals of their students.

34

Figure 24.32. The gift-opportunities book, excerpted here, appeared in the flap of the case statement

Toward the 21st Century

The future of our nation and the world rests on the courage and commitment of a relative handful of individuals who have the knowledge and resources to create that future. Today's investment in education will determine whether or not our children are able to meet the unprecedented challenges that await them.

The mission of the University of Miami — to educate eager minds, to conduct research to increase humanity's wealth of knowledge; and to strengthen the community — responds to the incredible demands of our age. The University's record of research, teaching and public service is outstanding. That a great university now stands where 60 years ago there was none is a miracle of higher education. The University of Miami is in the right place at the right time. And with each success, its responsibility grows to provide the fertile ground for still more achievement. To meet this responsibility, the Campaign for the University of Miami was launched, a $400 million fund-raising drive to enhance the curriculum, strengthen the faculty, provide scholarship and fellowship assistance to students, and construct new facilities.

The Campaign for the University of Miami is an opportunity to participate in the establishment of a truly world-class university in a great international city. Gifts to the University are essential to maintain its vital role as Florida's only major private research university and its primary intellectual resource. Friends of the University are being asked to make an investment in those areas where it will bring the greatest return and where the donor's interests and concerns may be reflected. At this decisive moment in the University of Miami's history, donors can shape the University for the next decade and into the 21st century. Their names will join those who live in perpetuity through their generosity — names such as Calder, Cox, Curtiss, Glaser, Hecht, Jenkins, Knight, Leach, Mailman, McArthur, McKnight, Meyer, Palmer, Richter, Rosenstiel and many others. Because of its leadership role, the University of Miami offers a unique opportunity for great and lasting impact with every donor's gift.

The opportunities outlined here are based on the University's Strategic Plan, which establishes a clear path for a globally oriented University. Private support will enable the University of Miami to achieve the goals put forth in the Strategic Plan: to move into the front rank of American universities and to realize a vision for the University as a center for the educational, economic, and cultural aspirations of the region.

The following pages identify Campaign goals and the gift opportunities that fulfill them. Specific ways are suggested of associating the name of a person, family, foundation, or corporation with the University of Miami in perpetuity.

1

Gift Opportunities for Shaping the Future

THE CAMPAIGN FOR THE
UNIVERSITY OF

Miami

Endowment Support

> The best use of life is to invest it in something which will outlast life
> **William James**

Campaign Goal: **$150,000,000**

The heart of the Campaign for the University of Miami is the generation of endowment. the University's reserve fund which offers financial security and annual income through careful investment management. Since 19—, the annual return on the endowment has averaged 15.8 percent, ranking the University in the top 6 percent of nearly 3,000 major funds measured by a national brokerage house. University policy permits the spending of a constant fraction of the endowment's value, with additional earnings reinvested to safeguard the fund's permanence throughout changing economic conditions.

Endowed chairs, scholarships and fellowships, research and educational funds, and library acquisition funds are crucial to the quest for knowledge. Opportunities are available to endow an entire school or college, which may be named according to the wishes of the donor. In 1969, the University's Institute of Marine Science became the Rosenstiel School of Marine and Atmospheric Science in recognition of a major gift from the Rosenstiel family. Endowment funding, the mechanism by which great private universities have built their enduring quality, is crucial for the University to develop the strength of its programs and advance the diversity and intellectual breadth of its faculty and student body.

Creation of Endowed Chairs

Campaign Goal: **$75,000,000**

The gift of an endowed chair is among the most important contributions that can be made to the University of Miami, for the stimulation and sustenance of academic excellence begin with the faculty. The prestige of endowed professorships enable the University to attract and retain the best and most dedicated faculty. These gifts underwrite participation in teaching and research of uncompromised vigor, the most vital and fundamental activities of the University. A fully endowed chair will be named according to the wishes of the donor.

University Chair

$2,000,000

Those who hold a University chair are internationally respected scholars whose activities transcend the boundaries of traditional academic disciplines. A University Chairholder is a person who symbolizes appreciation for the accumulation and sharing of knowledge, for both their own sake and for the advancement of the human condition. A University Chair is not bestowed lightly, and it is not expected that more than two or three will be created by the University. Endowment of a University Chair provides for compensation for the chairholder and for the costs of staff and research support.

Graduate Fellowship Fund

$50,000 - $1,000,000

Graduate students, who are junior colleagues of the faculty and an important part of innovative faculty investigations, teach or assist in undergraduate courses.

Post-Doctoral Fellowship Fund

$500,000 - $1,000,000

Post-doctoral fellowships attract promising young scientists to the University by providing funds to continue a line of research and to work with the University's leading scientists and teachers. The fellowships also give the University the chance to assess potential new faculty members.

Endowment for the Libraries, Research, and Program Development

Campaign Goal: **$25,000,000**

One of the key functions of endowment funds is to preserve the spirit of venture at a university — to encourage new research, to explore new curricula, to provide new methodologies for learning, and to seek out new knowledge resources.

Instrumentation and Laboratory Fund

$150,000

Research laboratories throughout the University can only sustain their work if scientists have access to the most modern equipment. The ability to attract capable researchers depends in large measure on the University's ability to provide modern instrumentation maintained at peak condition.

Academic Program Funds

$100,000 - $500,000

Innovation within a progressive university is limited only by the availability of funds. Often, new programs can attract support through government or foundation grants once they are established. Academic Program Funds are, in effect, non-research seed money provided through endowment to fund broader or improved programs for students, the opportunity to obtain curriculum resources, and to provide outreach and service to the community. Programs identified for possible funding include: student exchange and study-abroad visits; a computer aided design laboratory; media and theatre productions; a trial advocacy program; and interdisciplinary medical programs.

Research Fund

$50,000 minimum

Basic and applied research seeks answers to fundamental questions of science, leading to advancement in technology, improvement in industry, progress in medicine, and understanding of human behavior. Endowed research funds support basic investigation in all academic areas. They are sought within the science, social science, and technology departments of the College of Arts and Sciences, the College of Engineering, and the School of Medicine; the Graduate School of International Studies; and in the School of Law. They are established by gifts of at least $50,000 to support the work of a

> All who have meditated on the art of governing mankind have been convinced that the fate of empires depends on the education of youth
> **Aristotle**

9

particular faculty member, to support a specific research project, or to support general work within a department, and may be named according to wishes of the donor.

Faculty Enhancement Fund   **$100,000 · $250,000 minimum**

These funds will create additional financial incentive for faculty members by using endowment income to supplement salaries of particularly distinguished professors, and to fund program-oriented projects of interest to faculty. Faculty enhancement endowments will help the University compete for and retain the best teachers and researchers.

Library Acquisition Fund   **$10,000 minimum**

The rapidly escalating cost of books and periodicals essential to research and teaching makes it difficult to acquire new titles. New books, monographs, and serials are needed to keep pace with the rapid advancement of knowledge in the various academic fields. Endowed book funds will be used to purchase books and other materials for the Richter Library, Medical Library, Law Library, and Marine Science Library. Acquisition funds will be acknowledged by a University Library bookplate, and may be established by gifts of $10,000. The Richter Library has set an overall goal of $8.5 million for book acquisition, and the Law Library has a book acquisition goal of $5 million.

Residential College Program   **$750,000**

Visiting Professor   **$50,000**

House Activity Fund

The University of Miami is committed to the expansion of a system of residential colleges to improve the quality of residential life and increase informal student-faculty contact. Patterned after successful residential college programs at prestigious institutions in the Northeast and Europe, the first residential colleges at the University have been met with tremendous enthusiasm by students. Gift opportunities are available to support activity within each college or to endow visiting professorships. Professors will live within a college for one term, and be available for informal programming and mentoring.

Facilities and Equipment

Campaign Goal: **$125,000,000**

Although increased endowment is the University's most pressing need, new facilities and equipment are required if the University is to attain the excellence envisioned in its Strategic Plan. Following are the most pressing capital needs facing the University of Miami — needs which must be addressed within the next five years. Each will be undertaken in accordance with the development of a campus master plan, assuring that new construction is attractive as well as functional. The University of Miami is committed to creating an architectural and landscaping atmosphere that reflects the uniqueness of being the only private research university in the sub-tropical United States. The gift dollar

The George W. Jenkins Building and the Elsa and William Stubblefield Classroom Tower of the School of Business Administration

---

Generosity to the University of Miami by individuals, families, organizations, and businesses is recognized in a number of ways. The most notable means of recognition is through the naming of a gift in accordance with the wishes of a donor. In this way, buildings, facilities, professorships, scholarships, and programs acquire names that honor or memorialize a person, family, organization, or business.

Recognition is also provided through membership in a series of University societies which represent levels of cumulative giving. Each year, members of these societies gather at the University's Donor Recognition Gala to welcome inductees. Individual members of the three highest recognition societies receive special gifts which signify their close association with the University of Miami. Organizations and businesses receive specially designed plaques which reflect their level of commitment to the University.

Membership in the different societies is also signified by medallions and ribbons worn by society members and presented to inductees at the annual Donor Recognition Gala. The highlight of the Gala is the induction ceremony publicly honoring the new members of each society.

Donor Recognition Societies

The George E. Merrick Society

The George E. Merrick Society honors those whose support to the University exceeds $1 million. In addition to a golden medallion on a golden chain, individual members of the Merrick Society receive a specially commissioned piece of Steuben crystal, in the shape of a tetrahedron, bearing the logo of the University of Miami and the society name.

Bowman Foster Ashe Society

The Bowman Foster Ashe Society honors those whose support to the University exceeds $500,000. Members of the Ashe Society receive a pewter medallion worn on a white ribbon and a specially commissioned piece of Steuben crystal, a Pyramid Block, bearing the University of Miami logo and the society name.

Ibis Society

The Ibis Society includes those whose total commitment to the University is greater than $250,000. Individual members of the this Society receive a copper medallion worn on an orange ribbon and a unique bronze sculpture of an ibis in flight created by artist Larry Hoff.

Society of University Founders

The Society of University Founders honors those whose total commitment to the University exceeds $50,000. Within this society, the level of Grand Founder recognizes those whose commitment exceeds $100,000. Founders are awarded a bronze medallion worn on a green and orange ribbon. The bronze medallions of Grand Founders are worn on a green ribbon.

Figure 24.33. A fact card on the University of Miami was not intended for general distribution but provided background for volunteer and staff activities

UNIVERSITY OF Miami
FACT FINDER 1987-88
INFORMATION RESOURCES
(305) 284-FACT

FOUNDED: 1925. Classes began October, 1926.

OFFICERS: Edward T. Foote II, President; James W. McLamore, Chairman, Board of Trustees.

ACCREDITATION: Southern Association of Colleges and Schools; 12 professional accrediting agencies.

SCHOOLS: The Coral Gables campus comprises two colleges and nine schools. The Schools of Medicine and Nursing, in Miami's civic center, form the hub of the fourth largest medical complex in the U.S. The Rosenstiel School of Marine and Atmospheric Science (RSMAS) is on Virginia Key in Biscayne Bay.

RESEARCH: Sponsored project expenditures totaled $68.3 million (1986-87). Ranked among top three percent of institutions receiving federal funds.

PROGRAMS: Approximately 180 undergraduate and 175 graduate and professional areas of study.

DEGREES AWARDED: 1,813 bachelor's, 620 master's, 426 JDs, 185 MDs, 118 other doctorates (1986-87).

STUDENT ENROLLMENT - FALL 1987

School (Founded)	Undergrad Degree	N-Deg	Grad	Prof	Total
Architecture ('83)	351	0	13	0	364
Arts-Sciences ('26)	3,124	0	437	0	3,560
Business ('29)	2,196	0	695	0	2,889
Communication ('85)	788	0	29	0	817
Cont Studies ('74)	0	208	0	0	208
Education ('29)	47	15	557	0	619
Engineering ('47)	1,147	0	196	0	1,343
Graduate ('41)	0	0	621	0	62
Int'l Studies ('83)	0	2	93	0	95
Law ('28)	0	0	0	1,426	1,426
Medicine ('52)	0	0	204	642	846
Music ('26)	529	7	173	0	709
Nursing ('68)	151	0	83	0	234
RSMAS ('69)	0	0	173	0	173
TOTAL	8,333	241	2,703	2,068	13,345

Full-Time	7,524	36	1,268	1,997	10,825
Part-Time	809	205	1,435	71	2,520
FTE	7,946	112	1,894	2,040	11,992

[1] Joint degree and interdisciplinary graduate students only.

Can't find the right fact?
Call (305) 284-FACT
Office of Planning and Institutional Research
University of Miami
Coral Gables, Florida 33124

(12-87)

NEW FRESHMEN STANDINGS: Over 40 percent graduated in the top fifth of their high school class with a combined SAT score of 1100 or higher.

HONORS PROGRAM/SOCIETIES: 1,445 students participating in the honors program (Fall, 1987). Nine campus-wide honor societies including Phi Beta Kappa.

CLASS SIZE: Over 50 percent of classes for undergraduates have fewer than 30 students; over 75 percent have fewer than 35 students.

RESIDENT STUDENTS: Approximately 3,800 live on campus, including over two-thirds of new freshmen and 42 percent of all undergraduates (Fall, 1987).

SPORTS: Men—baseball (1982 & 1985 NCAA champions), basketball, crew, cross-country, football (1983 NCAA champions), golf, swimming and diving, tennis, and track. Women—basketball, crew, cross-country, golf (1984 NCAA champions), swimming and diving, tennis, and track.

ALUMNI: Live in all 50 States and over 100 foreign countries; 39,000 reside in Florida, including 34,000 in Dade and Broward. More than 90,000 in UM's history.

COMPUTING FACILITIES: Ungar Center has an IBM 3081-KX, DEC VAX cluster 8650 and 8530, MicroVAX II, terminals and PCs. Additional hardware/student labs in residential colleges, library, and schools.

LIBRARIES: Richter (central facility), Law School, Medical School, Music School and RSMAS. Combined holdings of 1.6 million volumes, 16,000 periodicals, and 900,000 microforms (excluding government publications).

DEVELOPMENT: Five-year, $400 million fund-raising campaign announced December, 1984. $359 million (90 percent) pledged and/or received as of November, 1987.

ENROLLMENT BY GENDER - FALL 1987

	New Freshmen	Undergrad Degree N-Deg	Graduate & Prof	Total
Male	1,017	4,733	98	2,018	7,447
Female	717	3,600	145	2,153	5,898

RACIAL/ETHNIC DISTRIBUTION - FALL 1987

	New Freshmen Count	%[1]	Undergrad (Degree Only) Count	%[1]	Graduate & Prof Count	%[1]
White	1,186	72	4,835	60	2,432	66
Hispanic	301	18	1,980	25	759	21
Asian	47	3	587	7	264	7
Black	117	7	601	7	208	6
Amer Indian	2	0	18	0	10	0
Unknown	81	--	312	--	1,098	--
TOTAL	1,734		8,333		4,771	

GEOGRAPHIC ORIGINS - FALL 1987

	New Freshmen Count	%[1]	Undergrad (Degree Only) Count	%[1]	Graduate & Prof
Dade	435	25	3,320	40	2,555	54
Broward	152	9	707	8	423	9
Other Florida	200	12	667	8	305	6
Other U.S.	815	47	2,531	30	817	17
International	132	8	1,078	13	531	11
Non-U.S. Campus	0	0	30	0	52	1
TOTAL	1,734		8,333		4,771	

[1] Percentages may not total 100 due to rounding.

ANNUAL STUDENT COSTS

Tuition	1987-88
Undergraduate (12-18 Hrs)[1]	$ 9,787
1-11 Hours (per Hr)	395
Over 18 Hours (per Hr)	395
Graduate (per Hr), except RSMAS	400
RSMAS (per Hr)	9,878
Law (Day Program)	13,560
Medicine (MD Program)	
Room and Board[2]	$ 4,010

FINANCIAL AID AWARDED - 1986-87 (In Millions)[3]

Pell Grants and Federal Campus-Based Aid	$ 9.3
Federal Loans Certified by the University	16.7
State Funds (excluding Contract Programs)	5.4
Institutional Maintenance of Effort Funds	27.0
TOTAL	$58.4

UNIVERSITY-OWNED FACILITIES

Campus	Buildings	Sq Footage
Coral Gables	118	2,670,804
Medical School	26	979,359
RSMAS	7	246,489
South	18	43,049
Other Facilities	44	55,333
TOTAL	213	3,999,984

[1] Both semesters, including undergraduate fees.
[2] Based on residential college (double occupancy) and 20-meal plan.
[3] Revised awards may change some accounts slightly.

NEW STUDENT ENROLLMENT - FALL 1987

	Applied	Accepted	Enrolled
Undergraduate New Freshmen	4,430	4,550	1,734
New Transfers	1,800	1,185	660

Home School	New Freshmen	New Transfers	Total
Architecture	56	15	71
Arts-Sciences	862	228	1,090
Business	381	177	558
Communication	152	74	226
Engineering	187	83	270
Music	90	56	146
Nursing	6	27	33
TOTAL	1,734	660	2,394

CREDIT HOURS TAUGHT - FALL 1987[1]

Teaching School	Undergrad	Grad	Prof	Total
Architecture	4,222	167	0	4,389
Arts-Sciences	60,137	2,925	0	63,062
Business	24,207	6,300	0	30,597
Communication	5,995	121	0	6,116
Cont Studies	73	0	0	73
Education	2,649	3,097	0	5,746
Engineering	10,367	1,223	0	11,590
Int'l Studies	357	478	0	835
Law	0	0	20,587	20,587
Medicine	980	1,691	11,574	14,245
Music	7,550	1,175	0	8,725
Nursing	1,102	645	0	1,747
RSMAS	346	790	0	1,136
TOTAL	118,075	18,612	32,161	168,848

[1] Special plus regular credit hours taught.

FINANCIAL HIGHLIGHTS - 1986-87 (In Millions)[1]

What We Own	
Cash, Cash Equivalents and Investments	$ 168.0
Receivables	84.7
Land, Buildings and Equipment	352.9
Other Assets	18.2
TOTAL ASSETS	$ 623.8

What We Owe	
Services and Operating Expenses	90.0
Bonds and Notes Payable	90.4
TOTAL LIABILITIES	$ 180.4

Balance (What We Own Less What We Owe)	
Current Unrestricted Funds	$ 6.9
Current Restricted Funds	16.7
for Designated Purposes	7.8
Loan Funds	27.0
Endowment and Annuity Funds	115.6
Equity in Plant Funds Assets	286.1
TOTAL FUND BALANCES	$ 443.4

Sources of Current Revenues for Operations	
Student Tuition and Fees	$ 120.8
State Appropriation–Medical School	10.0
Gifts to All Funds: Endowment	28.2
Investment and Interest Income	97.8
Grants and Contracts, including Research	34.4
Auxiliary Enterprises	104.1
Patient Care	
Other Sources	2.6
TOTAL CURRENT REVENUES	$ 397.9

[1] From the University Annual Report for the fiscal year ended May 31, 1987.

FULL-TIME PERSONNEL - 1986-87[1]

Classification	Men	Women	Total
Faculty			
Architecture	17	2	19
Arts-Sciences	225	45	270
Business	85	11	96
Communication	18	7	25
Cont Studies	0	0	0
Education	26	10	36
Engineering	60	0	60
Int'l Studies	4	0	4
Law	37	10	47
Medicine	538	194	732
Music	52	10	62
Nursing	0	35	35
RSMAS	67	6	73
Other (Libraries)	19	33	52
TOTAL FACULTY	1,148	363	1,511
Administrative	374	445	819
Professional/Non-Faculty	138	206	344
Secretarial/Clerical	146	1,352	1,498
Technical/Paraprofessional	260	348	608
Skilled Crafts	104	1	106
Service/Maintenance	127	59	186
TOTAL PERSONNEL	2,297	2,774	5,071

[1] Affirmative Action Report for the fiscal year ended May 31, 1987. At time of publication, 60 additional administrative and 419 clerical/technical personnel are reported for Bascom Palmer Eye Institute.

Figure 24.34. A campaign newsletter was circulated throughout the effort

UNIVERSITY OF MIAMI   SUMMER 1988

CAMPAIGN CONTACT

CAMPAIGN TOPS $400 MILLION MARK

In 1984, when the University of Miami announced its five-year Campaign to raise $400 million, skeptics said it just could not be done.

Granted, the UM is a top-flight institution, and the community's primary cultural and intellectual center. But how could a 58-year-old university, with more than half its alumni having graduated since 1972, raise that kind of money? Many thought it unlikely that such a young university could succeed at what was then the second most ambitious fund-raising campaign in the history of higher education.

The skeptics were proved wrong. Very wrong. In fact, the Campaign for the University of Miami had reached $403.9 million as of April 9, 1988, surpassing its $400 million target 19 months ahead of schedule. But this does not mean that the Campaign is over. The five-year fund-raising effort will continue until its December 1989 completion date.

"This is a great day for the University of Miami," James W. McLamore, chairman of The Campaign for the University of Miami and of the UM Board of Trustees, said in announcing the achievement at the Donor Recognition Gala on April 9. "Though we are celebrating the advent of this milestone today, tomorrow we go back to work to meet the many needs that still exist. We have only 19 months remaining in which to secure the additional support necessary to meet our goals."

"We are extremely grateful to our friends and neighbors in South Florida for their commitment to making

the University of Miami one of the nation's truly great universities," said Edward T. Foote II, president of the University of Miami. "This would not have been possible without Jim McLamore and the hundreds of volunteers who are doing a superb job."

More than 75 percent of the financial commitments to the University of Miami's Campaign came from individuals, corporations, organizations and foundations in Dade, Broward and Palm Beach counties. "This broad-based community support for a fund-raising effort this large is incredible for a university that is only 61 years old. One would expect this from a much older school, which has several generations of alumni to support it," McLamore added.

An unusually large portion of the Campaign's commitments were made by individuals who are not alumni — some 45 percent of the 131,000 commitments made to the Campaign.

"We haven't yet really contacted alumni," said McLamore. "We've just launched the very important alumni phase of the Campaign. Headed by Charles Rice, president, chairman and CEO of Barnett Banks, Inc., it will give alumni an opportunity to give something back to their alma mater."

In addition to attracting most of its support from the community, the Campaign has amassed several other accomplishments. Between May 1983 and May 1987, the University of Miami's endowment grew from $66 million to $112 million as a result of Campaign gifts and en-

▲ *University of Miami President Edward T. Foote II, and Campaign Chairman James W. McLamore toast the University's supporters for helping the Campaign surpass its $400 million target at the Donor Recognition Gala.*

dowment management. During the same period, annual cash gifts and grants to the University of Miami increased 142 percent from $24 million in 1983 to $58 million in 1987. Thirty-six new endowed chair funds for distinguished professors will raise the University's total from 15 to 51.

With 67 donors committing $1 million or more, the Campaign's largest benefactor is the Harcourt M and Virginia W. Sylvester Foundation, whose $32.5 million commitment — $5 million of which recently topped off the Campaign — should generate more than $77 mil-

lion over 30 years. This is the largest complete gift in the history of the University. These funds will go to build the Sylvester Comprehensive Cancer Center, establish three endowed chairs and provide medical faculty support.

A charitable trust formed by James L. Knight will generate $56.25 million for the University over a period of 27 years. Only $20 million, the present value, has been counted toward the Campaign. The Knight gift will provide support for the Bascom Palmer Eye Institute and

Continued page 2

Figure 24.35. Prospect profile

```
                       UNIVERSITY OF MIAMI
                       INDIVIDUAL PROFILE
                          CONFIDENTIAL
            (Prepared by the Office of Development Research)

     NAME:

     HOME ADDRESS:

     POSITION:

     BUSINESS ADDRESS:

     BIRTHDATE:

     EDUCATION:

     FAMILY STATUS:

     CAREER HISTORY:

     CORPORATE, FOUNDATION & PROFESSIONAL AFFILIATIONS:

     UM AFFILIATIONS & SPECIAL FACULTY/STAFF RELATIONSHIPS:

     UM GIVING HISTORY:   Personal:

     UM GIVING INTERESTS (OVER $200):

     GIFTS TO OTHER INSTITUTIONS:

     INDICATORS OF WEALTH:    (When blank, information not available)
     Estimated Net Worth
     Home Value:
     Known Stock Holdings:
     Known Dividend Income:
     Other:

     CIVIC, SOCIAL, POLITICAL & RELIGIOUS AFFILIATIONS:

     POSSIBLE CULTIVATORS/SOLICITORS:

     CULTIVATION RECORD:

     COMMENTS:

     Development Research
     CSB:
```

Figure 24.36. Progress report

```
                                          Progress Report Worksheet
                                          Revised June 23, 1988


              THE CAMPAIGN FOR THE UNIVERSITY OF MIAMI

                      PROGRESS   REPORT

                     _____ 1988




                    Nucleus Fund    Cumulative                    Cumulative
                       as of          as of                         as of
                    November 1984  _____ 1987    _____          _____ 1988
                                                   1987

GIFTS AND PLEDGES:  $ xx,xxx,xxx   _____   _____    _____

PLANNED GIFTS:        xx,xxx,xxx   _____   _____    _____

TOTALS:             $ xx,xxx,xxx   _____   _____    _____

Percent of Goal:                     _____%                      _____%




                                                                   as of
                              MEDICAL                            _____ 1987

                      GIFTS AND PLEDGES:                         _____

                      PLANNED GIFTS:                            _____

                      TOTAL:                                    _____

                      Percent of Campaign Total                  _____%




Prepared By:  Development Services
              Report #1

              _____
```

Figure 24.37 Cumulative report work sheet

CUMULATIVE REPORT SUMMARY WORKSHEET   REVISED June 23, 1988

Cumulative through _____

	(3)+(4)+(6) TOTAL COMMITMENT	(3) + (5) TOTAL CASH	(3) GIFTS & GRANTS	(4) PLEDGES	(5) PAYMENTS	(6) PLANNED GIVING
ANALYSIS BY SOURCE:						
Alumni						
Non-alumni Individuals						
Corporations						
Foundations						
Organizations						
TOTALS						
TRUSTEE ANALYSIS:						
Trustee Individuals						
Trustee-related Entities						
TOTALS						
ANALYSIS BY PURPOSE:						
Endowment						
Facilities & Equipment						
Current Operations						
TOTALS						

NOTES:
Columns (3) & (5) represent all gifts, grants and payments received since 6/1/83, and those to the President's Contingency Fund received since 6/1/81.

Column (4) represents all pledges received since 6/1/83 and pledges to the President's Contingency Fund received since 6/1/81.

Column (6) represents irrevocable gifts held in trust outside the University received since 6/1/81, and documented bequest reports from testators over age 65 and received since 6/1/81.

Prepared by: Development Services
               Report #2
               Date

Figure 24.38. Planned giving report

```
                        UNIVERSITY OF MIAMI
                     DIVISION OF DEVELOPMENT
                      PLANNED GIVING REPORT
                      (Strictly Confidential)

                      as of XXXXX XX, 1989
                           Total Backlog

    Bequest Receivables¹                        $   XX,XXX,XXX²
    Gift Annuities                                  XX,XXX,XXX
    Trust Receivables¹                               X,XXX,XXX

         Total                                   $  XXX,XXX,XXX

                           Total Campaign

    Bequest Receivables¹                        $  XXX,XXX,XXX³
    Gift Annuities                                  XX,XXX,XXX⁴
    Trust Receivables¹                               X,XXX,XXX⁵

         Total                                   $  XXX,XXX,XXX


    Cash Received from Matured Bequests & Trusts
       Unrestricted                             $  XXX,XXX,XXX⁶
       Other Purposes                              XX,XXX,XXX⁶

         Total                                   $  XXX,XXX,XXX

                    Total Fiscal Year-to-Date
                     (06/01/88 - 04/30/89)

    Bequest Receivables¹                        $   XX,XXX,XXX
    Gift Annuities                                  XX,XXX,XXX
    Trust Receivables¹                                X,XXX,XXX⁷

         Total                                   $  XXX,XXX,XXX


    Cash Received from Matured Bequests & Trusts
       Unrestricted                             $  XXX,XXX,XXX
       Other Purposes                              XX,XXX,XXX

         Total                                   $  XXX,XXX,XXX
```

¹ The word "Receivables" means that this amount is reduced as cash arrives.
² Includes Bequests in Probate.
³ Includes Bequests in Probate and documented Bequest Reports from testators over age 65 and reported since 06/01/81.
⁴ Includes Gift Annuities received since 06/01/83. Recorded in "Cash" on Campaign report.
⁵ Includes Trusts received since 06/01/83. Includes Lead Trusts. XXXXXX Trust included at $20 million.
⁶ Includes Cash received since 06/01/83.
⁷ Does not include Lead Trusts according to CFAE standards.

Prepared by: Development Services
              Report #7
              May 16, 1989

Figure 24.39. Goals report

```
                                                    REVISED June 24, 1988


                              GOALS REPORT WORKSHEET


                              _____



                                                                    % OF GOAL
SOURCE:                         GOAL              ACTUAL            REACHED

Corporations              $  45,500,000      $ _____        _____%

Foundations                  28,700,000        _____        _____%

Individuals & Organizations 325,800,000        _____        _____%

     TOTALS               $ 400,000,000         _____        _____%




PURPOSE:

Endowment                 $ 150,000,000      $ _____        _____%

Facilities and Equipment    125,000,000        _____        _____%

Current Operations          125,000,000        _____        _____%

     TOTALS               $ 400,000,000         _____        _____%




Prepared by:   Development Services
               Report #4
```

Figure 24.40. Gift-range work sheet

REVISED June 24, 1988

GIFT RANGE TABLE SUMMARY WORKSHEET

Cumulative through _____

RANGE	NUMBER OF COMMITMENTS	FOR A TOTAL OF	NUMBER OF COMMITMENTS	FOR A TOTAL OF
$ 25,000,000 - +	1	$ 25,000,000	_____	_____
15,000,000 - 24,999,999	2	30,000,000	_____	_____
10,000,000 - 14,999,999	4	40,000,000	_____	_____
5,000,000 - 9,999,999	6	30,000,000	_____	_____
3,000,000 - 4,999,999	10	30,000,000	_____	_____
2,000,000 - 2,999,999	15	30,000,000	_____	_____
1,000,000 - 1,999,999	25	25,000,000	_____	_____
	63	$ 210,000,000	_____	_____
500,000 - 999,999	100	50,000,000	_____	_____
250,000 - 499,999	200	50,000,000	_____	_____
100,000 - 249,999	300	30,000,000	_____	_____
	600	$ 130,000,000	_____	_____
50,000 - 99,999	300	15,000,000	_____	_____
25,000 - 49,999	600	15,000,000	_____	_____
10,000 - 24,999	1,000	10,000,000	_____	_____
5,000 - 9,999	2,000	10,000,000	_____	_____
	3,900	$ 50,000,000	_____	_____
Below 5,000	MANY	$ 10,000,000	_____	_____
TOTALS		$ 400,000,000	_____	_____

Prepared by: Development Services
Report #5

Figure 24.41. School report

THE CAMPAIGN FOR THE UNIVERSITY OF MIAMI

REVISED June 24, 1988

CONFIDENTIAL

SCHOOL REPORT

cumulative through 1989

SCHOOL	TOTAL COMMITMENT	PERCENT OF CAMPAIGN TOTAL TO DATE
Architecture	_____	_____._____
Arts & Sciences	_____	_____._____
Athletics	_____	_____._____
Business	_____	_____._____
Communication*	_____	_____._____
Continuing Studies	_____	_____._____
Education	_____	_____._____
Engineering	_____	_____._____
Graduate School	_____	_____._____
International Studies	_____	_____._____
Law	_____	_____._____
Library (Richter)	_____	_____._____
Medicine**	_____	_____._____
BPEI	_____	_____
Mailman	_____	_____
Music	_____	_____._____
Nursing	_____	_____._____
RSMAS	_____	_____._____
Other***	_____	_____._____
Unrestricted****	_____	_____._____
TOTALS	_____	_____._____

*   Prior to 6/85 included in Arts & Sciences

**   Includes: Bascom Palmer Eye Institute and Mailman Center

***   Includes: Lowe Art Museum; Residence Halls; Student Affairs; Financial Aid
          (scholarships not restricted to schools); Campus Beautification;
          Citizens Board; Pledges where payments go to various areas; gifts
          awaiting designation.

**** Includes: Unrestricted Endowment listed under Endowment in other reports

Prepared by: Development Services
          Report #6
          Date

Figure 24.42. A pledge-aging schedule was used to estimate income per year from these pledges

PLEDGE AGING SCHEDULE

DONOR NAMES	OVERDUE	FY 89	FY 90	FY 91	FY 92	FY 93	FY 94	FY 95	FY 96	FY 97	TOTAL
Doe, John M.		5,000									5,000
Smith, Betty S.			2,000								2,000
Doe, John M.		5,000	5,000								10,000
Smith, Betty S.		2,500	2,500	5,000	2,500						12,500
Doe, John M.			2,000								2,000
Smith, Betty S.	10,000	10,000	10,000								30,000
Doe, John M.	7,000	2,500	2,500								12,000
Smith, Betty S.			1,630	10,000							11,630
Doe, John M.			8,000								8,000
Smith, Betty S.			2,000	2,000	2,000						6,000
Doe, John M.	2,000		2,000								10,000
Doe, John M.	2,000	2,000	2,000								6,000
Smith, Betty S.		2,000	2,000	2,000	2,000						8,000
Doe, John M.			1,000	1,000							2,000
Smith, Betty S.	15,000	10,000	10,000								35,000
Doe, John M.	1,000										1,000
Smith, Betty S.	2,000										2,000
Doe, John M.		1,000	1,000	1,000		1,000					4,000
Smith, Betty S.		2,000	2,000								4,000
Doe, John M.			10,000								10,000
Smith, Betty S.		2,000	2,000								4,000
Doe, John M.		2,500									2,500
Smith, Betty S.				500	1,000	2,000	2,000	2,000			7,500
Doe, John M.			1,000								1,000
Smith, Betty S.				1,000					1,000		1,000
Doe, John M.		200	200	200	200						800
Smith, Betty S.			100	100	100	100	100	100	100	100	800
Doe, John M.	10,000	10,000	10,000	10,000	10,000	10,000					50,000
TOTAL	**$37,000**	**$49,200**	**$89,930**	**$32,800**	**$21,300**	**$13,100**	**$3,100**	**$3,100**	**$1,100**	**$100**	**$250,730**

Prepared by: Development Services

Figure 24.43. This briefing paper was used to help introduce the university and the campaign to new corporate prospects. It was updated monthly and personalized for specific companies.

THE UNIVERSITY OF MIAMI:

A BRIEFING PAPER

FOR

THE CORPORATE COMMUNITY

UNIVERSITY OF MIAMI
Development Division
Coral Gables, Florida
AUGUST 1988

I. INTRODUCTION

No world-class community has anything less than a world-class university. The University of Miami is making remarkable strides in becoming such an institution, by advancing the quality of its student body and enhancing its standing as a private research university with a global focus.

The process of transformation from a sub-regional to truly national institution is reflected in the Campaign for The University of Miami. What follows is a general description of the University of Miami, the progress it has made during its brief history, the process being undertaken toward entering the top-rank of American universities, and the fund-raising effort underway to meet the cost of advancement.

II. THE PROGRESS OF THE UNIVERSITY OF MIAMI

Only 61 years old, the University of Miami is the largest private institution of higher education in the southeastern United States and the only private research university in the state of Florida. It has a solid core of excellent faculty, dynamic academic and administrative leadership, and a record of sound fiscal management. The University has operated within a balanced budget for ten of the past eleven years. The total operating budget for 1988 is $418 million.

The University of Miami has always served South Florida as its primary institution of higher learning. (Until 1972 it was the only university in South Florida.) More than 34,000 University of Miami alumni live and work in South Florida. An economic study by Coopers & Lybrand indicates that alumni in Florida earn an additional $357 million annually because of their education. As a direct economic entity, the University has an impact of about $1.25 billion on the region's economy; it is the fifth largest private employer in Dade County.

The University stands among the top three percent of all American colleges and universities in receipt of federal support for research and other programs. Sponsored research project expenditures were $82.5 million in Fiscal Year 1987. Many members of the faculty have won international recognition for their academic work. For example, Isaac Bashevis Singer, the 1978 recipient of the

Nobel Prize for literature, is a lecturer on the English faculty as is novelist James Michener.

During the fall, 1987 semester the University provided undergraduate, graduate, and professional education to 13,345 credit-seeking students. Among this number are 1,741 international students representing 115 countries. The University's fourteen academic divisions offer 133 undergraduate and 175 graduate degree programs. The basic academic divisions of the University are architecture, arts and sciences, business, communication, continuing studies, education, engineering, graduate studies, international studies, law, medicine, music, nursing, and marine and atmospheric science. These are supplemented and strengthened by interdisciplinary centers in law and economics, quality, molecular and cellular evolution, theoretical studies, child development, medicine, energy, international studies, and marine and atmospheric science.

Increasingly, the finest students are choosing to attend the University. Over the past seven years the average combined SAT scores of entering freshmen has climbed from 100 to 200 points above the national average, and presently stands at 1106. Since 1984, more high school valedictorians and salutatorians of Florida high schools chose the University of Miami for their college careers than any other Florida college or university. This past fall, the University attracted 54 valedictorians (including 32 from Florida high schools) among its 1,734 freshmen. Some 30 percent of the freshman class graduated in the top ten percent of their high school class. Among freshmen, 7.1 percent are black and 18.2 percent are Hispanic. In 1983 the University of Miami became one of the small minority of institutions to shelter a chapter of Phi Beta Kappa, and in the fall of 1987 the first award of a Rhodes Scholarship was made to a University of Miami undergraduate.

III. THE LOCAL, REGIONAL AND NATIONAL ROLE OF THE UNIVERSITY

For the first 46 years of its existence, the University of Miami was the only institution of higher learning in South Florida, functioning as would a public university for Greater Miami. The University helped organize the first professional orchestra in the area, and opened the first art museum. The School of Music continues to present more than 300 performances a year by its students, faculty and visiting artists, and the Lowe Art Museum houses the major art collection in South Florida. For all the good work done by the other important educational, charitable, cultural and civic organizations in

greater Miami, none can begin to compare to the breadth and scope of the influence of the University of Miami.

The University of Miami has always provided — and continues to teach and train — many of the managers, teachers, doctors, lawyers and judges, scientists and researchers, engineers, architects, musicians, accountants and countless other professionals needed in Florida. The major change over the past several years is that the University is also helping to educate and train a growing number of students from markets all across the nation.

In particular, the southeast United States, as it becomes increasingly urbanized and more international in its outlook, is becoming increasingly dependent on the University of Miami to provide specialized talent and expertise. The University is committed to serve the community by its charter, and the degree of service has progressed in stride with advancing academic strength.

Public service is perhaps most obvious through the University of Miami School of Medicine/Jackson Memorial Medical Center which provides sophisticated services such as the Burn Center, High Risk Neo-Natal Intensive Care Unit, Spinal Chord Injury Rehabilitation Unit, and sophisticated diagnostic and treatment facilities through many of its departments. These capabilities have made the University of Miami/Jackson Memorial Medical Center a major medical resource for the southeastern United States, the Caribbean and Latin America. The reputation of its ophthalmologic services at the Bascom-Palmer Eye Institute draws patients from around the world. The School is consistently recognized as one of the finest in the United States, with a wide range of strength in teaching, research and patient care. The Medical Center is ranked sixteenth among the top 25 such facilities in the nation.

As an integral part of a city that is a center of international business activity, the University of Miami functions as a global institution. Virtually every department of the University contributes to the education or betterment of the surrounding community and to the international themes of the region. For example:

* The wide range of research at the Rosenstiel School of Marine and Atmospheric Science helps protect and improve the quality of Biscayne Bay and helps to investigates global issues in science and policy involving the interaction of sea and air;

* The School of Nursing has one of the few gerontology nursing courses in the country and a trend-setting program in cross-cultural nursing;

* The School of Education provides a wide range of consulting, technical assistance and training services for Dade and Broward County Public Schools, and special training projects for school districts throughout Florida and the Caribbean;

* Professional seminars, special programs, and continuing studies reach about 17,000 people a year in presentations held on-campus, at the Knight Conference Center in downtown Miami, the Koubek Center in the Hispanic community, and at other locations within South Florida;

* The Executive Conference Program gives top and middle managers the opportunity to interact with experts in business, education, and government about problems facing the business community;

* The International Business and Banking Institute provides research and consulting services on matters of international business and finance;

* The Corporate Affiliate programs of the School of Business Administration and the College of Engineering provide general and technical information, consulting services, and recruitment assistance;

* The issues of productivity, quality, and the ability to compete internationally are being addressed by new interdisciplinary programs being developed within the College of Engineering and the School of Business Administration;

* The School of Law presents extensive international legal expertise in its curriculum and through special seminars;

* The Graduate School of International Studies specializes in regional studies, data collection, and policy studies on Cuba, Latin America, the Middle East, and Eastern Europe.

* The HERE Program (Higher Education/Relevant Experience) is specifically designed to help assure access to private higher education for black students by providing scholarships, part-time and summer employment, and a mentor from the business community;

* MEDD, a program involving the schools of Continuing Studies, Education, and Medicine, provides training in microcomputer education and helps find jobs for the "employment disabled".

* The intercollegiate athletic program consistently fields nationally competitive teams in football, baseball, basketball, crew, cross-country, golf, swimming and diving, tennis and track. National championships in football (1983 and 1987), baseball (1982 and 1985), and women's golf (1984) have been an immense source of pride for the entire state.

IV. THE CAMPAIGN FOR THE UNIVERSITY OF MIAMI

The University of Miami is now conducting a comprehensive campaign, scheduled to conclude in December 1989. It is presently the fourth largest fund-raising project now underway at an American university and is rooted in a clearly defined set of needs and priorities. The funds will be used to increase endowment significantly, expand and improve facilities and equipment, and enhance operating support.

The needs to be addressed have been defined through an intensive and continuing process of self-examination and analysis. The result of this two-year effort was a five-year Strategic Plan for every segment of the University. The plan was first published in 1983 and is updated annually. It relates to the University's commitment, to "reshape itself into a highly selective private university which offers programs of the highest caliber to discerning students seeking a quality education." Conscious decisions were made to become a smaller, more academically elite institution, and to reposition the University from a predominantly sub-regional institution to one of significant national impact and international stature.

The Campaign is specifically designed to reduce dependence on tuition to finance annual operations and to increase funds for program enhancement. Over a long period of time, increased endowment funds -- both restricted and unrestricted -- will produce significant income that can be used for operating expense. That is why the Campaign is seeking to increase endowment by $150 million. (At the beginning of the Campaign the total endowment value was $75 million. Through gifts and appreciation, its value is now approximately $120 million.) The other broad goals of the Campaign are $125 million for facilities and equipment and $125 million for operating support during the period of the Campaign.

The Campaign has enjoyed stunning success. By the end of July 1988 the Campaign had reached $414.9 million in total commitments. of this amount, 14.5 percent -- $60.8 million -- has come from corporations. Examples of major corporate support (including subsidiaries and corporate foundations) are:

[insert list of corporations and amount of campaign support]

6

Despite this success, much remains to be accomplished. Critical needs continue for new buildings, for new laboratories and equipment, endowed faculty positions, and endowed scholarships. Projected cutbacks in federal funds for student aid, program development and basic research must also be anticipated.

VIII. CONCLUSION

The University of Miami welcomes the responsibility inherent in seeking to become a great university. Greatness, however, is unyielding in its demands, and requires a full complement of resources. Although the success of the Campaign is helping to advance the University, much remains to be accomplished. The University of Miami is pleased to invite the continuing interest of the corporate community in the University's progress and its participation at this critical moment in this remarkable philanthropic enterprise.

Figure 24.44. The development office staff at Miami produced a basic planning document for the campaign wthat was revised annually

UNIVERSITY OF MIAMI
Development Division

Revised
Goals and Action Plans

FY 1987-1990

A. Plan, execute and manage the Campaign for the University of Miami

1. Generate 1987-88 cash returns of $50 million (+25%) and annual increases thereafter of at least 15% (1987-88 goal minimum: $66 million). (Status: In 1987 generated $58.4 million; up 46.6%)

2. Increase the pool of rated prospects to 750 for gifts of $100,000 and up by May 31, 1988. Increase the pool to 1,000 by May 31, 1990. (Status: little progress made to initial goal of 900 by 1987; a continuing process)

3. Complete initial solicitation on 40 prospects for gifts of $1 million or more by May 31, 1987. Complete initial solicitation on 40 prospects for gifts of $1 million or more per year through 1990. (Status: 22 solicitations accomplished in 1987)

4. Conduct solicitation of at least 30 prospects by each fund raiser, and three prospects by each volunteer. (Status: new)
Estimated One-Time Cost: none beyond budgeted expense
Estimated Recurring Costs: none beyond budgeted expense
Anticipated Benefits: increased use of development officers in direct fund raising, for review for goal setting in FY 1989

5. Secure funding for sixteen endowed chairs within fiscal 1987 and again in 1988. (Status: goal for 1987 achieved)

6. Secure funding for two additional residential colleges by May 31, 1987 and two more by May 31, 1988. (Status: not accomplished)

7. Establish President's Fund as vehicle for raising unrestricted funds, with an initial goal of $2 Million (Status: new)
Estimated One-Time Cost: none
Estimated Recurring Costs: approximately $96,000 per year for staff and recognition activity
Anticipated Benefits: increase acquisition of unrestricted funds

8. Increase commitments for scholarships, fellowships and loan funds by 20% to $1,500,000 in 1988, and by at least 15% per year thereafter through 1991. (Status: new)
Estimated One-Time Cost: none beyond budgeted expense
Estimated Recurring Costs: none beyond budgeted expense
Anticipated Benefits: increase available student financial aid

9. Increase commitments for laboratories and equipment by 15% to $4,000,000 and increase by at least 15% a year thereafter through 1991. (Status: new)
Estimated One-Time Cost: none beyond budgeted expense
Estimated Recurring Costs: none beyond budgeted expense
Anticipated Benefits: stimulate lab renovation, the equipping of new facilities, and help faculty recruitment

87-90 Goals and Objectives - Development Division   2

10. Implement the new prospect tracking system and evaluate its effectiveness as a tool for the management of prospects in the $100,000 and above range. Refine as appropriate and train staff in its use by May 31, 1987. (Status: accomplished)

11. Include at least 500 major and leadership gift prospects at no less than one event annually. Action being changed to inclusion of 100 Leadership Gift prospects in primary events for 1987-88. (Status: actual number was approximately 125 in 1987, including Major Gift prospects.)

12. Initiate an annual series of five President's Forums for select groups 20 prospects each. (Status: two conducted in 1987; they will continue to be held)

13. Assure that 40 solicitations occur through the Major Gifts Committee and 20 occur through the Corporations Committee for 1987 and 1988. (Status: 15 Major Gifts solicitations conducted)

14. Increase by 50 the number of volunteers actively engaged in Campaign committees. (Status: not achieved; a continuing objective)

15. Establish the volunteer structure for the School of Medicine component of the Campaign by May 31, 1987. (Status: accomplished)

16. Increase by 25% annually the number of donors who qualify for recognition at levels of $50,000 and above. (Status: increase of 16 percent in 1987; a continuing program)

17. Inaugurate the alumni phase of the Campaign through establishment of the National Alumni Sponsoring Committee by May 31, 1987. (Status: top leadership recruited; structure being put into place)

18. Plan and implement a rating and screening framework to identify alumni prospects with gift potential of $10,000 and above, by May 31, 1987. (Status: being implemented)

19. Plan and implement a planned gift marketing program that will include solicitations for current gifts and create a recognition society for bequestors and life insurance donors by May 31, 1987. (Status: deferred; new target date is May 31, 1988)

20. Update and/or create necessary Campaign publications and audio-visual material. (Status: a continuing process)

21. Reassess Campaign goals, progress and priorities on a quarterly basis each year. (Status: being done on schedule)

87-90 Goals and Objectives - Development Division   4

for development officers and support staff occurring on a regular basis)

2. Continue to develop increasingly effective quantitative mechanisms for measuring progress, recognizing trends, and developing forecasts. (Status: a continuing process)

3. Continue the development/University Relations interactive on-line database project for completion in 1986-87 and train staff in its use by May 31, 1987. (Status: phase one on-line; phase two set for completion by 12/87)

4. Improve employee working conditions by correcting the severe deficiencies of the Ponce Building. (Status: new air conditioning system installed; renovation scheduled for January-February, 1988)

5. Develop in-house capability to develop large-scale, stratified mailings by May 31, 1988. (Status: on schedule; tied to phase two of the database project)

9/5/87
ddc

87-90 Goals and Objectives - Development Division   3

B. Initiate additions and refinements to programs in order to accelerate high yields during the term of the Campaign and set the stage for post-Campaign fund raising.

1. Improve the Annual Fund donor acquisition and donor upgrading programs to generate $1.5 million cash (+15%) by May 31, 1987, and annual increases thereafter to generate $3 million by May 31, 1991. (Status: on target and on schedule)

2. Create a new recognition society to improve cultivation and solicitation of annual donors of $1,000 and above by May 31, 1987. First year target: 500 members. Target increases by 25% per year through May 31, 1992. (Status: cultivation and implementation underway)

3. Improve alumni telephone campaign results by training volunteers in solicitation and gift upgrading techniques. (Status: accomplished; results improved by 26.1%)

4. Increase the percentage of alumni response to solicitations to meet the national average (26%) by May 31, 1989. (Status: up to 20% for 1987)

5. Institute a parent involvement program by May 31, 1987. Increase parent gift total by 15% by May 31, 1987 and by 20% annually thereafter through May 31, 1992. (Status: program instituted in 1987 and continuing)

6. Improve alumni records by reducing the percentage of lost alumni from 21% to 16% by May 31, 1988. (Status: lost alumni remain static at about 22%)

7. Conduct an alumni survey by May 31, 1987 preparatory to publishing an alumni directory by September 30, 1988. (Status: deferred for further review later this year)

8. Develop and deliver at least 150 proposals to foundations and corporations annually through Coral Gables Campus. (Status: 65 sent in 1987; 150 is the continuing goal)

9. Develop improved procedures for clearing proposals to foundations and corporations. (Status: some progress made; will continue in cooperation with Provost's Office)

10. Increase fund raising of schools and colleges by 45% by May 31, 1987. Increase by 15% per year thereafter. (Status: accomplished)

C. Improve the effectiveness and productivity of Development Operations.

1. Enhance staff professional skills and knowledge through an annual program of education and training. (Status: education and training

A Final Word to Those Who Would Succeed

Make no little plans. They have no magic to stir men's blood and probably themselves will not be realized. Make big plans; aim high in hope and work, remembering that a noble, logical diagram once recorded will never die, but long after we are gone will be a living thing, asserting itself with evergrowing insistency. Remember that our sons and grandsons are going to do things that would stagger us. Let your watchword be order and your beacon beauty. Think big.

Daniel Burnham

Acknowledgments

Many people provided materials and thoughts for this book, but I particularly want to thank a few who helped significantly: Janice Fritsch, who helped prepare the first draft and saved the disks; Martha Hewson, the editor who brought clarity and organization to the project; Jackie Balthaser and Steve Hirt, who helped in the transition to Taft; Bob Elster and Chuck Lean, who guided Taft's input, and Dave Dunlop, who shared the basics about major gifts fund-raising with me over the years. Also the following people who took considerable time to provide materials and to review the case histories: Brodie Remington, Anne Adriance, Donna Wiley, Vince Spinelli, George Lukac, Fred Lintner, Rita Bornstein and Rick Schuster.

Figures

For Further Reading

American Association of Fund-Raising Counsel. *Giving USA*.
    American Association of Fund-Raising Counsel Trust for Philanthropy, annual editions.
Andersen, Arthur & Co. *Tax Economics of Charitable Giving*.
    Arthur Andersen & Co., annual editions.
Ashton, Debra. *The Complete Guide to Planned Giving*. JLA Publications, 1988.
Brakeley, George A. Jr. *Tested Ways to Successful Fund-Raising*.
    AMACOM (Division of American Management Associations), 1980.
Broce, Thomas E. *Fund-Raising: The Guide to Raising Money From Private Sources*.
    University of Oklahoma Press, 1979.
Conrad, Daniel Lynn. *How to Solicit Big Gifts*. Public Management Institute, 1978.
Conrad, William R. and Glenn, William R. *The Effective Voluntary Board of Directors*.
    Swallow Press, 1976.
Dove, Kent E. *Conducting a Successful Capital Campaign*. Jossey Bass, 1988.
Fink, Norman S. and Metzler, Howard C. *The Costs and Benefits of Deferred Giving*.
    Columbia University Press, 1982.
Hauman, David J. *The Capital Campaign Handbook: How to Maximize Your Fund-Raising Campaign*.
    The Taft Group, 1987.
Hodgkinson, Virginia Ann and Weitzman, Murray S., eds.
    The Charitable Behavior of Americans: A National Survey. Independent Sector, 1986.
Jenkins, Jeanne B. and Lucas, Marilyn. *How to Find Philanthropic Prospects*.
    Vol. I. Fund-Raising Institute, 1986.
——————— . *FRI Prospect-Research Resource Directory*. Vol. II. Fund-Raising Institute, 1986.
King, George V. *Deferred Gifts: How to Get Them*. Fund-Raising Institute, 1980.
Lord, Benjamin W., ed. *Fund Raiser's Guide to Private Fortunes*. The Taft Group, 1987.
Lord, James Gregory. *The Raising of Money: Thirty-five Essentials Every Trustee Should Know*.
    Third Sector Press, 1985.
Mai, Charles F. *Secrets of Major Gift Fund-Raising*. The Taft Group, 1987.
Moerschbaecher, Lynda S. and McCoy, Jerry J., eds.
    The Experts Guide to Generating Major Gifts. Little, Brown & Co., 1986.
Nason, John W. *The Nature of Trusteeship: The Role and Responsibilities of College
    and University Boards*. The Association of Governing Boards of Universities and Colleges, 1982.
O'Connell, Brian. *The Board Member's Book*. The Foundation Center, 1985.
O'Connell, Brian and O'Connell, Ann Brown. *Volunteers in Action*. The Foundation Center, 1989.
Panas, Jerold. *Born to Raise*. Pluribus Press Inc., 1988.
——————— . *Mega Gifts: Who Gives Them, Who Gets Them*. Pluribus Press Inc., 1984.
Quigg, H. Gerald, ed. *The Successful Capital Campaign*.
    Council for Advancement and Support of Education, 1986.
Schneiter, Paul H. *The Art of Asking, Second Edition*. Fund-Raising Institute, 1985.
Seltzer, Michael. *Securing Your Organization's Future:
    A Complete Guide to Fund-Raising Strategies*. The Foundation Center, 1987.
Seymour, Harold J. *Designs for Fund-Raising, Second Edition*. Fund-Raising Institute, 1988.
Strand, Bobbie J. and Hunt, Susan, eds. *Prospect Research: A How-to Guide*.
    Council for Advancement and Support of Education, 1986.
Trenbeth, Richard P. *The Membership Mystique*. Fund-Raising Institute, 1986.
Tueller, Alden B. *The Planned Giving Deskbook*. The Taft Group, 1987.
Williams, M. Jane. *The FRI Annual Giving Book*. Fund-Raising Institute, 1981.

About the Author

M. Jane Williams has been in the fund-raising field for more than 20 years, serving in development positions at five higher-education and health-care institutions. She is now senior vice president and partner in the consulting firm of McPherson, Schultz & Associates Inc, which has offices in Philadelphia, Los Angeles and Boston. The firm provides marketing, development and planning counsel for nonprofit organizations.

Prior to that, she served as vice president for development at New York University Medical Center in New York City, where she headed a development program that raised more than $50 million annually.

For more than 10 years, she was on the staff of the University of Pennsylvania. As assistant vice president for development and alumni relations, she played a key role in planning a $1 billion university-wide capital campaign. Her work at Penn emphasized developing cultivation and solicitation strategies for major individual prospects.

Jane's other development positions included serving as assistant vice president and campaign director for Temple University's first major capital campaign for $60 million. She has also worked on the development staffs of the Medical College of Pennsylvania and Haverford College.

As an advisory member of the Fund-Raising Institute, Jane directed its conference program. She has also written seven books on fund-raising for FRI.

Jane has been a faculty member at Temple University and the University of Pennsylvania, teaching non-credit courses in fund-raising. She has also taught at the New School in New York City.

Jane has a B.A. in history from the University of Pennsylvania, and an M.B.A. and a master's degree in education from Temple University.